LADIES' MAN

Also by John A. Jenkins

The Litigators: Inside the Powerful World of America's
High-Stakes Trial Lawyers (1989)

JOHN A. JENKINS
LADIES' MAN
THE LIFE AND TRIALS
OF
MARVIN MITCHELSON

ST. MARTIN'S PRESS   NEW YORK

Design by Glen M. Edelstein

Library of Congress Cataloging-in-Publication Data

Jenkins, John A.
    Ladies' man : the life and trials of Marvin Mitchelson / John A. Jenkins.
        p.   cm.
    "A Thomas Dunne book."
    ISBN 0-312-07856-0
    1. Mitchelson, Marvin M. 2. Lawyer—United States—Biography. 3. Trials (Divorce)—United States. I. Title
    KE373.M535J46   1992
    346.7301'66'0269—dc20
    [B]
    [347.3061660269]
    [B]   92-3154
                                    CIP

First Edition: August 1992

10 9 8 7 6 5 4 3 2 1

To Joe Parker Rhinehart and Dick Lee, two men
who set me on my way;
And my son, Gregory, with greatest love.

RESEARCHERS

Michael John Seeley
Los Angeles

Allison Porter
Susan Raleigh Jenkins
Laura Harris
Washington

Maureen A. Jung
Sacramento

CONTENTS

A NOTE TO READERS

Marvin Mitchelson didn't want this book to be written. "What's your working title?" he asked me derisively when I first telephoned him in February 1989. "Marvin Mitchelson Does It With Mirrors?"

I was calling not so much to propose the idea as to get his involvement; not to seek his permission but rather to give him an opportunity to cooperate in the writing of this book.

I told him he was, after all, arguably the best-known lawyer in America, if not the world. He'd forever changed the divorce law landscape by successfully making the case for palimony, a legal protection for live-in lovers now recognized by forty states. And his clients over more than three decades had included some of the world's wealthiest women—always made richer by the cases he'd won.

"You want to write a bestseller," he punched back. "And a bestseller isn't white bread."

Well, he was right about that. At this time, Marvin Mitchelson was being sued and publicly accused of rape and fraud by numerous clients—allegations which, if true, surely warranted his disbarment. He had been the object of a major exposé by CBS's "60 Minutes." And yet he had managed to *dodge every bullet* for a period of what was then more than three years.

So, yes, I told him, I *do* think your life and career warrant a more thoroughgoing journalistic examination than they've ever had.

But Mitchelson wasn't ready to help.

First, he wanted some money: "If I'm gonna do it, it becomes a financial thing. I want to be part of it, too. What's in it for *me*? I mean, it'll make a difference if I'm being paid for my story."

His unwillingness went far beyond the financial, though. Mitchelson, the lawyer who never met a television camera he didn't love, suddenly found himself fleeing from the kind of press attention he used to crave.

"Look," he told me that very first afternoon we spoke, "whenever somebody comes in and says, 'I'm gonna do this whether you cooperate or not,' I know what they're gonna do. A hatchet job! I'm a realist. I'll bet you ninety-nine cents to a penny it'll be a negative thing. I know how these things go. You'll talk to some jealous competitor like Raoul Felder"—the famous New York divorce lawyer who lately had been eating Mitchelson's lunch—"and he can't stand anything he's not connected with. I know the kind of competitiveness!"

Go ahead, Mitchelson concluded. Write your book. But write it without me.

Long before any writing begins, a biographer has played the disparate roles of detective and confidant. Facts have been gathered, sifted, analyzed. Stories, sometimes incredibly sad and sometimes never before told, have been listened to.

The biographer's job is daunting enough in its own right, but it becomes immensely more so when the subject of the research refuses to cooperate. The doors of friends and relations are also slammed and, inevitably, a rich history is lost.

So, even though I began my research early in March 1989 with the presumption that Mitchelson wouldn't be cooperating, I never totally lost contact with him. If nothing else, we kept hearing each other's footsteps, and on each trip West I attempted—always unsuccessfully—to meet with him.

By July, our cold long-distance relationship began to thaw. Mitchelson had heard from enough people who'd been contacted by me or my researchers to know that a serious work was in progress, and that his refusal to cooperate would not stop it from being written. (Ultimately, more than a thousand interviews were conducted; 104 key sources were interviewed multiple—in some cases, dozens of—times.) It was then that he authorized his two older sisters, other family members and friends, and some loyal clients to talk to me. His sisters spoke individually with me for many hours and provided otherwise unobtainable letters and pictures from the family scrapbooks. In the end, I wasn't aware of anyone he told *not* to talk to me.

Although he still refused to see me, we occasionally spoke by phone. And the fact that the ice was breaking without our ever having met conjured up in Mitchelson's vivid imagination a picture of another noted recluse who feared the outside world.

"Hello," Marvin would say puckishly to my answering machine, in his unmistakable raspy voice, "this is Howard Hughes. Please call me." The first time I called him back, he was like a mischievous little boy, demanding to know how I knew it was he who had left the message.

"Are you looking forward to meeting me?" he'd ask with a conspiratorial giggle. "This really is becoming a Howard Hughes thing, isn't it?"

Despite his many promises to the contrary, though, Mitchelson still refused a face-to-face meeting until a full year after my research began. "I'm going through a hailstorm," he'd say, referring to all the charges that still pelted him. "It really hurts."

The story of Marvin Mitchelson is one of a heroic figure whose image was tarnished by drugs, women, and his own arrogance. Mitchelson—who, like you, will be reading what follows for the first time when this book comes out—will not always be happy with what he sees. The truth can be painful. But it can also be fair.

Readers should know that neither Mitchelson nor anyone else interviewed was paid or otherwise compensated for his or her cooperation. No promises of special treatment were made (other than, where appropriate, pledges to respect the confidentiality of certain names, statements, or documents), and no one who was interviewed was allowed to review any part of this manuscript prior to publication. My only obligation was to the facts, wherever they led. Although he spoke to me, Mitchelson provided me nothing else except one old newspaper-clipping scrapbook and a few dozen other loose newspaper clippings and photographs. The approximately thirty-two thousand pages of documents that had to be collected and reviewed during my research were obtained from the National Archives, the California State Archives, the Library of Congress, the U.S. Supreme Court, other federal and state courts, private lawyers, the morgue of the *Los Angeles Times*, and other sources.

On our third day of interviews, I told Mitchelson I thought he had finally agreed to meet me because he couldn't resist a challenge: He didn't know how much, or how little, I really knew. And the only way he was going to take the measure of my knowledge was to come face to face with me.

The funny thing was, I didn't expect him to so readily agree.

"Yeah," he replied. "It's a challenge. There's always that"—he groped for the right words—"competitive spirit."

Two days earlier, he had flashed it for me.

"Look, if you're looking for the smoking gun, like, Am I a drug addict? The answer is, No, I'm not. Am I an alcoholic? The answer is, No, I'm not. Am I a secret rapist? No, I'm not. Do I defraud people? No, I don't. That's not the flaw. You're not gonna find it. And you can talk to seven thousand people and you'll never find it. That's not what it is. But there's gotta be a flaw.

"There's [such a thing as] enigmas. *Marvin Mitchelson is many different people*. It's true. And *you* don't know the half of it! There really is a book here, but *no one* will ever write it."

He was wrong, of course. But all I could do, seeing that raw nerve twitch, was to stare steadily back and wonder what in the world he thought he was hiding that I didn't already know.

Washington, D.C.
February 1992

Acknowledgments and Notes on Sources appear at the conclusion of this book.

PART ONE
I Wanted To Be Famous…

1

Los Angeles was seldom like this: starry, clear, smooth at the edges. The early spring rains had cleared out the smog, and now the evening was lavish in its crispness. It was going to be one of those rare nights. Marvin Mitchelson could already tell that as he drew his Rolls-Royce to the curb.

Inside, it was opening night at Noa Noa, a splashy crystal-and-chrome eatery on North Bedford Drive in Beverly Hills.

Instant hot. Invite the celebrities and watch the place light up. To make sure things started right, a white-suited, unfailingly kissy maitre'd had invited his best customers to dine free and dress up the place.

Mitchelson's Friday-night guest was his sometime business partner, a pretty, thirty-five-year-old former model named Tashi Grady. She was twenty-eight when they first met at a Paramount screening; he was fifty-three and then, as now, very married. But Mitchelson was drawn to this tall young woman with carefully touseled brown hair, just as he'd been drawn to others before. She had perfect earlobes. He told her that.

Tashi and Marvin were digging their way to the Hollywood gold: They had their own film production company. Never mind that they'd never made a movie in the more than five years they'd been running Oakenlee Productions out of Mitchelson's law office. Here, you worked your connections and bet on the future. And after more than three decades as *the* divorce lawyer to the stars, connections were the coin of Mitchelson's heady realm.

"Oh, God!" Mitchelson's murmured exclamation telegraphed his boyish glee. Another genuine Hollywood presence had arrived. Mitchelson himself was one, of course, and yet he never seemed to remember that when he started celebrity watching. "It's Jackie Collins! And who's that with her? Her husband? Who else?" He had plopped down in the strategic seat, a plate-glass window to his left and the front door dead ahead. Everybody who came in, he saw first. Tashi, her back to the door, tried to swing around. But by now Mitchelson had already bolted from his chair to embrace and kiss the author, a heavier, denser image of her sister, Joan. Jackie's dark hair was swept straight back in a leonine flip, and an unstructured dress that flowed from her shoulders to the floor disguised the years underneath and seemed almost to undulate along on its own. A gaggle of guests—Mitchelson did not immediately recognize them—trailed behind to a table nearby.

"Thanks a lot for what you did for my sister." The doyenne of the Tinseltown novel smiled wanly as she said that, but Mitchelson veritably beamed right there in the aisle. The Joan Collins divorce case had kept Mitchelson and his client in the headlines for much of 1986 and 1987. After everything was resolved, there'd been a big party for the "Dynasty" star, and Aaron Spelling, whose company produced the series, walked up to Mitchelson and gave him a friendly punch on the shoulder. Spelling gushed about how happy he was, and what good work Mitchelson had done, because the divorce had improved the ratings of the show. It was one of the ironies of his law practice. Only in Hollywood could a messy divorce actually *help* someone's career.

Seated once more, Mitchelson discreetly scanned the Collins table, searching his memory for names of the other celebrities he was sure were there.

"That's Morgan Brittany," he now whispered to Tashi, nodding toward an attractive auburn-haired woman. "From 'Dallas.' I think I represented her once on something. Next to her is Sammy Cahn. I thought he was *dead!*"

Still very much alive and looking dapper as could be in a houndstooth jacket and a Nivenesque moustache, the frail, seventy-six-year-old Cahn was a Hollywood legend, a lyricist whose slow love songs had earned him four Oscars. He and Mitchelson knew each other, too.

"I've never heard of him. Or his songs," Tashi said.

Well, Tashi was young. Flush with the evening, Marvin smiled and leaned across the table toward her. "I'll be seeing you," he crooned, not the least bit self-consciously. "In all the old familiar places. . . ."*

The world of Marvin Mitchelson had always been a world of scandal and indiscretion. But always somebody else's. Mitchelson was, after all, the most famous lawyer in a specialty that many in America who were rich and well-known probably couldn't do without.

Divorce.

The word's sonorous ring masked the pain, the anguish, and the humiliation that stood behind it. And, of course, the greed.

Sooner or later, divorce invariably came down to that. Two former lovers in one last battle, a metaphor for every fracas that ever led to irreconcilable differences. But even though the agony of divorce gave no special consideration to wealth or one's station in life or anything else that set people apart, the law certainly did. If you were wealthy and getting divorced during the 1970s and 1980s in the community-property state of California—a state that would slice a billionaire's assets straight down the middle during a divorce, just as it would anybody else's—you needed what was known, in the divorce lawyer's peculiar vernacular, as a "bomber": a master of hard bargaining and legitimate dirty tricks. A lawyer who would do almost anything to gain an advantage over his foe. Marvin Mitchelson.

The inevitability of it all meant Mitchelson could afford to wait. He knew that the right clients, propelled in his direction by the fruits of unrelenting press agentry, would undoubtedly seek him out.

If divorce were a high-stakes game, it was also one in which Mitchelson, years earlier, had come to control the action. Los Angeles was his home but he moved around the world signing up new clients—the wives of the rich and famous, mostly—and feasting on a percentage of their gross. He stayed in the spotlight through clever use of publicity and outrageous antics, the kind of boisterous tricks that scandalized the bar but were beloved by the tabloids and, who knew?, maybe even by the stars he represented. The man who embedded "palimony" into America's liberated consciousness was himself a household name. So were many of his clients: Michelle Triola Marvin, Joan Collins, Tony Curtis, Bianca Jagger, Sonny Bono, Mrs. Bob Dylan, Carl Sagan, Mrs. Marlon Brando, even the mistress of the bullfighter El Cordobes. Marvin Mitchelson had his own press agent, a fast talker out of New York named Sy Presten. Ask Mitchelson why he worked so hard to keep his name in the papers and he'd simply answer, "I like publicity," but, Christ, Marvin Mitchelson loved it, needed it to survive among the other sharks he swam with.

It got him noticed. Late at night, driving west on Hollywood Boulevard, Mitchelson pulled his Rolls up at a traffic light alongside a black 280Z. Two young men inside had their stereo cranked up full blast, so loud that even the Rolls shook with every bass note.

Mitchelson leaned out the window, bobbing his head and snapping his fingers in time to the music. The dudes probably weren't more than twenty-two years old, but instead of laughing at this white-haired fat cat, they gaped in awe at the spectacle.

"Hey!" the driver shouted. "I think I've seen you. Are you a lawyer?"

"Yes, I am. Maybe you've seen me on television."

"You're Marvin Mitchelson!"

"Thank You!" Mitchelson yelled back as the driver hoisted a Bud in a street salute. "Thank You!" Then he turned and took in vain the name of his biggest competitor, a New York divorce lawyer who earned nearly $3.8 million a year. "Betcha that's *never* happened to Raoul Felder!"

It was like old-home week for Mitchelson at Noa Noa. Perched at his strategic viewing post, he spotted fellow lawyer Howard Weitzman even before Weitzman came through the door.

Weitzman was one of the best criminal lawyers in the country, having won an acquittal in 1984 for automaker John DeLorean on charges DeLorean conspired to sell and distribute $60 million worth of cocaine. What was astonishing about the trial—what, in fact, made the compact, combative Weitzman as much of a celebrity as his client—was that the feds had seemingly caught DeLorean red-handed. They had more than a hundred audio and video tapes, including a crucial last tape where cocaine was brought to DeLorean by undercover cops. For his good work, Weitzman got, among other things, a $2.5 million San Diego ranch in payment from DeLorean. The automaker, meanwhile, got divorced. And now Weitzman was at Noa Noa with DeLorean's former wife, the model and local television personality Christina Ferrare.

Mitchelson and Weitzman kissed each other on the cheek, but this chance meeting wasn't between old friends. The two lawyers, each among the elite in their respective fields, had done some serious business together several years earlier.

Mitchelson had been accused of rape. It was hard to believe Mitchelson would rape a woman. He fancied himself the quintessential ladies' man—their courtly protector by day and their escort-of-choice by evening. But that's what the accusation was, and he'd brought in Weitzman to fight it for him.

Such an allegation was serious enough in its own right, but it was potentially devastating to someone like Mitchelson, who'd built a hugely successful practice on the reputation of being a sensitive, liberated defender of women.

2

The prospect of impending doom has a way of clearing the mind. And that is what it must have done for Marvin Mitchelson as he reached for the telephone on Friday afternoon, January 31, 1986.

The client's name was Kristin. She had a pert round face and short auburn hair, and when she spoke in her soft, childlike voice she sounded at first like a thousand other clients he'd nursed through the rough times with that dippy let's-get-you-back-on-the-road-to-recovery-honey bedside manner of his. Well, so she was a wreck. No, she was absolutely devastated. Mitchelson already knew that. And angry. Yes, yes, of course she was angry, too. "They get that way," he'd chuckle with a wave of his fat Monte Cristo cigar in steadier days when one or another of his clients couldn't cope. "Crazies!" That was vintage Mitchelson, too.

He liked to talk about "the closeness that develops between the lawyer and his clients"—his *female* clients—in a divorce case. "Sometimes, my clients feel they're falling in love with me." He would give them champagne and sympathy, but Mitchelson insisted he had not done even that with the client who now sought her vengeance.

Thirty years of representing so many women in divorce actions had given Mitchelson a well-developed personal radar that served him well when trouble lay over the horizon. But he could only listen in horror now as this client of his sobbed into the telephone. There was no placating her.

Unbeknown to Mitchelson, Kristin Barrett-Whitney had walked into the West Los Angeles station of the L.A. Police Department at 11:30 that morning and told an LAPD detective of being raped by Mitchelson on the floor of the bathroom adjoining his office, and of being forced almost immediately thereafter to perform more sex acts on him—masturbation and oral sex—in that same bathroom and in his Rolls Royce going to and from the courthouse.

What Mitchelson also didn't know was that the cops at that moment were taping his comments—comments an assistant Los Angeles district attorney later said made "the hair on the back of my neck stand up" when he heard them on the tape.

"Now, without acknowledging that anything happened anyplace, I don't intend in any way to become personally involved. . . . That's not what I need or anyone else needs. I just wanted to help you and represent you; try to settle the case. That's all I wanted," Mitchelson assured her.

"I know," Kristin answered.

"And I can tell you something," Mitchelson continued. "You know, without referring to you or me, you know, there are people, I mean, let's take a doctor—a doctor may be an excellent surgeon. Maybe he even becomes involved with the patient. . . . But he's still able to—he's a great surgeon. He's able to perform a cataract. I'm a lawyer. I know what I'm doing. I think I do. I'm able to settle cases." Mitchelson went on, saying, "We start a new slate. And, you know, I don't intend in any way to traumatize you, nor would I want to. Nor did I ever have that in mind."

"Because—" Barrett-Whitney made one of many attempts to break in.

"I have no bad feelings against you, and I wasn't in any way trying to traumatize you," Mitchelson continued. "And I'll just say to you that I won't. You know, of course, I won't. . . ."

"I just can't—nothing against you or anything—it's just—" Barrett-Whitney kept pressing for an admission, but all Mitchelson would say was:

"Look, I understand."

"I am, I'm emotionally, can't have situations like the bathroom," Barrett-Whitney went on.

Later, Mitchelson would call her a nut case who, he claimed, used thirteen aliases and filed seven other suits totaling $300 million, "all claiming the same thing," against different doctors, dentists, psychiatrists, and lawyers who, like himself, were only trying to help her. He fought back, because no amount of press-agent wizardry would be able to undo the damage if her claim of rape and sodomy stuck.

Barrett-Whitney did, indeed, have some skeletons in her closet. But she had a way of compensating for them with tenacity and boldness. The bad news for Mitchelson was that she would get more articulate before this was over; her allegations would be taken seriously enough to be investigated by the district attorney, the state attorney general, the grand jury, and, unavoidably, considering the characters involved, the CBS television show "60 Minutes."

Mitchelson refused to be interviewed on camera with Mike Wallace. Indeed, he begged Wallace not to run the piece at all, offering him what he said were "ten great stories" if CBS would just pass up this one.

Then, he broke down and cried.

That was an essential part of the Mitchelson persona, too, another manifestation of the sensitive-male image he tried to craft. Five years earlier, sitting at his corner table at Le Cirque, spooning his crème brulée and talking to a woman he'd just met, Mitchelson propped his hands under his chin and explained as sensitively as he knew how, "You know, my wife Marcella and I don't see each other often. A professor once told me, 'You know, the law is a jealous mistress.' And he was right. My work is my life. One of the most gratifying experiences I have is when I lecture at law schools. They really appreciate me there. They see what I'm doing. They *understand* palimony." And then, inexplicably, Mitchelson started weeping.

Mitchelson wiped away the tears with his napkin and gave his guest a big smile of apology. Then he leaned in close and coyly whispered into her ear: "Let me tell you something few people know. I'm an adventurer. I like to make forays into the world of the unknown."

At night, from his pricey office high up in a Century City tower, Mitchelson could push a button to automatically part the drapes covering three huge floor-to-ceiling windows. Below him, Beverly Hills and Santa Monica Boulevard spread out and away toward the Pacific. And on the ceiling, at the flip of another switch, floated the gossamer image of Botticelli's *Venus.*

Mitchelson had a fascination not only with the goddess of love, but also with the divinely beautiful model that Botticelli had used for his Venus-on-the-half-shell portrait, her hair flying back in a way that invited you to look but not to touch. The model had been the mistress of the two towering figures of the Italian Renaissance, Botticelli and Michelangelo, "at the same time," Mitchelson marveled. "She expresses something romantic in women. There is something regal about her. I like her."

He had worn her visage on his belt buckle and set it into his ashtray. But his *pièce de résistance* was a photographic transfer of the artist's fantasy, placed onto a glass panel and then set into a huge recessed light fixture above his desk. Mitchelson liked to tell people that the luminescent portrait was his favorite possession in the whole world.

Off to the side of his office was his private bathroom, a large sanctuary with black marble fixtures, erotic wallpaper, and its own view of Los Angeles. Mitchelson veritably relished the way his oddball, even egomaniacal, indulgences like the bathroom drew the attention of the tabloids and the ridicule of his peers. He'd even done a television interview grinning from the bubbles of his bathroom's oversized tub.

At night, once in that tub, phones turned off and everybody else gone, he relaxed by resting his head on a pillow that pictured not Venus, but rather his elderly mother, Sonia, a Russian emigré who Marvin said had struggled when he was a little boy to give her only son something better than the hardscrabble life she'd had.

Mitchelson had, in a sense, finally found in his own garish lifestyle—with the excesses that the black-marble tub typified—the kind of Hollywood notoriety he'd aspired to from the moment his penurious family came west from Detroit during the Depression. Mitchelson's outrageousness and the attention it commanded were the constants in his life, his assurance that he'd arrived.

"Then I get out of the tub, dry off, and put on this black robe," Mitchelson explained now, pulling a velour robe off his coat rack. "I go back into the office. I dim the lights way down." A million dots emerged in relief beyond the windows. "It makes an interesting effect with the Botticelli *Venus*," floating there, above everything. "She reflects in the windows. She's floating over the city. She's so—ethereal."

And then Mitchelson would do something that those who'd seen it couldn't possibly put out of their minds. Camoflaged against the night in his black robe, watched over by his own private angel, he'd put a symphony on the sound system and crank it up full blast.

"And I get my baton, and I face that view, and I conduct."

He liked *Rigoletto*, "a beautiful opera by Verdi, beautiful in the sense that it has a message of protection of women." And if you knew Marvin Mitchelson you didn't have to ask why he wanted sung at his funeral an Italian song of anguished love called "Core 'Ngrato" ("Ungrateful Heart"). You already knew.

Patricia French was one of those who didn't know him. Lured by all the publicity about the *Marvin vs. Marvin* palimony case, she came to Mitchelson's office one day in late 1981 to retain him in a palimony case she wanted to file.

According to French, Mitchelson met her in his robe. And, she said, as they talked, he asked her if she'd like to see his bathroom. *The* bathroom.

"I stepped just a tiny bit inside. And before I knew it, he slammed the door, [and] he became a totally different person," she would tearfully say later on. "I didn't know what happened. Somehow, I was on the floor; he was on top of me. He—well, he lifted my skirt up and he raped me in the bathroom. And I got up and I said, 'Let me out!' I just put my things back on and then he just started acting ridiculous, like he was leading an orchestra or something."

Mitchelson denied it all.

But other women who sought his counsel later said they'd experienced inappropriate sexual advances. And when a lawyer hired by Barrett-Whitney started poking around, he found others who said they'd earlier been too afraid to step forward.

The LAPD sent its file over to the district attorney's office, but the D.A. refused to prosecute because of what the office considered insufficient evidence. Controversy swirled around that decision. Barrett-Whitney's lawyer pressed for reconsideration by the California attorney general's office, but, again because it found insufficient evidence, it didn't take any action, either.

Barrett-Whitney and her lawyer went to the grand jury, which voted

23 to 0 to proceed with its own investigation anyway—only to have the state attorney general refuse to provide a lawyer to facilitate the investigation. And when one of the grand jurors then complained publicly that the district attorney's office was obstructing justice by lobbying to prevent the appointment of an independent counsel, a judge ordered the grand juror off the Mitchelson case and threatened to have him arrested for contempt of court if he violated that order.

There was no indictment. With pluck worthy of his nickname, the lawyer whose cable address was "Marvelo" dodged another bullet. But there would be more.

Two California appellate courts fined him a total of $40,000 for bringing frivolous appeals and the California Bar prepared its own charges accusing him, among other things, of misappropriating clients' trust funds, failing to return unearned fees, and charging unconscionable percentage-of-the-gross fees of a type that even Mitchelson said, in a book he wrote, were prohibited.

Having long ago lost some Palm Springs property and his glitzy house on Sunset Heights Drive to satisfy a hushed-up $1.5 million malpractice and breach-of-trust settlement with a client, there now was also the matter of some $590,727 in back taxes he owed the Internal Revenue Service and the California tax authorities, plus about another $1 million or so he owed Sotheby's auction house for some of the Duchess of Windsor's jewels he'd bought but never paid for. The Bar was accusing him of moral turpitude and threatening disbarment.

A former secretary who said she'd once had a long-running affair with Mitchelson came forward to talk about what she said was his addiction to cocaine and the prescription painkiller Percodan. Somebody else who'd been a drug-detoxification patient at the Beverly Glen Hospital in 1983 claimed that Mitchelson had been there at the same time.

It had been more than four years since the first allegations of wrongdoing against him. But Mitchelson's denials of wrongdoing were so categorical, so vociferous, that even skeptics seemed to *want* to give him every benefit of the doubt. Where a man's good name was at stake—particularly someone as well known as Mitchelson, and particularly a lawyer with a reputation for suing right back when he was cornered—the watchword was caution.

So Mitchelson kept up appearances and went about his business, as he dodged the charges and continued his highflying ways, Marvin Mitchelson's world seemed at times to have changed not at all. He had this placidity, almost like he was set apart from the whole sordid mess. And he could still get cases; still get the calls from "Nightline" and Larry King. That was the amazing thing. Just when you thought for sure the collapse had begun, he'd pop up on some talk show, garrulous as ever. When he talked about his problems at all, it was often in bitter allusions to "all that free publicity I've gotten," or sarcastic disavowals of the charges: "Can I tell ya? I can't remember *anything*! Now, maybe I'm a *sleepwalker*!"

Just one day before Barrett-Whitney went to the LAPD with her rape complaint that day in 1986, Mitchelson was still riding high in his career as the divorce lawyer of choice for the Hollywood lovelorn.

He had achieved a new record on January 30, 1986: He'd gotten the largest palimony settlement in history, $3.5 million for Veronica Miramontez, the longtime companion of Korbel champagne magnate Adolf Heck. The two lived together for twenty-three years, even though he was still married to his wife, Richie Heck. Heck left Miramontez a mere $50,000 when he died, and she'd only get that if she didn't contest his will. It took the threat of a messy palimony trial against the Heck estate to set things straight.

Mitchelson's own share of the Miramontez money came to about $700,000—a 20 percent payment, called a contingent fee in lawyer's parlance, was Mitchelson's customary minimum in palimony cases.

Mitchelson's career wasn't built just on chutzpah and cleverness. A dose of greed had a place in the grand scheme, too. Nevertheless, he owned little in his own name, not even the $5 million Hollywood mansion he lived in. The place was titled to his dead mother; so was Marvin's Rolls-Royce. "Let me ask you," Mitchelson would explain, turning the tables on his inquisitor. "What if it isn't in my name? Is that so I'm going to defeat the creditors? Or is that estate planning?"

Mitchelson's mistress was known to the federal authorities as a "C.I." A controlled informant.

It was on Tuesday, January 3, 1989, the first day of business after the New Year's holiday, that she walked into the criminal investigation offices of the Internal Revenue Service at 6230 Van Nuys Boulevard and asked to speak to the Treasury agent in charge.

She told him she wanted to reveal the crimes of Mitchelson. He deserved retribution, she believed, for welching on promises to her—even if that meant inflicting pain on the person she still considered a hero, and still loved.

She could give corroborating names, dates, and places. She'd consent to a tap being placed on her phone. And, since she and Mitchelson were still lovers and saw each other all the time, she'd consent to concealing a hidden microphone that would record his incriminating statements when they were together.

The mistress expressed the depth of her anger to another former Mitchelson girlfriend a few months later, telling her, "his worst nightmare just came true. . . . I am going to have him disbarred. He is going to go to prison. He is going to die in there, broke."

Mitchelson suspected nothing. "In her next life," said a federal agent who listened to their amorous conversations from an automobile parked outside, "she better come back as an actress."

The massive, throne-like chair behind Mitchelson's desk once belonged to Rudolph Valentino, the darkly handsome actor who sent chills down millions of female spines but died a tragic, early death. Sitting in it, Mitchelson gazed across his desk into a propped-up volume of Shakespeare, open to *Hamlet*, and talked about his own travails.

"Well, right now I'm not as happy as I was. Because I've had to take up arms against a sea of troubles, to quote half a Shakespeare line, and suffer the slings and arrows of outrageous fortune. And some misfortune. . . .

"You know something? I think I wanted to be the total Renaissance man. A man for all seasons. I wanted to be heroic to people. I wanted to accomplish something. I wanted to change the law. I wanted to be famous for the right reasons. Not just to amass the publicity. But I wanted to be known for things like [arguing before the Supreme Court and making new law in palimony]. I wanted to do more of those. . . . But I think it's too late, probably."

PART TWO
Sonny

3

Many years later, Marion Mitchelson would recall her younger brother Marvin as being "an odd combination of slightly shy and very bold." He was a boy-man whose closest friends sometimes seemed to be his own imagination.

And his mother.

As a Ukranian immigrant, life had not been easy for Sonia Knoppow, and she wanted it to be better for the three babies she'd had quickly after her marriage to another immigrant, Herbert Michelson. (The "t" was added later.)

Marvin was her youngest, the boy child that Sonia dearly wanted. She played back from memory the exact moment of Marvin's birth on May 7, 1928.

"It's a boy, Herbert?"

"Yes," her husband smiled back. "It's a *boy*!"

But things had not gone well after that. Money was short in their Detroit home. Then, when Marvin was only a year old, Sonia's oldest girl, May, fell ill with polio. The disease turned her parents into refugees all over again. The whole family fled Detroit for Los Angeles in search of a cure for May. Helping her was the most important thing.

Sonia's family ran a string of paint, wallpaper, and varnish stores in Detroit, and Herbert Mitchelson went to work as a paperhanger when he arrived in Detroit from Gdansk, Poland, to marry Sonia. In Los Angeles, Herbert reestablished himself as a paperhanger and painter. He worked long hours and was a remote figure to his children.

"Sonny" was the nickname Sonia gave their little son, and she called him that for the rest of her life. Herbert gave young Marvin another nickname: "Windy." The moniker described Marvin's unceasing penchant for cooking up grandiose schemes that couldn't possibly be realized anywhere but in his own vivid imagination.

"My father called him 'Windy' because he couldn't settle down!" May recalled. "He had ideas, and he lived a lot with his imagination. But he also could put his imagination into reality if he spent enough time at it.

"He would blow around; scatter his energies. Marion and I were always *amazed* at his success. We'd say, 'How come people don't know him the way *we* know him?'" She laughed. "How can these people confide in him, and how can they depend on him, and how can they risk their lives and all with *Marvin* being in charge? It was just amazing to us!"

May conjured up an image of her little brother with platinum-blond curls, toddling along behind his sisters and begging to be included in the bigger kids' games.

"He needed a pal. He needed another boy." But there wasn't anyone else. "[There was] my dad, but he was always at work.

"And then, I guess, [there] was my mother. My mother understood.

"I think that was it. Mother understood Marvin. Marion and I didn't. We became buddies, Marion and I. Marvin was on the outside."

He found ways to compensate. Marvin mixed well with adults, loved a challenge, and came to life before a big crowd.

Young Marvin organized neighborhood charity circuses in the Mitchelson backyard, first getting all the "acts" together and then walking up and down the streets in the neighborhood talking them up. He was also a slick enough talker to be able to persuade the other neighborhood kids to give him their toys to "fix." He always returned them—minus a few parts that he couldn't figure out what to do with.

The Los Angeles River ran along the edge of his neighborhood near Glendale. Most of the time it really wasn't much more than a drainage ditch, but the river swelled during occasional torrential rains. With the river rising to flood level, Marvin persuaded a classmate that they should build a Huck Finn–style raft and sail it right out to the South Seas. Marvin called it "the typhoon tug." They laid three logs lengthwise, nailed a big wooden garage door on top of them, and built a cabin on the whole contraption, only to find that it was so heavy they couldn't even push it the few steps to the river.

"You knew that he was going to be a *salesman* or something," childhood pal Bobby Arbogast said, "because if there was something we didn't want to do, in an hour, he'd give us enough reasons to do it.

"I remember the one thing we *never* wanted to do was go to Echo Lake (near what is now Dodger Stadium) and fish for sunfish. Marvin talked us into it. We caught a bunch and fried them up with potatoes, and we all got *violently* sick!

"What always struck you was his *charm*: the absolute ability to, usually in a humorous way, talk you into anything he wanted. He was charming and glib. I don't think anybody didn't like him."

The irony was that in spite of his gift for mingling and persuading, nobody really got to know young Marvin very well. He created his own reality; lived a great life in his mind. A nut about sports, young Marvin would make up the perfect football and baseball teams and then follow his players' progress during the season through a labyrinth of homemade charts that filled the walls of his bedroom and stretched right out the door.

"I remember Marvin sitting for hours and hours and hours, going over football scores and listing them all," Marion said. "He knew all the things on football scores and football teams and football players."

He ingratiated himself to adults. Marion swore that Marvin took the Boy Scout oath so seriously in grammar school that he hung around street corners in their neighborhood just so he could help old ladies cross the street or carry their groceries home.

From the surprisingly early age of 11 on, Marvin worked an array of odd jobs: clerk at a bike-rental concession; pin-setter at a Glendale bowling alley; dishwasher at the country's first Bob's Big Boy double-decker hamburger stand, a ten-stool affair on Colorado Street in Glendale. Marvin used to play catch with the malt glasses—until the cook fired him for throwing one through the skylight.

In many ways, this was an idyllic time in Los Angeles. There was no smog, a great climate, and the very first freeway, to Pasadena, wouldn't be built for another eight years. There were still vast stretches of open land where coyotes howled at night.

The family's first house was in the East Los Angeles immigrant neighborhood of Boyle Heights. But the Mitchelsons kept trading up until they bought, sometime around 1935, a little Spanish-style stucco bungalow on Glen Feliz Boulevard. It was on a pretty, Sycamore-lined middle-class street. There was a roomy detached garage in back where Herbert could park his truck and keep his painting stuff. The house was within sight of the hills of Griffith Park. The park was urban Los Angeles's counterpart to Central Park, a huge recreational green space with canyons, an observatory, golf courses, tennis courts, and the Greek Theater.

Marvin's neighborhood was called Atwater Village, and it was situated between the Los Angeles River, which curved lazily around the neighborhood's southern boundary, and Glendale. Just on the other side of the river were the rambling, million-dollar estates of palm-lined Hillhurst Avenue, the street leading into Griffith Park.

Each summer, Sonia, the girls, and their aunt Gwen—and Marvin, of course—took a rental at Venice Beach, with the four women and Marvin all living in a single room with a kitchen. Herbert kept on working in town and commuted out to the beach as his work permitted. Holidays that were just a week long in the beginning soon stretched into a month as Herbert's business grew.

"Pretty horrible surroundings," added Marion. "Really horrible. But livable for a week or two or three in the summertime. And then my father would go back and forth in old jalopy cars." Sonia didn't drive at all.

Sonia told the kids the sand on the California beaches wasn't anything like what it was on the Baltic. There, she said, "it was like sugar." They'd run down to the beach in the morning, the girls playing under their aunt Gwen's watchful eye, Sonia floating on her back in the water.

But Marion knew Marvin had a different agenda from the women of his family. He'd leave them and "gravitate toward the Muscle Beach guys." There really *was* a Muscle Beach there, a famous place of rippling bronzed bodies and assorted hangers-on. Marvin became one of the Muscle Beach groupies during his vacations, and he got a kick out of how he was able to catch on with this older, wizened crowd. "He would always find people—older people than he was—to hang around with," said Marion.

"His idea of a good time was not finding other kids his age to play with, but finding older people who would patronize his desire to hang around them, and from whom he could learn something. . . . He liked being around older people. And mature people."

One on one or in small groups, Marvin could be quite shy. He didn't show much of himself. But, as articulate as he was, if he could step into a role—carnival pitchman, neighborhood rogue, Muscle Beach groupie, good little boy for the grown-ups—he could be the center of attention.

"I don't think he was self-conscious," observed May many years later. "I can't remember *ever* that he was self-conscious."

Young Marvin's quarter-a-week allowance was supposed to cover his weekend treks to the movies. But on Friday nights, he and his buddy Bobby Arbogast would hustle some extra money by standing outside the Atwater Theater, heads down, forlornly pacing the sidewalk. It wouldn't be long before some well-meaning grown-up would walk up to them.

"What's wrong, boys?"

"We've lost our movie money."

Out would come two quarters. "We'd knock down eight dollars every Friday night!" Arbogast chuckled. "And then we wouldn't even go to the movies! It *always* worked."

Marvin also had excellent instincts about how to survive in the schoolyard. It wasn't easy being a Jew in his neighborhood during the height of World War II; Mitchelson remembered one of his neighbors wearing swastikas. And as one of the only Jews at the Glen Feliz School, he sometimes became the butt of anti-Semitic humor.

Arbogast explained how, when people made fun of Marvin, "he pretty much went along with it. But nobody was putting anything over on him. He let them *think* they were. Maybe to make them like him. Maybe because he thought if they knew how smart he really was, they wouldn't like him. He had to play the fool on purpose."

Marvin, suffering from asthma and not anywhere near the five feet ten, 180 pounds he'd be as an adult, also made friends with all the rough guys. Not because he wanted to be like them, but because he wanted to make sure they left him alone.

Marvin was bitten by Hollywood. While the stories penned by his classmates contained accounts about the more mundane elements of a sixth-grader's existence—things like worms, fish, bee stings, and permanent teeth—Marvin was already in the thrall of show business. He signed up to be the assistant movie critic of his grammar-school paper, _The Bugler_, and wrote short blurbs that could have dressed up any marquee. Darryl F. Zanuck's _Drums Along the Mohawk_, with Henry Fonda and Claudette Colbert, was "an exciting picture. . . . interesting and romantic."

Marvin raved about Walt Disney's _Pinocchio_, too, even though, as he warned his classmates, "there are no movie stars in this picture for it is a full-length cartoon."

But Marvin wasn't about to just sit there in the audience _watching_ those stars. He was going to go out and meet them! That gift of gab that he'd been honing at the backyard carnivals and on Muscle Beach—that uncanny ability to win people over—was being wasted on the Glendale locals.

He and Bobby Arbogast thought the beach might be a good place to meet stars. Some had oceanfront places in Santa Monica, near the public beach. Arbogast and Marvin went there, waited until they saw some unsuspecting "star," then swam out into the surf and started rolling around yelling, "Help! Help!"

The ploy worked. Marvin was "rescued" by Cornel Wilde, who took the fourteen year old back to his house. And Arbogast was plucked from the breakers by Hollywood's Irishman-in-residence, sixty-year-old Barry Fitzgerald. Safely back to shore, the heavily accented Fitzgerald breathlessly asked if Arbogast was all right. And Arbogast, already set on an acting career and by now a quick study at imitating other people's accents, mimicked Fitzgerald's almost impenetrable brogue "and gave it right back to him and he _bought_ it! I never copped!"

But there had to be something more to this Hollywood bit than phony drownings that produced hurried, chance encounters with the first star that came along. Spotting Victor McLaglen, one of Hollywood's hottest actors, at a local restaurant, Marvin swaggered up and persuaded him to start a recreation club for kids.

The Victor McLaglen Kids' Club soon had two-hundred young members, and it wasn't long before Marvin had the whole group organized into Ping-Pong, tennis, badminton, and riding—and, of course, more circuses, with the proceeds helping to fund the Victor McLaglen summer camp for kids. Sonia became one of the adult sponsors, and she went along with McLaglen—the kids called him "Uncle Victor"—when he took the gang on annual trips to Catalina Island.

Marvin was meeting other stars, too. By the time he started high school, he boasted of being a favorite of Betty Grable and her new husband, trumpeter Harry James.

Marvin was fulfilling his dreams. He learned that he really could do that if he persevered. Just like his mother said.

He idolized the magic-fingered UCLA quarterback, Bob Waterfield.

So Marvin went down to the practice field, started hanging around, and became a "pal" of Waterfield's and a water boy for the team in 1942 when UCLA finally beat USC and got its first bid ever to the Rose Bowl.

"That was typical of the way that Marvin could talk himself into a situation," Marion later said. "That's what I mean by that 'Windy' business. . . . We thought it was all very exciting and fun that he would be kind of a mascot for the team. And he did it all by that personal charm."

Later, Marvin found another way to get into the games free. He and Arbogast, having noticed that all the white-trousered, white-shirted ushers at UCLA football games gathered at a particular gate well before the game, simply started showing up there, too. Dressed as ushers, they walked right through, then put on jackets and found themselves some empty seats.

Marvin's family got a vicarious kick from Marvin's pluck—up to a point. For Sonia, that point was reached when it became clear that, in spite of his winning personality, Marvin wasn't going to be much of a student.

Sonia believed that the key to success lay in a good education, and at Marshall High School both Marion and May (in spite of the latter's frequent absences due to polio) were excellent students with bright futures. Why can't you be like them, Marvin? Why can't you be like your sisters and get good grades?

Sonia nagged. She cajoled. She made it very clear that young Marvin was letting her down. The importance of an education was driven home even more forcefully when Herbert had his first heart attack in 1941, at age forty. His doctor told him he'd have to give up the painting business. But what else did Herbert know other than the hard work of a painting contractor?

Herbert wanted to open a kosher delicatessen—like the ones in his homeland—and that was what he did, right in the middle of Atwater Village. Herb's Los Feliz Deli was filled with wonderful European delicacies. Reluctantly, Sonia gave in to the idea. She cooked and Herbert ran the register.

But the ringing of the register was not a sound heard often in the deli, and Herbert's new venture soon went broke. "Terrible idea," Arbogast remembered. "A Jewish deli, right in the middle of a goyish neighborhood! Why *wouldn't* it go bankrupt? They were the only Jews in the neighborhood!"

Sonia and Herbert planned their recovery. With housing in short supply and prices rising fast because of the war boom, they decided to start buying fixer-uppers and begin doing what already came naturally to Herbert: renovating them.

Sonia found the properties; Herbert supervised the repair and redecorating. Equity from one job was rolled into the next. Suddenly the family was pulling up roots and moving somewhere new every three months. In the space of three years, the Mitchelsons moved more than a dozen times, never living in one place long enough for Marvin to make friends. But with each move, Herbert and Sonia were increasing their equity and getting into a better place. By the war's end, the Mitchelson family lived in a decidedly upscale home on Daniels Avenue, right on the edge of Beverly Hills.

After first enrolling at Marshall High, where his sisters went, Marvin transferred to Los Angeles High in 1943 and remained there through all the moves. It was considered academically superior to Marshall. But no matter what the caliber of the school, there was no talking to Marvin about schoolwork. He simply refused to study hard. Marvin certainly didn't leave much of a footprint at L.A. High. His sisters later said his attitude was a way of rebelling against the intense pressure that Sonia was putting on her only son.

Marvin was also having other problems with his mother. On one hand, she'd always been the surrogate for his absent, aloof father, and the pal to him that his older sisters never were. But her constant goading to make him a better person, if not to remake him altogether into the new boy-man of the house (replacing her infirm husband), was smothering Marvin's freewheeling, inventive spirit.

Marvin arranged to get his diploma four months early and announced that he wanted to join the Navy.

Good idea, said his father.

Sonia supposed she thought it was a good idea, too. He needed to "find himself," she told the family. Sooner or later, Marvin would wake up to what she'd been telling him.

In February of 1946, seventeen-year-old Marvin shipped out as a hospital corpsman aboard the cruiser U.S.S. Columbus, bound for Shanghai. One of his stock stories was about how he stepped into a line in boot camp for what he thought were people who wanted to be *signal* corpsmen.

The pressure to be better was still there from both parents when his ship returned to San Francisco from Shanghai the following year. And Mitchelson was still trying to please. On Mothers' Day, 1947, he wired Sonia a big basket of flowers and got a hearty "Well done" from Herbert. Sonia sent Marvin some money, and Marvin returned it to her. Herbert was impressed by that, too.

Marvin still yearned to be a big-time athlete. Even though he had only played second-string football during his senior year in high school, he'd managed to catch on with his ship's team in the Navy. By mid-October of 1947, the Columbus was berthed in Long Beach. Herbert went there to watch Marvin's team play; they took a 46 to 0 shellacking. Herbert was to return a few weeks later to watch his son again, and

Marvin expected to do better. But before that, on October 30, 1947, Herbert had another heart attack.

No one knew how serious it was. Marvin went ahead with his game, and this time his team won. But on Sunday morning, November 16, Good Samaritan Hospital called and told Sonia and the children to hurry over; there wasn't much time left. Sonia hadn't even finished dressing when the hospital called back at 9 A.M. to say her husband had died. Herbert Mitchelson was forty-six.

"I never got a chance to see him again," Marvin recalled. "My father never got a chance to see me play very well. I was trying to prove myself to him—I *needed* to prove myself to him—and I never had a chance.

"So I tried to prove myself to my mother. It's why I had to be a success. It motivated me. I guess I needed to be accepted."

For the rest of his life, Mitchelson would be locked in a love-hate struggle, trying to fulfill his mother's high expectations but also to rebel against the standards she set. That pattern had been established early on, but now, with his father's untimely death, there would be an even greater pressure on young Marvin to step in and become all that Sonia wanted him to be: a surrogate husband; someone to fulfill her high expectations.

It was almost as if two Marvins had evolved. There was Good Marvin, who did as he was told, looked after his mother, was contrite when she scolded him, and set his sights on the great things she had in store for him.

Then there was Bad Marvin, a rebellious child who misbehaved when his mother wasn't looking. And he could be very, very bad.

4

Shortly later, Sonia was home alone. Her daughters were married in a double-ring ceremony within a year after their father's death. And nineteen-year-old Marvin was off to the University of Oregon, to try to make it as a jock. He lived at the Delta Upsilon fraternity house and otherwise did his best to blend in. But he played in only one game on the freshman football team, as a reserve halfback. ("I was usually hurt.") This was not the place for him. Soon, Sonia summoned her beloved Sonny home.

When Marvin left the University, he never explained why, other than to say, "It was time to come home." But he became her reason to keep on living. The girls were afraid that Sonia had been so devoted to Herbert that she wouldn't last long without him. But in Marvin she found a new cause for her life.

Marvin took a job helping Sonia in her new occupation as resident manager of a sixty-six-unit apartment complex on Holloway Drive. A couple named Markowitz were building the apartments, and while their six buildings were being completed they leased one of the houses Sonia had fixed up. They liked this hard-working widow and made her an offer: Become our resident manager and we'll give you your own place, rent free. No wages; just a place to live in exchange for running the complex, and later, the income from five apartments she furnished herself at the complex.

Sonia accepted the offer. Marvin was her helper and was paid $100 a month. College would have to wait. Marvin and Sonia moved into one of the apartments on Holloway Drive together. And much later, in 1960 and 1961, she and the children bought two of the Holloway Drive buildings with an inheritance from Herbert's brother, Arthur.

"Sonny" was still Sonia's special nickname for Marvin; she'd called him that since his childhood. To Sonia, calling him "Sonny" was a way of expressing the special bond that existed between them.

But if Sonia had an idealized view of their time together, Marvin acknowledged that his mother's well-meaning guidance sometimes could, and did, become overbearing.

She even interfered with Marvin, who had grown quite handsome, when he took a strong interest in a woman named Doris, one of Sonia's female tenants.

"She was older. My mother suspected something," Mitchelson recalled.

One afternoon, Marvin and Doris were "in an amorous situation" when Sonia skulked up to Doris's apartment door and let herself in.

"I turned around one day and there's my *mother* standing in the doorway, tapping her foot! It was embarrassing! I was furious at my mother for invading my privacy, and I wouldn't talk to her. I was calling her names and she was almost fainting. A doctor came! It was a scene right out of an Italian movie!"

Sonia fretted about her beloved Sonny. She worried, for one thing, about his becoming involved with the Hollywood types who were her tenants. The Holloway Drive buildings were home to people like Michelle Triola, a sometime singer who Marvin would occasionally see nearby at Dino's Lodge, on the Sunset Strip. And China Lee, the future Mrs. Mort Sahl. And Sal Mineo.

"The range of personalities there was something completely new to my mother and brother," Marion Mitchelson recalled. "It was their first exposure to people who were sometimes real and sometimes phony: coming in and out of L.A.; short rentals, long rentals; living beyond their means or having much less money than we thought they had; dealing with all kinds of problems that my mother had never encountered in her narrow world."

Sonia thought she had to keep Marvin on the straight and narrow. She wanted to "keep Marvin in line," Marion recounted. "Keep him studying. Encourage him. . . . My mother was afraid that people like [the Holloway tenants], with phony values, would be an influence on Marvin, and she was always trying to bring him back into line and keep him anchored and doing his work."

If Marvin stayed out too late at night, his mother would lock him out. "If he did anything bad," Sonia once said, "I wrote him a letter and he had to read the letter aloud. It had more meaning that way."

Those letters were more than just an adult son's strange penance; they were intended to be a dagger in the heart of any evil demons Sonia thought might be lurking out there. Reading them, there could be no doubting the extent to which Sonia tried to rule the life of her only son.

She would also chide him in letters about his health and diet. It would strengthen her love, she wrote, if Marvin would just ease up and take better care of himself.

The interesting thing was that Marvin's sisters saw in their own family some of the same hypocrisy that Sonia thought pervaded Holloway. May saw it in the façade that Sonia maintained when her Orthodox Jewish parents came to visit. The whole house had to switch to being kosher, but someone would invariably forget.

"I stuck the meat knife into something," recalls May, "I forget what. It was considered not too kosher! And my grandfather jumped up from his chair, dashed outside, and plunged the knife—I remember this!—into the earth to cleanse it. And the knife blade broke, and I just laughed! All that hypocrisy. *That* was my first taste of it."

By the time Mitchelson was twenty-two years old he had made three more failed tries at higher education. He quit Santa Monica City College and its football team after one semester because Sonia wouldn't let him play on Jewish holidays; he dropped out of USC after only one semester; and he went to summer school at Los Angeles City College. In 1950, he set out again to realize his mother's ambition for him. This time his choice was the nearby local college, Occidental.

Still fantasizing about a football career, Mitchelson went out for the team but broke his wrist on the first day of practice. The injury ended his hopes that he might "become a famous sports star," and explained his complete omission from the college's annals of athletic lore. Occidental verified his attendance during the 1950–1951 academic year, but knew nothing else about his time there.

"I was devastated," Mitchelson said of his broken wrist. "I wasn't a brain success, and now I wasn't an athletic success. What was left?"

The answer was UCLA, to which he commuted the next academic year, finally earning a degree in history after attending summer school.

The whole family wondered what Marvin was going to do next.

So did Mitchelson. He had dreamed of becoming a doctor when he was in the Navy. Then he wanted to be a writer, like Hemingway or Jack London. Then a Hollywood manager.

"I didn't think I wanted to be a lawyer till I was in college, actually just toward the end [of college]. 'Cause everyone would say, 'Well, you yell and talk; you're very dramatic.'"

May put it another way: "[My father] thought that with Marvin's big mouth, he could be an attorney."

"So," said Marvin, "I decided like almost my senior year that I'd study law."

5

The study of law was one more thing that Mitchelson apparently didn't have time for. His grades during his first academic year at the UCLA Law School, from September of 1952 through June of 1953, were not good. UCLA placed him on academic probation and demanded that he repeat some courses. Instead, Mitchelson started over at one of the only law schools that would take UCLA's rejects: Southwestern Law School.

Southwestern held its classes in a dark old building in downtown Los Angeles, and at that time its program didn't even qualify for accreditation from the American Bar Association. But from Mitchelson's standpoint it had at least one thing going for it: It would let him in.

"Southwestern was the one place they didn't ask you much on your application," explained Ted Cohen, one of his classmates there. "All they said was, 'Can you pay the tuition?' And it was the only place where a working guy could go. We had a lot of policemen, court bailiffs, guys who had jobs and were older. People who were working and had families."

One of the interesting things about Southwestern was that it produced an inordinate number of good trial lawyers. The kind of people who could identify with the average juror were frequently the scrappy, independent lawyers educated there. Lawyers like that cared little for law books but they sure could make their cases sing to a jury. So in that respect it turned out to be a perfect match for Mitchelson.

In California, if you went to an unaccredited law school like Southwestern, at the end of your first year you had to pass something called the First Year Law Students' Examination, euphemistically called the "Baby Bar." It was a test in contracts, torts, and criminal law. Flunk it and you had to start all over and then take the exam again the following year. Having already taken all his first-year classes twice, Marvin managed to pass the Baby Bar the first time and continued in Southwestern's program.

Mitchelson was getting an education on Holloway Drive, too—in how to lead the good life.

One of his mother's tenants was a *Life* photographer named Bob Landry, and Mitchelson had done with Landry what he'd become so skilled at doing during his days as a kid hanging around Muscle Beach. He watched closely, took his cues, and insinuated his way into Landry's life. In doing so he found a role model whose super-slick modus suited him perfectly.

Landry was a swashbuckling man's man in Hollywood, and as far as Mitchelson was concerned his tall, blond photographer friend had it all.

Landry's most famous single picture was the one he'd taken of Rita Hayworth kneeling seductively on a bed in her nightgown—the fantasy pin-up for countless GIs during World War II. They'd spent the whole day together, Bob and Rita, and even went out to a Santa Monica hamburger stand for lunch. But as Landry took the famous shot his flashbulb failed to fire, producing the shadow effect that added an otherworldly dimension to Hayworth's already formidable curves.

Landry also had photographed the Japanese invasion of Pearl Harbor; he fortuitously happened to be on an American cruiser there. They were the first pictures of the U.S. Navy at war and the stuff of legend besides. He'd been to Casablanca. And it was Landry who accompanied the American paratroopers during the D-Day invasion of Omaha Beach in 1944. He was a hard-drinking, acerbic-witted guy who smoked two packs of Camels a day and drove a flashy white Packard convertible. On an assignment once, his office cabled that his then-wife had been in an accident with the Packard, but that she was not hurt. Landry fired a wire right back and ordered the office to find out: How badly is Packard damaged?

The *Life* photographer certainly had been around. He'd been in some movies himself, dated Ingrid Bergman, and had a well-publicized fling with singer Deanna Durbin. When Mitchelson knew him, Landry was even having an affair with a good friend's wife, and the friend was none the wiser. What a guy! With all his *Life* assignments on the Hollywood sets, to which Marvin sometimes tagged along as his assistant, Landry provided the excitement Mitchelson wanted.

Landry nicknamed his young friend "Muscles" because Mitchelson, impressed by what he'd seen on Muscle Beach, had embarked on a private weight-lifting program of his own. Landry also took Marvin on a trip around the country photographing golf courses for *Life*, teaching him another lesson that was never forgotten. When "Muscles" soon wearied of lugging around all the clothes he'd needlessly packed, Landry made him ship the excess back home. Decades later, a client would be horrified when Mitchelson, bragging about how "light" he traveled, got off a plane carrying a change of underwear in a plastic grocery bag, and nothing else.

Taking another cue from Landry, Mitchelson went out and bought himself a brand new white Lincoln convertible. "Marvin had the absolute best car in law school," remembered Ted Cohen. "A big boat. Everybody knew it. I thought he was a rich kid. He talked as if he came from big money. That's what people thought. That he was rich."

At the school, Cohen remembered Mitchelson as "an extrovert. Very charming. Everybody liked Marvin." He made friends with the owners of Hamburger Hamlet and they hung a photograph of him in a football uniform despite his lack of distinction on the gridiron. "But I never knew that he had any close friends. The guy was always smiling, always a glad hander. He could have sold cars! 'Hi, howya doin'!' Charming guy. He could talk to anybody. Marv didn't have any close friends that I knew of. I think he was friendly to everyone and never got close to anybody. That may be something that stuck with him for the rest of his life. I wouldn't guess that Marvin Mitchelson is close to anyone today. I would say the guy's just a loner."

Maybe there was a reason why he didn't let people get too close to him. They might find out the truth: that he wasn't really a rich kid after all, but rather a man living with his immigrant mother in a tiny apartment in one of the buildings she managed.

To pay for his new Lincoln and get the spending money he needed, Marvin took another job more suited to his aggressive personality. Presaging the career ahead of him, he became a part-time process server.

A lawyer used a process server to officially notify someone of a lawsuit, summons, or subpoena. In legal jargon, summonses and subpoenas are a form of "compulsory process," and that's where the profession got its name. It wasn't enough just to file papers in the courthouse. You had to make it official by putting your opponent on notice. This made them not the most popular people around—and made the loud-mouthed Mitchelson a particularly unpopular fellow.

As a server, Mitchelson worked on commission. He only got paid if he delivered the papers to their intended victim. And he got paid more often than not. When it came to difficult cases, Mitchelson was cunning. If someone refused to answer the door—which happened frequently—he had a standard ploy: He would simply open up the complaint and start reading it at the top of his voice.

"As I started to yell out the details of purported frauds, business misconduct, or marital indiscretions, passersby would stop to listen and neighbors' windows would fly open," Mitchelson said. "In seconds the door would be flung open and the paper snatched from my hands with accompanying curses." At Christmas time he wrapped the documents up in tissue paper and red ribbon and handed them out like presents.

His exploits became the stuff of myths for another reason. There were three process-serving firms in Los Angeles, and by secretly working for all three and thereby triple-dipping on the mileage fees he was paid ("I earned it"), Mitchelson was the most productive server in the whole city. He sometimes made more than $2,000 a month.

"We used to call him a 'mailboxer,'" Ted Cohen said with a laugh. Cohen was one of the servers, too. "You only got paid if you made the service. You worked on commission. So we used to accuse Marvin of mailboxing 'em, because he had too good a success rate. Everybody'd say, 'You must be leaving 'em in the mailbox!'"

Mitchelson would come home and regale his family with tales from the streets. There was the November evening in 1955 that he was out on a date and decided to drop off a subpoena at an address in Hollywood because it was on the way. He pulled his convertible up to the house and told his date to wait a minute; he'd be right back. He bound the steps, whereupon the ungrateful recipient proceeded to beat Mitchelson and tear his sweater off.

Mitchelson went racing back down the front steps and zoomed off in search of a phone booth. The cops were called. And then he came swaggering back with two of L.A.'s finest—who, along with Marvin's girlfriend, witnessed Marvin's first citizen's arrest.

Mitchelson, described then by the *Los Angeles Times* simply as a twenty-six-year-old "bespectacled law student," was back in court a month later to make sure the guy got convicted. Which he did.

"I'll tell ya," his Uncle Mack marveled, "that Marvin's *aggressive*."

Joan Collins was a twenty-two-year-old English starlet. Now she was on the lot at MGM playing what she thought of as her first "all-woman" role, that of Crystal in *The Opposite Sex*. It was a remake of *The Women*, a big success during the 1930s, and Collins's character was the queen bitch in a story about Hollywood's familiar territories of sex, men, husband snatching, gossip, and back-biting.

Collins had to do a scene in which she luxuriated in a bubble bath while talking on the telephone to her boyfriend. But after two days of rehearsing the scene using real bubbles—a mixture of dishwashing detergent and Lux soapflakes that the prop men kept whipping up—Collins's flesh was so tender that by the time the *real* shooting began, a contraption had to be rigged up that kept all the bubbly bathwater from touching her. The prop department did that by encasing Collins in Vaseline, bandages, and a set of men's long johns, topping the whole ensemble with a waterproof rubber sheet.

It was slow, tedious going. Then, as the cameras rolled, in rushed a maniacal stagehand.

"Joan Collins?"

"Er, yes—er, maybe," Collins replied, looking frantically at the assistant director as if to say, Get this madman out of here before he hurts me!

"Cut! Cut! What the hell's going on here?" yelled the director, David Miller. "Who is this jerk?"

Mitchelson handed divorce papers to Collins and got her to "sign here" just as three assistant directors hustled him off the set.

Collins called him a "jerk," too—a far cry from what she'd be saying about Hollywood's best-known divorce lawyer thirty years later. No matter. He was back home that evening with another tale for his family. When Sonia heard such stories, it just reaffirmed the value of the sacrifices she was making for her Sonny.

One of Sonia's relatives was nonplussed at her devotion. "You intend to work *this* hard, [just] so Marvin can go to law school?" he asked incredulously. "I would *never* do it!"

Sonia's response always came as if by rote: She would always work hard to help Marvin achieve his goal of a good education.

Sonia and Marvin made quite a twosome, and his mother never seemed to lose the chance to underscore just how much he meant to her—no matter what kind of histrionics attended each demonstration. Only Sonia could accidentally "overdose" on sleeping pills while her son was away at his law school classes, then "awaken" hours later and crawl to the telephone, where she first tried to reach her sister, Gwen, and then her daughter, May.

No answer at either house.

Sonia called for an ambulance, and just as the attendants came charging up the stairs Marvin returned.

"Where are you taking her?" Marvin cried out. "She's my *mother!*"

Suddenly, everything was better. Marvin had arrived in the nick of time. They kissed each other and then Sonia let the attendants take her to the hospital to have her stomach pumped. All the way there, she kept assuring Marvin: "All will be well."

When Sonia's doctor came in and asked her, "Why did you do it?"—meaning, Why did she try to kill herself?—she looked him straight in the eye and gave him a Sonia-style tongue lashing: "Doctor, Marvin is in *law school!* How can you think that I would attempt something so foolish while he's in *law school?*"

In between the purple hearts he was earning as a process server and his mother's accidental overdose, Mitchelson managed to pass enough courses at Southwestern to graduate in 1956. Now it was time for the last crucible of Sonny's education: the three-day Bar exam.

The California Bar exam was one of the country's toughest. Mitchelson spent day after day boning up for it. But after untold hours of copying his notes, writing his practice essays, and doing whatever else an aspiring lawyer thinks he has to do to jump that last hurdle, it was Marvin's turn to go into hysterics.

Sonia was asleep in bed when she awoke to see Marvin kneeling beside her, weeping aloud.

"Mother, my shoulder is in pain! I can't write anymore."

It was long past midnight, but Sonia got a neighborhood doctor to open up. He looked at Marvin's shoulder.

"Hot compresses," the doctor said. "Apply hot compresses."

They went back home, and Sonia stayed up all night putting the hot compresses to her Sonny's shoulder. For each of the next three mornings, she had their family doctor give Marvin a shot in his arm to deaden the pain.

But Marvin failed the bar exam just the same, and Sonia told him he was just going to have to keep on going to Southwestern until he could pass the test.

Sonia had already borrowed money from her father for Marvin's law school tuition, and now all she had between her and total poverty were five $1,000 government bonds. The bonds are to help you finish your education, no matter how long it takes, she told him. Sonia cashed in the bonds and Marvin returned to Southwestern—this was going to be the start of his *fifth* year in law school—and then took the Bar exam again.

As Sonia later recalled it, the news from the State Bar came on a Saturday. Marvin was cleaning the basement, so he didn't see the long envelope that the postman slipped into their mailbox. Sonia did, though, and she hurried to take the envelope into the bathroom to open it herself—to receive the first shock if the news were bad. But this time it was good news: Marvin had passed.

Her feet shaking, Sonia went to Marvin and yelled joyfully: Marvin, you made it! Marvin, you are an *attorney*!

Marvin didn't know whether to laugh or cry as he fell to the floor with relief. He said, "Mother, *we* made it! *We* made it!" As always, Sonia felt that everything she'd done for her son was worth it.

Sonia was so anxious for Marvin to start his legal career that she persuaded a few Holloway Drive tenants to hire him. She worked out a space-sharing arrangement for him with another tenant who was a Beverly Hills lawyer. She also furnished his first office with a desk, lamp, and chairs that she'd skimmed from the various furnished apartments she managed. Mitchelson's only up-front investment was $15 for a couple of lithographs.

Even after he passed the Bar exam, though, Marvin kept right on living with Sonia for several more years at her Holloway Drive apartment. It wasn't until August of 1960, when Sonia married her first cousin, Benjamin, that he moved out for good.

On the day he was admitted to the Bar, in June of 1957, a square-jawed, handsome Mitchelson posed with his mother in front of the courthouse and again outside the law office he'd rented in Beverly Hills. He certainly looked like a lawyer. It remained to be seen what he was going to do now.

6

Marvin Mitchelson handled the run-of-the-mill cases that were the fate of any first-year lawyer, picking up much of his business at the Melody Room cocktail joint on the Sunset Strip. For his very first fee, one of the waitresses there gave him a $100 retainer to represent her on a bad-check charge.

Marvin went all the way home and showed her check to his mother.

"A *check*? You took a check on a *bad-check* case?" Sonia couldn't believe it. "Go back and get *cash*, Marvin!" Mitchelson did.

He also had a seventy-five-year-old client, a cook at the Melody Room, who'd gotten hit in the groin by a bundle of newspapers thrown from a *Herald-Examiner* truck. Mitchelson claimed the man's sex life was ruined, and he told the newspaper's lawyers that his client's girl-friends—plural—would be testifying to that at trial. The case was settled for $800.

But it was a routine auto-accident case, filed on behalf of a jazz musician's wife, that would soon push this willing young lawyer into a whole new world.

Years later, after *Marvin vs. Marvin* and the slew of other high-profile cases he'd handled, there'd be a certain after-the-fact obviousness to Mitchelson's uncanny knack for capitalizing on an opportunity before it became apparent to anyone else. His gift was his ability to see a great cause in a seemingly routine case, and then to be able to make it cry out for redress.

This keen sensitivity to the hot buttons of a case was something that couldn't be taught in law school. Having it meant knowing how to orchestrate all the players in the comedy or tragedy that a trial invariably was. Judge, jury, plaintiff, defendant, the media: Their lines got written as they went along. The difference between a journeyman trial lawyer and a genius was in the way the geniuses almost imperceptibly shaded the script. Years later, Mitchelson would call what he and other great trial lawyers did—the theatrics they engaged in—"acting for real," and if that sounded like a contradiction in terms, then you'd never been inside a courtroom when the stakes were high. You had to be able to stand in the shoes of your client and make his story—*your* story, now—come vividly to life for the judge and jury.

The best trial lawyers were chameleons. How else could they assume the colors of their clients? If you were a criminal defense lawyer you couldn't think too hard about why you were helping to put some low-life hoodlum back on the street. *You couldn't afford to be too moral.*

Marvin had what it took to be a good trial lawyer. Ask him to describe who he was and he'd offer a prophetic confession: "Well, at various times, I'm different people."

That was what made Mitchelson so well suited to the craft he'd chosen. Here was a man who had spent his entire life, from earliest childhood on, trying to please other people. He'd gone through his entire life with a well-developed awareness of what others thought and felt. He'd watched his role models closely—his mother, the older crowd at Muscle Beach, Bob Landry, the Hollywood people—and assumed their colors when he was around them. *Everybody* liked Marvin! But what you liked depended on what you saw, and what you saw depended on who you were.

"Can I tell you something?" Marvin Mitchelson asked. "In the strangest way that people never realize, I've led one of the most private lives you've ever seen. *No one knows me too long.*

"I'll tell you why. Because that's the nature of my life. I'm just always on the move. I mean, that's where my business takes me. It takes me for a week here. I mean, I'm here three days in New York. You know, last night I went to a function. Everyone was nice. There were ten thousand cameras there. But no one really knew me. I said Hello and posed with a few people, and it was nice, and off I went. Yet someone will say, 'I knew Marvin Mitchelson.' And I just came back here and I was gone and no one knew what happened to me. . . .

"It's lonely. I'm here right now [in a hotel suite]. And I have one of the most lonely lives you can ever imagine in your life. I mean, you cannot believe how lonely it is. That's why I like to talk to people. That's why I like to go to the opera. Yes, that's why I like to talk to women sometimes. I like to talk to people. I like someone's company. You know, it can be love of the spirit."

The jazz musician responsible for his first big break was named Shorty Rogers. Rogers' wife was Mitchelson's client, and she had a black housekeeper who had a sister who had a problem. As a new lawyer, Marvin took on the cases he could get, and now Farena Douglas was sitting in his office, tearfully pleading with him to "help my boy. He's not a murderer."

That wasn't what the district attorney said. If you believed the D.A., William Douglas and his older friend Bennie Will Meyes had been on a crime spree that ended with a dead cop.

During the summer of 1958 a team of stick-up men had taken their own cut of the illicit poker, numbers, bookie, and crap games that locals knew where to find in Watts, the toughest black neighborhood in Los Angeles. The cops thought one of the robbers was Meyes, a thirty-three-year-old parole violator who'd been in and out of reform schools and prisons since he was fifteen, and who'd done three prison stints since he was twenty-three for different robberies and burglaries.

Meyes's partner, an informant told the police, was a twenty-nine year old named "Bill," but the police didn't know anything else about the second man or either's whereabouts until a hot lead came to them from Meyes's girlfriend.

The detective assigned to the case, Sgt. Walter F. Bitterolf, had been leaning hard on the girlfriend. Now, on the evening of Monday, October 20, she told the cops about an apartment where she said the other man, "Bill," lived.

Four cops went to the apartment building that evening. Two stayed outside as Bitterolf and his plainclothes partner, Gene T. Nash, pulled out their .38-caliber service revolvers and walked inside. Nash was new to the robbery detail. It was the very first day the two men had worked together.

Bitterolf rapped hard on the front door of the first apartment. "Open up! It's the police!"

Virgil Lee answered the front door, and Bitterolf, his voice raised to a command, immediately asked him, "Is Bill here?"

Lee, another man, and two women friends had been watching television. Lee said No, there was no one there by that name. Bitterolf started crowding him at the door, telling Lee the police wanted to have a look around and shoving him back into the apartment.

When Bitterolf stepped inside, he flicked off the television and started asking the others if they knew "Bill." Bitterolf knew at least one of them did because he recognized a woman who'd once fed him some information about "Bill," but he didn't say anything. The other woman present told the cops that the only other person in the apartment was her small child, asleep in the back bedroom. Nash said he'd walk back there and check.

The kid was still asleep when Bennie Meyes and William Douglas heard the strange voices, and when the television went dead and things got quiet, they both became concerned. At the time, Meyes had Douglas's .38 stuffed into his waistband, previously fetched from between the mattresses of Douglas's bed.

Bitterolf was still in the living room when he heard the pow! pow! pow! of 11 gun shots in rapid succession. He raced back down the same hall Nash had entered only a few seconds before, encountering first one empty bedroom and then an empty bathroom before running into the horror he knew he'd find.

Nash was down, lying on his back, his feet in the doorway. He was still grasping his pistol in his right hand, and he was still conscious. But he'd been shot three times in the chest and abdomen and once each in the left arm and right hand.

One of the back-up cops outside charged in when he heard the shots, and Bitterolf yelled at him to radio for an ambulance.

There were two men, Nash told Bitterolf. He'd shot them both. One was still hiding in the closet; the other one had jumped out the bedroom window.

Bitterolf went over to the closet and saw a man who turned out to be the wounded William Douglas doubled up on the floor. Nash had fired five times, and one of his shots had entered almost at Douglas's rectum and tore straight up to his chest. Bitterolf thought Douglas was dead, and went back to Nash.

There was an almost surreal, cinematic pathos to the conversation between the two partners.

"How is it, Gene?" Bitterolf asked.

"Real bad."

"Don't worry," Bitterolf responded. "Relax. An ambulance is on its way."

"Don't kid me," Nash told him. "I know I'm done for. I know I'm going to die. Cancel the ambulance." (He died at Central Receiving Hospital a few minutes before his widow, Cindy, arrived.)

It was only now that Bitterolf noticed that Douglas wasn't dead after all. Douglas's eyes were following Bitterolf as he walked over to the window where the second man had jumped. Outside, Bitterolf saw a shoe, a gun, and the punched-out screen.

So did one of the back-up cops who came running up the alley. He also saw a trail of blood spots that snaked around a garage in back of the building, under a clothes line, and over a fence. On the other side of the fence, the spots got larger, until, a block away, they actually formed footprints. Shot clean through the left thigh and in the right hand, Bennie Meyes had lost so much blood that he'd passed out on the floor of what would have been his getaway car.

In 1958, there was no such thing as a *Miranda* warning; no *Escobedo* requirement that an attorney be provided during an interrogation. Even in California, which prided itself on being progressive, there was no guarantee of an attorney for someone charged with a crime. In parts of the United States blacks still sat in the back of the bus, and restrooms and water fountains were still marked "White" and "Colored." If things were better in California, it was by only a matter of degree.

The cops started questioning Meyes in the ambulance. Meyes, who was under the impression that both Nash and Douglas were already dead, did what any self-respecting crook would have done: He concocted a story that blamed everyone else.

His story was unbelievably simple: Meyes hadn't seen anybody shoot at anybody, but he'd heard the shots and "hit the road" because he didn't want to get caught for the parole violation.

Douglas, who said he'd been told during his interrogation that he might as well confess because he was going to go to the gas chamber anyway and ought to make it easy on himself, had given the police a story that probably came closer to the truth. He said Meyes had the gun and shot Nash. Douglas said he was crouching on the floor, trying to hide beside the bed, when he was hit—a story consistent with the wounds he received.

Douglas and Meyes were being kept at opposite ends of the county hospital. Each thought the other was dead. But a week after the shootout the police decided it was time the two men confronted each other. They pushed Douglas, in a wheelchair, out into the main corridor and in due course wheeled a stunned Meyes alongside him.

"Isn't it true," an officer now asked Douglas, "that Meyes shot Nash?"

Meyes screamed at Douglas: "Are you going to let me go like that, ride that?"

Now it was Douglas's turn to show he'd been watching too many Cagney movies: "You're going to fry, Bennie! And you're not going to take me with you!"

Meyes just glowered back at Douglas and didn't say anything.

The D.A. wasn't messing around. Both men were going to be tried together on the murder charge starting the day after Christmas, 1958.

Mitchelson had been a lawyer just one year, and he'd hardly had time to get inside a courtroom let alone handle a murder case. But he was attracted to the elements of Douglas's case: The man was poor, he was black, and he'd been branded a cop killer. Douglas's mother paid Mitchelson forty dollars a month, all she could afford.

Meyes was represented by an aloof thirty-one-year-old deputy public defender, Paul G. Breckenridge.

"It was a tough, emotional case," Breckenridge recalled. "They wanted the pill [gas chamber], at least for Meyes. And you've got to remember, it wasn't like it is today. In those days, people *died* in the gas chamber."

The deputy district attorney who intended to send them there was Joseph Lester Carr, a tall, husky prosecutor with white, thinning hair. At age fifty-three, Joe Carr had been sending murderers away since almost before Mitchelson and Breckenridge were born.

The defense lawyers' primary objective was to beat the death penalty.

The problem was that neither Meyes nor Douglas presented a sympathetic picture to a jury. Meyes, who had by now confessed to shooting Nash, albeit in self-defense, had three prior felony convictions. And although Douglas didn't have a prior record, the cops were trying to pin the robbery spree on him.

So Breckenridge did what he always did when he had a capital case. He psyched himself up to take on the unfairness of "the system"—the system that would surely kill his client unless Breckenridge saved him. That moral outrage was what he needed the jury to see.

Breckenridge saw in his cocounsel Mitchelson "just a young, enthusiastic guy, not too long out of law school, scratching for work. When we'd talk about the case, he'd be full of ideas and strategies about it. His weakness was that he couldn't tell which of his ideas were good and which weren't."

One of the things Breckenridge stressed to Mitchelson was the importance of winning in the trial court. They had to make their case to the jurors, because the appeals courts weren't punctilious in reviewing death sentences. "It's unlikely there'd be a reversal," Breckenridge counseled, "and with three priors, my client isn't going to get a lot of help from the governor." If Meyes went down for the big one, Douglas probably would, too, because under California law anyone involved in a crime that resulted in a homicide was equally guilty of the murder.

The defense lawyers got a post-Christmas continuance, but when they asked for a second one in February of the following year, the judge refused and ordered them to start picking a jury. The case of *People of the State of California vs. William Douglas and Bennie Will Meyes* was going to go to trial as scheduled on February 24, 1959.

In thirteen days of trial, Mitchelson and Breckenridge managed to cast enough doubt on the state's case to produce a jury that became hopelessly deadlocked after four-and-a-half days of deliberation.

In a retrial, the terrain of a case has already been well charted. Surprises are rare. Opponents have been sized up and are warily regarded. Each side knows the other's strengths and weaknesses and crafts its strategy accordingly.

This kind of familiarity produces not a speedier trial but rather a more deliberate one. With the first verdict as feedback, the weak points of a case can be reinforced and the strong ones built up more.

That was surely what was happening in the retrial of Douglas and Meyes. What had been little more than a one-day process of jury selection now consumed, before a new judge, Herbert V. Walker, the entire first week. It produced, just as it had in the first trial, a panel of eight women and four men.

Just as during the first trial, prosecutor Carr led off with the closest person he had to an eyewitness: Detective Bitterolf. The detective's testimony was the spine of Carr's case. After Bitterolf, just as before, Carr would bring up an array of doctors, police officers, and ballistics experts to further describe what had happened, and to tie Douglas, Meyes—and Douglas's gun—to the crime.

The retrial was in its second day on Tuesday, May 19, when Carr asked Bitterolf what Douglas said in the moment right after the gunplay, when Bitterolf first noticed that Douglas was still alive. Carr, of course, knew only too well what the answer was; well-rehearsed testimony was the essence of a good direct examination.

"I asked [him] what his name was," the detective began replying. "He said something I didn't catch. I asked him again. He said, 'It's Bill Douglas.' I asked him where the gun was. He said . . . 'You're going to find out sooner or later; Bennie Meyes got my gun. That's the gun he used to shoot the officer with.'"

Bitterolf had recited this same story so many times that it rolled out in a just-the-facts-ma'am narrative. He didn't even wait for Carr's next question before continuing:

"I asked him how many jobs [robberies] he had been on—"

Mitchelson was on his feet in an instant.

"I ask that that be stricken! I am going to object to this part of the question and answer. It is incompetent, irrelevant, and immaterial as to how many 'jobs' he's been on!"

What was interesting to see was the obvious growth of the young lawyer's confidence in the courtroom. What they'd taught him about trial law at that unaccredited law school had clearly made an impression.

"It has nothing to do with the killing of this police officer, or the death of this police officer, and I am going to ask that counsel be restricted to ask *questions*; that [Bitterolf's testimony] not be in narrative form, but by question and answer so that I can properly make my objections," Mitchelson demanded. "I have no objection to any part of the conversation that pertains to how this shooting occurred, but I do have an objection as to what jobs he had been on, that kind of question."

The prosecution saw it differently. Although Meyes and Douglas were only on trial for murder, avoiding arrest for their robbery spree provided the motive for *why* they would kill an officer.

Jurors are only supposed to hear the evidence, not the lawyers' impassioned objections, so the judge called all the lawyers to the far corner of his bench where they argued Mitchelson's point in a colloquy known as a sidebar.

Mitchelson pointed to Gene Nash's dying declaration that Meyes was the trigger man. Since it wasn't the prosecution's contention that Douglas did the shooting, the only purpose to Bitterolf's testimony would be "to inflame and impassion the jury. . . . I think it is entirely irrelevant and immaterial! I will state right here on the record in trial [that] I want to urge every objection to keep some of these irrelevant matters out."

Fine, said the judge. Just don't "reurge something I've already ruled on."

"You haven't yet ruled on this!" Mitchelson kept petitioning, and the judge kept slapping him down. But the Mitchelson moxie was definitely showing.

Mitchelson did what he could with Bitterolf on cross-examination, bringing out the fact that Nash was inexperienced on the robbery beat; that the officers hadn't had any reason to suspect Douglas of wrongdoing before they'd heard about "Bill" on the day of the shooting; and that the police had neither a search warrant nor a warrant for Douglas's arrest when they entered the apartment. But none of those points really helped Douglas.

With a case like Mitchelson's, the only strategy left was for him to put the other side on trial: in this case, to raise any questions he could about Bitterolf's motive for wanting to send Douglas to the gas chamber. But even though Mitchelson gave it his spirited best, the state's first and best witness proved unshakeable.

After cross-examining Bitterolf about his earlier account to the grand jury of his first conversation with Douglas, Mitchelson suddenly and unaccountably declared: "You *also* recall telling him, 'I ought to kill you.'" It wasn't so much a question from Mitchelson as an affirmative declaration.

"No, I do not."

"Do you recall kicking him?"

"I did not."

"Are you sure you didn't kick him in the thigh?"

"I am positive I didn't kick him any place."

"In the back?"

"No place."

"Did you say, 'Go ahead and die, you black bastard'?"

"No, I did not."

"You were pretty angry, were you not, Sergeant?"

"Well, not so angry. No, I don't think so."

Carr objected to what he thought were the insinuations in Mitchelson's questions. "Are you attempting to create the impression that this is [Bitterolf's] testimony that [Bitterolf] gave at the last proceeding?" Carr asked.

"No," said Mitchelson with the seeming ingenuousness of someone who in later years would become very proficient, indeed, in the lawyerly art of character assassination. "I'm not attempting to do anything of *that* sort."

During the trial, Mitchelson's style was to confront prosecution witnesses with whatever dirt he thought he had, and then to walk all over the witness' denials in hopes that the jury only heard his subliminal message. Five days into the retrial, his act was wearing quite thin with Carr.

"You are a bookmaker, are you not?" Mitchelson asked Frank Stevenson accusingly.

Stevenson, who'd been robbed of $130 and swore that his shoe-shine stand wasn't a bookmaking front, nonetheless blurted out that he had "been accused of that" so quickly that Carr didn't even have time to object. As the jury watched, Carr asked the judge to cite Mitchelson "for misconduct in asking the question."

"Just a minute!" Mitchelson yelled back. "I have every right to ask such a question."

Again, Carr cited him for misconduct.

"Oh, nonsense!"

Again, Carr tweaked Mitchelson, this time letting the jury know that "as time goes on" the feisty young lawyer wouldn't make such silly mistakes and then call his elder's objection nonsense. "However [Stevenson] got the money, he had better title to it than they had."

"I cite counsel for misconduct for making speeches!" Mitchelson now shouted back.

The judge called a recess and sent the jury out of the room. "Remember that you are in a lawsuit," he told Mitchelson. "This isn't a boxing match or anything else."

Mitchelson apologized, and when the jury returned, the judge permitted him to ask his original question.

The pivotal issue in the trial was, Who fired first?

Douglas and Meyes claimed Nash did, shooting Douglas while Douglas crouched behind the bed, then firing at a frightened Meyes as Meyes tried to get out the window. The men said they thought Nash, in civilian clothes, was an intruder. The D.A.'s contention, by contrast, was that Meyes had emptied his six-shooter first, as soon as he saw Nash.

It was a matter of credibility, and neither side had very much. The defense eyewitnesses were the accused themselves; what did the jurors expect them to say? And the prosecution had no eyewitnesses at all.

As far as Mitchelson was concerned, though, it didn't matter who shot first. Alongside Meyes, Douglas looked like a choirboy. Douglas had no criminal record, and he not only hadn't fired a shot but had almost been killed in the melee.

So Mitchelson, during the nearly six weeks that the second trial consumed, merely had to do one thing reasonably well: inculcate in the jurors a mental picture of the hapless Douglas cowering there on the floor and being shot in the back when he had no gun. It wasn't hard to do. If the jurors got that picture, they'd almost surely find Douglas not guilty.

His best witness turned out to be his own client. The mere sight of Douglas was enough to evoke sympathy. After three operations, he still had a big scar and an open wound on his stomach, along with a lump above his navel where another bullet still rested, too close to vital organs to be removed. He also just had some teeth pulled and could hardly talk. Even the judge acknowledged in front of the jury that Douglas was "on death's doorstep."

Mitchelson brought out that Douglas was wearing a black shirt with metallic threads on the evening of the shootings, and that the shiny threads reflected the light when Nash pushed open the bedroom door. The shimmer from behind the bed could have startled Nash enough to make him fire at Douglas.

"All right, now, you say there were some shots?" Mitchelson asked as he walked Douglas through his testimony on direct examination.

"Yes, sir."

"Were you hit on the first shot?"

"Yes, sir."

"All right, what did you feel; what did you experience?"

"I felt something dull hit my body and start—just felt like something floating in me. . . ."

"Did you see Bennie Meyes fire at anyone?"

"No, I did not."

Douglas testified that he'd been perfectly motionless, and that he hadn't said a word to provoke Nash before being shot. He also swore that the ambulance attendants said they were taking a roundabout route to the hospital "to let me die on the way," and said Bitterolf had kicked him and threatened him: "He said, 'I ought to kill you.' That was the first time he talked to me."

"What else did he say to you?"

"'Go ahead and die, you black bastard.'"

"Did he have his gun out?"

"It was pointed right at my face, sir."

Mitchelson got Douglas to recant earlier statements he'd made to the cops at the hospital in the hours after the shooting. "I had trouble breathing," Douglas said by way of explaining how he wasn't quite himself then. "And I had some kind of a plug in my rectum."

Just about the only thing Mitchelson *didn't* do to get the jury's sympathy was have Douglas pull up his shirt to show the jury some of his wounds—and he even tried to do that.

"No," said Judge Walker firmly. "Do you have any pictures?"

"All I want to do is show the jury," Mitchelson pleaded. "There is nothing repulsive about it. He doesn't have to take his trousers off. . . ."

Walker said, ". . . You've done everything I know of that you can do."

"Except show the scar," replied Mitchelson.

"I'm not going to let you do it!"

It was also during Douglas's testimony that Mitchelson gave an indication of why he had so much trouble with the Bar exam.

As Douglas was describing how he "fell heir" to a gun, the judge asked incredulously: "Fell *what*?"

"Fell heir," Mitchelson volunteered cheerfully. "H-I-E-R."

"H-E-I-R," Carr grumbled.

An incident that occurred toward the end of the trial showed just how different the legal and cultural climate was then.

There was great interest in the trial among blacks in Los Angeles, and it was being covered by the city's black newspaper, the *Tribune*. (The paper's slogan was: "The Vote is the Negro's Muscle; Register NOW.") The judge took note of the black spectators who showed up every day, and he became concerned when one of those regular spectators showed up at a juror's house one night.

"I don't know who that colored boy is, either," Judge Walker told the lawyers in his chambers the next morning.

"He was sitting there all of the time?" Mitchelson asked.

"A couple of days."

"I noticed the last couple of days there were a couple of them sitting together," Mitchelson volunteered.

Now Carr chimed in. "Meyes is supposed to have a pretty tough reputation around the colored area." The prosecutor said some police informants "indicated the word has gotten out from Meyes that, if and when he gets out, [the witnesses against him] can expect a *visit* from him, or from someone on his behalf." The witnesses were afraid, Carr said. This visit to the juror, he continued, "may constitute at least a psychological threat to the juror." The judge thought it plausible.

Mitchelson had his own concerns. "I am afraid of all of those people. I feel when I cross-examine them, they will waylay me!"

Even Breckenridge had a story to tell. "I got a call at midnight from some drunken colored person who told me about some woman that was going to come into court. Interrupted my sleep."

A plan was agreed on. "Should that person show up again . . ." Carr asked, "[can] the bailiff unobtrusively ask him who he is, or something like that?" Yeah, that would protect everybody.

The jury had deadlocked 10 to 2 for acquitting both Meyes and Douglas during their first trial, and crusty old Joe Carr was nothing if not a realist. It was going to be a lot harder for him to pick up ten more votes than it would be for Mitchelson and Breckenridge to get two.

Since the burden of proof was on the prosecution, Carr led off the closing arguments. Unlike in a civil case, where the burden of proof was easier to meet, a criminal case had to be proved beyond the reasonable doubt of every single juror.

Carr was going to need a spectacular closing argument to put his side over the top. His problem was that the facts he needed just weren't there to back him up.

He started out with a confusing, step-by-step description of the events that took place in the apartment right before and during the shooting. The fact was, nobody really could be sure *what* had happened in that back bedroom—and Carr's lengthy restatement just underscored that.

"Don't discount suspicions," Carr admonished the jurors. He was really saying: Even if you're not quite sure what happened in the back bedroom, just take a look at these two black defendants and draw your own conclusions about who's telling the truth.

"Suspicions have a very *definite* place in this case," he continued. "A suspicion is the start, and from the suspicion the seed grows into a plant and from the plant springs the flower."

Mitchelson had made much during the trial of the absence of a search warrant or an arrest warrant when the officers went to the apartment. But, Carr said, the police "don't go there with an orchid corsage."

Carr knew there was sympathy for Douglas. But he tried to turn it around, saying that even though Douglas was severely wounded, Nash was *dead*. Who deserved more sympathy?

There was also the issue of the questionable motives of the police themselves—the possibility that they were trying to vindicate their fallen comrade by harshly prosecuting Meyes and Douglas. The police categorically denied almost all the post-shooting misconduct Mitchelson and his client had accused them of, but one thing they admitted was lying to Douglas and Meyes to get them to implicate each other by telling each that the other was dead.

"You may say, well, it was unfair to play Meyes and Douglas against each other," Carr told the jury. "Well, you know there is an expression that the English use, that it is "not cricket.' Well, these people weren't even playing cricket, ladies and gentleman. It was very serious, a murder of a brother officer."

Carr rattled on like that for hours, but at the end of it all he still hadn't tied all these loose ends together.

Mitchelson was next. He hadn't spoken for more than a few minutes when it became so clear why his family and classmates thought him so well suited for the courtroom.

The white-haired, wizened Carr had lumbered through the case, picking his way across each and every piece of evidence and losing the jury in the process. But his boyish antagonist was going to show the jurors that he was just as confused as they were. All these conflicting stories were too much for Mitchelson, too! All *he* knew, Mitchelson told them, was that there sure was a lot of *suspicion* about his client. But suspicions didn't equal *facts*.

Then he cleverly turned around one of Carr's lines. "We have learned from the prosecution that the flowering tree started with the seed of suspicion. Now, I guess I can go along with that statement, the flowering tree that started with the seed of suspicion. But the seed of suspicion can also grow into a tree of fabrication."

It was pretty good extemporizing for a thirty year old whose first big case was for capital murder. Good enough that he kept returning to the metaphor through his closing argument.

"Now, let's check the *seeds of suspicion*," Mitchelson would say. "I think the prosecution would have you believe, ladies and gentlemen of the jury,"—Carr had called them *all* gentlemen, even though there were only four men on the panel—"that you are dealing with a couple of *animals* over here. . . . They don't do [normal] things, ladies and gentlemen of the jury. They just do things so they can have an *alibi*."

Mitchelson still hadn't talked about any of the conflicting facts of the trial when he got to the racial issue. Carr hadn't mentioned color because he didn't have to, but the threat of a backlash against the two black men was obviously there. Mitchelson had an effective way of demystifying it without directly challenging the jurors: He reminded them of a question he had asked one of the jurors during the *voir dire*, the jury-selection phase where prospective jurors are questioned about their backgrounds and possible biases.

"I think I asked the question, 'Do you believe that people have rights, despite whatever race they may belong to? [And that] they are entitled to the same consideration as other human beings are entitled to?' And his answer was, 'They are American citizens, aren't they?'

"Now, ladies and gentlemen of the jury, that is a very important comment, at least to me. Because it made me feel that there was going to be at least one on this jury, and I hope the rest of you felt the same way after I examined you, who would treat these people as human beings—as *individuals*—and would recognize that they have rights like anyone else."

It was only after setting up that sympathetic framework for his client that Mitchelson started discussing the specifics of the case against Douglas. And even then, he could glide over some of the evidence. A lot of it just didn't matter to him, Mitchelson seemed to say, because regardless of whether Nash or Meyes shot first, Douglas was about as close as he could get to being an innocent bystander.

C'mon, Mitchelson seemed to be exhorting them, my client has no criminal record, didn't have a gun, was shot in the back and was almost killed, and the state wants you to do *what?*

"I can't help but think," he concluded, "that God must have had his hand on this boy. He has seen him through three or four operations and He has seen him on death's door, as he tells us here. I can assure you, ladies and gentlemen of the jury, *only* because I believe completely in the innocence of this man, I implore you to return a verdict of not guilty."

On June 23, 1959, just as this jury's deliberations had entered their fifth day, a verdict was finally reached. Mitchelson's man, Douglas, was found not guilty. That was a huge defeat for the prosecutor, and an impressive victory for the up-and-coming Beverly Hills lawyer. "I stood toe-to-toe with the toughest prosecutor in L.A.!" Mitchelson boasted. "I stood toe-to-toe with Joe Carr!"

Meyes wasn't so lucky—or was he? He didn't get off; the jury found him guilty of second-degree murder. But Meyes's lawyer, Breckenridge, *had* achieved his primary objective: He'd saved his client from the gas chamber.

And Meyes, from the sound of things, was positively thrilled.

On the day of the verdict, he wrote Mitchelson a letter thanking and congratulating him and Breckenridge for the job that they had done. Meyes told Mitchelson he would always be on his side.

7

Through Bob Landry, Mitchelson had already developed a taste for things European. He started affecting the Landry style, a sort of pseudo-British snootiness that had them both hanging out at a "pub" on Sunset Boulevard called the Cock and Bull and doing things like calling an automobile hood the "bonnet." When Landry finally married again, in 1960, it was to a young Englishwoman who was a film publicist.

Between the two *Douglas* trials, Marvin jaunted to London, Genoa, and Paris and shipped back enough stuff to turn his apartment into what a gushing *Los Angeles Times* article called "a veritable antique shop." The media loved Marvin even then—loved him so much that the *Times* did a nearly verbatim rehash of its earlier story about his antique collecting a little more than two years later.

Among other things, Mitchelson had a penny-farthing bike used in the movie *Around the World in 80 Days*; a ten-foot-long shotgun that he called "quite a conversation piece"; a ten-and-a-half-foot-long cocktail table hand hewn from a yule log; a two-hundred-year-old wine cooler; and what Mitchelson boasted was the world's largest piggy bank.

"There are many things to do and see in European cities," he told the *L.A. Times*, "but antique hunting comes first."

Well, not quite. Now that the Douglas retrial was finished, he intended to head back to Italy. But his sights were definitely *not* on antiques.

Landry was already there, shooting publicity stills for *It Started in Naples*, a film starring Clark Gable and Sophia Loren. Marvin was to join Landry, ostensibly to prepare Landry's last will and testament, but also just to goof off with his good friend.

By the time Mitchelson caught up with Landry, in September of 1959, Landry was at the Blue Grotto, a romantic spot on the island of Capri. And he had big news for his up-and-coming bachelor friend from West Hollywood.

"There's a great-looking gal you should meet!" Landry told Mitchelson. Her name was Marcella Ferri, she was twenty-nine years old, and she had a part in the Gable-Loren movie.

There was just one problem: Marcella didn't speak English. Not a word of it. And Marvin's Italian wasn't any better than Marcella's English.

It was, they both later said, love at first sight.

"I started giving her lessons," Mitchelson explained. English lessons. They used sign language to communicate; to talk to each other they looked up words in dictionaries. They wanted to get married right then, but decided to wait until Marcella could get a student's visa to come to the States.

When Mitchelson came back and told his mother and sisters who he'd met and what their plans were, they couldn't believe it.

Sonia didn't approve. She was upset that the woman he said he loved and wanted to marry wasn't Jewish.

"Marcella was a starlet, sparkly and blond!" recalled May Mitchelson. "It was an interesting period in our lives as well as hers, because we wondered why Marvin had to *import* somebody when so many American girls were crazy about him! They were standing in line!"

Good old Uncle Mack Marks may have been the only one who wasn't surprised at this latest turn in Marvin's life. "Nothing unusual about it," he harumphed. "You know, Marvin always was kind of a screwball, anyhow. Marvin's got a lot of guts."

Marvin and Marcella were married exactly a week before Christmas, 1960. The big Sunday wedding was in the Empire Room of the Beverly Hilton, with two-hundred guests, masses of red and white carnations, and a reception on the roof. Mitchelson used the bash to rise a few more rungs on the Hollywood social ladder by having his idea of impressive people involved in the wedding party: A lissome, twenty-six-year-old actress named Gia Scala was Marcella's maid of honor; his best man was the art director of the Getty Museum and the son of an MGM songwriter; and the guest list was sprinkled with judges, Italian luminaries, and Hollywood types.

But Bob Landry wasn't going to be there to see what a great match he'd made, for during one of Marvin's visits back to Rome—this time during the 1960 Summer Olympics—Mitchelson's office called to tell him that his best friend had died of an aneurism in London. Landry was on his honeymoon, and had been married only eight days.

Mitchelson flew up to London for the funeral. It was a typically overcast, bleak day, and there were maybe a dozen mourners there, mostly people who'd been sent by *Life*. Landry's wife didn't know any of them. The dreariness of it all was overwhelming.

This was the second time the most important man in Marvin Mitchelson's life had died unexpectedly. In the years to come, those premature deaths would profoundly affect him, leaving him with such a fear of dying that he refused even to make out his own last will and testament, "because it's a recipe for death sometimes." Herbert Mitchelson was only forty-six years old at his death; Landry just forty-five. How could Mitchelson trust friendships? Landry was the closest thing to a soulmate that he had. The only constants in his life now were the women: his mother, his sisters, and his wife.

8

Back in Beverly Hills after his victory in the Douglas case, Marvin settled down to the staples that were the fare of a rising lawyer.

He was accumulating a number of Hollywood clients, and with each came the kind of publicity that virtually guaranteed that more such clients would be walking through the door. He handled divorces (with tabloid headlines that read "LIPSTICK STAINS LEAD TO DIVORCE"; "ACTRESS CHARGES MATE HAS VIOLENT TEMPER"), child custody cases ("WOMAN WINS CUSTODY OF SISTER'S BABY BOY"; "MAN, 63, SEIZES BABY SON OF HIS WIFE, 17"), and just about anything else that paid the rent—even libel actions against the very tabloids that seemed to be so enthralled by his other cases.

There was the lawsuit Mitchelson filed against President John F. Kennedy—a case with enough media appeal to thrust him way beyond the tabloids. He'd sued Kennedy for $450,000 a few days before the November 1960 election, alleging that four Mississippi delegates to the Democratic convention earlier that summer had been injured in an automobile accident involving a car Kennedy had hired to take them to a Perle Mesta party in J.F.K.'s honor. His main client was a hack politician who'd once made a four-day donkey ride from Winona to Jackson, Mississippi, to win a campaign bet, and who now alleged he "will no longer be able to ride donkeys, or broncos and rodeo bulls." After amassing two years worth of publicity, including threats to take the president's deposition, an insurance company sent a check for $2,187.50.

He was also riding high on the tabloid-splashed case of Beverly Aadland and her mother, Florence. Seventeen-year-old Beverly was the pubescent playmate of Errol Flynn, who'd died the year before.

The prosecutors said they had secret tape recordings of Beverly's mother boasting that "nobody is going to make love to my baby for less than $100," and one witness claimed he'd been offered $5,000 by Florence to "take care of" one of Beverly's unwanted boyfriends.

Considering all the accusations against his client, it was amazing that the only charge Florence faced was contributing to the delinquency of a minor. But that's all it was, and Mitchelson took his client as he found her. Florence was decidedly less than charming: She was a tempermental, fifty-three-year-old bleached blonde (the tabloids almost never missed the chance to call her a "bleached blonde") with an artificial leg, and Marvin had all he could do to control her outbursts in and out of court.

The Aadland case stayed on the front pages for weeks, the newspapers chronicling one wild courtroom scene after another. Marvin thought one way to control Florence would be to kick her under the counsel table when she acted up. It was only after each kick produced a dull "thunk," but no discernable reaction from Florence, that he realized he was kicking her artificial leg.

With a flourishing practice and all the media attention his burgeoning ego could absorb, the last thing Mitchelson probably wanted to do was more charity work for Douglas and Meyes. But now there was another letter from Douglas's mother, Farena, reporting that the state had gotten its vengeance against her son after all, and asking for his help once more.

Scarcely a month and a half after Douglas had beaten the murder rap, he and Meyes were reindicted on thirteen robbery and assault counts, and a little more than a month after that they'd been found guilty on every count. What was worse, the two hadn't even been represented by counsel during the robbery trial. The whole proceeding was stacked against them right from the start.

"I was *broke* after that second [murder] trial," Mitchelson recalled. He'd been on the Douglas case the better part of six months by then. "I couldn't put in a number of weeks [more] on it." But he also couldn't resist the pleas of Farena Douglas.

Sonia had recently married her cousin, Ben Knoppow. He was also a lawyer. So Mitchelson ordered the transcript of Douglas's robbery trial and asked his new stepfather to have a look.

Ben Knoppow came back and told him: It's just like Mrs. Douglas says it is. Her boy was railroaded.

That was all Mitchelson needed to hear. He remembered what he'd told the jury about the robberies during his closing argument in the second murder trial. "They're going to try Bill Douglas for every robbery they can think of" if he walks on the murder rap, Mitchelson said then, "but I want to say to you right here and now that he is not guilty of those robberies, [and] I hope I'm there to defend him! . . . Those witnesses are so bad, so poor."

There was no federal constitutional requirement then that an indigent criminal defendant in a state court action be provided with a lawyer. Nor was there a constitutional guarantee that a lawyer be provided for such a defendant appealing a criminal conviction.

California thought of itself as progressive when it came to those two things, though. The state already had public defenders in its trial courts, and if a destitute defendant filed an appeal the court of appeals could ask the county bar association to find an attorney for him—but only if the chief judge found a meritorious issue to appeal. Such was the extent of the state's *noblesse oblige* toward the destitute.

Paul Breckenridge was already familiar with the robbery charges from having represented Meyes in the two earlier murder trials. But he was so wrung out from those trials that he asked to be reassigned. With both of their original lawyers thus out of the picture, Meyes and Douglas had been given a new deputy public defender to share for their robbery trial. Their new lawyer was Norman R. Atkins. He was thirty years old, and he considered his two clients "particularly ugly and loathsome characters who spent their lives figuring out ways of getting themselves out of jail. I didn't want anything to do with them. I don't know why *anybody* would."

Meyes and Douglas felt the same way about Atkins. They'd both become adept jailhouse lawyers—by now, they'd been in jail almost a year, and they'd been putting their idle time to good use. On the day the robbery trial was to begin, Meyes complained that Atkins was so overworked and unfamiliar with the case that he couldn't possibly provide a decent defense. And Douglas demanded private counsel because he said the public defender had a conflict of interest: Meyes, after all, was a convicted *murderer*; but Douglas had been found *innocent* of that charge. Forcing the same lawyer on them both presumed, incorrectly, that they ought to rise or fall together.

"Say, your Honor," Douglas interjected as prospective jurors were being questioned. "I'd like to address the court."

"No!"

Douglas said, "I am denied the right to obtain a private counsel!"

Bayard Rhone had also presided over their first murder trial. He wasn't going to tolerate their interruptions, and to make that clear he threatened to gag them and strap them in their chairs. When Meyes and Douglas fired Atkins (much to Atkins' pleasure) to make their own point, the judge instructed them: "You will have to carry the defense of the case yourself; have to ask all of the necessary questions and do all the cross-examining."

"We aren't lawyers," Meyes replied. "We can't fight Mr. Joe Carr. . . . We are not ready for trial, your Honor."

Rhone replied, "Very well. Call your first witness."

"We cannot defend ourselves. It's illegal, this procedure," said Douglas.

Meyes ended up getting a lifetime ticket to Folsom Prison. Douglas was sent to San Quentin.

Neither man was permitted a lawyer for his appeal. But Meyes, on behalf of himself and Douglas, got a jailhouse appeal going anyway. By the time Marvin stepped back in, there was only one appeal venue remaining: the U.S. Supreme Court.

Mitchelson had agreed to help the two men, but he was an astute enough judge of his own skills to know that, however good he might be on his feet, he certainly wasn't very good in the library. Appellate work was heavy on the research, and that took a lot more than just heart. Trial work was often just the reverse. Mitchelson was going to need a cocounsel—somebody to pull the laboring oar when it came to brief-writing and all the other paper-handling that went along with an appeal to the nation's highest court.

Burton Marks had been Marvin's classmate during the first, abortive year at the UCLA Law School. He had put himself through the law school by working nights as a cashier at a downtown striptease joint.

Two years younger than Marvin, Marks was an affable, fun-loving, stout guy, about six-feet-one and 250 pounds, with slightly receding black hair and a booming baritone voice. But the appearance Marks presented was deceiving; his garrulous style masked a superior intellect. Marks loved his law books, and he was already making a name for himself as an articulate, respected appellate lawyer. Marks had his heart set on being a judge someday.

In years to come, other lawyers would often come in whenever Mitchelson had an important case. You could win a case in the courtroom, after all, but that meant little if you couldn't protect it on appeal through the gritty, unglamorous work that was the appellate lawyer's stock in trade: precedents, theories, the written word.

All through his career, Mitchelson used his appellate gnomes brilliantly, and there were times when he was told, point blank, to just stay out of the way and let them do their stuff. He paid them well and took credit for their work, but everybody seemed satisfied. They were his heavy ballast; when their work was done, he could sail off to his next big headline.

It was in the appellate courts, Mitchelson would later write, "that attorneys get down to practicing real law, because it is the law itself, its meaning and interpretation, that must be argued on appeal." The trial court simply resolved matters of fact, but appellate courts *defined* the law.

The Supreme Court seldom agrees to hear any appeal, but the odds of the High Court accepting a pauper's appeal—an *in forma pauperis* petition, in the Court's peculiar vernacular—were almost nil. When it did accept such a petition, the Court advanced the expenses of the appeal itself, and agreed to waive some of the strict rules that applied to ordinary petitioners.

The eight-page typewritten *in forma pauperis* petition that Marks, acting for Douglas and Meyes, sent to the Court on April 6, 1961, came at a critical point in the evolution of criminal law. The important decisions of the 1960s—decisions like *Gideon*, *Miranda*, and *Escobedo* that would be synonymous with new due-process safeguards for the accused—were just over the horizon. The Warren Court's judicial radar was scanning "cert" petitions to find the right ones to make new law. And when they spotted the petition for a writ of certiorari in the case of *William Douglas and Bennie Will Meyes, Petitioners, vs. The People of the State of California, Respondent*, the justices picked it up.

Give Mitchelson credit. As would be apparent in the *Marvin vs. Marvin* case more than a decade later, he had a knack for sensing when the law was ready to change and then helping to move it in that direction.

Up to that point, the 1942 Supreme Court decision of *Betts vs. Brady* controlled. It said, quite clearly, that there was no universal assurance of a lawyer's help in a state criminal trial.

In his petition, Marks wrote:

> The principal questions presented for review is [sic] whether the petitioners William Douglas and Bennie Will Meyes were accorded due process of law under the United States Constitutional Amendments V and XIV in that:
> A. they were denied the right to independent counsel at time of trial;
> B. they were denied the right to any counsel at the appellate level;
> C. they were denied the right to prepare their defense for trial; and
> D. they were denied, severally, access to transcripts and records upon which to base their appeal.

Marks thought the best chance for getting the convictions overturned lay in arguing that the men were unconstitutionally denied the assistance of counsel in prosecuting their appeal. He found a passage in a 1956 Supreme Court opinion that raised, but didn't resolve, the same issue, and told the justices in his cert petition that the *Douglas* petition ought to be accepted because it presented "a new and novel question never passed upon before by this Court."

The California attorney general's office thought so little of Douglas's and Meyes's chances to win that it didn't even bother to rebut the cert petition. But on June 15, 1961, the assistant clerk of the Supreme Court wrote to the attorney general in San Francisco and told him to send a response to the petition before July 24. The justices were seriously considering granting cert, even though that wasn't known by either Marks, who, having heard nothing from the Court, wrote on June 22 to ask what was going on, or by Meyes, who did the same a week later. ("Further inquiries of this nature should be directed to your attorneys," the Court's assistant clerk stiffly replied.) On October 9, 1961, the Court air-mailed a notice to Marks that it had agreed to hear *Douglas*.

Because this was a pauper's case, the High Court would be absorbing the substantial expenses associated with printing Douglas's and Meyes's lower-court record and their Supreme Court briefs. But Marks and Mitchelson wanted to be paid, *too*, for all the time they were about to put in on *Douglas*, so they started petitioning the Court to formally appoint them as the paupers' counsel.

Denied, the justices ruled. Mitchelson and Marks had come this far without compensation; they ought to be able to see the case through the rest of the way. The two lawyers couldn't even get their travel costs back to Washington picked up.

Only in oral argument before the Supreme Court did the public actually observe any part of the decision-making process of the nine justices. Everything else they did took place in total secrecy; even the law clerks were sometimes excluded.

It was also the closest thing that the judicial branch had to a spectacle. In the Court's high-ceilinged, ornate chamber across the street from the Capitol, the solemn call to order—Oyez, oyez, oyez!—came precisely at 10 A.M.; then began the lively sparring between lawyer and justice. The justices didn't look with favor on lawyers who read from a prepared text. This was a time for extemporizing, made all the more so by justices who had a penchant for interrupting a lawyer at will with questions that invariably derailed any well-rehearsed presentation. There was a saying among appellate lawyers who considered themselves old hands at the Supreme Court: You could never win a case on the strength of an oral argument alone, but you sure as hell could lose one.

The oral argument in *Douglas* was scheduled for Tuesday, April 17, 1962.

"I figured, after the Court agreed to review *Douglas*, that they were going to bury *Betts vs. Brady* and bury us, too," recalled Jack E. Goertzen, then a strapping, blond young deputy California attorney general.

"The state of California always appointed a lawyer for an indigent at trial, even though it wasn't federally required," Goertzen went on. "But in the old days, the [California] court was stingy and didn't want to spend the money to always furnish a lawyer for the appeal. So I was defending the system of the appellate court reviewing the transcript and making its own decision about the need for counsel on appeal. I knew I was fighting a drift against the position we were taking. I just didn't want to look like a fool [during the argument]."

The drama of it all had its effect on everybody. Goertzen and another more experienced state lawyer, William E. James, were going to argue the state's case for keeping the status quo. James had previously argued before the Court and was thus already a member of its bar, but the other three advocates had never been to the Court before. Goertzen went out a day early for his swearing in, which was a formality but one attended by a bit of pomp, too, only to find President Kennedy, Attorney General Robert F. Kennedy, and Defense Secretary Robert McNamara already there: It was the first day on the bench for their good friend, Byron R. ("Whizzer") White. Mitchelson and Marks were sworn in the next morning, sponsored by their putative nemesis, Bill James. Advocacy sometimes made for strange bedfellows.

Sonia and Marcella were in the audience, too—the latter wearing what Goertzen later recollected was a full-length sable coat, even though it was the middle of April.

Chief Justice Earl Warren called the case in his gravelly voice, mispronouncing Meyes's name as "Meyers" and mumbling through the rest of the case name.

By prearrangement, Marks and Mitchelson had agreed that the more experienced appellate advocate should go first. Each side had an hour. Marks planned to use most of their hour, with Mitchelson returning for a rebuttal after the California attorney general's lawyers had spoken.

Marks started off in his resonant voice. "It's our contention," he said, "that petitioners were denied assistance of counsel, and thus due process of law, at *both* stages,"—the trial as well as the appeal.

Marks maintained that it wasn't enough for California to say it had adequately protected a poor man's rights when all it did was have an appellate judge review his trial transcript. A judge, Marks said, cannot also be an indigent's lawyer.

Justice Hugo Black started swamping Marks with questions right away. Black seemed much more interested in the trial than the appeal, and now he wanted to know why the public defender had been fired by Meyes and Douglas.

Because he wasn't prepared, Marks replied.

Well, why not? Black wanted to know. "It's a pretty common thing for lawyers to say they haven't had time to prepare," Black drawled. Marks was getting antsy to return to his line of attack, but Black, who spoke like he had a mouthful of small pebbles, kept needling him with question after question about the prep time for the trial. Why wasn't thirty-nine days sufficient to prepare for trial? How long had Atkins been a public defender? How long had he been a lawyer? What was so peculiar about this case for the public defender not to be able to prepare adequately?

When Marks got back on track, he finally cited what was the core of his case: Goertzen's brief wrongly argued that a bunch of skilled appellate judges, being conscientious almost to a fault, would be better able to decide whether the defendants needed counsel on appeal rather than a court-appointed attorney who might view his appointment with irritation.

"I'd rather have a novitiate attorney review my record on appeal than any appellate justice," Marks intoned. "And the reason for that is because appellate justices *are not advocates*! They're not out to determine error or find error. They're *judges*!"

The chief justice broke in, "Would you mind stating to us what the record shows about conflict of interest?"

Marks replied, "This was Mr. Mitchelson's portion of the argument." Mitchelson was saving that for the planned rebuttal.

Let's have it now, Warren ordered.

Marks first tried to give a clear, heads-up reply himself: "If I'm sitting here with two defendants, I may decide that it would be better not to have defendant Meyes take the stand. Because if he takes the stand, he can be impeached—by the murder conviction and the prior robberies. Defendant Douglas can't. How can I, as a counsel, who must conscientiously devote myself—my entire zeal and energy and devotion—to one client, stand there and talk about Mr. Douglas as being 'a nice clean young man who really has no record, but look, on the other hand, at Mr. Meyes.' You just can't do it! You cannot say this man is good and this man is bad and represent them [both]. It is a conflict of interest."

"That's all you can point to about conflict of interest?" Warren asked, seemingly incredulous.

Marks asked, "May I ask Mr. Mitchelson to take over that part of the argument?"

Marks had been speaking for about half an hour. Now, much sooner than he or anyone else expected, Mitchelson walked to the well of the Court.

Mitchelson had a cold, and his voice was hoarse. It certainly wasn't starting out as one of his better days. "An attorney must have his mind free and *cluttered*," Mitchelson began, a noticeable tremelo in his voice. "Free and *uncluttered*, excuse me! He must not worry about being embarrassed when he argues for a second party. . . . This is conflict if I've ever seen conflict in a case."

Warren: "Would you please point out to me in the record how the conflict was presented to the court?"

Mitchelson fumbled around. "Yes, your honor," he said, dragging each word out as long as possible. "I think I can point that out to you—"

Even his opponent felt sorry for him. "Page thirty-six," Goertzen whispered from the counsel table.

Mitchelson replied, "Page thirty-six would be one instance!" He turned to the page and read from it.

The justices were full of other questions, questions totally unrelated to the conflict-of-interest issue that Mitchelson was supposed to be addressing. But, instead of inviting Marks back up, Marvin just stood there and took all the shots.

"What happened is, you've got an hour, and they just started asking question after question," Goertzen laughed. "I could see poor Marks over there, just going *crazy!*"

Mitchelson equivocated on most of the tough legal points but regaled the justices with all kinds of war stories from the trial. "I can still hear myself referring to the jury!" Mitchelson rattled on as the justices all sat there silently. "I've never seen a collection of witnesses like this! One of them couldn't see fifteen feet! Didn't have her glasses on at the time of the alleged robbery. [She was] talking about instances that happened two hundred feet from her. Positively refused to identify Douglas!"

A red light in front of him blinked on. "I see by that, your Honor, that my time is up," Mitchelson said abruptly as Marks stewed. "I guess I better sit down." Marks never got a chance to stand up again.

Behind the scenes, Justice Black was one of the strongest proponents of a universal right to counsel in criminal matters, and his testy questioning of Goertzen, when it was time for the state to argue, now left little doubt about where he stood:

"How long did it take the defendants to offer their evidence at the murder trial, and how long did it take 'em to offer it at the robbery trial?" Black demanded to know.

Goertzen: The defendants offered no evidence at all in this robbery trial. At the murder trial the witnesses were thoroughly cross examined.

Goertzen spoke in a nervous, reedy voice. It seemed so ill-suited to his big frame. He sounded like an officious pipsqueak.

Black: How *long* did they offer testimony in the murder case?

He sounded hostile.

Goertzen: On the robberies?

Black: On *anything* in the murder case.

Now he sounded real hostile.

Goertzen: Oh! Both defendants took the stand and testified at great length in the murder case. . . . Mr. Mitchelson can vouch for that.

Mitchelson saw his opening. Without giving Goertzen a chance to start talking again, Mitchelson hurried to Goertzen's side. "Yes they were, your Honors." Yes, Mitchelson was happy to come back to the microphone—again—to vouch for that particular fact. Yes, indeed! His voice had a smug intonation that put it somewhere between a Boy Scout and a teacher's pet.

"They were on the stand a *great* while." Mitchelson cheerfully babbled on as Goertzen stood there. "But there were two trials, also. So it was not just two hundred and sixty-seven pages of transcript [as Goertzen had mentioned], it was *five hundred,* 'cause there were two trials and there was different testimony at each trial." The point of Mitchelson's answer was to show that Meyes and Douglas couldn't possibly have had proper representation, because, if they had, their trial would have taken a whole lot longer than three days.

Warren: The two trials took twelve weeks?

Mitchelson: Yes, your Honor.

Goertzen had logged forty-one hours at night preparing for this argument, but in spite of all that hard training he was punchy from the blows Mitchelson had just gotten in. "Oh, I didn't know that myself. I thought the second trial took the twelve weeks."

Mitchelson: The second trial took about eight weeks. The first one took about six. [That didn't add up to twelve weeks, but nobody said anything.]

Black: I was asking him the question on this basis. They claim that they were not properly represented. Now, here you have a case that heretofore has been referred to as being very much the same. It took eight weeks and four weeks [sic] to try the two murder cases. Three *days* to try the robbery cases, where the defendants did not have lawyers. Does the fact that they didn't have lawyers have anything to do with that?

Goertzen vehemently denied that it did. But then Justice William Brennan jumped all over him.

"Am I right?" Brennan intoned scornfully. "These defendants basically stood mute through the trial after Atkins had been dismissed?"

Goertzen: Oh yes, you're definitely right.

Brennan: They didn't cross examine any witnesses.

Goertzen: Right. They didn't do a thing.

Brennan: They didn't sum up to the jury.

Goertzen: They didn't do a thing.

Brennan: They offered no witnesses of their own.

Goertzen: Absolutely nothing.

Brennan: They didn't take the stand.

Goertzen: They did absolutely nothing. Nothing. And our whole basic contention is, they had no right to dismiss that public defender. And I submit that the citations in the record that I've given your Honors adequately support—

Brennan: I take it the three days [of proceedings] includes all the time up to Atkins's dismissal, does it?

Goertzen: Yes. The three days include everything.

Brennan: The trial itself, when they finally got to taking testimony, took how long?

Goertzen: I believe that took a day. Maybe. A trial day, let's say.

Goertzen was pretty well bloodied by now. He tried to continue his argument without giving Brennan a chance to ask anything more.

"These men weren't inarticulate defendants. You read that record. Patently, these men might be able to get on the 'David Susskind Show.' At least Meyes. He used some pretty large words, there. And he knew what he was doing, I submit."

Brennan: Well, it doesn't follow that they knew how to defend themselves.

Goertzen: . . . They were adequately warned [that they shouldn't have fired their public defender].

Now Black jumped back in. "What you have is . . . the Court exercised his judgment and decided that they could take him or have nobody."

Goertzen: That's about the complexion of things.

Black: And they defended themselves about like people without a lawyer usually would. They didn't argue the case, did they?

Goertzen: No, they didn't.

Black: There's no question.

Goertzen: After each witness, they'd jump up and yell they wanted counsel and that they were being railroaded.

Black: As to whether that violated due process or not, I presume, looking at it from this significance, having happened, it might have been better if [the judge had] waited a few days and seen if he could get 'em a lawyer, wouldn't it?

Goertzen: I submit Judge Rhone followed the state penal code in this case.

It was becoming clear where the majority of the justices were going to come out on *Douglas*. But the interesting thing would be how they were going to get there, because even though the state of California didn't have the justices on its side, the state *did* have the support of the existing precedents of *Betts vs. Brady* and its progeny.

As Goertzen later explained it: "I said, when I wrote our briefs, How can they claim federal due process requires separate counsel on *appeal*, when *Betts vs. Brady* still says there's no federal right to counsel at *trial*? I mean, they were going to have to deal with that. Nobody could argue that having guaranteed counsel on appeal was more important than having a lawyer at your trial."

It soon became obvious that the justices saw that dichotomy too, for as the term was ending, on June 25, the justices set *Douglas* over for reargument in the new term that would begin the following October. It was to be argued on the same day as another important case. A few weeks earlier, they'd granted an *in forma pauperis* petition from a Florida prisoner named Clarence Earl Gideon. The case of *Gideon vs. Cochran* (later, *Gideon vs. Wainright*) clearly presented the issue of the right to counsel at trial; in Florida, the only indigents who were guaranteed counsel were those facing the death penalty.

Gideon was destined to become one of those rare cases that symbolize a major turning point in the slow evolution of the law. Its place in history was to be all but assured. The justices had asked one of Washington's most respected attorneys, Abe Fortas, to represent Gideon before the High Court, an illustration of just how important they viewed the case to be. (Not too many years after that, Fortas himself became a Supreme Court justice.)

Mitchelson and Marks figured that if they were going to have to come back to Washington for the reargument, they might as well try again to get their first-class airfare reimbursed. And, in their own serio-comedic way, the justices again rebuffed the duo with what was by now their standard one-liner on the subject: Denied.

Not that it made any difference, of course. The two lawyers certainly weren't going to turn down their second shot at glory.

The *Douglas* case finally came up for reargument on Wednesday, January 16, 1963. Fortas, who argued *Gideon* a day earlier, on January 15, held a dinner that evening at the National Lawyers Club for all the other advocates in what now was a melange of similar cases being argued that week. Mitchelson and Marks both went, as did Goertzen, who was sorry he turned down Fortas's offer of a ride back to the Mayflower Hotel when he later saw the classic Rolls-Royce that was the wealthy Fortas's transportation.

It was decided that Mitchelson would speak first. Having written all the briefs* and with his own reputation on the line, Marks wanted to be the one to charge in off the bench. Mitchelson had taken more of their allotted hour than Marks wanted him to during the first argument, but for the reargument Marks must have somehow become convinced

---

*Before the reargument, Marks brought in three lawyers from the American Civil Liberties Union to help with the legal research.

that letting his counterpart go first would get him up and out of the well quickly.

The result, instead, was that Mitchelson held the floor for more than thirty-three minutes, never once addressing the central issue in *Douglas*—whether there was a federal guarantee of counsel on appeal. Even when Justice White subjected him to a virtual cross-examination that was flagrantly intended to get Mitchelson to the point of things, he didn't get on track.

Which wasn't to say that Mitchelson didn't do well. In fact, he'd gotten over the stage fright that was so evident early in his first argument, and he spoke forcefully, even eloquently, to a Court that seemed ready to overturn *Betts vs. Brady*. What he could do was to speak with a fervor that Marks couldn't possibly have, because Mitchelson had been there. He'd *seen* the injustice.

"I happened to try both murder trials. I represented Douglas, and I gained an acquittal for him. . . . They were thoroughly impeached, these [robbery] witnesses [against Douglas and Meyes]. And very badly discredited. And I feel, quite frankly, in all earnestness, that this cross examination of these witnesses helped gain an acquittal for Douglas. So, when a statement is made by the judge, who tried the first case and knows the testimony from these witnesses, and the prosecutor who was the same prosecutor on both murder cases, that there was no conflict, that both defendants were positively identified by all these witnesses in every respect: that just is not the truth of the matter. . . .

"I would ask my brother Goertzen, who he'd have rather represented. Here's a man [Meyes], on one hand, who has four prior felonies. And Douglas, who has a clean record. Has no felonies. Douglas, who has just received an acquittal for murder; Meyes, who's been convicted for murder. And these two were thrown into a trial together. And, almost naively, the prosecutor says: There's no conflict.

"Your Honors, there isn't any doubt in my mind that this whole proceeding is a result of the bias by the Los Angeles Police Department. This is a tragic event, the death of a brother officer. But here they have two trials, where finally Douglas is acquitted. Meyes is found to be a habitual criminal. You can't give a man more than life! What was the necessity of bringing Meyes back for the robbery trial? He's a habitual criminal. He's sentenced to life imprisonment. After the second murder trial, the result is the same. He'll be there for the rest of his life! So why do they bring him in on a robbery trial? So obvious! They want to put him back together with Douglas. They want the taint of Bennie Meyes to rub off on Douglas!"

When the opinions in *Douglas* and *Gideon* were issued by the justices on Monday, March 18, 1963, it was *Douglas* that was announced first. When the justices read their opinions, which is almost always on a Monday until the load gets heavy toward the end of the term, they go in order of the most junior to the most senior justice. Justice William O. Douglas had written the 6-to-3 opinion in the case of his ironic namesake, and it was a workmanlike, straightforward disavowal of the appellate process California had used in *Douglas*. "There has been discrimination between the rich and the poor which violates the Fourteenth Amendment," Justice Douglas's opinion said. The conviction of the two men would be erased. They would get new trials.* And Douglas would get his name on a Supreme Court opinion that was still the law of the land nearly thirty years later. Mitchelson and Marks had good cause to be proud of what they'd achieved.

The reading of the result in *Douglas* telegraphed the result that would soon be announced by Justice Black in *Gideon*. If *Betts vs. Brady* were overturned as to the guarantee of counsel on appeal, then it logically followed that *Gideon* would overrule *Betts* as to counsel at trial. And that is precisely what Black's opinion did.

If there were anything for Mitchelson and Marks to be disappointed about, it was that *Douglas* quickly became something of a judicial footnote to *Gideon*. *Douglas*, after all, raised the same issue of counsel at trial as *Gideon* did, and raised it earlier. But Washington was an insider's town: Fortas was destined for glory, and the Court's unanimous ruling immortalized Gideon and Fortas, not Douglas and Mitchelson. When Anthony Lewis wrote his celebrated book, *Gideon's Trumpet*, in 1964, the Douglas case wasn't even mentioned by name.

Even Jack Goertzen, the deputy California attorney general who lost the Douglas case, felt robbed of the greatness that he thought, win or lose, would be his. "By calling into question *Betts vs. Brady* when we did, our case was responsible for *Gideon*," he claimed. "They shopped around until they came up with *Gideon*. It always pissed me off that Fortas got all the credit."

But that didn't seem to matter so much to Mitchelson. Beverly Hills and Hollywood were a long way from Washington, and he had his own agenda for capitalizing on the case he'd just won.

---

*Douglas and Meyes were convicted of some of the crimes at their retrial. Douglas was discharged from San Quentin in 1969; Meyes from Folsom Prison in 1978.

PART THREE
Ticket to Ride

The Beverly Hills boutiques that became a national metaphor for conspicuous consumption were still years in the future when Marvin Mitchelson returned to his law office after the *Douglas* victory. Even though Beverly Hills wasn't the lima-bean field it had once been before the city incorporated in 1914, Rodeo Drive was still a down-home main street with a hardware store, cheap restaurants, and lots of beauty salons. Gucci would be the first to arrive, in 1968, with Van Cleef & Arpels soon after.

But there was still a familiar, lived-in feel to the place in the 1960s, and it extended to the fraternity of Beverly Hills lawyers.

"The lawyers who were here then were like the L.A. clique," explained Carey Caruso, a second-generation Beverly Hills lawyer whose father, Paul Caruso, became part of that monied club whose legal work greased the skids for Los Angeles's fantastic postwar expansion. "They got here at the end of World War Two, and it was such a smaller, more intimate town then. For a while, vets who'd gone to law school didn't even have to take the Bar exam. They could get passed by a resolution.

"These were the guys who *made* post-World War Two Los Angeles, from 1947 to the 1970s," Carey Caruso observed. "It's almost a biblical tale."

Paul Caruso's story was part of it. The elder Caruso had no sooner established himself in Beverly Hills than he was drafted back into the military during the Korean War. Lawyers at the Pentagon, which is where he was from 1951 until 1954, didn't earn what their silk-stockinged counterparts did, so when Caruso finally got back home he was anxious to make up his lost time and just as hungry for business as Mitchelson was.

"Through a series of fluke accidents, I met Pam and James Mason," Caruso remembered. James Mason was one of the film colony's steadiest workers, an Englishman with a knack for playing romantic villains. His younger English wife, Pamela, was a television personality and the outspoken doyenne of Beverly Hills society. She affected the same stiff British accent as her husband; it was "lovah" this and "dahling" that.

The Mason house on six acres was so grandiose it was called a château; their neighborhood behind the Beverly Hills Hotel so exclusive its only street was a private one named Pamela. And therein lay a problem for those very important people named Mason: Pamela Drive was *so* exclusive that the City of Beverly Hills called it a private right-of-way and refused to pick up the Masons' garbage—unless, of course, Pamela or James hauled it all the way out to a public street, three hundred yards away, which no self-respecting matinee idol was about to do.

So Pamela's brother, who also served as her personal manager, called Caruso and told him about their problem. "And [he] assured me they had a very good lawyer named Greg Bautzer, and that I shouldn't have any illusions about being their lawyer. [He said] I'm not in Bautzer's class. . . . My assignment [was] to have the City of Beverly Hills pick up their trash; their garbage."

"It just so happens I *specialize* in garbage cases," Caruso instantly replied. Effective at that moment, he was the city's leading legal expert on trash hauling. He used his connections to cut the red tape.

"And I *succeeded*. [So] I became their attorney."

It was just another example of cultural Darwinism, Beverly Hills–style: survival of the best-connected.

"Now, Pamela was the absolute queen bee of society. When I was in her favor, which was for about four years, she opened doors for me that you couldn't believe! Jack Benny. Zsa Zsa Gabor. Name them! I was there, meeting them! I represented Richard Burton and Laurence Olivier through her. Richard Burton on a drunk driving [charge], and Laurence Olivier on something. Richard Burton had been at their house at an all-night party. Got drunk. And on the way home, crashed into a tree. I got the case."

Then James and Pamela wanted a divorce. Caruso represented Pamela, and got her $20,000 a month in temporary alimony in 1962, which was virtually unheard of. Caruso had four young children, with another on the way, and this was his first taste of money. He went to Europe with his wife. He called the office one day to ask, "How're we doing?" And the reply came back: "We have bad news."

It seemed that "a hot-blooded Italian" lawyer in Caruso's office had insulted Pamela. "She had sent a telegram [as evidence in the divorce case] and we had not returned it to her." Pamela was irate. "[And] my young lawyer said, 'Go fuck yourself!' to Pamela Mason. . . .

"So she fired me—and found a young lawyer named Marvin Mitchelson. That was his first big break."

The Pamela Mason story had enough twists in its plot to be subtitled The Case of the Disenchanted Doyenne. Although everybody agreed that Caruso had been fired, each of the principals gave a different reason why. Caruso alleged it had to do with another lawyer's vulgarism, and Mitchelson said Pamela fired Caruso because "he was driving down

[Sunset Boulevard] in a convertible and her file fell out and left a trail all the way down to the beach!"

In any event, by the time Pamela walked into an Encino restaurant to attend a friend's Christmas party in 1963, she had been handling the case by herself, without any lawyer at all. And she was handling it poorly.

Against James's tough San Francisco attorney, Jake Ehrlich, Pamela was beset by a maze of legal and jurisdictional issues posed by her husband's living in Switzerland, sheltering his assets in Liechtenstein, and keeping scarcely a cent in the United States.

Mitchelson was at that Encino party, too, telling his tales about the *Douglas* victory of the previous March and generally being himself. Marvin particularly liked to describe how he'd preempted his compatriot, Burton Marks, during the first *Douglas* oral argument after Marks had addressed the justices for scarcely more than one minute. One minute! As Mitchelson related it, he had taken over for Marks and literally won the case single-handedly, arguing by himself for a full fifty-eight minutes. As Mitchelson repeated the tale again and again it grew to include a little sidebar about his dropping all his papers while walking to the well of the court ("I was so nervous. . . . But I took my time picking things up. . . . I let them suffer with me. . . . I was looking for sympathy.") and an account of how the justices asked him to spend an extra half hour during the reargument so he could describe every last detail of how he beat Douglas's murder rap.

They were entertaining stories, and they were told with gusto. They also happened to be totally untrue—although only the few who'd ever listened to the Supreme Court arguments could possibly know that.

"He didn't seem the standard Hollywood slick talker," Pamela Mason later recollected in what was a rare exception to her ordinarily biting tongue and, some would say, ordinarily good judgment. "He waved his arms around when he was discussing things and had rather loud opinions on practically everything. He also had a fairly cozy manner. He confided. He charmed. He lied occasionally, and was suitably abashed when he was caught. I decided he looked like a fairly good bet."

Pamela Mason had a raconteur's reputation, too, having been dubbed "Mrs. Chatterly" by the local press for hosting her own daily radio and television talk shows. So Mason invited her new lawyer friend to be a guest on her TV show, there to be, Mitchelson suspected, a straight man for Mason's diatribes against lawyers.

He was right about that. But when his host started haranguing him about why there were so many whereases and wherefroms and wherefores in the wills lawyers wrote, Mitchelson came back with a zinger. The shortest will on record was just three words: "All to mother." Mitchelson later confided he'd been flipping through the *Guinness Book of World Records* just before the show.

Mason was sold on this lovable rogue. She hired him as her new lawyer, and he reached back to his process-server days for a stratagem aimed at inducing a settlement in the case of *Mason vs. Mason*.

The ploy was ingeniously simple. Two weeks before the scheduled trial, Mitchelson subpoenaed as prospective witnesses about forty prominent friends of the Masons. He didn't have any idea whose side they'd take or what they'd say, but he did know that there were two "Jane Does" in Pamela's divorce complaint and he presumed some of the witnesses would know about them, too. Mitchelson also let it be known that he was prepared to disclose, both to the media and in the courtroom, the details of private sexual matters that would embarrass James.

"I knew the result that could be expected," Mitchelson later wrote. "Immediate panic." Sure enough, the witnesses who wanted to be kept out of the middle started pressuring James, who wasn't exactly thrilled at these previews of coming attractions, either. On the weekend before the trial was to begin, Jake Ehrlich came down from San Francisco and announced that his client wanted to settle. After negotiating all day Saturday and into the wee hours of Sunday morning, Mitchelson had his deal: a $1.5 million settlement for Pamela.

The whole package was wrapped up and sealed in Santa Monica Superior Court the following Tuesday morning, September 1, 1964. Afterward, in the courthouse corridor, James called the settlement "a flea bite." After all, he was getting off the hook without giving her any alimony at all. But Pamela was ecstatic. Her settlement was one of the first ever to break the magic million-dollar mark, and Mitchelson had gotten her—and himself—a ton of publicity about it. ("$1.5 MILLION DIVORCE FOR PAMELA MASON," one headline screamed. "SPICY TRIAL AVOIDED BY SETTLEMENT").

The Mason case set the tone for the Hollywood divorces to come. Pamela was so grateful she did everything she could to make Marvin Mitchelson a household name. Pamela hired him eight months later for a $138,500 breach-of-contract suit against actress Loretta Young on behalf of Pamela's sixteen-year-old daughter, Portland. (He got a $2,800 judgment.) Pamela introduced Mitchelson to her divorcing friends, "all of whom were wildly delighted with the results," she later claimed. Pamela gushed about him in her book about marriage and divorce, and invited him back to her television show. She became Mitchelson's ticket to ride, his entree to those rarefied upper brackets of Beverly Hills and Hollywood. Years later, Pamela and Marvin were still doing gigs together on shows like Merv Griffin's—two publicity piranhas on stage at the Hollywood Palace.

"I am the one who *discovered* Marvin Mitchelson!" she proclaimed.

And he was grateful. Ten days after the divorce hearing, when their first and only child was born, Marvin and Marcella gave him the name of Pamela's nine-year-old son, Morgan.*

"So that's when I first heard of Marvin Mitchelson," Caruso explained. "First thing I know, Marvin Mitchelson, through Pamela Mason, is claiming full credit for the Pamela Mason divorce. Well, I got her twenty thousand dollars a month, . . . and that was called *temporary* alimony; . . . today, it'd be like fifty thousand dollars or a hundred thousand dollars a month. And I was shooting for two million dollars in a trial or settlement.

"So when Marvin stepped in, all the work had been done. Except that my young lawyer said 'Go fuck yourself!' to Pamela Mason.

"Marvin's always said, 'I owe you something. You got me the Mason case, indirectly.'"

Somebody had to be lying about who did all the work and deserved the credit for breaking the million-dollar barrier, because Mitchelson and Caruso both claimed it.

"When I took over the case, *nothing* had been settled," Marvin huffed, flatly contradicting Caruso's claim. ". . . All I can tell you is, Pamela wanted to get the proverbial one million dollars. That was a big settlement in those days. And I got her over two [million]." An exaggeration. "And she was very happy with what I did." Not an exaggeration.

Twenty-five years later, Caruso was still bitter. "I've watched Marvin's ascent, and to me it's amusing, because there's a cadre of family-law lawyers [in Los Angeles] and they have a laughing toleration [of Marvin], because he attracts more business in one week than all the other [big] names put together!

"He does the initial interview, gets the initial retainer, and then you can't find him! I remember I was taking an elevator to the second floor of the county courthouse about two years ago, and some woman about four-feet-eleven had Marvin pinned against the wall. And she said, 'You son of a bitch! You're not returning my phone calls! I gave you twenty-five thousand dollars and I can't get you on the phone now!'"

At least nobody denied Mitchelson had treated Pamela Mason a whole lot better than that. At $100,000, his fee for getting her a million-dollar settlement, he said, was "kinda small. In those days, I was quite humble."

---

*Their son's name is Herbert Morgan Mitchelson; he goes by his middle name.

10

Publicity was the coin of Marvin Mitchelson's realm, and just as bankable as any fat fee. He knew that it was his "Protector of the Stars" routine that gave his act its cachet. That's what attracted media attention, which in turn brought in more clients. But no lawyer, not even Mitchelson, could live solely off the fees from divorcing stars and starlets. So a pattern was established early on. Mitchelson didn't just represent the stars; for a price, he'd represent has-beens, wannabes, used-to-bes, and never-weres, too—anyone who hoped to bask in the reflected glow of the Divorce Lawyer to the Stars. What a client needed in order to get his attention was enough money to pay his five-figure retainer, and a healthy amount of community property from which the remainder of his fee would be paid.

The retainers, which could run to $25,000 and more, were "non-refundable," and some clients complained that Mitchelson would keep the whole thing when they fired him, even though he hadn't earned it all. In years to come, some would also accuse Mitchelson of taking on far more cases than he could possibly handle. But that was not a rap against Marvin Mitchelson in the early years of his career.

His reputation then was simply as Hollywood's budding ambassador of bad will, a bomber who embodied a system that thrived on sensationalism for the sake of everything *but* marriage.

The long, echoing corridors of the Los Angeles Superior Court had something of the look and feel of a hospital. The place was all institutional drab, with lawyers and clients parked on the corridors' oak benches and the overflow leaning against tile walls. Each courtroom was connected to the corridor by a varnished oak door with a gun-port-sized window.

Hugh McIsaac was the director of family court services at the Superior Court. "There's sort of a strange synergy between Mitchelson and his clients," he observed. "They *both* need publicity." McIsaac was reminded of the symbiosis whenever Mitchelson sashayed past the waiting press with an arm around some starlet "for a motion that could have been done over the phone."

It had been like that all through his career. For an entertainer, preserving one's marquee value was frequently more important than saving a marriage. Which meant that somebody like Marvin Mitchelson, who was part lawyer but also part publicity agent, was often just what a fading star needed to rejuvenate a career. "If you've got a failing movie career, there's nothing like a steamy divorce to get you back on track!" McIsaac jibed.

Howard Weitzman, the outspoken Los Angeles lawyer who was Mitchelson's sometime buddy and sometime nemesis, saw his own role clearly. In a high-profile case, Weitzman explained, "sometimes the image—and how the public perceives the client—is more important than winning or losing a case. Because, you know what? [In a divorce,] you're only dealing with dollars and cents for the most part. Or, you're dealing with [child] visitation, which we view as a major thing. But in that client's mind, their *career* is the major thing. *That's* what really counts. My experience with high-profile people is that their career really comes first—even in family law matters; even when you're dealing with custody of kids. I'm not saying they'll give up custody. But they're much more flexible. [They'd rather be flexible than get] into an open forum, exposing their whole lives."

Weitzman represented boxer Mike Tyson in his divorce from the twenty-four-year-old television actress Robin Givens. The Tyson-Givens case was a gossip columnist's dream, made all the more so because of the lawyers involved: Weitzman for Tyson, and Mitchelson and Raoul Lionel Felder for Givens.

Mitchelson and Felder had once been friendly. In 1983 they talked about combining their practices into what would have been a bicoastal divorce firm. The scheme progressed far enough that Felder even had an office set aside for his California colleague, and Marvin was planning the kick-off party at "21." Felder remembered it well.

"He once said to me, I'll never forget: 'I know you don't think much of me as a lawyer, but you've gotta admit, I have a wonderful sense of P.R.!'"

Actually, both lawyers were masters on the public-relations front, and both worked hard at it. They also spent a ton of money to employ their own publicity agents.

Felder earned $3.8 million a year and paid out a $4,000-a-month retainer to the New York superflaks Howard J. Rubenstein & Associates. They were a high-powered group that represented, among many others, Donald Trump, media magnate Rupert Murdoch, and later, Robin Givens and Marla Maples.

While Felder favored the buttoned-down, well-modulated style of the Rubenstein agency, Mitchelson went with Sy Presten, the old-time press agent whose style was as much a contrast to Rubenstein's as the flamboyant Mitchelson's was to the subdued Felder's.

"Sy What's-His-name," Felder called him. Presten looked like he would have been more at home with Walter Winchell than anybody the media could offer up today. He was also the publicist for *Penthouse* magazine and had been the same for its now defunct cousin *Viva*, too. That was how Mitchelson first met him in 1979, when Presten was doing the publicity for a Mitchelson interview. At five-feet-four, Presten stood just about eye-to-breast with the statuesque *Penthouse* Pets of the Month he squired around to press appearances. Photographs of him with the Pets—dozens of them, each taken with Presten grinning at bust level—adorned the dining-room wall of his apartment, which doubled as his office. There was a pool table where the dining-room table should have been. Presten looked, according to one of his friends, "like a little Glenn Ford," but his wisecracking manner was all Henny Youngman's. ("How old are you? . . . Christ, I've got *ties* older than you!") Not surprisingly, he also had a picture on his dining-room wall of himself with the Borscht Belt comedian.

What Presten mainly did was to feed a little photocopied sheet to the New York gossip columnists with items about each of his clients. He'd been planting tidbits like that since the days when he was a publicist for the Copa and the Stork Club in New York, getting the clubs' names in the tabloids with stories about the doings of the celebrities who'd been there the night before.

"I must be doing something right" in Mitchelson's eyes, Presten said, and there was no doubting that. Although the checks from Mitchelson came irregularly, Presten averaged about $2,500 a month from Marvin, but in a good year, like 1986, Presten could be paid as much as $100,000 by his white-haired client.

"I remember what Sherman Billingsley, who owned the Stork Club, told me about my job," Presten remarked. "Don't confuse effort with achievement. You can have the greatest idea in the world, Billingsley told me, and it doesn't mean a thing unless you get it noticed!" Billingsley also told Presten: "The celebrities are my floor show."

Those were the credos Presten lived by when he planted items for Mitchelson. "You've got to have celebrity clients! You can be the best goddamned lawyer around, but how're you going to get into the paper if you've got Joe Schmuck as a client? Marvin gets the celebrity cases. That's what the columnists like Liz Smith in the *News* and Page Six in the *Post* want."

According to Mitchelson, Felder was hot for the bicoastal collaboration in 1983, but at the last minute Marvin backed out. He thought Felder was too small. "Felder suggested we do this, to be in partnership. But that's when I was riding pretty high. . . . I think he was envious of me all along," Mitchelson recollected in 1990. "He just wanted to be in that spot, and [maybe] he got there. [But] I think if you ask ten people across the country if they've heard of Raoul Felder and Marvin Mitchelson, they're gonna say Marvin Mitchelson.

"That's an ego thing," Mitchelson admitted.

Ego, certainly. But there was more to it than just vanity. Through all the publicity and public recognition he commanded, this lawyer who'd flunked the Bar also found a vindication of his own prowess. Deprivation and humiliation were his silent partners, but he did his best to crowd them out with reams of newsprint and scripts from a thousand newscasts.

The self-image he possessed could be chilling. It was Marvin Mitchelson against an uncaring, unloving, insensitive world. He struck back by trying to outsmart and outhustle the rest of the world.

In his mind, nobody played the angles better than he. "I think I took advantage of almost every situation I ever had. I don't mean I stepped on some little person. I *saw* opportunities. I *played* them all the way." Looking back on his career, Mitchelson became infused with all the energy of his past. He visualized his biggest cases as he spoke. "I could see a case that was interesting, that was controversial and that deserved to be put out there in the court.

"And, yes, I recognized its potential for its publicity and its value for *many* reasons. But that was never the only reason. [Why did I] take the *Marvin* case? My God! Because I thought it was right. . . .

"It's my *destiny* to do that! You see, that's the way I felt about things. I tread where men fear to go." It certainly was true that Mitchelson seemed to relish saving himself when his back was to the wall. "I took a lot of cases, believe me. I'll never forget the *Marvin* case. There wasn't one person who believed that I could make a change. There wasn't one! [Not] my mother. No one believed me! But *I* believed. . . .

"I felt it was my destiny to do that, and nothing would stop me. I was totally *relentless* in my pursuit. . . . I've paid my dues."

He recalled his uphill struggle in *Douglas*, "where the judge said 'Dammit, counsel, you interrupt [the prosecutor] one more time and you're going to *jail!*' Meanwhile, the tears are coming down my face and I'm trying to carry on and trying to match objections with Joe Carr, a veteran of thirty years, the toughest prosecutor in L.A."

But his blind spots were as big as his oversized ego, and if you asked him to discuss his shortcomings he was suddenly at a loss. If he had a flaw, Mitchelson would finally concede with studied guilelessness, it was that he tried too hard to make people believe in themselves, and in their cases. And, even though he didn't say it, probably in Marvin, too. "And if it doesn't happen, you've failed them. Love turns to hate."

The relationship between Mitchelson and Felder was certainly strained by the time the Tyson-Givens case came up. It erased much of the residue of friendship that hadn't already been rubbed away by the intervening years of rivalry.

After the Mitchelson-Felder collaboration fell through, Felder hadn't given up on the idea of creating a national practice, and by 1988 he'd finally pulled it off, linking up with lawyers in New Jersey, Florida, and California. The Rubenstein agency's hallmark was publicity stunts, like floating a helium King Kong over the Empire State Building to advertise the big building's observation deck. So it was decided that Felder would do his own dignified stunt, trumpeting his new nationwide collaboration at a celebrity-studded cocktail party at Elaine's, a posh New York Upper East Side watering hole. The summons for the affair was literally that: an ersatz subpoena that was as official-looking as Felder could make it. And just in case Felder's presence and that of the other celebrities wasn't enough to entice the 350 guests, he had some back-up: music by The Drifters.

The big bash was set for Tuesday, October 11, 1988. But Mitchelson intended to trump Felder with a publicity coup of his own. He had beaten out Raoul by snaring Robin Givens as a client. On the prior Friday, he filed the Givens divorce against Mike Tyson and held the wildest-and-wooliest news conference the Los Angeles courthouse had seen since the Joan Collins days. The publicity war was on.

Both lawyers knew the Tyson-Givens case was going to be pure gold while it lasted. And when Mitchelson came into the Tyson-Givens bout, he had precisely the kind of high-profile case he loved. But, as David Margolick of the *New York Times* pointed out, "by the lawyer's clock he lasted about as long as Max Schmeling against Joe Louis, or Michael Spinks against Tyson himself. Within four days he'd been dropped. His replacement? Raoul Lionel Felder."

Now it was Felder's turn to gloat.

"He had some problems at that time," Felder deadpanned. "His timing was *very* off."

And among high-stakes divorce lawyers, just as with boxers, timing could be everything. The problem in this case was that two days after Mitchelson's splashy news conference for Givens, the Sunday *Los Angeles Times* ran a magazine piece that catalogued the parade of public and private horrors that had been plaguing him: the allegations of unconscionable fees, dissatisfied clients, drug use, and rape. Givens and her mother, Ruth Roper, saw the article. That kind of publicity, they didn't need. They dropped Mitchelson on the spot.

Felder was Mitchelson's replacement. It didn't hurt that Felder and Givens had the same publicist.

"[Mitchelson] had just signed up Givens, and that Sunday a big piece came in the *L.A. Times Magazine* about him!" Felder savored his upstaging of his California rival. "[Marvin] had gone public right before this with Givens. A cynic might say that maybe that [news conference] was part of some plan to offset the article he knew was coming. But he didn't warn *them* that it was coming, and they were most unhappy about it. . . ."

"Next thing Felder knew, in the middle of everything, for whatever reason, Mitchelson is flying to New York on the case. I can't understand why! He's been *fired!*"

Mitchelson had Givens's file with him. Felder left word at Mitchelson's hotel for him to have the papers delivered to him. "But *no!* He insisted on coming here and bringing the papers. So he comes here and he says to me he can be very helpful in the case."

Mitchelson saw the case as a ticket into the headlines, and he sure didn't want to lose it.

"He insists upon coming here. He says, Why not leave him on the case. I could be lead counsel. Let him stay in the case, he could be very helpful, and so forth. So I said, 'Marvin'—it was an awkward conversation—I said, 'Marvin, I'll leave it to the clients.' I said, 'It's okay with me.'

"He says, 'You'll be the lead. You'll call the shots. Let me stay on the case.' It was embarrassment at this point."

Marvin left, but within ten minutes, he was calling Felder from a public telephone on the street. It was a pathetic call, and Mitchelson sounded like he was about to start crying. "Listen," Mitchelson pleaded. "I'll do anything, I'll do anything! Let me stay on the case! I'll help you."

"Marvin, I'm gonna try, I told you. Just relax," Felder replied. "Very sad call."*

Without his really planning it that way, Felder's publicity ploy had become a hat trick. Mitchelson was on the skids; Felder had a notable new client; and the bash at Elaine's that night was so hot it made all six New York newscasts.

Mitchelson wrote off Felder's account of the Tyson-Givens divorce as nothing more than the raving of a "jealous competitor." Said Mitchelson: "I understand what he's doing. He's always wanted to be where I was. He was always jealous of me. I've been there. I've been at the top. He's got a ways to go yet."

Meanwhile, Weitzman, representing Tyson, claimed victory in this three-way publicity war. He bragged about how he could "neutralize" reporters by giving interviews to favored journalists. As to the others, he said, "I don't make any bones about it. If you wanna misquote me, if you wanna say things that are less than accurate about my client, don't bother calling me. Make it up." In the Tyson case, he boasted of having mounted such an effective publicity offensive that neither Mitchelson nor Felder could ever do much for their client.

---

*Mitchelson later sued Tyson again, this time on behalf of a woman who claimed he was the father of her 16-month-old son. The lawsuit sought $11 million.

The whole thing was wrapped up in a matter of months, with Givens signing a divorce agreement on February 5, 1989, on terms favorable to Tyson—terms that Weitzman said were pretty much foreordained by the good publicity he got for the champ. That was how Weitzman's world worked.

"You really *can* control the situation," he contended. "But you have never dealt with a more avaricious, aggressive group of people until you deal with the press hot on an item that they think will get them some space on the nightly news or in the morning newspaper."

But regardless of how many other lawyers tried to capture the limelight, no one did better than Marvin Mitchelson. The stars got what they wanted when they came to him. Hire him and you weren't just hiring a lawyer—you were hiring a show.

"I have to tell you," Mitchelson boasted. "The best press agent I ever had was Marvin Mitchelson! . . . Because I used to do this myself. I know how to do this!"

No matter how trivial the cause of action, if he found an angle, he could turn it into a story. And in the early days, when his client list was still thin, he could gin up publicity by filing an oddball lawsuit himself.

Long before Mitchelson made it to the big time, there was a tiff over the coloring given to one of Marcella's wigs. The year was 1964, Beatle wigs were the rage, and Marcella wanted hers dyed again. Joanna Winograde, the owner of Joanna's Wigs, had already changed the color of Marcella's wig once, and she laid down the law: No more free dye jobs.

Marvin went to the proprietor and pleaded for reconsideration. He explained that Marcella forbade him from paying even one cent for the dye job; that he would, indeed, have to sue Joanna's Wigs just to maintain domestic tranquility at the Mitchelson house.

It was not a heavy-duty case. But Mitchelson knew that Man Bites Dog was what sold papers. Years later, he'd be grabbing headlines by suing for a husband's visitation rights to his two rare pianos. And for a mistress's right to be impregnated by her married lover. And for a cowboy's custody of his horse named Larry. But this was 1964, and he had to work with the material fate sent him. When they got to the courthouse, Joanna was surprised to find the media waiting.

"If I lose the case," Mitchelson said, "my wife's going to make *me* wear the wig!"

Sometimes, Mitchelson had a much better sense of his clients' newsworthiness than they did. That was certainly the case with Patti Lear Corman, the daughter of Learjet designer William P. Lear and the wife, in 1976, of a California Democratic congressman named James G. Corman.

There was a capricious side to Patti Corman. Her whimsies were an endearing quality most of the time, but not, in her husband's eyes, when she decided to run for the neighboring congressional seat held then by Rep. Barry Goldwater, Jr. (R-Calif.). A congressional wife running for a colleague's seat went against the clubby rules in the House, and Jim Corman made it clear that if she insisted on doing that, it would be as Patti Lear, not Patti Corman. He made good on the pledge with a three-page poetical request for divorce penned on House Ways and Means Committee stationery.

When Patti Corman rang up Mitchelson one Friday evening, at the suggestion of a girlfriend, he told her to meet him at his office at ten o'clock that night. Corman's best friend tagged along.

"It was my third marriage and I was distraught. My whole world was coming to an end! I trusted him. I'd been told he was all-wise and all-great.

"When I met him, he was in his bathrobe. I thought, So what else is new? My father was extremely eccentric, too."

Mitchelson told Corman he wanted to file her divorce papers on March 10. What he knew, but she didn't, was that March 10 also was International Women's Day, and that the Corman case—with a woman who could, and did, honestly say that her husband "doesn't want me in the House, he wants me at home!"—was too great a story for the newspapers to pass up on that particular day.

He took Corman to dinner the night before the suit was filed. Then he drove her down to the courthouse the next day in his Rolls-Royce to file the papers. When they got back to his office, Mitchelson nonchalantly asked Corman to come up for a few minutes. She did—and, in his office, she encountered a passel of reporters who were waiting to take down her story. Even if Marvin Mitchelson wasn't yet a household name, Lear certainly was.

"He'd called the AP, UPI, and every other P there is!" she recalled. "It was a natural!" But after the news conference, Corman had the same complaint as so many other of Mitchelson's clients. "He dropped me. . . . He wouldn't respond to my phone calls. He'd had his fun." She eventually gave up on Marvin and hired another lawyer.

Mitchelson did, indeed, have a publicist's knack for the headlines. When the Beatles needed a Hollywood lawyer in 1964 to fight a $1 million breach-of-contract lawsuit by an entrepreneur who claimed he had the exclusive right to distribute paintings of them, they chose Mitchelson. He settled the nuisance case, but not before piously warning in the newspapers that there could be a "riot" in Beverly Hills if the mop-haired boys were forced to come there for a deposition.

In the immediately ensuing years he represented, and sometimes out-headlined, Mrs. Aldo Ray, Mrs. Van Heflin, Mrs. William Shatner,

Mrs. Peter Fonda, the third Mrs. Groucho Marx, and the third Mrs. Eddie Fisher, Connie Stevens.

But Mitchelson was ready for anything. On behalf of the former Mrs. Gig Young, he succeeded in getting the Santa Monica Superior Court to rule that the sixty-year-old actor was, indeed, the father of their eight-year-old girl—even though Young had been sterilized thirty-four years earlier!

And when a young, rifle-waving twenty-year-old AWOL Marine hijacked a TWA jet over California, forcing it to fly to Denver, Colorado, New York City, Bangor, Maine, and finally to Rome, it was Mitchelson who volunteered to take the case. The Marine's name was Raphael Minichiello, his parents Italian-Americans. Mitchelson said he was concerned for the young man's constitutional rights.

There were questions from the start about what Marvin was doing in a case that could get Minichiello the death penalty. *Time* magazine cryptically noted that Mitchelson "normally represents Hollywood clients," but the real controversy came when he hurried to Italy to meet his client. Suspicious Italians, believing that Mitchelson was grandstanding for publicity, harassed him and picketed him in the streets. He was, their signs said, a "PUBLICITY SEEKER." Another sign proclaimed: "MITCHELSON IS AN EXHIBITIONIST! GET ITALIAN LAWYERS FOR RAPHAEL." There was more criticism when Marvin four weeks later was reported to have sold to *Time* the notes he'd made of his prison conversations with Raphael. Excerpts were published under the headline: "ANATOMY OF A SKYJACKER." For his part, Mitchelson claimed that the information he gave *Time* was given with the permission of Minichiello and his family and that the money received from *Time* would go into a trust fund for the hijacker. Mitchelson always made a point to say that he hadn't gotten a cent from the penurious Minichiello, which was undoubtedly true. But all that publicity added up to millions of promotional dollars. Those images of the gallant young lawyer squiring Raphael's immigrant parents around, or cooly fielding questions from dozens of reporters at impromptu airport news conferences, were priceless in their publicity value.

It was heady stuff for a guy barely forty years old.

11

Alan Jay Lerner had a creative gift. His Broadway musicals—*Brigadoon, Paint Your Wagon, Camelot*, and *My Fair Lady* among them—became monster hits, and when he tried his hand in Hollywood with films like *Gigi* he was equally successful.

But all was not Camelot in Lerner's life, and by 1964, the dapper songwriter, with an eventual eight marriages, was well on his way to becoming the most divorced man in Hollywood.

Lerner had written *Gigi* in 1958 for his pretty Parisian wife, Micheline. Six years later, they had a son, Michel, and a marriage that was coming apart. Both sides had filed lawsuits that were pending in New York, but Mitchelson would get in on the act before *Lerner vs. Lerner* ended.

New York's divorce laws didn't necessarily favor Micheline. Because New York was not a community property state, Micheline was not automatically entitled to one half of the millions of dollars in assets Lerner had accumulated during their marriage. And because of New York's archaic divorce laws in those days, one of them was going to have to prove that the other was committing adultery.

For a case like that, Micheline needed a fighter. And that's what she had, because when it came to shameless bravado and dirty tricks, Roy Cohn acted like he didn't know any better. Somebody once called him "the Legal Executioner," and when you considered where he'd learned his stuff, that was an apt description.

Cohn's notoriety stemmed from his years during the early 1950s as counsel to red-baiting Senator Joseph McCarthy (R-Wisc.). McCarthy leapt in 1950 from the obscurity of a congressional back-bencher to the national headlines with a speech declaring that Communists had infiltrated the State Department. He never produced any evidence to support his allegations, and the department was cleared in a Senate investigation. But that didn't matter to the junior senator from Wisconsin. With a devilish young Roy Cohn at his elbow, McCarthy, by 1953 the chairman of the Senate Permanent Investigations Subcommittee, made new allegations and recklessly used his power to ruin the careers of those he said were Communists or subversives. Nobody really stood up against him until the senator claimed he had evidence that the secretary of the Army had tried to conceal espionage activities that Cohn and his minions had supposedly uncovered at Ft. Monmouth, N.J. The Pentagon fought back, and when everyone from President Eisenhower to Edward R. Morrow joined the Army's side in the fray it was clear that the senator's red-baiting days were numbered.

As often happened in Washington, what finally brought McCarthy down actually had little to do with the bad things he'd *really* done. The senator and Cohn had, after all, used baseless allegations to wreck scores of lives, and they'd suffused an entire generation with a fear of Communists. When the Army finally turned the tables on McCarthy and Cohn, it was for the tawdriest of misdeeds, accusing them both of trying to gain special favors—things like an officer's commission and an exemption from boot camp—for Cohn's friend and nightclubbing companion, an Army private named G. David Schine. Cohn was a closet homosexual, although his staunch denials meant that it would be years before the whole story was out.

The story of Cohn's malevolence was actually a whole lot longer than the one about his old boss. In December of 1954, the Senate condemned McCarthy in a censure vote, and he died a drunkard's death in 1957. Cohn, on the other hand, landed on his feet in New York City at the well-established law firm of Saxe, Bacon & Bolan. The firm had a good client list but its name partners were aging or gone. A twenty-nine-year-old comer seemed just what the place needed to get back on track.

Cohn catered to the wealthy clients who needed his eclectic assortment of services. Roy was a fixer, a Republican maven with superb access to the powerful. The people who couldn't be fixed, he could sue. As a litigator, Cohn collected a healthy array of detractors and more than his share of malpractice suits. But when it came to scorched-earth litigation—the dirty lawsuits where McCarthyite tactics still prevailed—he was a master. When he represented a fat-cat husband, which was what he mostly did when he took divorce cases, Cohn would hire a private detective to collect all the dirt he could on the wife; stonewall rather than disclose the husband's income and assets; and try, in essence, to use the quickly collected dirt to blackmail the wife into a fast settlement before she found out the true extent of her husband's wealth. Since it was usually also the husband who paid the wife's legal fees, Cohn intimated confidentially to the wife's lawyer that the husband would be "generous" with the fees if things got over quickly. They got the message.

While Roy Cohn usually represented husbands whenever he took a divorce case, when he and Mitchelson first met in 1964 it was through their joint representation of Micheline Lerner—the fetching blond woman whom the headline writers were calling Lerner's "Fair Lady."

Micheline had brought their son west and moved into the Beverly

Hills Hotel. It made sense, of course, for her to try to shift the divorce venue to a community-property state, but there first was the matter of which California lawyer to hire.

It had been just days since Mitchelson had gotten Pamela Mason her million-dollar settlement, and already she was returning the favor. Pamela knew a friend who knew Micheline, and Pamela passed word to her that Marvin Mitchelson was the man to see. He met Micheline, she hired him as cocounsel, and he traveled east to meet the lawyer he would come to admire.

Part of the attraction to Mitchelson was that Cohn played by his own set of rules. He was a mama's boy, too. Cohn was also a fixer and a lawyer who didn't pay his taxes. He had thoroughly scammed the IRS by a tactic that was at once the stuff of legend and yet pathetically simple: He took almost no wages and just lived off the pseudo-deductible expenses provided for him by his law firm. Moreover, he had been able to stave off New York State disbarment proceedings for, literally, almost an entire lifetime.

"He was a stand-up guy," Mitchelson said of Cohn again and again. He loved that about Roy; admired it just as much as he did the publicity Cohn got in spite of—or because of—his reputation.

"I liked him in spite of himself. Regardless of his other problems, he was a stand-up guy. A guy who was mercilessly attacked throughout his life and stood up to it. . . . He was a *celebrity* to me."

Mitchelson told of attending one of Cohn's parties, where he met Jake La Motta, the former boxer. Marvin had seen the 1980 film *Raging Bull* by then. The Robert De Niro flick was all about La Motta's battles in and out of the ring. (Mitchelson had also represented in a divorce case the husband of De Niro's *Raging Bull* costar, Cathy Moriarty.)

"Jake La Motta had a very good looking gal with him that night," Mitchelson said with a glow in his voice. "It turns out she's a paralegal. Very pretty girl. . . . She's impressed and wants to talk to me. I tell her what I know about family law. I want to invite her for lunch or dinner, you know, but I *don't* want to offend La Motta! She says, 'No, no, we're [just] friends.'

"So I take her to dinner at Le Cirque." It was a Cohn haunt that Mitchelson also favored. "We're having a nice time. Talking. Smiling. You know, I'm trying to be charming. And all of a sudden, two drinks come up, and there's a note with them: 'What are you doing with my girl? Signed, Jake La Motta.'

"Fear went through me of paralytic proportions you can't believe! I hear this guy's still a raging bull. And I look up, and it's *Roy Cohn!*" Cohn had a big grin across his face. "And my heart [had just] stopped! I thought the Raging Bull was going to come right back there and kill me!"

When he wasn't out on the town or at his country house in Green-wich, Connecticut, Cohn lived and worked in a townhouse office at 39 East 68th Street. Mitchelson put the address of Cohn's Manhattan townhouse on his own stationery and called it his New York office.

Linda Acaldo, who was Marvin's secretary and sometime lover from 1973 to 1978, thought his feelings about Cohn verged on hero worship. "He told me he thought Roy Cohn was so great. It was all money and power.

"He remembered once he was riding with Roy Cohn in his car, he told me. And Roy Cohn was on his car phone. [Roy] had to put some-body on hold in order to take a call from Paris. Well, Marvin thought that was the greatest thing! And all his life he wanted to be able to have a car phone and put somebody on hold in order to take a call from Paris! Just like Roy Cohn had done."

Cohn clearly was much more important to Mitchelson than Mitchel-son was to Cohn, and it said something about them both that although Cohn could put down Mitchelson as a publicity-hungry lawyer with cases that Cohn thought were "crazy" or "ridiculous," Marvin never seemed to mind. After all, as Marvin's friend, the writer Martha Smilgis, put it, "I'm not sure Roy kissed up to anybody, except for presidents. . . . Truly! They had to be presidents!. . . Somehow, Roy and Marvin worked some deals out [representing clients together] and they were okay together. Marvin was never screwed by Roy. And Mar-vin's conscious of that. I think he is conscious if somebody screws him."

The lawyer representing Alan Jay Lerner was the formidable Louis Nizer, and since Cohn hated him (the feeling was apparently mutual), he lost no opportunity to try to embarrass or vilify Nizer in court. In court papers drafted by Cohn and filed by Micheline, Nizer and Alan Jay Lerner were accused of trying to drive Micheline insane by their conduct in the case.

Meanwhile, with New York remaining as the venue of the couple's divorce action, Alan Jay Lerner was pressing a contempt-of-court mo-tion against his wife for taking their son to California. Because Lerner didn't dare set foot in California, lest that invite the community-prop-erty courts there to take jurisdiction, the upshot of Micheline's move to L.A. was to prevent her husband from seeing his son.

Michel was three thousand miles away, in Los Angeles, on the day of the contempt hearing in New York. But for some reason, Mitchelson later recalled, Lerner expected his son to be right there in the court-room, and when he didn't immediately see him Lerner asked Cohn: "Where's Michel?"

"Why, he's right here, under the bench," Cohn replied, mocking Lerner with glee. "Come on out, Michel!"

Lerner bent down to look under the bench while Cohn glanced at

Mitchelson with a smirk. Poor Lerner, Mitchelson thought. Roy's making him look so foolish.

Both sides had hired platoons of private detectives, with Nizer's men spying on Micheline and Michel at the Beverly Hills Hotel and keeping detailed dossiers on their movements so as to formulate a plan for spiriting the boy back to New York. Cohn's detectives spied on the spies.

Nothing if not a man of tradition, Cohn was said to have used a plethora of dirty tricks to gain an advantage for his winsome client. The divorce case was tinged with insinuations that the oft-married Lerner was really a homosexual. Cohn, who always professed hatred of homosexuals, had a tap placed on Lerner's telephone to get the scoop on Lerner's sexual proclivities.

Cohn's tap revealed intimate conversations between Lerner and a New York publicity agent named Harvey Mann. "They had all this shit on tape," Mann told Cohn's biographer, Nicholas von Hoffman. "You know, Alan saying he loved me and all this garbage. But that wasn't admissible in court."

Since the taped conversations couldn't be used as evidence, Cohn dispatched Mitchelson in what turned out to be an unsuccessful attempt to get a signed declaration from Mann saying he'd had a homosexual affair with Lerner. Mann said Cohn offered him "a hundred thousand dollars cash and I still wouldn't do it." But Mann's refusal didn't stand in Cohn's way; Lerner was falsely told that Mann had, indeed, signed.

"He told Louis Nizer or Alan, or Micheline told Alan, that I had signed, and Alan till the day he died never spoke to me, or when we saw each other he was absolutely crazed," Mann later said. "And it's sad, because Alan never knew really who his friends were. I just idolized him."

By the time the case came to trial in March of 1965, both sides had been bloodied. Nizer got hold of a diary full of "fantasies" that Micheline had been keeping. The front-page headline in the next morning's *Daily News* shouted out: GRILL LERNER'S WIFE ON DIARY.

"Did you write that you wanted a lover, handsome and young?" Nizer asked Micheline.

"Yes, because I was disgusted with my husband. . . . He advised me to take a lover."

"A lover, beautiful and young?"

"A woman thinks such things."

One of the principal characters in Micheline's French diary was a young actor named Peter.

"What did you mean when you wrote, 'One has to defrost Peter constantly, and I get enough of that'?"

"He was often sad and morose."

"And when you wrote, 'He comes after dinner and I have two husbands instead of one'?"

"I enjoyed his company. We had many of the same interests."

"When Alan was out in California, didn't Peter occupy Alan's bed and wear his clothes?"

"I swear that is a lie! I loved Peter only as a friend."

"DEFROSTING BOTHERED HER," read the *Daily News* picture caption the next morning.

Both sides had had enough, and over the weekend they reached a settlement that gave Micheline custody of their son, a $1.5 million settlement that included $78,000 a year in alimony and child support—a vast sum by 1965 standards—and a Nevada divorce. Cohn, Lerner, and Nizer despised each other so much that it fell to Mitchelson to preside over the division of the couple's art objects and belongings at their three-story townhouse.

Mitchelson recalled Lerner's last, poignant gesture at the townhouse: He "sat down at a piano, which was disputed property, and played most of the *Camelot* score for me. This led him to recall his visits to the White House when John F. Kennedy was president. And he wistfully concluded, 'You know, Camelot doesn't last forever.'"

12

Claire Allen [name changed] remembered what it was like being Mitchelson's secretary in 1965.

"The huge ego was already there. I remember, he was doing a lot of traveling, even then. . . . He would call me collect, from Rome. At home! To find out what was happening, and to hide stuff from his wife. Part of the job was covering up his indiscretions. He was a wild man." She laughed.

The indiscretions were not only diverse, they also very early formed a pattern of deceit that continued right up to the present: assorted sexual liaisons, love interests, and mistresses that were an open secret in Mitchelson's office and elsewhere.

Mitchelson had slept once with Claire, who was then in her early twenties. It was spur-of-the-moment sex, Marvin following her into her apartment after driving her home, one thing leading to another and neither of them apparently giving it very much thought afterward.

"He came, went, and 'Bye!' I remember him putting on my bathrobe and wanting to walk around. Then, the next morning, nothing."

His secretary knew about his financial problems, too.

"At the time I was there, he was representing an Italian man who I think had visited Beverly Hills, and been in an automobile accident.

Marvin represented him in the personal injury case. And he settled it. Because of Marvin's need for money, he was borrowing from the trust account. Borrowing *desperately*!

"He was trying to convince this man, by correspondence, to allow him—to allow Marvin—to invest the funds for him and to let Marvin pay him interest. The underlying reason, of course, being that he really didn't have the [settlement] money!

"I got very nervous during this time. I was a kid. And I kept thinking, My God, I don't wanna have to go to the Bar! They're gonna call me to testify. Because he was kiting. He was doing more than kiting checks."

Mitchelson was among a number of young Los Angeles lawyers who were hustling publicity in those days. Another in that pack was Robert Steinberg, then a thirty-year-old Beverly Hills lawyer practicing a few blocks from Mitchelson up Wilshire Boulevard. People called him Bobby.

Steinberg's partner, Samuel Brody, was Jayne Mansfield's boyfriend in 1967, and it was as lawyers opposing each other in a case involving the thirty-four-year-old Mansfield that Steinberg and Mitchelson first met. (The two shared an eye for aberrant cases; in 1970, Steinberg represented one of the witnesses in the Manson Murders case.)

Mansfield had been booked to appear in an eight-week, $8,400-a-week tour of some British night clubs, with her boyfriend Brody tagging along. Mitchelson had been picking up some British legal work since defending the Beatles in the 1964 nuisance suit, and now David Jacobs, the British lawyer who had fed him the Beatles business, gave him the task of firing Mansfield after she showed up two days late for her rehearsals.

Mitchelson complied. But when word of her firing hit the London tabloids, complete with her every vital statistic, it accomplished more for Mansfield's career than anything a horde of publicists could have done. Suddenly, she was a hot property, and now that she was being let go amid so much furor, a bidding war ensued among other clubs anxious to book the breathless, dizzy blonde. Even six-hundred lifers at Leeds Prison—"the loneliest men in Britain," one broadsheet sympathetically called them—clamored for her act. As one paper put it, "she doesn't sing like Doris Day and she doesn't dance like Betty Grable. But then, nobody expected her to."

Back in Los Angeles after the Mansfield episode, Mitchelson discovered some common ground with her lawyer, Steinberg. They moved in the same circles and had some of the same favorite haunts: an Italian place, Frascati, at the corner of Wilshire Boulevard and Beverly Drive; the Luau; La Scala; Señor Pico's; and the Cock and Bull pub.

Mitchelson switched sides and became Mansfield's lawyer. As Steinberg would later recount it, Mansfield and her boyfriend, Brody, had a wild, tempestuous relationship in 1967, the year they both died in a ghastly automobile accident in New Orleans. "Jayne and Sam fought." Jayne had a place on Carolwood Drive in Bel Air, and Steinberg was there once after they had a big spat "and Jayne called Marvin. He didn't get there right away, and when he finally did arrive, he came up in this limousine and started banging on her gates. He wanted to protect her rights! But by the time he got there, they'd made up and all was fine. She wouldn't even let Marvin in! He just kept banging and then he left.

"He was doing his protector-of-the-starlets routine! But I had to give him credit. He worked real hard at it. He was a real go-getter."

13

Not everything Mitchelson did in those early days of his career was for the benefit of women. Years before he claimed the high ground in the women's liberation movement with *Marvin vs. Marvin*, Mitchelson was making the tabloid headlines in America and Britain with a red-hot case that some called a blow for *men's* liberation. And it was through this representation of a jilted millionaire named Ralph Stolkin—a millionaire who wanted nothing more than his gifts returned—that he got close to a young lawyer who supplied him with drugs.

Stolkin was an enigmatic entrepreneur who'd made a fortune in enterprises as diverse as real estate, cattle ranches, greeting cards, mail-order selling, television cabinetry, chemicals, and Texas oil. He'd also once been president of RKO Pictures, and his businesses had gone far enough south of the break-even line that Mitchelson had represented him in a 1968 bankruptcy proceeding in Chicago. "He came out of it with twenty-two million dollars," Mitchelson said. "And he thought he was *broke!*"

But Stolkin seemingly had recovered from those financial reversals by 1971, the year that a British society lady named Patricia Wolfson walked away from their planned marriage with $600,000 in jewelry and other gifts.

Stolkin wanted them back, not because he needed the money—one account put his net worth at close to $300 million that year—but because only legal retribution could give him comfort. It was a classic Mitchelson case of man-bites-dog, and *Stolkin vs. Wolfson's* six days of trial in London were laced with testimony of illicit sex and secret tape-recordings of a smitten millionaire who should have known better and a debutante who'd been a friend of Princess Margaret, a courtier to the Aga Khan, and a modern-day Mona Lisa.

Stolkin got back most of his gifts in a midtrial settlement. As salacious as the case was, though, much of the publicity about it was devoted to Marvin's wife, Marcella, whose outré Hollywood getups seemed to fascinate the British photographers, and to Mitchelson himself, who was still being fêted for the Pamela Mason divorce. They were curiousities in dreary London. "At forty-three," effused the *Daily Mirror* after it finished warming over the Mason divorce story, "he is considerably more than a film-star divorce attorney. He is proud most of the fact that he is responsible for a United States Supreme Court ruling giving the equivalent of legal aid to convicted persons so that they could appeal. It is considered one of the most important decisions of the Supreme Court of the past hundred years."

It was through Ralph Stolkin's daughter, Kathy, that Marvin met Kathy's husband, attorney Bruce Perlman. Perlman was tall and handsome, with blond hair and blue eyes. He was also one of the first of Mitchelson's friends Linda Acaldo met when she went to work for Marvin in September of 1973.

"That was when he [Mitchelson] initially started using me to go pick up his cocaine. I remember distinctly the very first time he sent me to get the cocaine."

Mitchelson was cooking up a scheme to invest about half of the $12 million that he had just gotten in a divorce settlement for a woman named Bonnie Grant. Her ex-husband, Robert, was a wealthy developer who owned the Santa Anita Race Track.

According to some, Marvin had been wooing Grant throughout her divorce proceeding, and an extensive court file would later demonstrate how completely he had won her over. Although their original agreement was for Mitchelson to charge $75 an hour against a $5,000 retainer for Grant's divorce, a little more than two weeks later Grant agreed to pay a flat fee of $750,000 for the dissolution of a trust, which Mitchelson treated as a separate matter. It was an amazing amount of money for just seventeen days work, but Mitchelson said he deserved it because he'd been able to quickly break an irrevocable trust that might have kept Bonnie from getting her share of the racetrack assets. Then, in October 1973, Mitchelson got Grant to agree that she owed him another $500,000 for selling all of her stock in Santa Anita back to one of her ex-husband's companies, thereby finalizing the division of assets in the divorce. In a little more than a year, he thus was paid $1,250,000 by Grant—an amount which, at his customary billing rate, he couldn't otherwise have earned in *eight* years!

In May of 1973, Marvin got Grant to set up a 50–50 investment partnership that used exactly $5,542,012 of her money and none of his. From Mitchelson's standpoint, the deal could hardly have been sweeter. The risk of loss was all Bonnie's, but Marvin would get 50 percent of any gains or profits in their La Radiana partnership over and above the first 5 percent, as compensation for his advice to, and management of, the partnership. And since over $4 million of La Radiana's assets were in promissory notes that paid 7 percent a year, he'd even be tapping into money Grant would have gotten without him.

Mitchelson wrote up their partnership deal in a letter full of careful legalese. She signed at the bottom of the letter that she "agreed, acknowledged, and confirmed" everything he'd written.

Within a few months of Mitchelson's writing that letter, Acaldo was having an affair with Mitchelson—an affair that Acaldo said resulted in her having an abortion late the following year.

Mitchelson, she said, wanted her to have the abortion, "and I certainly didn't want to have Marvin Mitchelson's kid, knowing what I knew about him.

"He came and picked me up from the hospital, Century City Hospital. He offered, but he never paid me back for it, either. I had to pay it all by myself.

"He drove me there and he picked me up. Of course, he was two hours late picking me up. He was always two hours late. Everywhere we go. Every restaurant he ever had me meet him in, I'd be sitting there an hour and a half before he showed up. Such an embarrassment. Inconsiderate jerk."

Mitchelson had set the La Radiana deal up right before Acaldo started working for him, and she said she saw right away what was happening.

"I mean, this poor woman . . . totally believed him. Completely. Had no idea!

"And Marvin, when I first went there, that first month or two, he used to sit there and make me work late and I'd be taking dictation, and he would put [Bonnie] on a speaker phone, have her pour her heart out, and he'd be just *laughing* at her. And she's such a nice lady.

"Anyway, about the third time out, I said 'Listen, I don't want to be a party to this. It's too sadistic. I can't handle it.'"

Mitchelson was closeted with his plans for the La Radiana investments on the day Acaldo first spoke to Bruce Perlman. "I remember answering the phone, and Marvin was in conference. A very charming voice on the other end says, 'Tell Marvelito it's Bruce Perlman, and he'll take the call.' I said, 'He said he's not to be disturbed,' And he says, 'He'll talk to me.' I said 'OK,' and I put him through and of course he did.

"So he took the phone call from Bruce, and then he called me in and gave me a check, and said I was to go pick something up from Bruce. . . . I was transporting cocaine, and I didn't even think about it!"

Acaldo went to Perlman's office elsewhere in Century City "and I handed him a check and he handed me a little coin envelope . . . sealed at both ends. I think it had his initials on it. Bruce did a lot of dope dealing. Marvin was not his only customer." Once, Acaldo said, she saw Perlman cutting down a block of cocaine.

"And so I brought it back to Marvin. . . . Marvin opened the envelope—I was taking shorthand—and started snorting it!

"I still really didn't pick up on it. I didn't pay an ounce of attention to this incredibly serious thing I'd just done.

"Marvin looked up and said, 'You don't even know what this is, do you?' And I just sat there for a minute. . . . Marvin just laughed and kept on snorting. And that's when I knew what I had picked up."

Acaldo said Mitchelson was a daily cocaine user then with a habit that appeared then to be costing him $100 a day. He also had a drinking problem that he tried to bring under control through Alcoholics Anonymous. Mitchelson could be a mean, sloppy drunk. He liked vodka or schnapps straight, with a beer chaser.

Mitchelson also abused the prescription narcotic Percodan, Acaldo said, relying on a particular doctor—"a scriptwriter" in drug lingo—to prescribe for him all the Percodan he wanted.

"He would take four or five of them. I could always tell because he'd get scratchy and jumpy." Acaldo imitated the way Mitchelson often fidgeted and scratched at his eyebrows. "When he's on Percodan, I've seen him scratch himself until he bled.

"And when he's coked up, I've seen him on talk shows sometimes when his lip is so stiff he can't smile. . . . His lip wouldn't move!"

Mitchelson insulated himself, she said, by using Acaldo or a junior lawyer in the office to fetch his cocaine from Perlman or other sources. After Acaldo became sexually involved with Mitchelson ("No foreplay. Just plows right in. You're sleeping with the wonderful Mr. Mitchelson! It was really quite boring."), she got close enough to see a drug connection between Marvin and one of his good friends who was one of Hollywood's best-known celebrities as well as a client of Mitchelson's.

The celebrity would "occasionally visit Marvin when Marvin had just scored." The two of them, Mitchelson and Acaldo, also visited the celebrity's Bel Air mansion a half-dozen times, she said, with Mitchelson sometimes explaining that he was going to get some cocaine because he'd run out, but that Acaldo "better never tell anybody."

"When we would get there, what would happen is [Marvin's friend], having more sense than Marvin, would say, 'Will you excuse us a moment?' and step into another room with Marvin. And then Marvin would come back and wink at me, and we'd leave."

For Mitchelson, part of the excitement of the drug scene appeared to be the challenge to keep it clandestine. "He'd do it in court! He'd carry it in court and go into the men's room and do it," Acaldo continued. "In fact, he came in laughing once, telling me how he snorted it in the judge's chambers. He was very proud of himself!

"He took [cocaine] with him almost all the time. . . . What Marvin

would do is go on what I call a toot. Stay up all night. Then he couldn't
come in the next day. He'd sleep that off, then he'd come in the following day, work great, and go off on another toot. . . . There was a lot
of cocaine. A *lot*! I used to find it hidden *everywhere*! In his shoes. All
over." He secretly stashed some of the dope between the towels in his
office bathroom, according to Acaldo, who later told fellow prosecutors
in the Los Angeles D.A.'s office that she wouldn't be surprised if he
turned up dead from an overdose.

A number of clients said Mitchelson had used cocaine with them,
or in front of them. One client, who also said she had sex with Mitchelson during the early 1980s, told the Los Angeles Police Department
that Mitchelson confided that his habit then was costing him $30,000
a month—an extraordinarily high amount. Another client during the
1970s said she witnessed him purchasing drugs:

"We were on our way to the office, and he said, 'I have to stop and see
Bruce Perlman.' We drove into [the garage of] Bruce's offices, in a bank
building, and as I recall, Bruce came down to the car. Marvin got out of
the car, and opened the trunk of the car, and they were talking. I got out
of the car, something like that, and they slammed the briefcase closed very
quickly. I saw [Marvin] put a package in the briefcase.

"So I said to him, 'What was that all about?'

"He said, 'Oh, just a little business.'

"I said, 'Are those drugs?' I knew, because the rumors were pretty
strong about the drug business.

"He said, 'Yes, but I'm not gonna take them. I'm gonna throw 'em
away. I told Bruce this is the last time.'"

Finally, Acaldo refused to act as Mitchelson's cocaine courier anymore. One afternoon, though, Acaldo heard Mitchelson turn the lock
in his door, "and there wasn't a girl in there, so I knew he was probably
snorting coke. So I waited. We used to wear, back in those days,
wooden shoes that were real popular. And I went in and took my key
and I opened the door real fast, and there he was with so much cocaine,
he had it in an old antique inkwell. . . . He was just standing over [it],
starting to snort, and I said, 'Put it down.' And he said, 'Linda, please!'
And I said, 'Put the motherfucker down!' And I took the inkwell and I
threw it on the wooden [trim] around the carpet. I raised my foot up
to smash it, and he said, 'My God, not that, it's an antique!' And I just
went *swoosh* and smashed the whole thing, and cocaine was everywhere, intermingled with glass.

"He owed me money!" (Mitchelson had borrowed $8,000 from her
and at that time still hadn't paid it all back.) She thought, "Christ, if
he's going to do all this coke, he can pay me!

"So [when] I smashed it to the floor, I just put all the glass splinters
in his cocaine for him, so he couldn't use it anymore. I said, 'There!
You want it? Get down on the floor and sniff it up!'"

Acaldo later got her night-school law degree and went to work for the Los Angeles district attorney's office. She realized she couldn't have gotten that job if she'd been convicted of carrying cocaine. "You know what Marvin would've said if they caught me and I told them it was really for him? 'I don't know what she's talking about.'" As it turned out, Acaldo wasn't too far from wrong.

On October 6, 1975, Bruce Perlman died suddenly of what a resident physician at the UCLA Medical Center diagnosed at the time as blood poisoning caused by a ruptured colon. Perlman was thirty-two years old. He had been at the UCLA hospital for five days.

Acaldo believed Perlman's death was really drug related. Although there is nothing in the death certificate to substantiate her conjecture, the attending physician later called Perlman's blood-poisoning death suspicious. "It should not have killed him," he said, "unless he was immuno-suppressed." American doctors didn't even know what AIDS was when Perlman died, but some researchers at UCLA now believe that undiagnosed AIDS actually caused the death of clusters of young men who died at the hospital as early as 1975.

Asked about Perlman's death, Mitchelson answered a question that hadn't even been asked: "He didn't die from drugs. He was strong as an ox."

Although he did not talk about whether Perlman ever gave him drugs, Mitchelson vehemently denied that Perlman ever sold him any. "Never sold me a drug in his life. And you can quote me on that one!

"I mean, never in his life did Bruce Perlman sell me anything. And no matter who you heard it from, you're not hearing the truth. Since Bruce is dead and can't defend himself, far be it for me to say that Bruce was a drug user or did this.

"In those days, in that era, many people tried drugs, or did them once in awhile, or did 'em at parties. I don't think I know of hardly anyone who didn't. I mean, I'm sure you didn't. . . . But most people at one time or another tried something like that.

"That's as far as anything went. No one was into selling or dealing. That's just bullshit. Bruce Perlman came from a very, very wealthy family. His father-in-law was my client. And, I handled a bankruptcy for him in Chicago. . . .

"These were very wealthy people. And Bruce was a lawyer. He had a law practice. As far as I know, he wasn't a drug dealer at all. That's all I can tell you about him."

Just as he found a mentor of sorts in Roy Cohn, so, too, was Marvin even then a mentor to other up-and-comers.

Martin Klass came to Mitchelson as one of those. Klass was short, with a receding hairline that he later tried to cover with a hair transplant, and he aspired to greatness.

Soon after signing on as Marvin's young associate, he bought a
Lamborghini. Later, he had a Rolls-Royce with the vanity license plate
KLASS.

"I remember [he copied] Marvin as soon as he could," Mitchelson's
secretary from the period, Claire Allen [name changed] recalled. "He
started living very lavishly. And he bought a Lamborghini. People
would say, Here comes this guy! He wanted them to recognize his car.
He'd seen what a Mitchelson could do, and he wanted the same
thing. . . . He was an attorney, so he could make court appearances
[for Marvin]. He could be a good lackey. . . .

"[Marty] tried to emulate Marvin, as a role model. It was hard
enough to deal with one, but when Marty tried it, I rebelled! I wasn't
very nice. I said, I'm not going to put up with an ego like that in a
pischer. So we didn't get along too well."

Klass, according to Acaldo, also replaced Perlman as one of Mitchelson's drug suppliers. Eventually, Klass went off on his own, first renting
space in Mitchelson's office suite, then moving out to establish his own
Century City law practice.

On October 17, 1987, Klass died from what his physician reported
was a cancerous tumor of the chest, but which some suspected was
AIDS. He was forty-seven years old. Mitchelson acted almost like he'd
never even heard of him.

14

There was a saying among the cognoscenti of the criminal courtrooms: It was there that you'd find bad people on their best behavior.

If that were true, said Family Court Director Hugh McIsaac, it was
in his divorce courtrooms that you'd find *good* people on their *worst*
behavior. "Anybody in a divorce is in a position of diminished capacity."

Nobody questioned that divorce brought out the worst in the
2,314,000 people whose marriages ended each year. "These are pathetic people," said the East Coast's master of divorce, Raoul Felder.
"They are just pathetic human beings."

"This used to be fun," Felder said of the divorce-law business. "It
was more of a game. There was the question of guilt and innocence,
and it required ingenuity to get evidence. It was like a chess game,
thrust and counterthrust. You'd get caught up in the cases; you felt you
were doing something right. You believed in your clients and your clients believed in you. Now, the client hates you. There's a big antago-

nism toward lawyers today. So you've got a client that's not particularly crazy about you, and all the fun is out of the cases. It's really a dull area of law. It *is* very lucrative, though."

Felder had learned a lesson that Mitchelson hadn't. "I have a very simple expression here: Today's client is tomorrow's enemy. We do a professional service. We don't get involved with these people. We keep them at arm's length."

Mitchelson's method was the antithesis of that. In fact, his steady business was very much dependent on his getting close to the vulnerable females who came to him. He was a ladies' man with a finely tuned "sensitive male" act. His female clients did not come to him for love and attention, but Mitchelson was very much aware that many of them needed that. And, in his way, that's what he gave them, as long as there was money to be made. He could turn on the charm or turn on the tears, and Marvin had the advantage because only he could know whether it was just an act.

Marvin had a standard line he used on new women clients: "I'm your knight on a white horse." It was an advertisement and a promise, and it was his way of gaining a client's confidence.

"I think that anytime anyone is in a very strenuous situation, it's not uncommon for women to fall in love with their doctors, their psychiatrists, their lawyers; anyone who can help them through a very troubled time," commented Joan Shepherd, for whom Mitchelson negotiated a $40 million settlement in the biggest divorce in Japan's history. She tried to explain why women who hired Mitchelson would later make accusations against him. "Now, a lot of time their mental balance has a lot to do with it. It's distorted. They need love. Marvin's like a father figure."

"The thing that he does is, he has people who are vulnerable," added Veronica Buss, whom Mitchelson represented in her divorce from the very wealthy owner of the L.A. Lakers. "In other words, nobody else really cares, but *he* cares. That type of thing. And, really, you *do* believe it because I guess all people believe what they want to believe. You really do want to believe that there is a nice person out there who really is going to help you in the ways that we have, by law. Do you see what I mean? I didn't go to him for a *date*, or a *romance*!" (Nor did she have either with Mitchelson.)

And yet, as Martha Smilgis saw it, her friend Marvin's affairs were just "part of the show."

"[The celebrities] love him. And you know why? It's a *show*! You're not just hiring a lawyer, you're hiring a press conference. You're hiring a stage. You're making a performance. And that's what they live for, and they *love* it!

"Marvin's a confluence of a lot of different feelings and emotions going on at one time. Some of his motivations are childish; infantile to the nth degree. And it's really 'Mommy, look at me now!' . . . Other times, he's got a brilliant mind, and he's the shrewdest fox in the world. You rarely see them in operation at the same time. . . .

"I think we're always children until we die. . . . But with Marvin, it's like you're dealing with a seven year old in emotions a lot of the time. He *is* like a kid a lot of the time. But he's also got a very fine intellect. So it's this weird combination. . . .

"He has to be on show. He loves the audience. He's really more of an impresario. He's in his own movie. He likes to conjure up stories. It's not only that he's a player in the story, he wants to make the story happen. He has a thousand fantasies and he likes to play them out one by one in his mind."

Mitchelson liked to do things for their shock value: He dressed flamboyantly, sporting a cape and a beret as he sashayed through the lobby of the Plaza Athenée.

"He has this great eye," marveled Smilgis. "He wants drama; he wants it to be exciting."

Smilgis wasn't the only one who said that. Nobody knew Marvin for very long without reaching the unavoidable conclusion that he was an excitement junkie for whom life held no interest, no thrill, unless he placed himself in jeopardy. It was as if every time one side of Marvin tried to show his worth, the other jumped out to prove him unworthy.

Smilgis thought she could see, in Marvin's circle of acquaintances, those who in his mind assumed the roles of mother and father. Marvin wanted to be scolded by the mothers and to show them how much he was trying to please. He wanted to challenge the fathers, to show them they could not bring him down.

"He wants [his father figures] to challenge him. Make him fight. He wants to push you as far as he can go to make you mad at him. He wants to push you to the edge."

"I'm his mother," Martha Smilgis observed. "Watch. You'll be his father. Trust me."

Such was the sex appeal of Marvin Mitchelson. From the moment he represented Pamela Mason, he'd been the leading man of the Hollywood divorce. His office, with its steady stream of women clients, was the place where motive met opportunity.

"He's always said, 'I love women. And all I want to do is help them,'" said Kathryn Cleary [name changed], who hired Mitchelson to handle her divorce, and who gave him a lot more of her money than she later thought she should have. "And some poor woman who's getting divorced says, 'This is what I need. An attorney who has sympathy for me.'

"He tried everything in the book. You wouldn't believe it. . . . I was married for twenty-five years. I didn't know people like that existed. And a lot of women walk into his office. . . . You could write for the rest of your life and still not get all the way to the bottom of things. People go to him because they think, 'Well, he's really a good attorney. He's tough. He's going to fix my husband.'"

"He comes on. He cares about you," explained Claire Allen [name changed]. "He can help you. He can make you feel better. Father. Husband. Lover. Friend. All those things. And the people who come to him are vulnerable. They're looking for someone to care. And there he is. He's famous and all that. . . .

"It was not something that would ever have occurred to me before that day; you know, sleep with *Marvin*? Since then, I've realized it's not an uncommon thing to do."

After her own experience, Claire figured that Mitchelson was constantly on the prowl. "He was living at the outer limits all the time. *All* the time. I don't know what started it, I don't know if it was his childhood or where it came from, but there was probably *never* a normal person there [in Marvin]—somebody who was living a normal life with an occasional fling. With him, it was a constant fling. And his face shows the ravages of time. His face now is very fleshy and pouchy and puffy. Otherwise, he would be very attractive, with the gray hair and the bearing that comes from being successful.

"He always used to have designer shirts, custom made shirts, from Nat Wise, the shirtmaker over on Sunset. Even if he couldn't afford them, that's what he'd get. And he'd never deprive himself.

"He'd always have top-line tickets. He'd go to brokers, or scalpers. Anything he wanted, he'd have an account to buy it. Sometimes he'd buy his tickets at the health club; somebody would be scalping tickets there. But the same man who never deprived himself would also call me collect from Italy! I would get paid, but I'd have to get myself reimbursed. . . .

"He's more than a Casanova. He's more than a gigolo. He's more than a Dr. Jekyll-Mr. Hyde. He's a combination of many personalities. What drives him? I don't know.

"He's managed to stay out of jail. He's managed to stay alive, and he's managed to make money. And he's not had an irate husband or boyfriend kill him, which I'm [surprised at]. I figured, with the percentages, it'd have been the other way."

The Marvin Mitchelson who slept around was like the little boy who still sneaked around behind his mother's back. And now he had another strong woman to hide from: his wife, Marcella.

Sonia, who brought chicken soup to his office and offered her apartment as a safe haven where he could sleep all day Sunday with the telephone turned off, only wanted to see her son's best side. "She was

this nice little, white-haired lady," commented Maureen Hancock
[name changed], "and as soon as she came into the office he'd revert
to being a sweet little boy around her." Sonia was oblivious to anything
the least bit off-key about her son. She refused to listen to criticism of
him, even if that criticism came from her own daughters.

Marvin's mother was so devoted to him that she sometimes would
even talk to his clients herself. Who wouldn't trust the little lady with
the funny accent when she said her Sonny was the right man for the
job? One client, who said Mitchelson raped her, but whose name was
never made public, later tearfully related how Sonia had earlier assured
her that Mitchelson was a fine attorney.

"He said, 'Hold on, I'll put my mother on.' She spoke to me in
Russian," said Rose Mishkin [name changed], who was also an emigré
from Eastern Europe. "She said, 'My son is good. Trust him. He's a
wonderful son. He's going to take care of you. Don't worry. Trust him.'
Then we met. She looked like a bag lady; like she had been cleaning
houses. This was how he was treating his own mother!"

Claire Allen remembered the day in January of 1967 when some
headboards and bed frames fell on top of Sonia while she was shopping
in Beverly Hills. "The store called. Well, hysteria! I mean, the end of
the world. He was running and carrying on." Mitchelson filed a
$25,000 lawsuit right before the statute of limitations ran out. "There
was a tremendous closeness with his mother."

Sneaking around his wife, Marcella, must have posed an entirely different challenge. Marcella was the intensely suspicious type. "It's in the
Italian blood!" Marvin would say, laughing. It didn't take his wife long
to wise up to Marvin's hyperactive libido.

Whether Marcella knew it or not then, the real threats to her marriage didn't come from the clients that Marvin carried on with. Business
was business, after all; nothing more. No, the serious contenders were
elsewhere, and when Marvin finally did meet the new woman of his
dreams in 1969 he fell extraordinarily hard. Some thought it was probably the only time he'd ever truly fallen in love, though others wondered
even about that.

15

Catherine Mann was a dark-haired beauty, a twenty-five-year-old honors graduate from Michigan State who was traveling the world as the New York Summer Festival Queen. Marvin was forty-one.

As Mayor John V. Lindsay's personal emissary to promote tourism in the Big Apple, Cathy Mann visited Japan, the Philippines, Australia, and New Zealand. She was making the rounds doing TV interviews, and met Mitchelson the day they both showed up for guest spots on the local KABC news show in Los Angeles. The meeting was fate; after that, lust took over.

Marvin was smitten by degrees until he was totally gone and, Marvin's friends said, so was she. Before long, Cathy moved to Los Angeles and got a job writing for *Teen* magazine, and eventually Marvin filed for a divorce. There was only one problem: How would he explain this to Marcella?

He *couldn't* explain things to his hot-blooded Italian wife. So Marvin carried on as best he could for as long as he could, sneaking around with Cathy and taking her on his frequent out-of-town trips.

There was, for instance, the time that Marvin took Cathy with him to London. When Marvin returned, he told his secretary about how he and Cathy had stayed in a ritzy hotel and were having a great time. One morning, Cathy wanted to leave the hotel while Marvin was still asleep, so she stuck a note to the bathroom mirror: Darling: I've gone to get my hair done. Be back soon. Love, Cathy.

As Mitchelson described it to Acaldo, it was a scene right out of the Marx Brothers. Marcella decided to surprise her husband by flying over to London. She told the front desk clerk, "I'm Mrs. Mitchelson and I want the key to my husband's room," and he gave it to her. As she opened the door, Marvin opened his eyes and saw Marcella. He jumped around and messed up the bed, to make it look like he'd been rustling around alone instead of sleeping there with someone else. He somehow managed to convince Marcella that the note stuck on the mirror was from the people who had the hotel room before him, and that he just hadn't bothered to take it down!

When asked about the story later, Marvin made no attempt to deny it. "You can say I responded with a knowing laugh! No, say it was an *appreciative* laugh."

Marcella became suspicious enough that she developed what seemed like a sixth sense about where she'd find Marvin and his beloved. She caught them once at Stefanino's, the "in" place on Sunset to have dinner and be seen back in 1970. Marcella came flying through the doors of the restaurant and, in front of Steve McQueen, Don Rickles, and Van Heflin, bellowed at Cathy: "You're sitting with my *husband!*" Whereupon, Marcella grabbed Marvin's Rolls-Royce keys from the table, tore off a wig Cathy was wearing and threw it in Marvin's linguine, and then dumped a bowl of Caesar salad over Cathy's head. After a struggle, the restaurant's owner and two other waiters were able to bustle the three out of the restaurant.

Marvin told Acaldo another story: How Marcella had once caught the duo coming back to the Los Angeles airport after another trip to Europe. Mitchelson had Cathy beside him in the Rolls as he headed for his Century City office, but when he spotted Marcella following him he started calculating the risk and decided he and Cathy should split up. At least one of them would get away.

As Marvin later described it to Acaldo, Cathy was to take refuge at the Century Plaza Hotel; Marvin told her that Marcella would follow his Rolls, not her. He turned into the driveway of the Century Plaza and slowed down enough for Cathy to jump out. "Run!" Marvin yelled. But Marcella didn't take the bait. She pulled up in front of the hotel and chased Cathy into the lobby, and there was another altercation. Marvin tooled away.

"She'd *always* go after the woman," Marvin chuckled smugly. He'd known that all along.

But by early 1970, Cathy was making her own demands on the man she apparently wanted to marry. She wanted Marvin to make good on his promise to leave his wife, and Marvin figured she wasn't kidding.

Mitchelson cleared out of his house on a Friday night. The following Monday, he had Arthur Barens, a twenty-five-year-old lawyer in his office, file a divorce petition for him. From the looks of that petition, Marvin was willing to be very generous to his putative ex-mate, offering to give her custody of their five-year-old son, Morgan, pay her attorney's fees, and do whatever else the court required. But within two weeks, he yanked the divorce petition back without serving it on Marcella.

By the end of 1970 Cathy Mann was giving Mitchelson an ultimatum: leave Marcella, or Cathy would be out of his life. So, he filed yet another divorce petition. Harold Rhoden was his attorney.

Two days before Christmas, Marvin also sought an order against Marcella, restraining her "from annoying, harassing, threatening, or molesting" him, and from telephoning his clients or entering his law offices. Mitchelson claimed that Marcella had:

> followed Petitioner [Marvin]; repeatedly threatened Petitioner with physical violence; disturbed the peace in public places by insulting

Petitioner in a loud and vulgar manner; humiliated Petitioner in front of his clients and friends; appeared at Petitioner's law offices and disturbed him and his clients; telephoned Petitioner's friends and associates and embarrassed Petitioner with various false accusations.

Cathy was friendly with Rhoden because she'd introduced her friend and coworker, Sheila, to the much older Rhoden and *they* were going to get married. Acaldo said that Cathy phoned for reassurance: Was Marvin really going through with the divorce this time? Yes, yes, it's been filed, Rhoden assured Cathy.

Has it been served yet, Hal? Cathy demanded to know.

Nope, Rhoden replied. Marcella still didn't know Marvin had filed for divorce.

As Acaldo recalled the events surrounding this divorce petition, Mitchelson kept telling Rhoden: "Don't serve her, don't serve her." He'd say, "I'll bring her into the office to do it." Finally, Rhoden telephoned Mitchelson. It had been six weeks. "I can't wait any longer. We've got to serve her." So Marvin arranged to have the papers served on Marcella at five o'clock at his office.

The process server had her description. But when he showed up, Acaldo said, Mitchelson silently pointed out his secretary. She matched Marcella's physical description. Mitchelson tiptoed out of the office and let the process server make his mistake.

The unknowing server reported his success. Rhoden told Cathy the good news. Marvin had bought another month's time, since that was how long Marcella would have before she had to file an answer with the court.

As Acaldo described it, when the month passed and Marcella hadn't answered the divorce papers, Rhoden called Mitchelson. "We're going to have to take a default."

"Hal, just give her a ninety-day extension," Mitchelson replied. "She's so broken up, she is so distraught, she doesn't know what to do." Finally, Hal got tired of being in the middle. He called Marcella and asked her when she intended to answer the divorce papers. And she said, "He filed another divorce? I'm going to *kill* him!"

Recalled Acaldo: "Marcella used to go down and check the divorce records every so often, to see if he was tricking some other girl into hanging on to him. That's the kind of marriage it was."

Marvin and Cathy kept seeing each other for years after that, even during the time he was also going out with Acaldo. But Cathy was a realist by then; she must have known Mitchelson wasn't going to marry her, and after *Teen* she plunged into a career that gave her, in 1973, her first on-the-air television job with KCBS-TV in Los Angeles. Stints at stations in Minneapolis and Detroit followed. In 1980 she returned to Hollywood as an entertainment reporter, first for "PM Magazine" and then for "Entertainment Tonight." She got married, divorced, and married again—to an actor-turned-Republican congressman from Iowa, Fred Grandy. (He played Gopher for nine years on "Love Boat.") She had her first child at age forty-four. And she wrote two Hollywood novels, the first of which, *Tinsel Town*, seemed like a dead-on *roman à clef* with a supporting character named Tashi and a twenty-five-year-old protagonist, Cathleen, a *Celebrity* magazine up-and-comer who loses her virginity to "an aggressive, married, Jewish" guy who keeps absolutely, positively promising to get a divorce but never does.

There was no small irony to the way Mitchelson feared the most commonplace thing in his life: divorce. Even now, twenty years later, Marvin couldn't really acknowledge the way he'd let down Cathy, and, maybe, himself by giving in to that fear.

Marvin said his greatest dread when he filed for divorce was that he would lose his son; that Marcella would take Morgan back to Italy. He also was afraid of the recriminations from his mother and sisters. "I wanted to have a family. . . . No one in my immediate family's ever had a divorce." So Marvin did his husbandly duty and stayed married for the good of his son, while another man within him continued a vain struggle to break free.

"I *liked* Cathy Mann very, very much. And, ah, I *liked* her. She was, you know, a lovely person that I had some wonderful times with and I liked her an awful lot. . . .

"I think I furthered Cathy Mann's education. . . ." Marvin chuckled. "She was a university person. But, you know, she never knew what an opera was till I brought her to some.

"You know, see, I have to tell you this. I *am* married. I'm still married. And I've never, ever, ever. . . . Well, I've never said anything against my wife to anybody. I wish it hadn't happened. But, you know, there were a couple of times along the way that I genuinely"—he hesitated—"*liked* other people. I loved my wife, but I liked other people."

Marvin and Marcella somehow managed to keep the façade of their marriage intact. He claimed he and his wife shared the same bed and that he came home every night, but others said that was not so. Mitchelson gave his wife a $5,000-a-month allowance and left her to her own life. Harold Rhoden, who'd worked with Marvin longer than anyone, called the marriage "a farce" and his expression of love for Marcella "bullshit." "It's not lovey-dovey," cracked Marvin's publicist, Sy Presten, a few years ago. "It's twenty-nine years, for chrissakes!"

But as Victoria Molloy, the California Bar lawyer who brought charges against Mitchelson, pointed out, "They have what has been described as a marriage of convenience, but *somebody* hasn't gotten the message."

There was the time that, meeting lawyer Evelyn Gruen for a strictly business breakfast at a restaurant near his mansion, Marvin had to fend off an unbelieving Marcella.

"I met him outside his house at eight A.M. and we took his olive-green [Rolls] down the hill," Gruen recalled. "From their patio you have a full view of the parking lot, and Marcella saw us. [Next thing I know] she's jumping out of her own [Rolls], looking like a witch! He'd come in at two or three A.M. the night before, and he'd forgotten his key. She had *not* let him into the house that night; she'd locked him out. He'd slept somewhere in his suit. He looked mighty disheveled, but apparently, a man like Mr. Mitchelson doesn't lack for a place to sleep."

"There's *no* [open marriage]," Marvin declared. "Anyone my wife'd ever think I was involved with, she'd run 'em off! Run 'em down with a car! Anything! . . . Even to the point of embarrassing me with a client, on occasion. It's happened."

Marvin had so little credibility with his wife that he sometimes didn't think she'd believe the truth even if he told it to her. So when he wanted to walk a few blocks down Sunset Boulevard one day to get an ice cream cone, he told her a lie: "I'm going to see another lawyer I've got a case with. I'll be back in an hour." And she yelled back: "You're fulla *shit*!"

"Why did I lie?" Marvin asked himself. "Because the ice cream story sounded more fake than the story about the lawyer!"

Then again, even Marvin could be moved to jealous rage, as he was in 1975 when he suspected Marcella of having an affair. To get to the bottom of things, he had his own home telephone tapped by a private investigator named Robert Duke Hall. Bobby Hall ran a shady bugging and wiretapping operation that did, in Acaldo's words, "everything that Marvin needed done," until a low-life business associate of Hall's killed him with one shot through his open kitchen window in 1976. The police found Hall face down in an aluminum sauce pan with a fresh bing cherry in his mouth and four more clutched in his hand.

Acaldo couldn't believe that Marvin was tapping his own phone to see whether his wife was cheating on him. "But mostly she talked to girlfriends in Italian, and we didn't know what the hell she was saying."

The sad truth was that Mitchelson's family was far from the model family. Their adult son, Morgan, although married, still had many characteristics of an adolescent.

"It's a very strange relationship," he explained without any apparent sadness. ". . .I like to have a family. But we've got a strange kind of a family. No one eats at the same time. I regret that."

16

The lawyer who'd seen as many of Marvin Mitchelson's sides as anyone was Harold Rhoden. He'd known Marvin since 1962, when Mitchelson moved from the shared office Sonia originally found for him. His new quarters were just a few blocks away, right in the heart of Beverly Hills at the corner of Wilshire Boulevard and Beverly Drive. A younger lawyer named Donald Sterling (he later became an entrepreneur and the owner of the Los Angeles Clippers basketball team) had a suite on the eighth floor of the Bank of America building and was subleasing some of the space. Besides Mitchelson and Sterling, there was a third lawyer, Harvey Strassman, and a fourth, Rhoden. Strassman soon went into partnership with Mitchelson, although, after a few years, Marvin broke up Mitchelson & Strassman as he viewed his business-getting abilities outgrowing his partner's.

Rhoden was an enigma. He was a bantam-sized man's man, a tough-talking, leathery-skinned guy who boomed out his words in a staccato machine-gun rhythm. Rhoden was five years older than Mitchelson and ten years older than his other two office mates, and those extra years meant a lot in terms of experience. Already nearly forty when he moved into the offices in 1962, the Chicago-born Rhoden had been a B-24 tail gunner during World War II. Shot down in 1944, he'd spent thirteen months as a prisoner of war in Germany. Returning to the States as a twenty-two-year-old wartime vet, he got a GI-bill education and then began his legal career in 1953 as a deputy D.A. in Los Angeles, switching to defense work the following year.

It would have been hard to find two people more seemingly dissimilar. Mitchelson chased the stars, and Rhoden, as much a lawyer's lawyer as he was a man's man, considered him a poseur. He derided Mitchelson behind his back for being a mama's boy, and was critical of the narcissism that spurred Mitchelson to amass a thick scrapbook of clippings about himself.

But the two had an affinity from the start, because each knew that the other had invaluable skills; one hand washed the other. As the *Douglas* appeal had already proved, Mitchelson needed someone to do all his heavy legal work—the brief writing, the library research, and all the other boring things that came with practicing law. Rhoden could handle that and didn't mind if his cohort got the credit. What Rhoden experienced in return, if he ever admitted it, was the vicarious thrill of

Marvin's life on the edge. Nobody really ever got close to Mitchelson, but Rhoden came as near as anyone did to being his soulmate.

Everybody seemed to have an opinion on what bonded them. Mitchelson's friend, Martha Smilgis, noted, quite simply and quite accurately, that "Marvin can't do it without people like Hal."

"They had a working relationship . . . ," commented Veronica Buss, who had been a client of both lawyers. "As with anyone, you go where the money is." She didn't consider them to be friends, and, when pressed about it, Rhoden seemed to agree. But he needed Mitchelson, just like Mitchelson needed him.

"Marvin *made* Hal," added Michael Krycler, a forensic accountant who worked on cases where Mitchelson and Rhoden split the fees as cocounsel. "That was the attraction between them. They had a symbiosis. Marvin got all the big cases and Hal did all the work and made a lot of money from them. Marvin was the showman and Hal was the worker."

But their affinity went far beyond that. There were those, like one of Mitchelson's former law-office associates, who derided the notion that Mitchelson could be responsible for whatever success Rhoden attained. Maureen Hancock thought it was just the opposite.

"Hal *made* Marvin," she said. "Hal knew what Marvin was. He was the one person whose ass Marvin kissed. Hal was the *real* Marvin Mitchelson. Good God! Marvin couldn't sit still long enough to write the briefs in *Marvin vs. Marvin.* And Marvin knew that.

"Marvin was so flamboyant. He was everything that Hal Rhoden wasn't. And I think Hal was kind of in the thrall of that, too.

"What they had was a love-hate relationship."

Rhoden could be brutally honest, or just plain brutal: "I've always known, in any relationship I've had with Mitchelson, what he would *not* do. I've always known he was never going to do any legal work. *He* knows he's not going to do any legal work. Because why does he want me, if he can do that? . . .

"The only time Mitchelson really comes to me is when he needs something. Really, now, what's wrong with that? What's bad about that?

"We don't have a lot of things in common. We don't have the same—what'll I say? I've gotta watch it now!—we don't have the same feeling about what is right and wrong. And I may be wrong in my attitudes. He may be entirely right in his. But we do disagree a lot.

"The only place where we're really comfortable is when it comes to humor. He and I often laugh so much on the telephone, it's hard to keep talking. [The kind of laughter] where your stomach begins to hurt. Laughing at things that happened in these different cases, with people. Opposing lawyers, things of that kind."

"He's not what I'd call a friend, at all. We don't go out to dinner; we don't socialize. We're not friends.

"I guess what we share is, we both like Puccini. I've gone to the opera with him. That's all. And I do things for him; for money." Rhoden called theirs "an odd relationship." Rhoden had once considered writing a biography of Mitchelson. "But I don't see how I could do it and not tear him to pieces. Or else, it would have to be a puff job. But I wouldn't do that for anybody, and surely *not* for Marvin."

Ask Rhoden to enumerate Mitchelson's redeeming qualities and he'd reply with another gleeful dig: "I will tell you! He and I have one thing in common: We both love the music from Giacomo Puccini. Therefore, he can't be all bad! We've been to the opera together a couple of times. I'd have my wife, and he'd have a lady friend. And we'd go to the opera. . . . *La Tosca*, we saw. We [also] saw *Turandot*."

Who Marvin brought with him depended, Rhoden said pointedly, "upon which opera, what year. Never the same person. The one person he *never* took was his wife. But this isn't a secret! The guy's there, people can see him, he's well known, he's a face that everybody seems to recognize, and he's with a lady who's not his wife.

"Redeeming features. . . ? *Seriously* redeeming qualities? Mitchelson is able to stand by and look at himself with incredible honesty in view of the weaknesses he has. He can joke about these bad things he does. He can laugh at them. . . . With me, for example, he can actually laugh at the things he does: his penchant for personal publicity. . . . His habit of always being late. His habit of publicly going out with women other than his wife; not making any secret of the fact that"—Rhoden paused dramatically, then lowered his voice to a basso-profundo—"he's a *philanderer.*"

"He has problems in life occasioned by his romances with women. These problems often were financial problems occasioned by this. Something he's able to laugh at." Rhoden marveled that, despite Mitchelson's prodigious earning capacity, his compatriot was "always flat broke. Can't get a credit card.

"He would live on a standard of living that was shocking, constantly taking planes to Europe, Paris, London, New York. *Constantly!* He's here Monday. He'll say, 'I'll see you for lunch on Tuesday, I gotta talk to you about a case.' That Tuesday, he doesn't show up. I go, 'Where in the hell is Marvin?' 'Oh, Marvin went to Rome.' 'When will he be back?' He'll call me from Rome: 'I'll be back Friday.' Well, he never comes back on a Friday. Then in the middle of the week: 'I'll see you tomorrow. I gotta talk to you about this case.' 'Okay, Marvin, you give me a call.' The next day, he doesn't show up. Where is he? He's in New York. He lives like this.

"Now, he travels well, he eats well wherever he goes, he stays in the best hotels, and you've got to pay these bills on the spot. You can't just owe it. And all the money that comes in, goes out. And if he earned $3 million in a given year, he spent $3 million and something more. And a lot of his expenditures did involve ladies.

"Mitchelson, I'll believe you'll find, is a shopper. He takes ladies shopping in department stores. He buys things. Now, you might say he's generous. Maybe he's generous to ladies. Hey, that might be a good quality if you're looking for good qualities! Maybe he's generous in buying expensive gifts for his girlfriends!"

Rhoden pondered once again the prospect of his writing a Mitchelson biography. "There are an awful lot of people who despise him. Actually, that's a compliment. The word 'despise' is rather mild.

"People are afraid of libel suits. But I know Marvin could never sue anybody for libel because he's *already* bare-assed naked. *Nobody* could besmirch Marvin's reputation."

Mitchelson actually reveled in his well-cultivated reputation as a rogue. That was part of his show, too, as was the absentmindedness that he sometimes affected. Mitchelson could seem frazzled by his own peripatetic lifestyle, or possibly by life itself, and when his Poor Soul act was turned on it seemed like he needed his clients even more than they needed him. People sometimes felt so sorry for this lawyer who earned well over $2 million a year that they ended up gassing up his Rolls, buying him dinner, or loaning him money.

But the devil-may-care abandon with which Marvin flouted legal convention also masked an extreme sensitity, and no one knew that better than a lawyer named Steve Landau. Landau sublet an office in Marvin's Century City digs and made an excellent living handling his overflow cases.

Landau was also a big tease. He would do things such as seeking out one of Marvin's friends and confiding, in a stage whisper that Marvin was sure to hear, "Listen, did he tell you about the four paternity cases that he's had to pay child support in? Did he tell you about all the children that he's supporting? Four of his clients, who he *never* had sex with, have sued him and now he's supporting their children!"

This was Landau's idea of a joke. But it got Mitchelson fuming. Marvin really *had* been sued by a twenty-seven-year-old woman for paternity in 1982, in a suit filed against him by his old nemesis from the Jayne Mansfield days, Bobby Steinberg. Mitchelson claimed he wasn't the father, and when he finally got around to taking the test—"he just *hates* needles," a colleague said—it proved him right.

And so it was nothing unusual one day when Landau and Mitchelson got into one of their customary screaming matches, with Marvin finally stalking off after awhile to his own office at the end of the hall. But Landau muttered something sharp as he walked into his own office, and the next thing the rest of the staff knew, Marvin was storming into

Landau's office right behind him. Then, in a flash, both men came rolling back through Landau's double stained-glass doors. Mitchelson was clutching Landau's throat, strangling him, as Landau, eleven years younger, pummeled away at Marvin's body.

Vicki Howard, Marvin's cute receptionist, started screaming. And a young associate burst out of his cubicle to break the two men apart.

"No harm, no foul," the young lawyer proclaimed. The two men later hugged each other and apologized to their coworkers.

"We had a little fight," Marvin explained later. "Yeah. But it didn't last very long. We argue about things. I can't remember what. . . . Just a temper loss."

He grinned broadly and added with perfect timing: "Vicki liked it."

Everyone had Marvin stories. There was Marvin the Hypochondriac, the character who rushed to the doctor to have his cholesterol measured after a simple conversation with someone about fat levels in the blood. Gas pains in a strange city sent him rushing to the hospital for a full EKG workup. He worried that his father's early demise presaged the same for him.

Marvin had reported enough false "heart attacks" to keep a paramedic squad busy for weeks. When Linda Acaldo and Marvin got into a screaming match, she related, Marvin's typical retort was: "You know my father died early of a heart attack. And you know I'm using coke. And you're *yelling* at me!"

One of Marvin's clients then was the singer Barbara McNair, and his entanglements with her and her mobster husband caused another of Mitchelson's imagined heart attacks. McNair had been performing in 1972 at the Playboy Club in McAfee, New Jersey, when a delivery boy brought a package to her dressing room and asked her to sign for it. The package contained a half-ounce of heroin, and the delivery boy turned out to be an FBI agent. McNair got busted, and soon Marvin was flying east.

"Marvin took the case for five thousand dollars," recalled Acaldo, and called a news conference where he said, "The government did this. They set her up because she's black and they just sent her the heroin through the mail and tricked her." The government dismissed the case. "He just thought that was the neatest thing in the world."

But his quick success created a problem. He'd gotten McNair off the hook so fast that her husband, a Chicago gangster named Rick Manzie, wanted back part of the $5,000 fee.

Who wanted to argue with somebody whose closest business associates had just been found stuffed into two 55-gallon drums sitting side by side on the Northwest side of Chicago? Not Marvin. He promised Manzie a $2,500 refund, but three years later he still hadn't turned over the necessary cash.

Manzie hadn't forgotten. He telephoned for Mitchelson.

"This is Rick Manzie," he rasped. "Tell Marvin I'm comin' to get my money!"

Explained Marvin: "I didn't back down. Except I didn't want to get killed, naturally."

When they were on better terms, Manzie, an avid gun collector, had given Marvin a favorite .38 revolver. Now, Marvin walked over the safe in his bathroom, opened it and took out Manzie's gun. "I was in my bathrobe. . . . I'm sitting there. I don't like guns. I never have. I looked through the [cylinder], and all the chambers were empty. Except the very top one was blocked off, so I figured there's only five chambers. So I held it up against the desk, I pulled the trigger, and there's this deafening, unbelievable shattering noise! The powder burns came back on my legs and everything, and I thought I'd killed myself! . . . I started screaming: 'I've been shot! I've been shot!'"

"I was out front typing," Acaldo recalled. "Pamela [Rushworth, his bookkeeper] was sitting at her desk. And all of a sudden we heard BOOM! So I looked at Pamela and Pamela looked at me, and I said, 'I'm not going in there.' And she said, 'I'm not going in there, either!'

"So from down the hall, we heard this plaintive, 'Linda, oh, Linda!'

"Here's Marvin, of course, in his robe and barefoot, as usual, with nothing on. And he's staggering around his desk, holding his heart.

"'I've shot myself!'

"'But Marvin, usually when you shoot yourself, there's blood and I don't see any.'

"'It's there! And I'm having a heart attack, too!'

"'Marvin, I still don't see any blood.'

"'I'm having a heart attack!'"

He'd shot his desk. It was just wormy chestnut, Marvin liked to joke whenever he told the story.

"That's the closest Marvin ever got to the Mob," Acaldo said. Manzie never did show up that day, and about a year later somebody bumped him off, underworld–style, in Las Vegas.

Much of what Marvin said and did—the outrageous getups, the audacious lawsuits and press conferences, and the heart attacks—were attempts to get attention. But sometimes his ploys backfired, as happened when he and the wealthy Kathryn Cleary [named changed] both went to New York to work on her divorce settlement. They were in separate hotel rooms.

"He called me and said, 'I'm having a heart attack! Come down and help me!'

"I called the hotel doctor. Then, I showed up and the doctor showed up. Well, of course, that wasn't what he planned!" Cleary figured what Marvin really wanted was to get her into bed, because Marvin shooed the doctor out of his room and then chastised his traveling companion for not coming alone.

"I said, 'You said you were having a heart attack. So I called the doctor.' But he plays those games."

Mitchelson was also vain. Smilgis remembered the day he permed his thinning hair. When she saw him, "he looked like Nero!" Smilgis, giggling, asked him why he'd done it, and Mitchelson sheepishly replied, "Because I wanted to make it look thicker."

Marvin also had his prematurely gray hair dyed brown, along with his thick eyebrows. "He looked like Dracula when he came back!" Acaldo recalled.

Vanity drew him to the stage. Mitchelson once left his only associate alone in Los Angeles with three weeks of work that had to be accomplished in *one* week, while he flitted off to New York for what he said was an audition for a role in an Off-Broadway Shakespearian drama. He came back and told everybody he'd won the role and then declined it. But he couldn't remember the name of the character he was going to play, the theater, or the producer, and the one witness he said could corroborate his dramatic prowess, the New York publicity agent Sy Presten, didn't know what in the world his employer was talking about. Mitchelson just guffawed when he was told there was no possible way to verify his story.

"I really got the part. . . ," he insisted playfully. "I'll think of it. . . . It might be Lear."

Was Mitchelson lying? Was his tale just one more example of how he created his own fanciful world, just as he had as a child?

"Never believe *anything* he says," Acaldo warned. "He loves the supreme feeling it gives him of tricking people. Remember poor Bonnie Grant on the speaker phone? And then [another time] he got off the airplane [from Las Vegas] in thongs and gave me this big cock-and-bull story about how he lost his shoes in a hotel room! Then later on he said, 'Linda, when I tell you how this *really* happened, you're gonna laugh and say, Marvin, you *lie* when the truth would get you out of trouble!'

"And I did! He had actually been to Pamela Mason's, spent the night or so, I guess, at her condominium in Las Vegas. According to him, he locked himself out of her house when he went to pick up the morning paper, and he didn't want to wake her up to let him back in. He rises very early. . . . So he conned a taxi driver into taking a check [for the fare to the airport].

"He called me from the airport 'cause he couldn't afford the cab fare home. . . . I went to pick him up and he was in thongs!"

One of Marvin's weaknesses was his sweet tooth for Key Lime pies and licorice. Victoria Molloy found out about the former when her famous quarry showed up in December of 1988 for one of the first days of depositions in his State Bar disciplinary proceeding.

"There was a parade of secretaries around the window, staring out: 'Oh, there's Marvin Mitchelson in his green Rolls-Royce!'

"'Course, I'd done a couple of depositions with him already. He was not particularly impressive. I went down to get him, to escort him up to the deposition room. And he had a Mother Butler pie box. And I thought, 'Well, that's kind of strange, [but] maybe he has some documents in the box or something.' He was carrying his little briefcase and his Mother Butler pie box.

"We got into the deposition room, and I offered to get him coffee, and he said, 'Oh, yes!' My associate went out for coffee for him. He opened up the box, and there was a whole Key Lime pie in the box! He took out his Key Lime pie and politely offered everyone a slice of pie. Everyone declined. It was ten o'clock in the morning! He proceeded to scarf down about a third of the Key Lime pie, eating it with a spoon! I mean, really shoveling it in! Very fast!

"By the time the coffee came, he was finished with his third of the pie. And then we took a break later, and he ate another third. This is all before lunch! He went out for lunch and came back—he had put it in his car—and proceeded to start eating the final third of the pie.

"Gail [Andler, another State Bar lawyer] said to him, 'It's a very hot day out. It's been in your car. I really don't think you should eat that. It might be bad.'

"And he said, 'Oh, no! It's fresh baked today!' And he proceeded to eat the remainder of the Key Lime pie that afternoon. He ate a whole Key Lime pie!

"And I thought the amusing part was that he came dressed in a green suit, which sort of matched his Key Lime pie! . . . You know what they're probably saying at the designer stores on Rodeo Drive? 'Get out all those old green suits that we can't sell. Here comes Marvin Mitchelson!'"

Marvin's outré clothing was intended as protective coloration in a town that celebrated the offbeat and the extraordinary. But even those who thought they knew him well saw the incongruity in Marvin's life. He wanted to mingle, to be part of the scene. But he'd never mesh with his glittery surroundings so long as he was still Marvin Morris Mitchelson from Detroit, one more ambitious young man from a poor family, trying to be rich and famous by riding the coattails of the rich and famous. Was that the self-image he battled?

May Mitchelson recalled how smitten Marvin was with the Hollywood scene. May simply thought it was "fake." She always wanted to talk to him about it, to convince him that there was nothing behind the glitter. But it was an untouchable subject, "because he knew the truth," even if he didn't admit to knowing it.

"That's why I think he's lonely."

Harold Rhoden saw the loneliness, too.

"I don't think he's happy," Rhoden said. "I don't think there's any love in his life right now. . . . His value is in the wrong place. It isn't [on] what he accomplished as a lawyer. But, rather, [on] how much press did he get."

Marvin Morris Mitchelson from Detroit. The lonely boy from a poor immigrant family was lonely still, but he became a crafty lawyer and found that his wiles took him where he wanted to go. He did good work, but soon he learned it was easier to cheat the system than to serve it.

The human psyche has its own ways of compensating for unhappiness and frustration. In Mitchelson's case, living close to the edge seemed to be a way of salving the pain.

Life was its own game. He liked to gamble; to call people's bluff. Here was an officer of the court who filed his tax returns *years* late and all too frequently was a scofflaw and a deadbeat.

To Mitchelson, this seemed to be a thrill. He appeared to thrive on excitement; the way he put himself in jeopardy just so he could squeeze out of a tight spot must have made life perversely interesting for him. But to confront Mitchelson about his obvious needs was to hear the evidence of inner conflict. He lived dangerously but professed to want tranquility.

"I know you think I like [living on the edge]. I really *don't* like it at all," he protested, "and I wish I didn't live on the edge. But sometimes you have to live on the edge when things don't go right for you. . . . You think I get some sort of a pleasure to see how far I can walk the line? You couldn't be more wrong. I don't like it at all. I wish I had peace. I really do."

But there was something most incongruous about the things like that that Mitchelson said and what he actually did. "It's the kind of life he's chosen for himself," Rhoden marveled. "He always lives on the edge. He *chooses* to live like this! He simply does things that way. No one *forces* him to live like this.

"With [his] problems, a lot of guys would not be able to function at all as lawyers. . . . A lot of lawyers would say, 'I've gotta go on vacation. . . . I can't function.' I don't know how he is able to go to Florida, to New York, to Tokyo, to Europe on these cases, [and] try to handle them when he's facing this kind of pressure." Rhoden couldn't see that constant traveling might be just another way of Mitchelson's avoiding his problems.

"It's his professional life," Rhoden added. "It's his life. He couldn't survive if he were kicked out of the Bar. It isn't just his ego, or the disgrace, which alone could kill him. How's he gonna earn a living? He *can't* earn a living doing anything else. Ever! What little money he's got may be all the money he's ever gonna have. If he can't practice law, the guy could not get a job selling hot dogs here in the mall. He couldn't get a job doing anything. And he's able to joke about it, and sometimes it cuts right into him and it hurts.

"I don't think if I were suddenly, metaphysically transposed into his shoes, I could say, 'Okay, I'll handle this case, that one, and that one. Whom do I see, what's my four o'clock appointment?' I'd say, 'Fuck it all, I'm outta here!' I'd leave the field. I'd stay home. I'd say, 'Gotta cancel the appointments.'

"He has a strength that, to me, is incredible."

Rhoden couldn't understand it, but that was just because Rhoden couldn't appreciate how thoroughly Marvin was controlled by the conflict within himself. Marvin wanted to be Sonia's son just as much as he wanted to be his own man. But there was a price to be paid for meeting his mother's unrelenting aspirations. They confined Marvin in a way that he must have secretly loathed.

So on one hand, Mitchelson seemed to keep up all the expected appearances, while on the other he found a release in getting away with his own secret games: drug use, financial improprieties, and casual sex.

Linda Acaldo gave vivid accounts of Marvin engaging in sexual threesomes. Another woman told of being invited over to Mitchelson's West Hollywood mansion when Marcella was gone. Then he got some thrills by making love to her in his wife's bed and by dressing her up in Marcella's underwear.

The woman initially resisted. "I said, 'Marvin, I have *never* done anything like that in my *life*! I've got to draw the line. It is one thing to make it with a married man, but to make it with you in your wife's bed, where you sleep, there is *no way!*' Well, he kept insisting, insisting, insisting. The only thing I can plead guilty to is that I was a colossal fool. I fell for all this.

"So then, we are in the bedroom. Finally, I agreed to do it. He said, 'Go in my wife's closet. It would really turn me on if you had some of her underwear on.' I said, '*That* is where I draw the line! I am not going to do that.'" But she did, of course, through repeated changings so Marvin could marvel at how well his wife's bras and panties looked on her.

"And he said, 'You have no idea how much it would turn her on! She would be going crazy.' Such a liar! She'd be madder than a hornet. She'd be mad at both of us."

The LAPD files also contained statements by women claiming sexual adventures with Mitchelson. The same woman who said she wore his wife's bras and panties also told the police she gave Mitchelson oral sex in September of 1988 in a stall in the men's room of a Century City restaurant, and two months later under the table at a Beverly Hills restaurant. Another client told the LAPD of giving Mitchelson oral sex in the back seat of a New York taxicab.

To prove what a regular guy he was, Mitchelson occasionally even told his own stories. There was, for instance, the time in 1981 when he met two women at Studio 54. He gave them a ride in his limousine back to their apartment, "and they were trying to entice me up to their place, and the whole thing. Yeah, they really were! . . . They wanted me to spend the night. I wasn't going to do that. [But] I walked them up to their place, and I was sorta eyeing them. And they were absolutely *beautiful!* They were *gorgeous!* Their voices, *everything!*

"So I went up and had a drink with them, but I kept my limo waiting. And then I heard one of them say something to the other one, and I realized they were *men!*

"There was a phone call or something, and one of them said, 'Tom can't talk to you right now.' I thought, 'Tom?' And then Tom says, to the other person, '*Charles*, why didn't you let me talk to him?'

"Their voices changed!"

Marvin was fast. He got up to leave, reassuring the two transvestites that he'd be back just as soon as he told his limo driver to go home for the night. Then, he said, he ran down the stairs instead of waiting for the elevator, hopped into the limo, and, "of course, never came back!"

Tom Rusk was a San Diego psychiatrist who'd spent much of his career counseling troubled lawyers.* Frequently, such trial lawyers had a bravado and a need for excitement that masked their deeper feelings of insecurity and low self esteem.

This was often called "narcissism." Superficially, the term connotes self-love, but there is a large quotient of self-*hatred* in the classic narcissist, too. Experts define the syndrome as a sense of self-importance alternating with feelings of special unworthiness, and although Rusk eschewed the label he didn't quibble with the underlying symptoms or their prevalence among the courtroom advocates who continually put their abilities on display and their reputations on the line.

"Trial lawyers are excitement junkies," he explained. "Now, we're *all* excitement junkies to some degree; otherwise, there'd be no Disneylands! We want to get excited, get a *buzz*, get scared—but we don't want to die, of course!

"It's just that some of us need much more [stimulus] than others to

---

*When I spoke with psychiatrists such as Rusk, they were aware that this was to be a biography of a famous lawyer, but they were not told the subject's name or the particulars of his background.

get excited or stirred up. Some people need a tremendous amount of buzz. It's like they have to have incessant background noise in their life. They actually get addicted to the buzz, because it distracts them from the discomfort they have about themselves and their life."

Narcissists could be also found among petty thieves and fighter pilots, prize fighters and politicians: people who put themselves on the line. Trial law promised clear wins and losses: The adulation of victory was always balanced by the possible ignominy of defeat. That's what gave life its buzz, its thrill of danger. Defeating an adversary was a lawyer's way of testing his insecurity. And if victory was an affirmation of self-worth, then defeat was just as much a denial of it.

What interested Rusk, of course, was the *why* of it all. Why do trial lawyers crave the risk? The source of that, Rusk and others theorized, was a conflict between good and bad that usually began in earliest childhood, and, in its classic typology, involves, as Rusk put it, "a father who's not a raging success in his wife's eyes, and a mother who plays out her own need to feel good about herself by vicariously living out her life through a child, usually a son.

"Often, you're dealing with an ambitious Jewish mother who bonds to her son and doesn't have a huge respect for her husband. The son becomes the admired man, and being the adored person just feeds his grandiosity.

"One of the basic ingredients is a brilliant, energetic spirit in the child—very high in intelligence, affability, sensitivity, vulnerability, perceptiveness, and energy. That makes the child likely to be a high achiever but also very suceptible to being wounded. Another ingredient is a family culture in which achivment and appearances and overprotection—through limits and controls, and rewards and punishments—have a much higher priority than respect and tenderness and understanding."

In other words, the combination of brilliant child and overbearing parents could create an obedient child who lived a life dictated by his parents and who was rewarded for doing what mom and dad wanted. But it also could cause unhappiness, fostering a sense of worthlessness in the child.

"There's an inner child that's still hurting inside these people, in adulthood," explained Rusk. "But if you don't understand why you're hurting, you see it as evidence that you've got a defect. You seek public acclaim to reassure yourself that you're okay. You try to compensate via escapes. But you always fear you're *not* really okay, and you're [so] afraid other people will discover that" that you actually try to validate your inner fears by putting yourself in jeopardy.

Outwardly, the narcissist craves adulation. Always, though, there is the need for excitement; the need to keep up the buzz. That is how the narcissist tries to escape the pressure of other people's expectations. The escape route might be through multiple extramarital affairs, drinking and/or drugs, workaholism, sexual perversions, or other avenues of great risk.

This was one way to explain the hidden side of Mitchelson's life. But it wasn't the only one. At the FBI Academy in Quantico, Virginia, a small group of behavioral scientists continually studied the criminal mind for clues to what made people good or bad. After years of interviewing criminals, the FBI agents had also come to some interesting conclusions about the kind of people who relished living on the edge.

"With these people," said one FBI agent, "it's a set of balls. That's what you're talking about. That's what they're trying to show."

The FBI's typology didn't differ substantially from Rusk's. The Bureau also found a correlation between the tortured life of the adult narcissist and a childhood typified by a weak or absent father and an unhealthy bond with a strong mother.

"In a world of givers and takers, these people are clearly the takers," explained the FBI's expert. "They're attracted to occupations where they can be independent. They have trouble taking orders and they don't think the rules apply to them, but if they become a doctor or lawyer, or run their own business, they can do well. They're extroverted. They're actors, always 'on.' They like to be the center of attention.

"When people like this become lawyers, they can channel their needs in totally legal, moral, and ethical ways. But some also channel it unethically, immorally, and right under the nose of the criminal justice system, screwing their clients and taking money from them. They become con artists and wheeler-dealers.

"A guy who sticks up a 7-Eleven is going to get caught, but a lawyer who cheats a client might not get caught because he's smarter," the FBI expert continued. "He appears to be a good guy. He looks right at you and flat out lies, which is, after all, a useful trait for any advocate.

"Practice makes perfect, and where that trait [deception] turns really bad is when the lawyer lies just for the hell of it; when his entire life becomes a game of manipulation.

"There are those [narcissists] who think day-to-day life is so boring they'd almost rather be dead. A lawyer who thinks like that may like the idea of having sex with a woman while her husband is in the outer office. Or, while the judge is in the next room. He might want to have sex in a broom closet. Or make pornographic films. I talked to one famous lawyer who said it gave him a tremendous kick that he'd secretly been in a porno film and that it was playing right down the block when he came into town to give a speech at Madison Square Garden!

"The more they do it, the cockier they become."

17

Who could blame Marvin for his cockiness? After all, as early as 1970 one of the things that distinguished him was his uncanny ability to turn a client's adversity into an opportunity for himself.

So it was in the tangled case of Forrest Earl Landers. She was a forty-eight-year-old woman then whose first marriage, at age fifteen after dropping out of high school, had ended in divorce. Her second, to a doctor nineteen years her senior, was on the skids, too. And the grocery store that her parents once owned, and which she was trying now to run, was in bankruptcy.

Forrest Landers hired Mitchelson as her attorney. According to her statement to her probation officer in a 1970 court proceeding, Mitchelson told Landers to deed her home over to him, which she unquestioningly did. It was sold for what was then the upper-bracket sum of $160,000. A little while later, she said, Mitchelson met Landers at her bank and had her sign a $15,000 money order, which she did without knowing what it was for. Mitchelson was also trying to sell, on Landers' behalf, her family's Sav-On Market, which was then in a Chapter 11 bankruptcy proceeding.

Landers was an attractive blonde who knew she didn't have a head for numbers, but she didn't think she needed to because managing her money was what she had entrusted Mitchelson to do. According to Landers, Mitchelson was supposed to be handling her financial affairs, and, indeed, she said that's what he told her he was doing. Landers told the probation officer that Mitchelson had constantly assured her that her account was flush with cash—right up until the time the Los Angeles police arrested her on the felony charge of writing $8,730 worth of bad checks.

Landers tried to tell the LAPD that it was all some kind of awful mistake, that surely Marvin Mitchelson would set the record straight. Mitchelson told the probation officer that his office had completely accounted for all of Landers' money. Landers, Mitchelson said, actually owed *him* $4,628.37. He did say that if he had any extra money, he'd be glad to loan it to his client, but, well, there was this case in Chicago that hadn't come through yet.

Paul Caruso came into the case after Landers had pleaded guilty to the bad-check charge at the behest of another lawyer.

"She was convicted as a felon! . . . The case is vivid in my memory.

"When I met Forrest, she told me she inherited two or three hundred thousand dollars from her family, who allegedly owned some supermarkets. And Marvin was handling her affairs. He said to her, 'We'll put the money in my trust account. You go ahead and write all the checks you want. If you need any money, let me know.'

"So she wrote some checks. As I recall, thirteen or twenty-four of them bounced. Each one was a separate felony! And so she was in a dither, and she called Marvin. He was out of town.

"So, believe it or not, she belonged to an auto club. So she called the auto club lawyer. [All he usually does is] go to the jail and put up bail for your parking tickets. She said, 'What do I do?' He said, 'Did you write the checks?' 'Yeah.' He said, 'They bounce?' 'Yes.' 'Well, plead guilty.'

"So this poor, simple woman pleaded guilty. . . .

"I was really pissed off. . . . I went to the D.A. and I said, 'There's a great injustice here.' I told him the story. He said, 'That's terrible.' We went to the judge. He said, 'That's terrible.' I said I wanted to withdraw her plea, *nunc pro tunc*. It's Latin for 'Then as now,' which meant we'd go back to the day she entered her plea. . . . So we withdrew the plea."

An investigation was begun. Now, the LAPD got into the act, interviewing Landers about what happened to the money she said Mitchelson was supposed to be keeping for her. The D.A.'s office also subpoenaed Marvin for questioning, and although the police had concluded that "there were serious irregularities in the handling of her affairs" by Mitchelson, they couldn't get enough evidence against him to warrant a prosecution. Instead, Marvin promised to make restitution to the victims of the bounced checks, and on the basis of that the D.A. dropped the bad-check charges against Landers and closed its investigation on November 19, 1971.

As Caruso told it, though, the D.A. investigation was only one of several problems Mitchelson faced. Landers, according to Caruso, also had managed to get the State Bar disciplinary machinery cranked up against her former lawyer, and Mitchelson was facing an investigation that could have led to his suspension or even disbarment. Stealing client funds is one of the most egregious ethical violations a lawyer can commit.

"Marvin called me personally," Caruso recollected. "He was desperate. He was pleading. He said, 'Paul, my license is in your hands. I need your help.'

"I felt sorry for the guy. I said, 'Marvin, I want to help you. I don't want to see you in trouble with the Bar'—because I don't want to see any lawyer in trouble with the Bar, unless he's an out-and-out bad guy. And I guess, looking back, he *was* a bad guy, because this woman had a felony she shouldn't have had!

"Anyway, I called the bunco squad and told them it was under control. Then I wrote the State Bar and said everything was under control.

"The State Bar called off its hearing. The bunco squad called off its investigation. Does Marvin owe me something? I think so.

"So we went to court, withdrew the plea, and this asshole, Martin Klass, [who was representing Mitchelson in the D.A.'s investigation] later said all they could scrape together was eighteen thousand dollars. And I think the amount missing was well in the two hundred thousands! Eighteen thousand dollars! And then Klass had the audacity to make a motion for my client to pay his fee of five thousand dollars, and I said, 'You've got to be kidding me! I'm not getting a penny. This poor woman has been fucked out of two hundred thousand dollars. You're giving her eighteen grand and I'm letting your client walk. And you have the audacity to want me to pay your attorney fees? I can't believe it!'"

As angry as Caruso was about the Forrest Landers affair, Caruso was not happy about criticizing another lawyer and he told his story reluctantly.

Mitchelson seemed to have an almost irresistible aura that gave his women clients supreme confidence in him. "He's as good at getting money off people as anybody I've ever seen," said his former associate, Maureen Hancock [name changed]. "Nobody can dance money off people the way Marvin can."

His own money problems were sometimes ferocious. Acaldo remembered a time when Marvin needed money so badly that he'd gotten a retainer fee from a new client at lunch and then called Acaldo to meet him outside his office building so she could run to the bank to deposit the money. His finances got so tangled, Acaldo said, that when she was acting as his bookkeeper in the 1970s she tried to impose discipline by making herself a cosigner of every check written on the office accounts.

Even then, she claimed, "I used to come in and the last check in the check book would be missing, and we'd be out five thousand dollars. He'd have gone to Vegas the night before, and I'd be writing bad checks all over the place, not knowing it—on the clients' trust accounts, too. You name the account, he'd spend it!"*

She said Marvin also wrote checks on a bogus Swiss account. His account at the Swiss bank had been closed for some time, but Mitchelson kept the old checks. Every time he wrote one, he knew he'd bought

*Mitchelson angrily denied this. He said he has "never taken one penny in my life, not a half a penny from a trust account. Ever. Ever. Ever. Ever. . . . I'd like to see her prove that I ever took a penny from a trust account. She's a goddamned liar."

himself the extra weeks it took the bad check to get back from Switzerland.

It was during the early 1970s that this lawyer who couldn't seem to hang on to a dime nonetheless began a sideline as an investor of his clients' money.

"Marvin would get a large settlement [for a client] and then presume to invest it or 'borrow' it," Acaldo has said. "He called them investments, and he'd give people ten percent on their money." The problem was, he'd often "spend the whole thing."

The little boy who tricked movie stars into "saving" him at the beach and who conned people out of pocket change outside the movie theater had grown up. "I used to accuse him of being a thief," Acaldo once said. "And he would say, 'Well, they're investing in Marvin Mitchelson, that's who they're investing in.'"

Still caught up in the pretensions of his youth and playing a poseur's role to the hilt, Marvin saw himself as some lord of the manor. He lived in a genuine, twenty-seven-room turreted castle once owned by the French actor Charles Boyer, and he even made plans to encircle his five-acre Hollywood estate with a real moat.

Marvin used someone else's money to indulge his fancy for buying and selling Picassos, Modiglianis and Van Goghs and other fine art. He did this by hitching himself to the substantial fortunes of his client, Bonnie Grant.

The vehicle for Marvin's big investments in artistic masterpieces was his 50–50 La Radiana investment partnership with Grant. The partnership had more than $5.5 million of her money, but none of his. By all accounts, Marvin made investments with an art dealer who was almost as adept as Mitchelson was at charming the wealthy out of their money.

In 1972, Frank Heller was the owner of the Sari Heller Gallery in Beverly Hills. His mother, for whom the gallery was named, was a noted art collector, and when she died Frank took over. He was just twenty-six years old then, but his manner and presence were that of a much older man, and his knowledge of art rivaled that of experts twice his age. He was an attractive, likeable guy, five feet, ten inches tall, with dark hair and intelligent eyes. Most of all, though, Frank Heller was a super salesman.

As scams went, young Heller's was so brazen that it was hard to believe he pulled it off: Heller sold the same paintings over and over again to different people. The customers were prominent bankers, lawyers, and sportsmen who perhaps should have known better than to fall for a get-rich-quick scheme. But everybody at the beginning was making tons of money.

Heller got his rich clients to become his partners in buying masterpieces. He found the Renoirs and Monets, and his investors put up the money to buy them. It was a foolproof investment, he confidently assured them. In fact, Heller *guaranteed* to buy back his investors' paintings for a return of as much as 138 percent a year.

It was easy to keep that promise as long as there were other unwitting investors waiting to buy the very same painting. Heller kept most of the "investment" paintings in his gallery for safekeeping, and when he needed to pay somebody back he simply "sold" one of the masterpieces again. He Ponzied the same paintings back and forth to several purchasers, using fictitious invoices. At least once, he sold a Van Gogh that didn't even exist. As long as it came with one of his gold-plated repurchase guarantees, buying a painting from Heller was as close to a sure thing as his well-heeled customers thought they could get.

When the prosecutors finally unwound all of Heller's transactions, he'd swindled his investors, who included Mitchelson and his partner Grant, out of at least $3.5 million.

"Heller was the most gifted con artist I've ever known," marveled Richard Moss, who was then a thirty-three-year-old deputy district attorney and who eventually got Heller sentenced to a year in jail for grand theft. "He would go to collectors and say, 'Here's this painting. I can get it for two hundred grand but it's worth three hundred and fifty. We'll sell it for that and split the profits.' Then he'd go to investor number two and say, 'I can get it for three hundred and fifty thousand dollars and we'll sell it for five hundred thousand,' and so forth." Heller later admitted that in some instances he'd inflated the paintings to three times their actual market value.

Once the scheme got rolling and young Heller's investors started leaning on him to make good on the outrageously high returns he still promised, Heller needed money desperately. "It was a fictitious circle that I couldn't get out of," he told the authorities after they arrested him in 1976, alerted by a $250,000 repayment check of his that bounced. "I was drowning and I would have signed a confession to being Adolf Hitler at that point. I was drowning. I was desperate."

What Heller also described was a business relationship with Mitchelson in which the buying and selling of fine art was a front for what, if Heller's account was accurate, amounted to Mitchelson's loan sharking.

In a deposition taken by the D.A.'s office in March of 1976—a deposition through which the prosecution hoped to unravel his complicated dealings—Heller testified that he "got involved with Marvin Mitchelson" because he was having trouble getting bank loans.

"Marvin's interest in paintings was strictly from the standpoint of the profits that could be made from their purchase and resale," Heller testified. He only ever saw Mitchelson with his eye on the balance sheet, never on the canvas. Mitchelson wanted to invest $3 million to $4 million of Bonnie Grant's money in art. When Marvin gave Heller money to "buy" a painting, it was always with the provison that the painting would be resold and the funds quickly paid back at an interest rate as high as 10 percent a month. As Heller described it, the Heller-Mitchelson-Grant relationship was not always what it seemed.

"Although Mr. Mitchelson's documentation indicates that he was a purchaser [of paintings], in each and every instance what I did was borrow money from Mr. Mitchelson," Heller testified. "Every time I got a dollar from Marvin Mitchelson I had to pay him back a dollar and ten cents thirty days later." He claimed Mitchelson made profits of $532,000 on all those "loans"; a later accounting put Mitchelson's profits at $703,500 on the $4.1 million of La Radiana's money he paid the gallery during the ten months between June of 1973 and April of 1974.*

Bonnie Grant wasn't happy. By late 1974, she wanted her money back—not just the huge divorce fee she'd paid Marvin, but also the La Radiana money he'd "invested" in Heller's art and in some Palm Springs desert real estate. In 1974, Grant complained to the State Bar, and in February of the following year she filed suit for fraud, breach of fiduciary duty, malpractice, and charging unconscionable fees.

The court file was replete with charges and counter-charges, and it read more like a long-running soap opera than a legal malpractice case. Sure, Grant wanted her money back—much of which was by then in the hands of the smooth-talking Frank Heller. But in Mitchelson's eyes, the subtext of her fight seemed to be about something else.

"Total revenge," Mitchelson called it. According to Mitchelson, "Bonnie Grant wanted me to divorce my wife to marry her. Well, I didn't want to do that."

Grant finally fired Marvin as her lawyer on May 22, 1974, after he confessed, as the stilted language of one of Mitchelson's court filings put it:

> [T]hat he had taken a three-day trip to New York with his wife, instead of taking a three-day trip alone to Oregon; and because, by May 19, 1974, Mitchelson had failed to keep several deadlines set by plaintiff for Mitchelson to move out of his house and leave his wife and son; and because of [Grant's] expressed threat to Mitchelson that for his "infidelity" to her, [Grant] would ruin him professionally and financially, and prevent him from again hurting another woman emotionally.

Grant later filed a petition charging Mitchelson with contempt of court for a 1:30 A.M.-to-dawn tirade in her living room and outside her

---

*Heller was such a con man that the probation officer's report was actually complimentary to him. Victims wrote in, asking that he be spared prison. In prosecutor Moss's unctuous words, "He was the *nicest* white-collar criminal I ever met."

apartment building just a week after she got an injunction prohibiting him from contacting her. Grant later claimed that, during Mitchelson's tirade, he threatened that if she didn't drop the fraud and malpractice charges against him, the gangster Rick Manzi was going to "take care" of her. Mitchelson sued back, charging Grant with attempting to murder him at 12:30 A.M. on the street leading to his driveway by lunging at him with a butcher knife.

All Grant will say about the whole sordid mess now is that "I can name six people that Marvin introduced me to that have all been murdered. Pretty good average, right? So he ran with a very nice group of people."

Mitchelson finally gave up fighting after four years of litigation and settled with her in 1979 for $1.5 million. Mitchelson called it "an amicable settlement," and maybe it really was. But after settling, he claimed he could not pay. To get her money, Bonnie Grant foreclosed on Mitchelson's Sunset Heights Drive house and on a 250-acre piece of Palm Springs real estate he owned in partnership with his friend Seymour Lazar.

Mitchelson's problems weren't over. When the Heller scheme collapsed, Marvin had at least four of the gallery's masterpieces in his possession. So he crated up the paintings—by Sisley, Matisse, Renoir, and Picasso—and shipped them to a Dutch bank.

"I didn't want to get twenty cents on the dollar," Mitchelson politely explained. The bankruptcy trustees of the Sari Heller Gallery didn't see it that way, and they sued Mitchelson for loan-sharking and fraud. The trustees wanted back those valuable paintings, and they wanted to punish him by making him pay over $13 million in damages—including triple the usurious interest he'd supposedly charged Frank Heller.

Marvin insisted he, too, was simply a *victim* in the whole Heller scheme—a victim who'd lost, he claimed, about $500,000 of his own money in addition to the considerable money that Bonnie Grant had put in. Marvin later even claimed that his mother, Sonia, had been fleeced out of $100,000 by Frank Heller, although his mother's name didn't appear on a grand jury list of witnesses in the Heller case.

To Moss, the deputy district attorney who was running the Heller grand jury, Mitchelson's claims didn't add up. He also thought Marvin was behaving oddly. When Moss asked him, as one of those who'd allegedly been swindled, to appear before the grand jury as a witness against Heller, Mitchelson showed up with his own lawyer and demanded to be given immunity from prosecution before he would testify.

"*Immunity?*" Moss replied incredulously. "What in the world for? We don't give *victims* immunity."

Moss initially figured Mitchelson was afraid of being indicted for criminal usury. He asked Harold Rhoden, who was acting as Mitchelson's lawyer, whether that was the problem. Nope, answered Rhoden. It's something else. The duo never told Moss what their concern was, although the deputy D.A. later speculated that it might have had to do with Marvin's fear of investigation into his handling of Bonnie Grant's money.

Marvin finally did testify to the Heller grand jury, and nothing else came of that. He waited out the Heller Gallery trustees for eight years on their lawsuit, though, before finally settling with them on the eve of trial for $100,000. That had to be a real deal for Mitchelson, considering that he boasted of having sold at auction a full five years earlier the Heller paintings he shipped out of the country.

To hear him tell it, he only settled out of sheer weariness. But getting Mitchelson to agree to a settlement and getting him to actually *pay* it off were two very different things, as Bonnie Grant had already found out. Even though he avoided a trial by agreeing to pay the trustees $100,000, he thereafter simply ignored the debt, forcing the trustees to spend another two years trying to attach anything Mitchelson owned in Los Angeles, Orange, Riverside, San Bernadino, and Ventura counties. The trustees finally found something: a Beverly Hills estate that Mitchelson had been given a part ownership in, in lieu of a cash fee, by Dena al-Fassi, the divorced wife of one of the richest sheiks in the world.*

18

Harold Rhoden was in Las Vegas. It was November 13, 1977, a week before the biggest trial of his life. Rhoden sat down and wrote out his Last Will and Testament:

As for my liabilities, I have the following:
1.) I owe the Federal Government in taxes approximately $100,000. Fuck them!
2.) I owe $50,000 to the First Los Angeles Bank.
3.) I owe Marvin M. Mitchelson, Seymour Lazar, and Steve Lan-

---

*In May 1986, more than two years after the settlement, the judgment was satisfied.

dau approximately $150,000 evidenced by numerous promissory notes.

Rhoden's big Las Vegas case was against the estate of the legendary Howard Hughes, and was the subject of a movie, "Melvin and Howard." It was the real-life story of how a gas station attendant named Melvin Dummar ended up with a one-sixteenth interest in the billionaire's disputed will.

Dummar claimed that he encountered a degenerate-looking man who called himself Howard Hughes lying alongside a highway in southern Utah. Dummar drove the man to Las Vegas, and gave him a quarter. All Hughes did was ask Dummar his name.

It was in 1976, after Hughes died, that Dummar noticed a strange man at his gas station. After the man left, a mysterious package appeared on Dummar's desk. It said: "Deliver to Mormon Temple." Inside was an envelope containing a three-page handwritten letter purporting to be the will of Howard Hughes. There were hundreds of millions of dollars in bequests to the usual good causes like the Boy Scouts and various universities for scientific research. But the truly surprising beneficiary was none other than Melvin Dummar, who was to get millions for saving Hughes's life. Noah Dietrich, the brains of the Hughes financial empire for thirty-two years until he had a bitter falling out with the billionaire in 1957, was named the executor.

Dietrich was eighty-seven years old. He needed somebody else to defend his interests, and he picked his trusted lawyer, Rhoden.

There was just one problem, Dietrich told Rhoden. "I can't cover the expenses for this."

"I know, Noah."

"Of course, when I'm in as the executor and you're my lawyer for the estate, there'll be *millions* in fees."

In the oil-drilling business, such a venture would be called an elephant hunt. Go hunting for the biggest game of all and you might come back with a trophy, but you'd more likely return with nothing. The story of how Rhoden hitched his fortunes to the disputed Mormon Will, as it came to be known, was a tale of advantages gained and possibilities lost.

Rhoden first hooked up with Dietrich in a case that began in 1959, when an entrepreneur named Emmett T. Steele sued Litton Industries and some of its executives. Steele claimed a founder's interest in the giant conglomerate, too, but he alleged that he'd been cut out of his rightful share. Steele claimed he was owed millions of dollars. Dietrich was tangled up in the litigation because, as someone who claimed knowledge of other unethical practices by one of the Litton people, he was one of Steele's main witnesses.

Steele's lawyer then was a thirty-four-year-old up-and-comer named Arthur Crowley. Crowley was to subsequently carve out his own niche as the divorce lawyer of choice for many of the male stars whose soon-to-be ex-wives had gone to Mitchelson. But in 1959 he was just another resourceful young lawyer. He hired Rhoden that year.

Rhoden worked as Crowley's assistant on the Steele litigation for three years. But in 1962, Rhoden abruptly quit and set up his own shop in the office-sharing arrangement with Mitchelson. Not long after that, Steele fired Crowley and hired Rhoden as his new lawyer on the case.

Crowley was mad. As he saw it, Rhoden had just stolen his case. Crowley claimed Rhoden turned his client against him by secretly bad-mouthing him to Steele. He also contended that Rhoden quit after having spent a month quietly studying a deposition that he thought would pave the way for a quick settlement. Crowley's claim boiled down to an assertion that Rhoden believed a settlement was imminent and wanted the big fee all to himself.

Crowley wasn't just mad. He held the trump card, a contingent-fee agreement that was absolutely ironclad. The law, as it then stood, was indisputably clear. Even though Crowley had been fired and Rhoden was going to do all the rest of the work, Crowley was still entitled to get *the entire fee*: at least one-third of whatever Rhoden won for Steele; 40 percent if the case of *Steele vs. Litton* went to trial for even so much as a day.

Rhoden had miscalculated. It wasn't enough to get the case; he also had to get the contingent fee. So, after quitting Crowley's office, he wrote some nasty letters to his old boss, threatening litigation to throw out Crowley's contingency agreement.

Crowley dared him to try, and Rhoden backed down. He figured that if he were ever going to induce Crowley to share Steele's fee with him, he'd first have to apologize to Crowley. He called Crowley and said he was sorry.

Crowley said that wasn't good enough. "The apology has to be in writing."

So Rhoden wrote what had to have been the most sniveling apology he'd ever composed—six single-spaced pages of pure mush in which Rhoden owned up, among other things, to being thoughtless, unfair, irresponsible, and foolish as well as a purveyor of bad taste.

It worked. The next week, Crowley agreed to split his contingency 50–50. Whatever happened, Crowley was off the hook as far as any more legal work was concerned. He could sit back and, if Rhoden won the case, cash what might be a big check.

The main problem for Rhoden was that the hoped-for quick settlement never materialized, and instead the Steele case weaved through the court system for more than a decade. Rhoden won a $7.5 million verdict for Steele in 1965 that would have given both him and Crowley fees of $1.5 million each. But that was reversed and a new trial ordered, and it spawned a slew of related libel suits and sundry appeals. Steele, Noah Dietrich, and even Rhoden ended up getting sued by the Litton board chairman, Charles B. (Tex) Thornton.

There was so much bad blood between Steele and the Litton people that a settlement was impossible. And the longer it took to push Steele's case through the courts, the worse the deal that Rhoden had made with Crowley looked.

Most important, Rhoden was running out of money. And money was a necessity in a contingent-fee case like this one, where the lawyer advances all the costs of litigation, recouping them only if he wins. Thus, he went to Noah Dietrich, who was still a friend and client of Crowley's. Crowley had gotten a big settlement against Hughes for Dietrich in 1959, in a suit over Hughes's firing of Dietrich. Rhoden asked Dietrich to intercede with Crowley. So Dietrich, with Steele, went over to Crowley's house one evening and begged him to come back into the case.

Crowley refused. "I have a rule," he remembered telling them. "I don't get back in."

Rhoden needed a loan to get him through the expense of the retrial of *Steele vs. Litton*. "He was almost *always* broke," Crowley huffed. And that was where Mitchelson caught the scent of an opportunity.

Rhoden needed $75,000, and Mitchelson was the man to loan it. He offered his pal Rhoden a deal that no bank would be allowed to make. Mitchelson would provide the $75,000 and do some consulting on the case. If Rhoden couldn't settle it and lost the retrial—an unlikely prospect, considering Steele's whopping first verdict that was overturned—then Mitchelson would forgive entirely the $75,000. But if Rhoden got a settlement or won, Marvelo would be paid the greater of either $575,000 or 10 percent of the gross recovery. In other words, Mitchelson was virtually guaranteed more than a 666 percent return on his money.

Just to make sure he got his money, Mitchelson made the loan repayable by Steele. That turned out to be a savvy move. When Steele died a little more than two months after agreeing to the repayment terms, Mitchelson locked in his $575,000 creditor's claim by filing it with the probate court.

The episode demonstrated how Mitchelson had a knack for turning somebody else's adversity into an opportunity for himself. On December 5, 1972—just 18 months after Mitchelson provided the $75,000 to Rhoden—the Steele case was settled for $2.4 million, and Marvin earned his full $575,000 payment from the Steele estate. (Mitchelson recalled only earning an additional $50,000 or $60,000 on the transaction.)

"It sure was a helluva lot more than he advanced," observed Arthur

Crowley. "But I don't fault Mitchelson. He was free to make any deal he could."

Under the terms of their earlier agreement, Rhoden and Crowley now were supposed to equally divide the 40 percent contingent fee on the Steele settlement. But considering what he'd had to go through—a six-month jury trial and seven years of preparation for the retrial—Rhoden's $480,000 half of the contingent fee was piddling. Crowley was going to get just as much although he'd done nothing at all on the case for ten years. And, by the precise terms of his loan agreement, Mitchelson was getting much *more* than either man, despite the fact that he was not the lawyer on the case.

Now, it was Rhoden's turn to show what he was really made of. Rhoden could let Crowley have what was legally his, or he could turn greedy.

Greed prevailed.

After Steele died, Crowley had followed the customary practice and filed his creditor's claim with the Steele estate for one half of any contingent fee that might later become payable. But just three days earlier, a landmark California Supreme Court ruling had *outlawed*, from then on, irrevocable contingent-fee agreements like the one Crowley originally had. Now, Rhoden had a slim argument he could use to repudiate the deal he'd previously written up with Crowley. The Steele estate thus objected to Crowley's creditor's claim, and when *Steele vs. Litton* was settled later that year Crowley's half of the $960,000 contingent fee was frozen while he and Rhoden battled in court over who the money belonged to.

There was a new cause of action now—*Crowley vs. Steele & Rhoden*—and there was little possibility of settlement. Where this case was concerned, two more stubborn lawyers couldn't be found. Rhoden's battle with Crowley also pointed up a big difference between Rhoden and his charismatic alter ego, Mitchelson. Where Mitchelson seemed to be able to wheel and deal with panache, nothing came less easily to Rhoden.

The two men fought with each other in court over Crowley's fee for a full fifteen years. Rhoden deserved credit: He was tenacious. He wouldn't let go of the case until he'd been absolutely, brutally beaten. That was how he was.

In September of 1988, Crowley finally got an order from California's highest court awarding him all that Rhoden had originally agreed to give. The original $480,000 had grown, over those fifteen years, to more than $2 million. "It turned out he did me a great favor," Crowley laughed. "All that money, sitting there, was like a great big pension fund. And the tax rate in 1988 was as low as you'll *ever* see it."

Harold Rhoden had lost his $2 million elephant hunt. On September

6, 1988, he wrote a one-line letter to Arthur Crowley acknowledging Crowley's total victory.

Crowley never replied. "He knew what I thought of him."

Mitchelson couldn't manage to hang on to money, but he always seemed to be able to get it from somewhere, at a price, when Rhoden had a need. It made for a strange affinity between Rhoden and Mitchelson—a bond by which each man let himself be used by the other, for specific reasons and to an explicit end.

Rhoden's new elephant hunt was the Mormon Will case. Noah Dietrich hadn't been much help in the Steele case, but, as the putative executor of the Mormon Will, his assurance to Rhoden held out great promise.

"Of course, when I'm in as the executor and you're my lawyer for the estate, there'll be millions in fees."

Dietrich appointed Rhoden as the will's substitute executor. Rhoden had become convinced that there would be $100 million in attorneys' fees if he proved that the Mormon Will was genuine. As in the Steele case, he agreed to advance all the litigation costs. It was bad judgment; the Mormon Will was just one of at least thirty-five different "lost" Hughes wills floating around!

The odds were stacked against Rhoden right from the start. And even in the unlikely event that the Mormon Will were genuine, Rhoden's hope for a big payday couldn't possibly eventuate. Probate fees never gushed; they just dribbled. And huge contingent-fee awards—the big money that Rhoden went after but seldom got—were non-existent. You couldn't get those in estate cases. No, if Rhoden won, the best he could hope for was to work for the Hughes estate by the hour, with all his bills closely scrutinized by a judge, the same as any other probate lawyer. It was a life more exciting than, say, an accountant's. But just barely.

Rhoden was caught up in the thrill of the chase. "We were just going to run the empire. Take it over. That was the deal," Acaldo recalled him saying.

This was where Mitchelson came in. Once again, he was going to be Rhoden's money man.

"Marvin was convinced that Hal Rhoden couldn't lose a case," Acaldo remembered. "He figured he'd be set for life."

Marvin did, indeed, help his friend. He loaned Acaldo to Rhoden; at Mitchelson's expense, she worked for Rhoden in Las Vegas all during the Mormon Will trial. And Marvin advanced another $300,000 to pay Rhoden's other expenses—money that Rhoden was expected to pay back if he lost the case.

Acaldo also remembered how much Rhoden chafed under the indomitable ego of Mitchelson. She and Rhoden, as the litigation team's only two Vegas full-timers during the trial, frequently went to dinner together, and when they did the conversation invariably turned to Rhoden's money problems. Rhoden used to proclaim that if he just had a $50,000 nest egg, he wouldn't have to owe Marvin anything.

Mitchelson also wanted to help on the case, and since he eschewed legal drafting and the other pick-and-shovel work that lawyers have to do before a trial, Rhoden assigned him to find some experts who would vouch for the authenticity of the handwriting in the will. The trial was going to be a battle of experts.

Mitchelson bankrolled the quest himself, paying one "questioned document examiner" several thousand dollars to meet with him and Rhoden. The examiner was *almost* convinced it was written in Hughes's hand—"almost" in this case apparently meaning that a little more money would do the trick.

That was Rhoden's initiation into the world of litigation experts. Although Mitchelson brought in five American handwriting experts and three professed it to be genuine, he couldn't seem to come up with a credible expert whom Rhoden was willing to put on the stand. That gave Marvin an excuse to satisfy his lust for things European. It wasn't long before he and his good friend, Seymour Lazar (who Marvin brought in over Rhoden's vociferous objections), embarked on a new search abroad for the experts Rhoden needed. He and Lazar hunted them down in Amsterdam, Paris, Marseilles, and Mannheim, Germany, and other points of interest. The best prospects were later interviewed by Rhoden, too.

Mitchelson's tourist French was awful, but he insisted on using it in Marseilles to talk to one of the experts he was interviewing.

"Doctor, see this shaky line in the will at the bottom of the *b* at line eighteen? *Regardez, s'il vous plaît*. You see it, *oui? Bon!* Now, *regardez* a shaky line in the *b* in the exemplar *vingt et un*. Now, do we have *la même chose?* Or do we have *la différence?*"

Not impressed, the expert replied through a translator: "Please, sir, confine yourself to English, which I cannot understand. Your French is *pathetic!*"

They found a European handwriting expert. When Mitchelson revisited him with Rhoden, the expert confessed that he'd been charged as a Nazi war criminal and served seven years of a fifteen-year prison sentence.

"I can see the headlines," Mitchelson moaned. "'Mormon Will Genuine, Says Proponent's Nazi Expert.' What if that little bastard is on the witness stand and the clerk asks him to raise his hand for the oath and he forgets where he is and gives the Nazi salute and a *Heil Hitler?*"

Early on, Mitchelson confided to Rhoden that he thought the Mormon Will was a fake. According to Rhoden, Mitchelson also believed that

Melvin Dummar and LeVane Forsythe, the man who personally deliv-ered the will to Dummar's gas station, were liars. Even so, Mitchelson was still willing to push on with the case, loaning Rhoden hundreds of thousands of dollars and traipsing the world for experts, because he thought Rhoden could win over a Las Vegas jury.

"Why are you in this, Marvin?" Rhoden asked when Mitchelson con-fessed he thought the Mormon Will was bogus. "Why waste your time? And your money?"

"Because I think you're going to win."

"You think this is a forgery but that a jury is going to be fooled into—"

"Not fooled! Persuaded! They're going to be persuaded because they're going to *want* to be persuaded. If this is a fake, at least seventy-seven percent of those billions goes to taxes, and the rest is split between some forgotten old aunt and some second cousins Hughes never heard of." Mitchelson was right about that. Twenty-two first cousins of Hughes were his closest surviving heirs. "But if it's admitted to probate, hundreds of millions go to medical research, and for orphans and for scholarships. They'll *beg* to be persuaded!"

It said a lot about Mitchelson that he was willing to stake so much on a case that he didn't believe in.

Arthur Crowley, still embroiled in his marathon fee dispute with Rho-den, didn't believe in the Mormon Will, either. But he also had other things on his mind.

In 1977, at the same time as Mitchelson and Rhoden were trying to put together their case for the Mormon Will, Mitchelson and Crowley were on opposite sides in the bitter divorce case between Mr. and Mrs. Mel Torme. In a rare switch, though, Mitchelson was representing the husband. Crowley's client was Torme's third wife, the British actress Janette Scott.

Jan Scott had walked out on the singer and sued him for divorce in London, which allowed Marvin to take trips there at Torme's expense. Jan had a new boyfriend, a Brit named Kevin Francis. After filing for the divorce, she returned to the Torme home in Coldwater Canyon in Beverly Hills with their two children. She and the kids moved into the main Torme house; Mel lived in the guest house in back.

Torme was a jumble of emotions—rage, jealousy, and self-pity—about the impending divorce. In the midst of it all, somebody tapped Jan's telephone in the main house. Marvin collected the tapes in his office. As the two of them sat there listening, Torme was incon-solable.

Even if the tapes proved adultery, they weren't going to save Mel any money on the property settlement. California had been a no-fault-di-vorce state since 1970, and that meant the Tormes' community property was just going to be split down the middle. But the tapes might have provided evidence that could have helped him get custody of his two children—something Marvin and Mel were fighting hard for—were it not for a serious blunder that blew the secrecy of the wiretapping.

The slip-up occurred when an incensed Mitchelson confronted Crowley one day in Superior Court. He claimed one of Crowley's other lawyers had bad-mouthed him to Janette Torme. He repeated exactly what had been said, and he told Crowley in no uncertain terms to cut it out.

"I went back to the lawyer and asked him if he'd said that," Crowley recalled. "He said, 'Yeah, but it was just in a phone call with my client!' That's when we knew [her phone was being tapped]. Marvin had been told the derogatory information, and, not being such a smart guy, he passed it right along." Crowley also recollected then that when Mitchelson had taken Jan Torme's deposition in Marvin's office, Crowley had seen a pile of tapes that were all labeled "Torme."

Crowley immediately took Mel Torme's deposition and peppered him with questions about the bugging—questions to which Mitchelson had his client invoke the Fifth Amendment. Crowley then used another tactic, petitioning the court to get the assent of the local, state, and federal criminal prosecutors in Los Angeles to granting Torme immunity from prosecution for wiretapping. When that had been done, Torme had no grounds for taking the Fifth.

Mitchelson appealed anyway. That was when Crowley began to suspect that Mitchelson was as concerned about his own neck as he was about Torme's. Teased Crowley: "We're not asking for immunity for *you*, Marvin!"

Marvin blamed everything on his client. "I didn't tap anyone. Mel . . . brought them in and told me he had these things. I got a little concerned when he did that."

Torme lost the custody of his children and had to pay a great deal of money in support and $168,000 in legal fees. He called the day of the divorce verdict the saddest of his life, and termed Crowley "the single cruelest man I have ever laid eyes on."

The truth was, Crowley seemed to revel in hearing that. But it wasn't enough for him to humiliate Mitchelson in the Torme case. He also savored trampling on Mitchelson's doomed contest for the Mormon Will.

"Hal's gonna lose that case, too," Crowley told Mitchelson in the midst of the Torme battle, "because . . . there's only one guy that Hughes hates more than Art Crowley, and that's Noah Dietrich." Hughes had said that *himself*, Crowley told Mitchelson smugly. The billionaire's animus toward Dietrich came from the multimillion-dollar lawsuit against Hughes that Crowley had filed for Dietrich.

"The minute I read about Dietrich being named [by Hughes] as executor, I just laughed. No way!" Crowley said.

The Mormon Will case finally came to judgment on June 8, 1978. Mitchelson already had the champagne on ice at the Sands Hotel. But he was so stunned when the jury verdict came in against them that all he could do was mumble something to Rhoden about winning a few and losing a few.

A stunned Rhoden looked wanly at his wife. "Sorry, baby."

Five years later, Melvin Dummar appeared on national television to take a lie detector test administered by the noted criminal defense lawyer F. Lee Bailey.

After the test, Bailey declared that there wasn't an ounce of truth to anything Dummar had said. "These charts are so bad, they would be excellent for freshman students in polygraph school just to show them how bad it can get."

Dummar was unfazed. "Bull," he replied.

The Mormon Will case became a turning point for the three principals—Rhoden, Acaldo, and Mitchelson—who'd put so much into it for two years.

Rhoden was the colossal loser. He'd invested $500,000 of his own money on the case, and that was all gone, unrecoverable. Rhoden lost his house in Sherman Oaks, his law practice (which he'd closed down to work on the case full time), his Cessna Turbo 310, and his lavish Century City office. What was worse, he owed money to a slew of people, including the $300,000 to Mitchelson. In humiliation, he had to move in with Mitchelson to work off the debt while trying to rebuild his client list.

Acaldo had to find a new life, too. A sparrow-like woman at exactly five feet tall and ninety-nine pounds, she broke off her relationship with Mitchelson and began law school at his alma mater, Southwestern. Mitchelson even wrote a letter of recommendation for her, just to show there were no hard feelings on his part.

But the same couldn't be said for Acaldo. Years later, while she was working for the Los Angeles District Attorney's office, she learned that Marvin was under investigation by some of the other prosecutors there. She saw an ethical responsibility to reveal her affair with Mitchelson—an affair that Mitchelson then denied ever happened "as far as I'm concerned." He dismissed Acaldo as someone who just wanted "her fifteen minutes of fame."

Rhoden could have told Mitchelson it was a big mistake to call an ex-girlfriend a liar. Particularly one who now was a public prosecutor.

"She's *very* mad at Marvin Mitchelson," Rhoden said. "Somehow, she had the opportunity to get him, and, boy, she got him!

"I think she wanted to be a part of his life, and he kicked her out.

There was just no way she was going to be his one and only mistress. I think he just simply didn't go for it.

"Marvin thinks it's jealousy. Resentment. A woman scorned. He thinks so. I don't know.

"I knew there'd been an affair between the two of them. I just frankly didn't care who fucked whom. I just wanted the work done, and, boy, she was good at that. Beyond that, I didn't care what she did. But she sure does hate him now."

While Rhoden worked off his debt to Mitchelson, Mitchelson returned to the divorce cases he knew best. He was about to embark on a celebrated elephant hunt of his own.

PART FOUR
The Prince of Palimony

The case of *Michelle Marvin, aka Michelle Triola vs. Lee Marvin* finally reached trial in January of 1979. By then, *Marvin vs. Marvin* was Mitchelson's annuity, a public-relations gusher that had produced millions of dollars worth of favorable ink since its filing in 1972.

This lawsuit to safeguard a mistress's rights was his ultimate credential as a protector of women, and his timing once again was impeccable. The decade of the 1970s was the decade of the feminist movement, and here was Marvin Mitchelson leading a celebrated battle for female equality. It made him a legend because *Marvin* was the one case that the media could use to encapsulate the feminine agenda. *Marvin* simply fit the times.

And so the gusher kept pumping, swamping the reality of Michelle Marvin's questionable claims in a sea of favorable ink—and bathing Mitchelson in adulation that would endure long after he had ceased to be worthy of it.

Marvin knew Michelle Triola from his years living with his mother at the Holloway Drive apartments. Michelle was a tenant there, too—one of the "Hollywood types" that Sonia often worried would lead her Sonny astray.

But that wasn't a concern of Mitchelson's. His friend Michelle was a sometime nightclub singer, a "working gal" in Mitchelson's lingo, and she earned a couple of hundred dollars a week on and off as a lounge singer and dancer. Sometimes she worked at Dino's Lodge, on the Sunset Strip, and Mitchelson went to see her there. It was just around the corner from the Holloway Drive apartments.

Michelle, a thirty year old with pert good looks, hired the handsome young lawyer to help her get a divorce from an actor named Rufus ("Skip") Ward.

In 1964, not long after Marvin helped unwind Michelle's four-months-and-six-days-long marriage, she went off to Europe. Maybe she could rebuild her career there. A few months later, though, Michelle was back in California, singing nights at The Little Club in Beverly Hills and working days as an extra on the set of *Ship of Fools*.

That was where she met Lee Marvin. Like so many of the characters he played, the forty-year-old actor was a gruff-talking, hard-drinking guy, but there was something about this star of *Ship of Fools* that she liked. Within two weeks, Lee and Michelle were lovers, but aside from the undeniable fact of their passion there wasn't much about the relationship that Lee and Michelle could agree on in later years.

As Michelle told it, they talked about marriage right at the start. Lee could talk all he wanted, after all, but he couldn't deliver because he was still *very* married to his wife of thirteen years, Betty. So Lee and Michelle did what they could, moving into a Malibu beach house and paying their bills out of various joint checking accounts as they traveled together to Lee's shooting locations. Meanwhile, Lee's career took off. He won the Academy Award for Best Actor in 1965, for *Cat Ballou*, and he starred in such films as *The Dirty Dozen* and *Paint Your Wagon*. Michelle cut a record, presciently titled "Promise Me Your Love," but it sank without a trace.

Lee Marvin's net worth increased from less than $50,000 when he started living with Michelle to more than $1.5 million by 1970. He'd earned $3.6 million during that six-year period. And, as Michelle would later assert (and Lee would vociferously deny), he'd told her, "What I have is yours, and what you have is mine." That was the slim thread her claim hung by.

It was also in 1970 that Michelle, perhaps sensing that her troubled relationship with Lee was about to break up altogether, took an important symbolic step: She hired Mitchelson to legally change her name to Michelle Triola Marvin. The way she looked at it, they'd always held themselves out as husband and wife, and everybody from the local Sears Roebuck salesman to a Catholic bishop in Oregon to the premier of Japan thought they were. From a strict legal standpoint, the name change didn't affect her status with Lee Marvin at all; she still wasn't his wife. But it took some of the moral high ground from Lee. Justified or not, Michelle could thereafter claim to be the one who gave up everything, even her own name, for the man who then spurned her.

One of Lee Marvin's lawyers, Lou Goldman, called Michelle into his office that same month she changed her name. He told her, "Lee is through with you. He wants you out of his life." But Michelle wasn't without options.

For one thing, Goldman told Michelle, Lee still intended to support her. "He doesn't want to leave you destitute." Lee Marvin would pay her $1,000 a month for five years, provided she just walked away, didn't bother him, and didn't talk to anybody else about what happened.

Neither side stuck to the deal. Michelle went back to the Malibu house and there ensued a hysterical scene with her and Lee Marvin, Goldman, and Goldman's law partner, A. David Kagon. Kagon allegedly threatened to call the police. Michelle sobbed: "What about the promises, the house, the babies I have lost! What about those?"

Having finally divorced his first wife, Lee married again. He was under great pressure from his new wife to cut Michelle off—and she gave him an excuse to do so in October of 1971.

Michelle filed her first lawsuit over their break-up that month—not against Lee, but against the producers of one of his movies. She wanted them to pay *her* a share of his earnings. As far as Lee was concerned, that was the last straw. She'd get no more money from him.

"Michelle was an old-timer on the Hollywood scene," recalled David Kagon, whose law firm of Goldman & Kagon had been taking care of Lee Marvin's business affairs for twelve years. "We knew her. We knew all about the relationship, the facts." The ruddy-faced, white-haired Kagon remembered that once, during some intense deposition questioning, Michelle had simply looked at him, as if amazed, and replied: "Dave, why are you asking *me*? You know the answers better than I do!"

As Kagon saw it, Michelle had brought on her problems by harassing Lee, who never wavered in his resolve not to pay Michelle once she went after him. "He was really angry. He was a very private person, and he felt he had done what was appropriate. He was only going to pay if she left him alone."

With her money cut off, Michelle Marvin once again turned to Marvin Mitchelson. Yet again, a cherished opportunity beckoned him.

Mitchelson had already heard the faint signals of an impending revolution in California divorce law, and he surely couldn't have been pleased. Always at his best in close, tough negotiating, and always able to raise the implied threat of outrageous courtroom accusations as an inducement to settlement, Mitchelson in 1970 had been confronted with a new California no-fault divorce law that threatened to make any high-stakes divorce lawyer an anachronism.

California's pioneering no-fault law was supposed to completely remove divorce from the adversarial realm. No longer would the guilty in a divorce be punished by the court's awarding most or all of the property to the innocent one. If a couple couldn't get along, all they had to do was say so, and their petition for divorce would be granted. The divorce court wasn't even allowed to favor one spouse over another in the property settlement: It had to be *equal*. Theatrical lawyers like Mitchelson who took their shot at a jury were replaced by skilled, ableit lackluster, professionals: tax lawyers and accountants who had a solid grasp of the tax code and the evolving law.

The first no-fault divorce law in the Western world would mean no more photographers snapping pictures of the cheating spouse in his love nest. No more humiliating allegations of adultery and mental cruelty.

And, perhaps, no more juicy cases for the flamboyant lawyers of Mitchelson's ilk.*

But in this case there was real promise. In *Marvin vs. Marvin*, Mitchelson could still use bomber tactics to contest all the moral issues of who-slept-where-with-whom. He could even plead his case to a jury if he wanted to—something even the old California divorce law didn't allow. And in a breach-of-contract case like this one he would be able to take a fat percentage-of-the-gross contingent fee, which was frowned upon, if not prohibited outright, in no-fault divorce cases.

If it took a leap of faith on most everyone's part to believe that he would really be able to pull it all off, that was just because nobody appreciated Mitchelson's gift for making the most of his opportunities.

The truth was, family law had been steadily and quietly evolving in favor of "mistress rights." Sooner or later the courts were going to affirm that live-in lovers did, indeed, have contractual rights that could be enforced against their paramours. If a spouse couldn't be penalized for being "guilty," Mitchelson reasoned, "then it seemed to me under equal protection of the law and due process that a non-married partner should not be penalized for the 'guilt' of 'living in sin.'"

Just as he had done in *Douglas* some ten years earlier, Mitchelson had sensed a coming change in the law—and he had arrived there ahead of it.

Initially, Mitchelson simply demanded that Lee Marvin reinstate Michelle's $1,000-a-month support. Lee Marvin turned him down flat, though, and his lawyers never lost an opportunity to mention that Michelle's claim to half of Lee's wealth had only been made after that.

Mitchelson filed Michelle's breach-of-contract lawsuit on February 22, 1972. He already had some things going his way. For one, the 1970 Family Law Act that instituted no-fault divorce in California also applied the state's community-property rules for the first time to common-law marriages. Two people who held themselves out as husband and wife thus had to divide their community property 50–50. That created a favorable climate for a greatly liberalized courtroom view of what constituted community property. Already making its way through the California court system when *Marvin vs. Marvin* was filed was another case, *In re Cary*, which was used by the California Court of Appeal in 1973 to underscore what would become the main principles in Mitchelson's case. The appellate judges said that the broad language of the new

---

*Every American state except South Dakota now has some form of no-fault divorce. Thirteen other states followed California's model and make marital breakdown the *only* ground for divorce. See *The Divorce Revolution* (The Free Press, 1985) by Lenore J. Weitzman.

no-fault divorce law could even encompass a live-in relationship where only *one* of the parties believed themselves married.

But because the appellate judges threw out a breach-of-contract claim similar to Michelle's and also ruled that *Cary* shouldn't be retroactively applied, Lee Marvin and his lawyers had the advantage. Mitchelson couldn't even get a trial of his case; it was thrown out the first time it went before a trial judge. Judge William A. Munnell took all of three minutes to do the job, then turned his back to Mitchelson and stalked off the bench. "I couldn't be happier," an indomitable Mitchelson exclaimed. "The judge's decision is clearly reversible error." Nineteen months later, the state appeals court affirmed the dismissal. "I actually never have been so happy about a ruling," Mitchelson said jauntily, "because this means the [California] Supreme Court will have to take it."

If nothing else, you had to admire Mitchelson's spirit. He was bank-rolling the case, advancing his own money, in the hope of getting a huge fee if Michelle won. "He was *extremely* tenacious," his adversary, Kagon, recalled with grudging admiration. "He just had a tenacity about carrying that case forward because he knew the direction the law was taking. There were increasing numbers of people living together, and inherent inequities in the law. It was almost inevitable in the progression of the law. If not *Marvin*, it was going to be another case."

To the world at large, *Marvin* was all Mitchelson's. But, just as with *Douglas*, Mitchelson had plenty of help. One of his associates, Donald Woldman, had the primary responsibility for drafting the original *Marvin* complaint. When the case went up to the California Supreme Court, it was David M. Brown, a local lawyer specializing in constitutional law, who drafted the brief and argued the case.

The publicity was all Marvin's, though, and he pushed the case for all it was worth, giving news conferences and handing out T-shirts that said, "It's Michelle's Money, Too!" For one television interview about the trial, he obligingly hopped into the bubble-filled tub in his office—to show how he relaxed amid the rigors of the case. During a *Newsweek* interview, he coined the term "palimony" to describe what he was after. In the charmed way that was Mitchelson's, the word became his talisman.

When the California Supreme Court finally handed down its ruling on December 27, 1976, the six-to-one decision was a clear victory. From now on, the California courts would have to enforce express oral or written contracts between live-in partners, unless they were sex-for-pay arrangements. Even if there weren't an express contract, judges could look to the conduct of the partners to see whether there was an *implied* contract. Courts would have the greatest possible leeway to divide the assets of the partners in a fair way.

Mitchelson had made important new law with his victory. Now, he had to apply the landmark decision to Michelle's particular situation. Seven years after he'd filed the original palimony suit, Michelle's celebrated case finally went back to trial in Superior Court in downtown Los Angeles.

It was on January 12, 1979, that Mitchelson at last strode into the courtroom of Judge Arthur K. Marshall to make his opening statement on behalf of Michelle Marvin. By then, he had also acquired a new factotum to handle the legal work that went on outside the theater of the courtroom. Seven months after the Mormon Will debacle, the beleaguered Hal Rhoden was still working for Mitchelson to settle his substantial debt. From a desk in Mitchelson's suite, Hal did the research and the writing; Marvin handled the trial itself.

Mitchelson saw his trials as great theater, but as his courtroom opponent, Kagon, laughingly put it, the trial of *Marvin vs. Marvin* was more akin to "a three-ring circus in a fishbowl."

There were the trademark news conferences, with Mitchelson holding forth and proving, with his well-timed one-liners, to be an adroit master of the press. "Publicity is good for business," he said unabashedly in the midst of the trial. "And there is no question about it, the *Marvin* case has exposed me personally more than the collective cases I've had. It's on the front page in Tokyo, Germany, and Italy." Mitchelson knew that because he had hired a worldwide clipping service.

"It's a just reward. I did it first. So I gladly accept the attention and recognition it's brought."

Lee Marvin, uncharacteristically sporting lawyerly pinstripes and carrying a briefcase to the trial, had said at the beginning that "the side with the better script" was going to win. But that turned out to be more than just an actor's turn of phrase. Having maneuvered so deftly to get this far, Mitchelson suddenly seemed to go flat. He'd wanted all along, for instance, for Michelle's case to be heard by a jury, but when the trial time came the master showman began to doubt his prospects. *Marvin vs. Marvin* would be a bench trial instead.

"I just didn't think a jury would go for it," he said wearily. "Know what I mean? I didn't think they'd go for it."

Marvin's opening statement to the judge was an uninspired recapitulation of Michelle's allegations—Lee promised this and Lee said that—and it dragged so far over his allotted time that at one point he had to assure Judge Marshall that "I really will sit down. I will keep my promise, speaking of promises!"

Kagon, slightly built, well-barbered, and as reserved as Mitchelson was flashy, came in with fancy charts and a few shopworn but effective metaphors to illustrate what Michelle was doing to his client. Lee Marvin had reached the "mother lode," after "sixteen years as a miner on his own claim. . . . Suddenly he sees it before him"—and just at that moment a golddigger shows up. It was a gentlemanly rebuttal to everything Mitchelson had said. Michelle Marvin's case was a fraud, Kagon said. "We're here today because there was no marriage, and no marriage intended."

For Mitchelson, there was an awful letdown in the trial itself. His glory days with *Marvin vs. Marvin* had been when he was the underdog, feasting on the publicity and battling all the way to the state Supreme Court to establish new rights for live-in partners. But now, having made such important new law, he had the daunting task of claiming those rights for the very woman whose case started it all. To try to meet the various tests of a *Marvin*–type relationship that the Supreme Court had established, Mitchelson and Michelle had to stretch things. Mitchelson called in his buddy Mel Torme and singer Trini Lopez to testify as expert witnesses that Michelle really was a good singer, and that she'd given up a promising career to stay with Lee.

But Michelle's allegations were sometimes easily refuted, as when Gene Kelly revealed on the stand that he'd not only never employed Michelle in the Broadway production of *Flower Drum Song*, but that he'd never even talked to her about it and that the play hadn't even been in New York City during the time Michelle claimed she worked for him there. Kagon made the same point to Judge Marshall in his opening statement: "This case, the one that has given its name generically to *Marvin*–type cases, is probably one of the worst *Marvin*–type cases on its facts. There are undoubtedly some good *Marvin*–type cases, but this is not one of them."

Mitchelson tried to prove otherwise, keeping the laconic Lee Marvin on the witness stand for days as he vainly tried to get him to admit that, yes, Lee really did want to spend the rest of his life with Michelle.

Lee wouldn't have any of Mitchelson's inferences. When quizzed about some love letters he'd written to Michelle, Lee simply testified that he hadn't meant what he said. They were just "an idle male promise."

"You told her you loved her even though you really didn't mean it?" Mitchelson inquired in stage-managed amazement.

"I might have said it on a number of occasions," Lee replied. "I might have meant it on some."

Mitchelson had an edge now. He wanted to know exactly *when* Lee had loved her, since it was Michelle's contention that Lee had expressed love for her when he made a *Marvin*–type promise to take care of her. Did he love Michelle in 1965? Mitchelson asked. How about 1966? What about 1967?

As Lee dodged the questions, Kagon jumped in.

"Your Honor," he protested in his unassuming way, "we are now talking about a subject matter that is as broad in scope as anything I can think of: love. What is love? If I say to Mr. Mitchelson, 'I love him' because of a job he's done, it doesn't mean I *love* him. I think we have to have a definition of the term, your Honor."

The sixty-seven-year-old judge agreed wryly. "Every writer in the world has a different meaning." Objection sustained.

If Mitchelson couldn't get Lee to make a straightforward confession, maybe he could tease an admission out of him.

"You don't love *me*, do you?" Mitchelson taunted, then added: "Strike that."

"Is that because you fear the answer, Counsel?" Judge Marshall rejoined.

"I'm too close to the witness, and I fear the answer, yes!"

As quick of foot and as sharp of mind as Mitchelson was, he was getting nowhere after nineteen full days of trial. The only other party who would have had knowledge of Michelle's and Lee's love contract was Lee Marvin himself, and he certainly wasn't going to help make Michelle's case, answering in grunts and evasions as Mitchelson pressed his rapid-fire examination. When Mitchelson finally was presented on the twentieth day of trial with a witness he could get his claws into, he ripped away.

The witness was a bit-part actor named Mervin Richard Doughty who'd privately told Kagon sometime during the prior November about a sexual affair he'd had with Michelle. The actor said he'd had sex with Michelle many times while she was living with Lee—sometimes making love to her while the unsuspecting Lee was in the house with them. He said Michelle had also told him about sexual affairs she'd had with other men, too. Michelle adamantly denied it all.

Doughty considered himself a friend of Lee's, and Lee had helped him get some movie roles. He said his decision to come forward was motivated in part by Mitchelson's brash persona. "I have seen you on television an awful lot recently," Doughty told Mitchelson, "and from your demeanor I feel that you are trying to railroad something through on Lee."

Kagon had been waiting to spring Doughty's testimony on Mitchelson and Michelle. And it promised to be dynamite, because the judge could well draw the inference from it that Michelle hadn't kept up her end of the contract with Lee. She had already testified under oath that during the entire time she lived with Lee, she never had intercourse with any other man. Mitchelson thus was doing everything possible to keep Doughty's comments out of evidence.

First, he brought out that Doughty had initially lied to Kagon, telling him that he *hadn't* slept with Michelle. Doughty said he had been keeping a promise to Michelle not to tell Lee about their secret sex, but when Mitchelson asked Doughty when he'd made that promise, Doughty couldn't remember.

"If you would like to give me some time, I'm sure I could go back and check on it," he replied helpfully.

"I don't want to give you anything," Mitchelson replied. Mitchelson claimed Doughty was just an "unmitigated liar" who'd come forward to curry favor with Lee Marvin.

Mitchelson fired questions wildly, apparently hoping that if he scattered his fire widely enough he'd hit a tender spot somewhere. "Did you notice anything peculiar about Michelle—her stomach, any peculiar markings?" Mitchelson asked, pursuing the question of what he called his client's "unusual" markings at great length but to no apparent purpose. His opponent wanted to know what "unusual" meant; Mitchelson hemmed and hawed and finally said the word meant anything that was, well, *unusual*. He couldn't otherwise define it, and he never said what he was looking for.

"How about when you had this alleged sexual intercourse with Michelle?" Mitchelson persisted. "You said yesterday you didn't use anything or wear anything, any contraceptives. Did you have to do anything *special* to yourself in order to enter Michelle?"

"No."

"Nothing at all, huh?"

"What do you mean by 'unusual'?" Doughty still didn't get it.

"Did you have to *prepare yourself* in any way? . . . Did you have to take any special preparation in order to enter her? Do you know what I'm talking about?"

Doughty didn't.

"You don't understand?"

"A little *special preparation*?" Doughty repeated the question incredulously. What in the world was Mitchelson trying to ask?

"Well, did you have to use any Vaseline, or jellies, or anything of that nature in order for you to penetrate her?"

Presto! Now Doughty understood.

"Never."

Whereupon Mitchelson was off on another, completely unrelated tangent, as if he'd never even brought up the issue of sexual lubricants: "Now, Mr. Doughty, you were kicked out of the Peace Corps, weren't you, sir?"

"That is absolutely incorrect!" Doughty had served in the Peace Corps on the Micronesian island of Belau, and it was there that he'd met Lee and Michelle, in 1969, while Lee was filming *Hell in the Pacific*.

"Weren't you accused of sexually molesting native women over there?"

"That is absolutely untrue!"

"Is it?"

"Yes!"

The *Marvin* courtroom became the heartland of sleaze, and Mitchelson was comfortable. If he'd ever worried about no-fault divorce cramping his style, he could relax now. The good old days of the who's-at-fault break-up were back. A palimony case like this allowed Mitchelson to use precisely the kind of outrageous tactics that the new divorce law intended to curb.

Mitchelson goaded the witness for more than a day, but he neither scored points with the judge nor shook Doughty's story. A frustrated Mitchelson held forth for the assembled media in the courthouse hallway and attacked Doughty's credibility with characteristic chutzpah. Doughty promptly sued Mitchelson for libel and slander.

"I warned him to watch those damned press conferences he was having because he might commit slander and be sued for it," Harold Rhoden said with the resignation of someone whose advice was invariably ignored. "And sure enough, he was. He made [a] smartass remark about one of the witnesses [Doughty], saying the guy was a liar, and the guy sued him for slander." As usual, Rhoden defended Mitchelson. They settled the case.

The *Marvin* trial was great theatre, all ten tear-soaked weeks of it. The testimony ran heavily to binge drinking, secret love trysts, hysterical break-ups, and abortions. It seemed that if Mitchelson weren't conducting some leering, sneering cross-examination of a witness, then he was doing something else that kept him in the spotlight—like collapsing in the courtroom from an asthma spasm as he cross-examined Lou Goldman, one of Lee's attorneys. There was a rumor sweeping the courthouse that afternoon that Mitchelson had dropped dead. A picture of him being rushed out of the courthouse on a gurney appeared in the next morning's newspaper under the caption: LAWYER STRICKEN.

He was back in the courtroom a day later, and it wasn't too long thereafter that Mitchelson was making a whispered petition to the judge to let him introduce more evidence about what he'd been so elliptically alluding to in his questioning the month before of Doughty. Mitchelson claimed that Michelle could only have intercourse if "the person penetrating used some sort of lubricant, such as Vaseline or something of that nature. And Mr. Marvin invariably did, and she would testify to that. She would also testify that she has a mole on her left breast and a mole on the left side of her back."

Mitchelson claimed that this testimony would prove Doughty was a liar. Kagon demanded a doctor's examination for Michelle. And the judge—well, the judge was just plain horrified at the prospect of "an undue elongation of this case." An explanation of Michelle's anatomical secrets would await another day.

When both sides began their closing arguments on April 10, 1979, Mitchelson lived up to his childhood nickname, Windy. He meandered all across the legal and anecdotal landscape for a full two hours, spinning yarns about his own family ("never been a divorce; no one has ever lived together"), and whittling away at Judge Marshall's patience without ever discussing in detail what the evidence showed about implied or express contracts. The judge told him to get to the point—and when Mitchelson finally did, it was lamely to suggest that maybe a fair compromise would be for Lee Marvin to set up a trust fund for Michelle. She'd get the interest and he'd keep the principal. Mitchelson dubbed it the "Marshall Plan," making a play on the judge's last name, saying Michelle should get "a half a tank of something, maybe regular gasoline," in return for Lee Marvin's "half a tank of love." Mitchelson would be glad for whatever he could get for Michelle.

Throughout the trial, the judge had played the bemused observer, expressing puzzlement at the public's fascination with the event. Once, after nearly being mowed down by a horde of camera crews chasing Michelle, he lifted his expressive eyebrows in amazement and wondered aloud, "What makes this case so interesting?" The judge apparently hadn't thought much of Mitchelson's case then, and he seemingly didn't now. On April 18, 1979, he ruled that there was neither an express nor an implied contract between the two Marvins. On that point, Michelle was entitled to nothing.

But there was a footnote in the state Supreme Court's *Marvin* decision that gave judges wide latitude to make monetary awards to live-in partners even when no express or implied contracts could be found. Judge Marshall reached down into Footnote 25 and awarded Michelle $104,000 "so that she may have the economic means to reeducate herself and to learn new, employable skills or refurbish those utilized, for example, during her most recent employment, and so that she may return from her status as companion of a motion picture star to a separate, independent, but perhaps more prosaic, existence." Judge Marshall rationalized the award as being equivalent to the highest amount Michelle had ever earned as a singer, $1,000 a week, times the two years it would take for her to get back on her feet. Kagon announced Lee Marvin would pay the money.

Mitchelson had been bankrolling the case himself for virtually the entire decade. Expenses alone were an estimated $100,000. But Mitchelson had, by his own admission, already "made millions out of it" through all the publicity. His out-of-pocket costs were really just a down payment on the new business his *Marvin* fame brought.

But now Mitchelson wanted Lee Marvin to pay Mitchelson's legal fees, too—all $500,000 of them. At that, Lee balked. He had his lawyers appeal everything, and in 1981, the state appeals court reversed Marshall and awarded Michelle and Mitchelson nothing.

Mitchelson, still using Rhoden as his silent draftsman, wanted Rhoden to take another appeal to the state Supreme Court. Rhoden told his friend the case was a loser. Forget it.

That's what they did.

By then, Lee Marvin was back in Tucson with his second wife, Pamela, enjoying a resurgence in his career that his agent said *Marvin* brought.*

Michelle, once destitute and on unemployment after breaking up with Lee, later had a new live-in partner in Malibu, actor Dick Van Dyke. Mitchelson had drawn up a palimony contract for them. But she also had a new legal problem: an arrest in 1980 for allegedly shoplifting three sweaters and two brassieres from a Beverly Hills department store. Mitchelson represented her in that criminal case, too. She was fined $250 and given six months probation.

Mitchelson profited the most from the celebrated palimony case, despite the fact that the client that started it all got nothing.

"What's the first thing the public thinks of when they think of Marvin Mitchelson?" asked Paul Caruso. "[*Marvin vs. Marvin.*] And they think he won the case, right? You know, and I know, that he *didn't* win the case. He *lost* the case. And the public doesn't know that."

Added Raoul Felder: "The public doesn't realize that the *Marvin* case was, in practical terms, a disaster. But much credit should be given to him for establishing the principle. It wasn't that revolutionary. To lawyers, it was a natural extrapolation. But the fact is, he created an awareness of palimony." Forty states now recognize palimony claims, and Felder and Mitchelson both were palimony record holders: Felder for the highest palimony verdict ever sustained in the U.S., about $400,000, and Mitchelson for the highest-ever palimony settlement, $3.5 million to Veronica Miramontez, the woman who had lived with Korbel winery founder Adolf L. Heck for twenty-three years.

Regardless of his loss in Michelle's case, Mitchelson knew he would be reaping the benefits of the case for many years to come. "There are still a thousand *Marvin* cases out there," he quipped on the day the trial verdict came down. "So, fellows, beware!"

---

*Lee Marvin died in 1987 at age 63.

Century City Office, Los Angeles, 1982. With Venus floating above and all of Los Angeles at his feet, Mitchelson conducts an imaginary opera. (Doug Menuez/Reportage)

Ripping a blank marriage license in the Las Vegas county clerk's office, 1978. Publicity-hungry Marvin retained a p.r. man, but he still boasted: "The best press agent I ever had was Marvin Mitchelson!" (Korody/Sygma)

Spoils of victory: Marvin, his Rolls-Royce, and his $5 million Hollywood castle. (Duhamel/Sygma)

Sonia, Marvin, and Marcella Mitchelson in Los Angeles, probably around 1980. Despite the facade, domestic relations between Marvin and his wife were said to be strained. (Joe Friezer)

Marcella blew out her birthday candles at Nirvana, New York City, 1985. Mitchelson twice filed divorce suits against her but apparently feared the outcome and pulled them both. (Ron Galella)

Marvin and Sonia celebrate her eightieth birthday. Century City, Los Angeles, 1982. (Ron Galella)

In court with Joan Collins as her divorce hearing opened, Los Angeles, 1987. Collins insisted Peter Holm sign a prenuptial agreement. "I never met a man yet who was able to take care of me," she testified. (Sygma)

Joan Collins and husband Peter Holm in New York, 1986. "Peter Holm was a fool," Mitchelson said, but Holm got a $1 million settlement. (Zuffante/Star File)

Collins and Mitchelson emerge from the courtroom after a judge ruled in her favor. Mitchelson relished the moment. Collins vowed: No more marriages. (Sygma)

Breaking for lunch with Michelle Triola Marvin during the trial *Marvin vs. Marvin*. Lee Marvin was on the stand that day. Los Angeles Superior Court, 1979. (Ron Galella)

Michelle Marvin and Dick Van Dyke in Los Angeles, 1988. The couple lived together in Malibu. (Zuffante/Star File)

Mitchelson arranged a news
conference for Roxanne Pulitzer at
Nirvana, New York City, 1983.
She saw him as her hot-shot
salvation but in the end became
disillusioned. (Chin/Star File)

Nancy Andrews sued Beatle Ringo
Starr for palimony, 1981. Marvin
showed her his handbook, *Living
Together*. (Ron Galella)

Carrie Leigh, in Mitchelson's office in 1988, later accused Mitchelson of supplying her with illegal drugs. (Sygma)

Mitchelson and client, jazz singer Mel Torme. London High Court, 1976. (Ron Galella)

Lydia Criss said Mitchelson offered her cocaine, or asked for it, just about every time they met. "Cocaine and champagne—those were the things that Marvin liked to do." They walked on her Greenwich, Connecticut estate in 1979. Later, she sued him for malpractice. (Grossman/Star File)

Veronica Buss, shown here with Marvin in 1983, said she once watched as her lawyer freebased cocaine. Thrown out of her house, she said he returned and tried to jump into her bed. (Ron Galella)

With client Marc Christian, whose AIDS lawsuit against Rock Hudson made international headlines, in 1985. (Ron Galella)

Sheikha Dena al-Fassi, Beverly Hills, 1982. Mitchelson pursued Dena's ex-husband for approximately $130 million, including $26 million in attorney's fees. (Ron Galella)

Special agent James Wilson of the IRS led a federal criminal investigation of Mitchelson. Santa Monica, 1991. (Ron Galella)

Harold Rhoden had worked with Mitchelson since 1962 and knew him as well as anyone. "There are an awful lot of people who despise him. Actually that's a compliment. The word *despise* is rather mild," he said. Superior Court, 1989. (Maria-Elena Cordero)

Mitchelson and his publicist, Sy Presten, at Roy Cohn's memorial service. New York City, 1986. (Star File)

Catherine Mann. Infatuated with her, Marvin teetered on the brink of divorce in 1970. (Celebrity Photo Agency/Scott Downie)

Mitchelson's mistress, Nina Iliescu, accompanied him to Geneva in 1987 for Sotheby's auction of the Duchess of Windsor jewels. Later, she became a federal informant, secretly tape-recording their meetings together.

Mitchelson's companion Tashi Grady. In the grand jury room she invoked the Fifth Amendment; later, she testified under a grant of immunity from prosecution. Poor photo quality due to California DMV microfilm.

Linda Alcaldo, Mitchelson's former secretary, lover, and cocaine courier, faced an ethical dilemma because she worked for the L.A. district attorney's office that was investigating him.

Chuck Lewis led the "60 Minutes" investigation of Mitchelson.

Mitchelson's wife and son stayed away from the Barrett-Whitney rape trial. Marvin arrived alone at the Santa Monica courthouse for the opening day of trial. (Jim Smeal/Galella)

Kristin Barrett-Whitney, entering the courtroom on the first day of the trial, was obsessed with fighting Mitchelson. (Jim Smeal/Galella)

Patricia French claimed she was raped by Mitchelson. While the California victims compensation board awarded her $12,000, a jury didn't buy her claim. Superior Court, Santa Monica, 1989. (Maria-Elena Cordero)

Felicia MacDonald became Mitchelson's client and said Mitchelson pushed her into having sex with him. Superior Court, Los Angeles, 1989. (Maria-Elena Cordero)

Century City, Los Angeles, 1981. (Ron Galella)

20

Marvin and his friend Martha Smilgis often went for morning jogs together on the track at Beverly Hills High School. It was work for Smilgis, who used Mitchelson as a source for the latest gossip that she could use in her *People* magazine stories. But the runs meant more to Mitchelson, who got to hang out with a woman with whom he was clearly smitten. Said Smilgis, "He used to follow me like a puppy."

Marvin's sagas of divorce among the rich and famous, described to Smilgis as they puffed around the track, were frequently laced with tales of the wealthy's eccentricities. Thus, it wasn't surprising when, one day in the spring of 1982, he arrived at the track announcing that he'd just met with "this nutty lady" who claimed she knew secrets that could bring down the government.

He told Smilgis her name was Vicki Morgan, and that she said she was the mistress of Alfred Bloomingdale. What do you know about Alfred Bloomingdale? Mitchelson asked insistently. He was turning the tables, using Smilgis as an information source. At first, Mitchelson didn't know anything about either of them, but as he learned more from Vicki in the days that followed he dribbled out a story that was, as Smilgis put it, "just too *delicious*." Vicki Morgan had more than a mere palimony claim. Mitchelson was on to something.

Vicki Morgan was a twenty-nine-year-old sex puppet, a woman who lived off of the men who used her. She was also a high-school dropout and a would-be actress who'd had an illegitimate son at age sixteen, three troubled marriages from age seventeen, and, by the time Mitchelson saw her, way too many miles on heroin and freebase.

If Vicki's paramour hadn't been Bloomingdale, the rest of the world wouldn't have noticed her, and if Alfred and his wife hadn't been the wealthy best friends of President Ronald Reagan and his First Lady, Nancy, nobody would have noticed him, either. But this was Tinseltown.

Vicki married a forty-seven-year-old man the first time. Shortly thereafter, seventeen-year-old Vicki met Alfred Bloomingdale.

Bloomingdale followed her into the Old World Restaurant on Sunset Boulevard in Hollywood. He wanted her telephone number—so his teenage daughter, Lisa, could make a date to play tennis, Alfred said disarmingly.

Vicki hadn't heard of the Bloomingdale's department store chain and didn't know that Alfred was rich. At first, she didn't want anything to do with this old man who telephoned her from five to twenty times a day, as she later described it, "for approximately two months straight." But she finally agreed to meet him twice more. It was when they got together for the third time that Alfred brought her to a house on Sunset Plaza Drive, to watch what she later described as being a kinky group sex scene between Alfred and two prostitutes.

"Alfred asked me, 'Wasn't this fun?' Alfred had a look in his eyes, believe me when I say this, a look in his eyes and his face that scared me to death. He was a different person, literally a different person, and I was scared to death to say anything but 'Yes,' and you better believe I said, 'Yes, this is fun!'" Then he had sex with Vicki and spanked her hard enough to make her cry. "Alfred didn't know from sharp love taps," she explained. Then they took a shower, and then Alfred asked her to be his mistress, which a compliant Vicki said she would.

As surreal as it all sounded, with Vicki Morgan it was real. Although she tried to act worldly, Vicki was still the lonely little girl whose father had skipped out on her when she was nine months old, and whose stepfather had died of a heart attack right in front of her, at a drive-in restaurant, when she was nine.

She wanted to be loved, and she thought she was falling in love.

Yet she was mere chattel to Alfred. He literally wanted to "buy" her away from her first husband, and, later, from husbands two and three as well. None of her marriages lasted very long, and although she continued to be kept by Bloomingdale and to accept his $10,000-a-month allowance, Vicki also hung out with a circle of expensive call girls and continued her straight and kinky sexual relationships with a multitude of other men, and at least one woman, in a way that made her equate having sex with being loved.

Jonathan Beaty, an investigative reporter for *Time*, described Vicki as Bloomingdale's Pygmalion project. Alfred set her up in fancy houses, bought her the obligatory Mercedes, and sent her to gourmet cooking schools, plastic surgeons (breasts and chin), and psychoanalysts (with Alfred often waiting outside while she had her session) in order to create the perfect hostess and companion. He arranged acting lessons with Mervyn LeRoy in the afternoon and at the Lee Strasberg Institute during the evening. Alfred even dispatched her to the same hairdresser, Ménage à Trois in Beverly Hills, as his wife, Betsy. There, the inevitable finally happened, and Betsy Bloomingdale spied Alfred with his mistress.

Even though Betsy Bloomingdale and Vicki had never met, much of Hollywood knew Vicki quite well. She'd flown to Las Vegas with Frank Sinatra in his private jet, made her own home movies of sex with one of the hottest Hollywood producers, slept with Cary Grant, and led the good life with King Hassan of Morocco.

The sexual schizophrenia of their lives should have dictated that Vicki's and Alfred's expectations of each other be less rigid than the norm. And yet Vicki's frequently were not. Having become the pleasure-seeking, self-centered person she was, Vicki could still be demanding when it came to somebody else's obligations.

When she threatened, in a 1974 snit, to sue Bloomingdale for failing to help her become an actress, her paramour just laughed and said, "I dare you!"

Vicki went to Paul Caruso and ordered him to file the suit. Caruso wrote one up alleging "interference with a business right." She must have dazzled him, because he took her case on a contingency and even guaranteed Vicki's payments on a new leased Mercedes. When she later stuck him with the unpaid debt, Caruso turned the tables and sued her. But his skip tracers couldn't find her, let alone any of her assets.

"That was when I started to realize how well protected she was. How very clandestine her life was," Caruso said.

Alfred and Betty were the Reagans' best friends, and on Inauguration Day of 1981, the Bloomingdales got a luscious apartment at the Watergate and settled in to reap the fruits of their White House connection. Within a month, though, Alfred was seriously ill with what would be diagnosed six months later as esophageal cancer.

Vicki panicked. Alfred had lately been giving her as much as $18,000 a month as an allowance, plus money for furnishings, rent on an expensive house, a car, and whatever else it took to keep her happy. Maybe she cared about Alfred, but she sure cared about herself, and she wanted an assurance that she'd be taken care of if Alfred suddenly died.

With Vicki and a friend of hers at his hospital bed, Alfred instructed his lawyer to give Vicki an interest in some real estate deals he was involved in. Three months later, Alfred met with Vicki and promised to pay her a $10,000-a-month allowance for five years. On February 12, 1982, he put the promise in writing: In the event of Alfred's death, Vicki's promised $10,000 a month was to come from Alfred's profits from his Marina Bay Hotel in Ft. Lauderdale. She would also get an interest in a start-up company called Showbiz Pizza. On paper, it sounded terrific.

Frail and unable to hear or speak, Alfred was discharged from the hospital for the last time in March of 1982, and he had what would be his last lunch with Vicki on June 16 of that year.

Vicki told a friend that Betsy didn't really give a damn about her and Alfred. Although Vicki visited the ailing Alfred daily, Betsy was, according to Vicki, just gadding about, "traveling around the world." Vicki mused to a friend that the only thing Betsy was really jealous about was being told by a servant that Vicki's Mercedes was newer than hers.

When Betsy returned from a trip abroad at the end of June in 1982, she took control of the Bloomingdale family interests, and on July 1 she stopped the $10,000-a-month payments that Alfred's lawyer had been making to Vicki.

Now it was Vicki's move. She wanted to use a lawsuit to fight back. With characteristic audacity, she went back to Paul Caruso, the lawyer she'd skipped out on before. Caruso couldn't believe she'd be shameless enough to come back, but he also was curious about what she was up to. He agreed to see her. After he heard her story, remembering how she'd stung him before, Caruso told Vicki to get another lawyer.

Vicki had known of Marvin Mitchelson's reputation ever since she'd moved out on her second husband, an aspiring actor named John David Carson. She'd eloped with Carson to Las Vegas and gotten married at daybreak on January 10, 1976; exactly nine months later, she moved back into a rental that Alfred had arranged for her on Basil Lane in Bel Air. Just as with Vicki's other brief marriages, the break-up of this one had been remarkably amicable—so much so that as a housewarming present for her new place, Carson even gave her Mitchelson's newly published anthology on his celebrity divorce cases, *Made in Heaven, Settled in Court*, with Carson's warm inscription wishing her happiness.

Vicki hadn't even read the book when she first got it. But now she took it out, more or less approved of what she saw as Mitchelson's aggressive style, and got in touch with him.

To Marvin, Vicki was an enigma: quiet, withdrawn, and sometimes not very articulate, but other times boisterous and demanding. He readily took her case but he knew the publicity would have to be carefully orchestrated: Her knockout looks had gone to seed and she drank too much. Mitchelson kept her away from interviewers and released an old, stunning photograph of her instead, swathed in a fox-trimmed coat that had been a gift from another of her lovers, financier Bernie Cornfeld.

Marvin's description of Vicki Morgan was a reflection of himself. "She had a certain mentality," he told Jonathan Beaty of *Time.* "This is hard to relate to other people, because you have to know her. She's not very bright. But scheming, and kind of cunning. Quiet. Always late. Every time, one hour, two hours, three hours! Never once was she on time! She had some nicer qualities, too. But [not when it came to] conscience things, really. She fucked Paul Caruso out of a car. She'd leave you in a minute [for] the next best deal, any place that would give her a good deal. [She'd] do anything."

In the aftermath of *Marvin vs. Marvin*, Mitchelson now was playing his new role as the protector of mistresses. Vicki's case seemed made to order: not necessarily because it neatly fit the *Marvin* criteria—in fact, it didn't—but, rather, because Mitchelson figured the Bloomingdale family would want to settle it quickly regardless of the merits. Just like his friend Roy Cohn, Mitchelson had learned that the threat of lurid publicity could sometimes quickly get a famous defendant to the settlement table. Much as he reveled in the publicity, it was these "quiet settlements"—sometimes paid even before a palimony suit was even filed—that he must have loved the most. He didn't have to do much legal work, so banking a big contingent fee was easy.

Mitchelson followed this basic strategy when he filed Vicki's palimony suit against Alfred Bloomingdale on July 8, 1982. Instead of using the suit to gun down the Bloomingdales with unfavorable publicity, Marvin saved his bullets. The suit was for breach of contract—Alfred having made some monetary commitments to Vicki that weren't being kept—and it didn't so much as even whisper about illicit sex or their twelve-year relationship, though it didn't *have* to mention that. Mitchelson wanted $5 million in damages. Betsy would know what was coming if she didn't settle fast.

But to Mitchelson's and Vicki's amazement, the Bloomingdale side would have no talk of settlement. Betsy was calling the shots for the Bloomingdales' Los Angeles lawyer, Hillel Chodos. When Mitchelson met with him and suggested that he get the payments to Vicki started up again in exchange for Mitchelson's backing off, Chodos curtly told him to forget it.

Rhoden was doing legal drafting for Mitchelson on Vicki's case. Now, Mitchelson came back from his meeting with Chodos and instructed Rhoden to bring out the heavy guns. Mitchelson would give the Bloomingdale side a dose of the scandal that Vicki could kick up.

On July 27, Rhoden filed a second $5 million lawsuit. But now the gloves were off. The new lawsuit said Vicki had acted "as a therapist to help [Alfred] overcome his Marquis de Sade complex." For the first time, Mitchelson used the words "friends and lovers" to describe Alfred's and Vicki's twelve-year relationship. He said Betsy had interfered with Alfred's payments because of her "jealousy of Alfred Bloomingdale's love and affection for, and devotion toward," Vicki.

The new suit was Mitchelson's shark bait. But Chodos's intransigence was puzzling. Instead of talking settlement, now Chodos was insisting on getting the palimony case to trial quickly, and he wanted to take Vicki's deposition.

Mitchelson had a one-third contingency on Vicki's case. He was so confident of his strategy for disclosing Alfred's secret sex life bit by bit that he let Vicki open up during her deposition.

But the strategy may have been miscalculated. By allowing Vicki to reveal all the lurid details of her affair, he lost his leverage. Having revealed everything, what was left to induce a settlement?

Even if he'd been smarter, though, Mitchelson still probably wouldn't have gotten his settlement. Betsy seemingly wanted revenge.

Besides, settling with Vicki might have encouraged the rest of Alfred's kinky entourage to come out of the woodwork, too.

Vicki didn't hold anything back in her all-day deposition with Chodos on Friday, August 13. Both Mitchelson and Rhoden were present, but they just sat to the side and let Vicki lay bare the whole crazy relationship with Alfred. There was only one limp objection from Rhoden, almost at the end of the day, about Chodos's persistent inquiries into Vicki's and Albert's sex life. "She's told me that she wished she could keep anything sexual out of this litigation," Rhoden explained politely, leaving unaddressed the obvious question of why her own lawyers had nevertheless sensationalized her case.

"Okay," Chodos carried on, totally ignoring Rhoden's weak protest. "Do you know who the Marquis de Sade was, or when he lived or—?"

Vicki answered tentatively. "I think it was the eighteenth century or something, wasn't it?"

"Do you know who Justine and Juliet are?"

No response.

"Do you know?"

Rhoden broke in. "That's assuming they are people. I object to the question on the grounds that it assumes facts not in evidence."

Chodos started in again. "Do you know who they are?"

"No."

"Have you ever read any of the books of the Marquis de Sade?"

"No, but I know about them."

"What do you understand a Marquis de Sade complex to mean?" Chodos asked.

"Someone that enjoys and believes that the other person enjoys getting pleasure out of hurting another person," Vicki replied.

"All right, and part of the deal, the original deal, was that you would act as a therapist to help Alfred over his Marquis de Sade complex?"

"Because he had a serious one, yes." Vicki helpfully explained that she would watch Alfred as he whipped his other sexual playmates, and that she would give him what she called "the look" if he got too rough.

"Now, Miss Morgan," Chodos finally interjected after Vicki had rambled on at great length about her "therapy sessions" with Alfred. "You never had a license to practice psychotherapy from the state, have you?"

"No."

The next day, from his hospital bed, Alfred signed his and Betsy's formal denial of Vicki's allegations in handwriting so feeble it looked as if he'd barely had the strength to move the pen. Within a week, Alfred was dead.

Nobody but Chodos apparently saw how devastating to her own case Vicki's deposition testimony had been.

Vicki came home that night and made one last entry in a diary that she hadn't written in since 1976. Her writing was childish and full of misspellings but the diary entry left no doubt as to what she felt. During the deposition, she had gone to hell and back "fifteen times at least." It was, Vicki wrote, the toughest day of her life.

Marvin still figured that Chodos would view the deposition as being detrimental to the Bloomingdale side. Taking Vicki to lunch the following Monday, as he liked to do with his hot clients, he reiterated his confidence. And Vicki said she now felt renewed self-confidence for having survived the deposition. She was planning to get her own revenge by writing a tell-all book that would reveal the whole story about her years with Bloomingdale.

Still expecting a settlement, Mitchelson had another unbelievably upbeat prognosis when he talked to Vicki by telephone on the evening of August 18, five days after her deposition.

Chodos and he had spoken again, Mitchelson explained. Chodos had laid out the theories he intended to use in a motion to dismiss the palimony suits.

"They want to vindicate themselves," Mitchelson said derisively. "They want to get a blow back in to show that they're devastated by the whole thing. Chodos told me, 'She's not a licensed therapist.' I said, 'Listen, you and I give therapy every day and we're not licensed therapists!'" Then Chodos told Mitchelson that the palimony suit was *res judicata*—legal language that meant "already decided"—because Vicki hadn't pursued the 1974 lawsuit that Paul Caruso filed.

Mitchelson dismissed his adversary. "He's looking for legal theories, but they're no good."

Chodos also claimed Alfred, days away from dying, wanted it that way. "Mostly vindication," Mitchelson related. "He wanted to see, before he died, that he got his name cleared."

Now Vicki, who hadn't said much, exploded. "That's not Alfred! That's *her!* I mean, he can't say more than five words a day! What the *fuck?*"

Their conversation showed that Mitchelson finally realized Vicki was damaging her case by emphasizing her sexual services. The *Marvin* case clearly established that a mistress couldn't enforce a contract for sexual services. Vicki needed to tell her story in a way that emphasized how Alfred's promises of payment were for her work as a confidante, business adviser, and therapist. Mitchelson wanted to make sure his client got that point.

"I said, 'She's *not* involved sexually!'" Mitchelson was getting his point across by relating more of his conversation with Chodos: "'This wasn't what the Marquis de Sade thing was. She *helped* the guy! She helped him by advising him. She got him over a problem.' I said, 'The more I think of it, the stronger this thing is!' That's really the case here.

Your [deposition] testimony shows you helped him. You didn't want to do it and you got him over it. It says you helped him with a problem. It's *not* sexual!"

It was also during this telephone call that Marvin revealed his feelings for the reporters who fawned over him. He had a reputation as a friend of the press, a guy who would always help with a quote if he could. The media had veritably bestowed his fame upon him. Now, unaware that she was taping every word, he was telling Vicki what he thought about all the reporters that chased him.

Mitchelson first predicted that Chodos would fail to win his motion to dismiss Vicki's case. "When he fails to do it, we're gonna look pretty good in the press, because the press is dumb! They're gonna think, Geez, we won some big victory!" Marvin giggled conspiratorially. "Whereas, all we really won was the right to go on with our case."

Marvin thought he had everything figured out.

"I personally like the shape we're in right now. I really like it. 'Cause we've got a lotta, lotta stuff comin' up, and we've got a chance to throw the White House book at 'em! And I really think, down in my little heart, that when they start seeing this shit come out, somebody's gonna say [to Betsy Bloomingdale], 'What in the fuck are you doing? You mean you wanna go into court and you want to hear all this shit with the Marquis, and all the whippings and the beatings and everything?' I just honestly don't think— They've got the bad edge of a two-edged sword! They're up shit creek! They're damned if they do and damned if they don't! And, believe me, this woman [Betsy] is so *social!* We'll show that her husband [was] a whoremonger and fucked the town! Is that gonna vindicate 'em? This is just *horseshit!*"

Vicki was spending most of her time holed up inside her house on Tower Grove Drive, collecting news about her case through marathon telephone calls. But when a few days passed in which her lawyer didn't phone—he was in Miami on another case—she became disillusioned. Vicki didn't think Mitchelson knew or cared about her case.

Seven days after her deposition, Vicki was already seeking more legal advice. She went to see Michael Dave, a forty-three-year-old Hollywood lawyer.

Vicki had known Dave and his wife, Lorraine, for ten years, and they'd taken a kind of parental interest in Vicki. Michael Dave even arranged for his brother and law associate, Jamiel, to handle her divorce from John David Carson.

Although Dave had the obligatory heavy gold chain, big diamond ring, Bel Air house, and rock-star clients, he wasn't the typical Sunset Boulevard shark: Dave was a vegetarian, a father of five (Volvo wagon license plate: 7DAVES), and a follower of the Hindu prophet Sathya Sai Baba, whose photographs were all over the Dave house that backed up to the edge of Stone Canyon and had a view all the way to the ocean. He also had a winning personality and a benevolent smile that told you he had nothing to prove. Vicki complained to Dave about "the P.R. stuff" that Mitchelson engaged in.

In a notebook she kept, Vicki wrote of Rhoden and Mitchelson: "Feel like killing." Early the following morning, though, Marvin telephoned her and told her he had a premonition that he was going to win her case. Vicki was skeptical, and wrote in her diary that she was depressed.

Chodos continued to bewilder Mitchelson. Instead of talking about a settlement, he filed a motion revealing all the shabby details of Vicki's deposition. The motion was couched in genteel legalese, but it unmistakably outlined a genuine soap opera. As a public document, it was also fair game for the tabloid press.

Even if it didn't presage settlement, Chodos's hardball strategy did seem to give Mitchelson some maneuvering room. The Reagans must have been furious about the embarrassment *they* were being subjected to. Not only was Betsy one of the First Friends, but Alfred had been appointed by the President to the prestigious Foreign Intelligence Advisory Board. How a person with Alfred's background could have passed a White House security check was beyond comprehension, but the implausible happened.

Sometime during August, Mitchelson arrived at the White House. Pamela Mason, the Hollywood wife who'd given Marvin his first big break, now had a son working for the President. Morgan Mason, twenty-seven years old, was Ronald Reagan's assistant for "political affairs." His White House meeting with Mitchelson apparently included a discussion of the White House's concerns about bad publicity in the case.

Marvin thought Roy Cohn would have a strategy for stopping the bad publicity. In fact, at one point, Betsy Bloomingdale may have considered hiring Cohn to represent her. Vicki Morgan told one of her lawyers that when Mitchelson filed Vicki's first palimony suit, back in early July, Cohn had flown out to Los Angeles and met Mitchelson at the Polo Lounge. The gist of Cohn's end of the conversation, as Mitchelson later revealed it to Vicki, was this: "I have a strange feeling I'm going to be on this case, and I'm going to tell her to settle immediately, because you and I know how to work."

That certainly was true. Putting Cohn and Mitchelson on opposite sides of the table was like asking a great boxer to fight his sparring partner for the world championship: Nobody'd get very bloody and both sides would still be standing at the last bell, but the winner would be a foregone conclusion from the start. Mitchelson admired Cohn. The two had just negotiated the largest divorce settlement in the history of South Africa: $26 million for the wife of billionaire tycoon John Schlesinger, one of the ten richest men in the world. Mitchelson was her lawyer. Cohn and Mitchelson traveled all over the world on that case. "We negotiated everywhere, including yachts and back alleys," Marvin gushed. "It was the James Bond of international lawsuits." It said something that Schlesinger celebrated his divorce settlement—and invited Mitchelson to the party at New York's fashionable "21." Later, Marvin went to Schlesinger's son's bar mitzvah, too. He couldn't afford not to go. His fee of more than $1 million had been paid by Schlesinger.

As it turned out, Betsy Bloomingdale didn't hire Cohn.

Vicki had been dubious all along. "Now, I know Betsy," she sighed and said when she first heard of the possibility of Cohn representing Betsy. "She's not the Roy Cohn type."

Mitchelson later told Vicki that Morgan Mason was talking to Betsy in September about the case. Mitchelson claimed that Betsy had promised Morgan to seriously consider a settlement—and to hire Roy Cohn to get it done quickly—if Chodos lost his forthcoming motion for summary judgment.

This did not impress Vicki. She had decided that she was being duped. Vicki renewed her resolve to get another lawyer. On the advice of a friend, she went to see Arthur Barens, thirty-eight years old then, who had an office on Santa Monica Boulevard. Barens had once practiced with Mitchelson. In fact, it was he who filed Mitchelson's first aborted divorce suit against Marcella.

According to Jonathan Beaty, Barens met with Vicki on three different occasions. He did not become her lawyer, although it is unclear why. Barens claimed he didn't trust Vicki—he saw her as someone "who'd call your wife up" after an affair. Vicki claimed, on the other hand, that Barens wanted her case but that *she* didn't trust him.

On September 10, Vicki again went to see Michael Dave. This time she took all her papers with her. Dave was her friend, albeit a man she also called "a nobody lawyer." But at least he was reliable. He would help.

Dave's analysis of her chances was sobering. He didn't think she had anything approaching a $10 million claim—Mitchelson's number—against Alfred. But he did think she'd be able to collect something on the contracts Alfred had signed. He and Vicki conferred on how to move Mitchelson aside.

Doing that was going to be tougher than Vicki first thought. Marvin was desperate to stay on the case. Moreover, Dave still saw some advantage to using Mitchelson's publicity tactics as a way of embarrassing the Bloomingdales.

Even though Dave viewed this media savvy as Mitchelson's only strength, Marvin's publicity tactics were also precisely what gave Vicki the most grief. Vicki had expected Mitchelson's orchestrated disclosures to evoke sympathy for her role as Alfred's "other wife"—that's what she called herself—but that hadn't happened, either. Nobody saw her as anything but an opportunist.

"The case developed a momentum all its own," said one of her friends. "Vicki quickly became out of control. She was a private person. To have those headlines just killed her. Virtually overnight, she became a leper. Her name was being bandied about in the media; she couldn't even go to the grocery store. She just wanted her due: what Alfred had promised her."

Perhaps coincidentally, or perhaps not, the same day that Vicki went to Michael Dave, the *Los Angeles Times* was preparing a story revealing for the first time that Mitchelson had conferred at the White House with Morgan Mason. The story looked like a Mitchelson leak. It advanced his line that a Reagan–induced settlement was likely, and led with his cryptic account of the White House meeting. But Vicki had heard all that before, and was still skeptical.

To firm up her resolve against Mitchelson, she wrote some notes to herself on an envelope and jammed them into her copy of his book, *Made in Heaven, Settled in Court*. She didn't want any more press "leeks" [sic] by Mitchelson, even if she had to get a gag order to stop him.

For a while, Michael Dave and Vicki considered letting Mitchelson stay in the case only if he survived Betsy's summary judgment motion and delivered a settlement within thirty days thereafter. Even then, they intended to make him give up half of his contingent fee to Dave.

Mitchelson was desperate to keep the case. During a long evening telephone conversation with Vicki, he bit right into the proposal, agreeing to slice his fee in half and to accept their other conditions, too. "I'll tell you on my son's life, I really want you to win this thing badly! You'll have the case settled within thirty days. You'll win it!"

He also bragged that he had clout when it came to Judge Christian E. Markey, Jr., who had presided in the Mel Torme divorce and who would also be deciding Vicki's palimony case. "It really is important to put me back in there with this judge and everything," he said. Mitchelson claimed Judge Markey had asked him to get back on the case. "Why would he want me on, just to throw the thing out of court? That was *dynamite!* . . . We can do it big!"*

Begging wasn't beneath Marvin when it was in the service of a potential big fee or a high-visibility case, and Vicki's case was both. He kept pleading with Vicki, telling her about the phone calls he said he'd had from Morgan Mason.

Mitchelson also claimed he was positive that Betsy was going to dump

---

*Markey categorically denied discussing the case with Mitchelson at all. "I repudiate it. . . . [It is] some kind of silliness."

Chodos and hire Cohn, unless Chodos won summary judgment.

"I cannot work with Hal Rhoden and you," Vicki said coldly. She acted as if she hadn't even heard Mitchelson. "You're a screamer, and I can't work with screamers. And every sentence out of Hal Rhoden's mouth is sarcastic. . . . You're a boy with his head in the clouds. And then I've got a chauvinistic pig [Rhoden] who has a snide remark for every sentence out of his mouth."

Vicki had another question for Mitchelson that night: She wanted to know the exact time of his birth, so that she could see what the stars told her about Marvin's continued presence.

"Mother? Mom? When was I born?" Mitchelson yelled to Sonia. His mother was around his house somewhere. Sonia picked up an extension. She still spoke with a thick, Eastern European accent. Her Sonny was born "on a Monday morning, pretty early. Like four o'clock in the morning."

"Are you studying my chart?" Mitchelson inquired playfully.

"I'm doing more than that, my dear."

The next morning, Michael Dave circulated a statement to the wire services saying that Vicki Morgan had fired Mitchelson. Marvin had seen it coming, of course, although he told the newspapers it was a surprise. The only shock was the timing: It was one of the wire reporters, not Dave, who gave him the first word that he'd finally been booted out of the case.

21

There were a few ways to look at the misjudgments Mitchelson made in the case of *Vicki Morgan vs. Alfred Bloomingdale*. Maybe he really believed he could win a huge verdict for Vicki. If that were true, he had been extraordinarily naive.

Less than two weeks after Vicki fired Mitchelson, Judge Markey did what Mitchelson had characterized less than a month earlier as a legal impossibility: He granted Chodos's motion to dismiss Vicki's palimony case.

Stripped of all its legal mumbo jumbo, Judge Markey's six-page opinion said that Vicki was a whore. And whores can't enforce a contract for their services.

The relationship between Vicki and Alfred, the judge wrote, was "no more than that of a wealthy, older, married paramour and [a] young, well-paid mistress. Moreover, their relationship was adulterous, immoral, bordered on the illegal at [its] inception, and was explicitly founded on meretricious sexual services [relating to prostitution] which formed an inseparable part of the consideration." *Marvin vs. Marvin*, the judge went on, wasn't going to be turned into a "Mistresses Recovery Act."

Mitchelson found that something to be proud of. "I loved that, because when I had the Marvin case it didn't rise to the dignity of *any* case. You know, I lived long enough to see some judge praise me for *Marvin* and tell me something wasn't as *good* as the Marvin case."

The only claims Judge Markey left standing were those relating specifically to the deathbed promises Alfred had made to Vicki: to pay her $10,000 a month for five years and to give her a 10 percent share of a company that owned an interest in the Showbiz Pizza franchise operation.

Michael Dave continued to press those two claims on Vicki's behalf. But Betsy had shrewdly seen to it that Vicki wouldn't get much in any event. She dissolved the Bloomingdales' interest in Showbiz Pizza within weeks of her husband's death, so that Vicki owned 10 percent of nothing. *

Judge Markey's opinion had the effect of immediately opening up to public inspection the full record of Vicki's case. Reporters pored over her Marquis de Sade deposition; every salacious detail hit the newspapers and television.

Vicki was out of money and out of luck. She signed a contract to write her memoirs with a Los Angeles author, Gordon Basichis. Anticipating some positive media exposure from this, the Daves signed up Vicki for public speaking lessons. Afraid of what people would think of her if they knew who she really was, she attended under the alias "Connie." It was her mother's name. But when she got up in front of the class, she forgot who she was *supposed* to be. "Hi," she said, "I'm Vicki, I mean I'm Connie, I mean Vicki—who am I?" It was so painful, she quit after the first class.

Vicki was depressed. She even made a half-hearted attempt in March of 1983 to kill herself with an overdose of pills.

A few years earlier, after the breakup of her third marriage, Vicki had gone into a depression. Alfred paid for her treatment at a mental health clinic in Los Angeles. In June of 1983, Vicki moved into a rented condo on Colefax Avenue with a thirty-two-year-old man she'd first met at the clinic.

Even by Vicki's standards, Marvin Pancoast was an unlikely housemate. He'd done at least nine stretches at mental hospitals since

---

*A civil jury later awarded Vicki's estate the balance of the promised monthly payments, a total of $200,000.

he was twenty years old, spending a cumulative total of 589 days being treated for severe emotional problems. Pancoast also tried to commit suicide on a number of occasions.

He had some serious problems. Vicki didn't realize she'd have to pay for them.

They'd lived together only a month. Pancoast told a detective he originally intended to strangle Vicki with the tie of a heavy velour bathrobe. But sometime around 2 A.M. on Thursday, July 7, 1983, he instead murdered Vicki Morgan by repeatedly hitting her with her son's baseball bat. Vicki's face and skull were crushed. She was thirty years old.

Around 3:45 A.M., Pancoast walked into the LAPD's North Hollywood station and confessed to the murder. "I just killed someone. . . . I hit her enough times on the head so she'd go to sleep," he said. He wanted to make sure that the officers knew *who* he'd just murdered; wanted them to know that he'd just whacked the palimony mistress herself. Her story, Pancoast said, was "very political."

Camera crews and press photographers swarmed about outside the condo and rang doorbells at the adjacent apartments. Detectives poked around with studied nonchalance. Jonathan Beaty, assigned to the story by *Time* magazine, called the events that followed Vicki's murder "Tinseltown at its tawdry best."

A number of lawyers suddenly appeared around Pancoast. One of them was Robert K. Steinberg—the same Bobby Steinberg who once had run with Mitchelson's crowd, and whose partner, Sam Brody, had been Jayne Mansfield's boyfriend at the instant of their deaths in a car accident. Steinberg, forty-six years old, had parlayed into moderate fame his role as a lawyer in the Charles Manson mass-murder case. He went into partnership with Manson's chief prosecutor, Vincent Bugliosi.

Steinberg wasn't the only familiar player. There was also Arthur Barens—the same Arthur Barens who once worked for Mitchelson and who, only the year before, talked to Vicki about taking over her palimony case. Barens was a friend of Pancoast's mother.

And, of course, there was Mitchelson. He'd been out of Vicki's case for almost nine months, but he was always a magnet for scandal.

The day after news of Pancoast's arrest hit the newspapers, Steinberg showed up at the county jail to talk to him. It was a Saturday afternoon, and he'd been asked into the case by a friend of Pancoast's.

After meeting with Pancoast, Steinberg left the county jail and almost immediately began calling reporters, telling them he was Pancoast's attorney (actually, Barens was) and suggesting that he had major revelations to make. Steinberg kept up his telephone press agentry on Sunday. On Monday afternoon, he told his story at a news conference.

Steinberg was full of delicious details: about the blond mystery woman who walked into his office that Saturday afternoon and brought him three Betamax videocassettes of "Vicki Morgan and some of her friends"; the unnamed dignitaries he'd identified on the black-and-white tapes; the sadomasochistic sex acts. It was just too lusciously bizarre.

Almost from the moment of Vicki's murder there was a conspiracy theory that had Pancoast taking the rap for somebody else. Given Vicki's Republican connections, conspiracy fanatics didn't find it hard to conclude that there must have been at least one bigwig who either didn't want to be blackmailed by her or, maybe worse, end up in the book she was going to write.

That Monday night, Steinberg was the featured guest on ABC's "Nightline." He told Ted Koppel he was going to destroy the tapes within twenty-four hours unless President Reagan asked for them.

Mitchelson was due at Pamela Mason's house for dinner that same evening. Throughout the day on Monday, he'd been getting telephone calls at his office from reporters who were asking about Steinberg's allegations. Were there videotapes?

"I knew nothing about it except for what I heard and read," he told *Time*'s Jonathan Beaty a few months later. "I think Steinberg gave this information out on Sunday, and I read it Monday morning. I thought: Shit, God, he couldn't have been making it up! To be making something like this up would be like having your head on a platter. I know some things about Steinberg, and I don't like him. He has this desire to be a big attorney; I don't blame him for that. [But,] I hear this. I believe it.

"Now, by the time I get over to the Mason house, Morgan comes over. He's very excited. *Very* excited." Mason had left the White House after the embarrassing disclosure of his meeting with Mitchelson to discuss Vicki's palimony suit. He was back in Los Angeles, working as a publicist.

Right away, Marvin asked him what he thought about "this Steinberg thing."

According to Mitchelson, Mason replied that he had just talked to an excited Michael Deaver, who was the chief White House public relations strategist. Deaver was one of Ronald Reagan's closest, most trusted friends and advisers. The two had been together since Reagan's days as the California governor. "Deaver says there are tapes," Mason confided. "[Edwin] Meese and [William French] Smith are on them. There are stories breaking out tomorrow in Washington and the *L.A. Times*."*

"I think we were all sort of astounded," Mitchelson recalled. "It was a hot story in the sense of: Wow! What happens next? Where does it go from here?"

Mitchelson believed that Vicki had some kind of sex tapes. The year before, when he and Rhoden were still handling Vicki's palimony case, they had subjected their client to the kind of cross-examination they thought she'd get if she ever took they stand. During that mock cross-examination, she had alluded to some blackmail material she had.

Given what Vicki had earlier told him, Mitchelson was convinced that tapes existed. But his next moves were entirely contrary to form. Ordinarily, he jumped right in and started hogging the limelight. Here, he actually had important, corroborative information to share, and yet he decided to keep quiet.

At Pamela's house that night, there was "a conversation on what is going to happen," Mitchelson confided a few months later. "[We wondered] whether we've got a Watergate–type situation, and if we're going to be called to give some answers as to what the meeting at the White House was all about. . . .

"We talked about it for a long time. And I really thought there were tapes, and [that] there was going to be a scandal. I really believed it. And then the next day, no story. And the day after that, no story."

The absence of a story made Mitchelson nervous in anticipation. He was, by now, even more firmly entrenched in the belief that it was only a matter of time before some Republican official was identified as being on Steinberg's tapes. He decided he better consult with the person he considered a world-class expert when it came to witch hunts like the one he expected.

Roy Cohn would know what to do.

"I think I discussed this with Roy at one time extensively," Mitchelson recalled. "Roy was a very strong supporter of the Reagan Administration. . . . I think his concern was, 'God! I hope this doesn't get out!' He was concerned it might be an embarrassment."

In Mitchelson's mind, the possibility existed that, as he gingerly put it, "people in high places" might somehow have stolen the incriminating sex tapes. "Power from the top is power from the top," Mitchelson pontificated. "That's how people live and operate, you know." Cohn agreed that a high-level theft was possible.

If that were true, it also explained the hot water Steinberg now found himself in. Having advertised that he had the sex tapes, he now couldn't produce them. Steinberg claimed he left them in a gym bag in his law library, and that one of the reporters hanging around his office on the Tuesday morning after Vicki's murder must have stolen them. He reported the theft to the Beverly Hills police.

The cops were skeptical that Steinberg ever possessed the sex tapes. After his news conferences, his story of a theft lost credibility. The D.A.'s office started its own investigation and filed charges against him for the misdemeanor of filing a false police report. These charges were later dropped when Steinberg pleaded no contest—the same as a guilty plea for sentencing purposes—to a misdemeanor contempt charge of failing to answer questions under oath about the tapes. Steinberg ended up paying a fine and restitution totaling $3,690.

Conventional wisdom was that the whole thing was a hoax. Even Steinberg himself later characterized the sex tapes scandal as "one of those strange, bizarre things. . . . Just total madness." Years later he still wouldn't discuss it.

Jonathan Beaty of *Time* had been working the Vicki Morgan story almost from the moment of her murder. He was a big bear of a man, intimidating at first but friendly to those who knew him. Beaty investigated life's seamy side—drugs, crime, murders, money laundering. His voice had an impassive, atonal quality to it that betrayed no emotion.

On November 5, 1983, four months after Vicki's murder, Beaty reported back to his editors at *Time* about what he had discovered: more odd pieces of the puzzle.

Beaty theorized that Vicki might have known too much; that it was only a matter of time before she was blown away by someone fearful of the information she had.

Beaty found numerous irregularities in the LAPD's investigation of the murder. He also located a playmate and lesbian lover of Vicki's who was said to be on some of the sex tapes.

Beaty's most stunning revelations came from Mitchelson and Barens. Mitchelson now claimed to recall more clearly what Morgan Mason reported that night at Pamela Mason's house. For the first time, Mitchelson named those who he said now possessed the tapes. But he also put that crucial information off the record, and Beaty never independently confirmed it.

Barens, it would seem, also knew more than he was letting on. But his was an altogether darker story. He privately told Beaty that he had known about the tapes. Vicki and Marvin Pancoast came to Barens two weeks before she was murdered, Barens claimed, with a plan to use the tapes to blackmail Betsy Bloomingdale for $1 million. Barens not only insisted he had viewed the sex tapes himself, he said he even had possessed copies of them. Barens now feared for his life, too, and he wanted an organization of *Time*'s stature behind him. *Time* could see the tapes, and could also get Pancoast's exclusive story, for $25,000—paid to Barens. *Time* considered the offer but turned him down.*

---

*Eight years later Barens categorically denied ever seeing the tapes or offering them for sale.

Beaty, a born skeptic, thought Barens was "mostly" telling the truth. But there were still too many loose ends to the story and *Time* decided not to do a piece. Beaty's report never saw daylight. Pancoast was convicted and got twenty-six years to life at San Quentin. Eventually, the Vicki Morgan case sank from view. Whatever she knew was safely buried now.

22

If the 1970s were Marvin Mitchelson's years of publicity, the 1980s would be the decade he cashed in on it.

He'd earned nothing on both the Vicki Morgan and the Michelle Marvin cases. But Mitchelson could afford that. Even in defeat, such cases had astounding publicity value. He could ride his notorious cases right into the bank.

There was the unusual case of Soraya Khashoggi. She was the ex-wife of one of the world's richest men, Adnan Khashoggi, and she wanted Mitchelson as her lawyer. God knows, she was going to need a *magician*, too, because Soraya's divorce case had some major problems: She was *already* divorced from Adnan, and had been for five years. Moreover, she'd been married and divorced *again* since then, and had given birth to a child out of wedlock.

Soraya knew of Mitchelson from all the publicity about *Marvin vs. Marvin*. Michelle's trial had barely ended when he agreed, in April of 1979, to meet Soraya for dinner at the Ritz Hotel in London.

What Mitchelson saw was a knockout: a thirty-three-year-old, dark-haired, ivory-complexioned, voluptuous Brit.

Soraya had married the older Adnan while she was still a teenager. She accepted the veil, moved to Beirut, and bore her husband four sons and a daughter. But the lives of the rich can be difficult. With Adnan flitting all over the world doing his arms deals and buying banks, he and his pretty wife eventually grew apart. By 1974, about the only thing they had in common was their height: Mr. and Mrs. Khashoggi were both five-feet-four, although, at two hundred pounds, Adnan was heavier.

The Islamic divorce that Adnan and Soraya got in 1974 had the intrinsic surprise of a sunrise. Khashoggi thought so little of the whole thing that he handled his part by proxy, sending an emissary to do the honors.

Adnan was generous. According to Soraya, he promised her

$400,000 in cash, and he also said he'd maintain her lavish lifestyle. But, Soraya told Mitchelson, Adnan had peremptorily cut her off.

Soraya wanted revenge, but she also wanted more money. Mitchelson's math spoke for itself. Khashoggi owned twelve lavish homes, three planes, and several yachts, including one later bought by Donald Trump and renamed the *Trump Princess.* Conservatively, Khashoggi was worth $4 billion. It didn't take an Einstein to figure out what that would mean to Soraya under California's community property laws. So Marvin started noodling around for a clever way to reopen the couple's divorce; maybe the Khashoggis weren't really divorced. After all, Adnan had done the whole thing by proxy. If they were still married, then Soraya's quickie British marriage to a government draftsman was automatically invalid.

Mitchelson, a $100,000 retainer from Soraya in hand, once again assigned Rhoden to do all the grunt work. Marvin's bantam sidekick drafted up not only a divorce complaint, but another one for palimony—using the just-established *Marvin vs. Marvin* doctrine—in case the divorce case failed. Mitchelson ran first to LAX and then to the Long Beach airport to serve the papers to Khashoggi aides aboard the rich man's private Boeing 727 and DC-9. Newspapers around the country ran photos of him nosing around the two planes, trying to find somebody to slap the complaint on. Marvin quipped that his experience as a process server was coming in handy.

For a while, Mitchelson was in heaven. The Khashoggi case was the biggest divorce in the history of the planet—Khashoggi was even richer than Howard Hughes—and Marvin was handling it. His friend Martha Smilgis did a big write-up for *People,* and there were other splashy stories and television pieces. One oft-used photograph had him walking up to the front of the Securities and Exchange Commission, his black limousine at the curb, escorting Soraya. This was Mitchelson's fill-in-the-blank photograph: the dark-suited protector at his comely client's side. You could ring down a new backdrop and put Joan Collins or Michelle Marvin or any of a thousand other beauties in Soraya's place. It was always the same Mitchelson, though, with his white hair limned against the darkness of his limo, his briefcase, his custom-made suit, and, in Soraya's case, her beauty itself.

Soraya was in Washington to give testimony about Adnan in an SEC investigation. If Adnan thought she was bluffing, now he had to have second thoughts. Soraya didn't have much of a divorce case, but she was cleverly employing the leverage she had. Her knowledge of Adnan's business was her trump card—a way of sending Adnan an implicit message: If he didn't play along, he'd have to start worrying about what she might tell the investigators.

With little chance of prevailing on either the palimony or the re-divorce petition, Soraya was using Mitchelson for the one thing he was still good for: causing hurtful, embarrassing publicity. She succeeded in humiliating Khashoggi and his entire family. But more than that, she got the attention of the Saudi royal family. They were Adnan's chief benefactors—their loyalty traced back to Adnan's father, who was the personal physician to King Ibn Saud. The royal family's unhappiness with Adnan was what finally brought him back to the negotiating table.

Without Mitchelson's knowledge, though, Soraya met alone with Adnan's lawyers in Salt Lake City and cut a deal that gave her, according to Khashoggi's biographer, Ronald Kessler, a lump-sum $2 million payment and $10,000 a month for life. "She made a deal behind our backs!" Rhoden howled. "We got *peanuts!*"

When reporters pried about how much money Soraya got, Mitchelson gave a vague reply:

"I'm *smiling*, aren't I?"

He had no choice but to smile through it all. There was no value in the publicity if he let on that his world-class client had cut him out.

Mitchelson liked to tell a story about how shocked his secretary was when he told her to type *nine* zeroes onto the Khashoggi complaint. Suddenly, those nine zeroes were nothing more than big fat goose eggs.

Soraya's case wasn't the only one where the hoopla and publicity didn't measure up to the fee. The same was true for Mitchelson's representation of Bianca Jagger when she got a divorce from her Rolling Stones husband in 1980. "What's her husband's name again?" Rhoden asked absentmindedly. "Mick?" According to Rhoden, their fee was "zero. A complete loss."

Then there was the divorce case of Sheikha Dena al-Fassi against her husband, Sheikh Mohammed al-Fassi.

Despite all his good work, the Fassi case became a hex and a jinx and just plain all-around bad luck for Mitchelson. And, as would later be apparent, it might have got him killed.

Dena was a twenty-three-year-old Belgian-born beauty. Her husband was a rowdy twenty-eight-year-old Saudi Arabian who was very, very rich. The Fassis were the proverbial jet-set couple, with far-flung possessions that included a yacht, a Boeing 707 jet and a companion cargo plane, thirty-eight automobiles, twenty-six Arabian stallions, a zoo, a Sunset Boulevard estate (complete with nude statuary the sheikh had repainted so as to feature red genitalia and black pubic hair), and at least ten other villas around the world. Mitchelson and Rhoden played the Lone Ranger and Tonto in the Fassi divorce, too. It was an easy case for them. The sheikh simply cut and ran once they sued him, taking his millions or billions—its depended on who you listened to—with him. Mitchelson quickly got a default judgment after Mohammed failed to show up to defend himself. It was a colossal judgment: $81 million was the sheikha's share of the community property.

When news of the victory hit the next morning, it rated a banner headline at the top of page one of the *Los Angeles Times*. As *People* earlier put it, Mitchelson had progressed from palimony to petro-mony. Given Mitchelson's 20 percent contingency, the Fassi case had the potential to be a real gusher. But it was just as likely to be another disappointment. The reason was that Mitchelson's huge judgment was just a worthless piece of paper unless it could be enforced. And since Mohammed fled from the country as soon as Dena filed her suit, trying to enforce the judgment was going to be like suing a wraith. Any of the sheikh's assets that Mitchelson could find and attach in this country were fair game. But outside of America, the sheikh could pretty much do as he pleased. Collecting anything approaching the full $81 million was going to be difficult.

Mitchelson had clients all over the country. In some states where he picked up cases, contingent-fee agreements in divorce cases were flatly prohibited. New York was one such state. Others, like California, considered them unethical except in certain circumstances where the divorce action had already begun. The reason was that the states didn't want to encourage divorces by giving the attorney a stake in the end of the marriage. Moreover, unlike in commercial litigation or personal injury cases, contingent fees weren't needed as an inducement for a lawyer to take a divorce case. A lawyer could expect to get paid in any event because, once the case was over, the judge had the power to decide what constituted an appropriate legal fee and then to pay it out of the marital assets.

Even Mitchelson, in his 1976 book, acknowledged what he said was the impropriety of contingent fees in divorce cases.* Yet this was precisely how he now made a lot of his money, and he became angry when questioned about it.

Mitchelson was eloquent whether his indignation was real or feigned. A contingent fee was only unethical, he said, if it clearly constituted profiteering. "The thing that outrages me more than any fucking thing in the world—just *outrages* me!—is that I've never done those things. And you take any one case I have that I have a contingency on, and I'll tell you the facts, and you then tell me if you think it could conceivably be unethical."

Mitchelson also vigorously defended his fee arrangements in non-divorce cases. "You know, these people who come in and sign up

---

*On page 176, he wrote: "Many states, including California, forbid lawyers to charge divorce clients on a contingency (or percentage-of-the-judgment) basis, which is common in many other types of lawsuits. Thus, divorce lawyers charge for their services on an hourly basis. . . ."

with me: Do you think I seek them out? Do you think I go around putting ads in the paper? They come to me because they really want me to help them! They *beg* me to help them! . . . I don't take huge contingencies. On palimony cases, I oftentimes charge twenty or ten [percent]. My colleagues charge a third, sometimes forty [percent]. I, who *invented* palimony, charge less than any lawyer I know for palimony! . . . A contingent fee isn't per se unethical at all."

Mitchelson lashed out at his critics. "Those big mouths! Those hot shots that like to do armchair quarterbacking! . . . No lawyer is worth, just on a purely hourly basis, four hundred and fifty dollars an hour. . . . *That's* unethical to me!"

In the Fassi case, Mitchelson's and Rhoden's 20 percent contingency was supposed to mean that they would take one fifth of whatever assets they could get for Dena. If they lost, they'd receive nothing. But Mitchelson never treated this as a contingent-fee crapshoot. Almost from the moment he filed Dena's case, he was concerned about how he would be paid.

Mitchelson wanted a retainer. Apparently, the sheikha didn't have enough cash, but she did have some exquisite jewels, and Mitchelson told her they would satisfy his monetary needs. She handed over an amethyst necklace, and he sold it for at least $50,000.*

Now, Marvin had working capital. He was going to need it: Marvin and the sheikha had been hot on Mohammed's trail, chasing him and the children and the couple's all-important assets first to the Diplomat Hotel in Hollywood, Florida, and then all over the globe.

By April of 1983, fifteen months after filing Dena's divorce complaint, he wanted more money. Mitchelson had obtained for Dena $75,000 a month in temporary support. Never mind that Mohammed wasn't paying *that*, either, and never mind that Mitchelson was still months away from his big win. Without altering the 20 percent contingency arrangement, he had Dena deed over to him and Rhoden a 20 percent interest in the painted-pubic-hair mansion she and Mohammed jointly owned on Sunset Boulevard.

The mansion was the couple's only valuable asset that hadn't already been spirited away, and Marvin latched on to the sure thing.

Mitchelson couldn't immediately record the deed, because the absent Mohammed was still technically a co-owner of the mansion, and he obviously hadn't approved the deal. It wasn't until twelve days after get-

---

*In a 1985 lawsuit, a cocounsel in the Fassi case whom he had failed to pay claimed Mitchelson had been given jewelry that Mitchelson valued at $500,000.

ting the $81 million default judgment, which gave Dena the sole ownership of the Sunset house, that Mitchelson recorded his and Rhoden's interest.

He now had ensured that he and Rhoden would get at least a million dollars for their legal efforts, and perhaps twice as much as that. The community property decree valued the Sunset property at $5 million, but it was already listed for sale with Rodeo Realty for $10 million. The listing was literally a fire sale, the main house having been gutted by an arsonist on New Year's Day of 1980. The sheikha had been living since then in a little gate house on the property.

Mitchelson now owned a valuable chunk of Beverly Hills real estate. The problem was that there was a slew of creditors chasing him. His strategy of placing almost nothing in his own name kept them at bay. But Dena's house now became their target of opportunity. Marvin's creditors showed up at the courthouse to slap the Fassi property with liens.

One of those whom Mitchelson failed to pay was a Bahamian lawyer hired as part of the global hunt for the errant Mohammed and the kids. The lawyer sued. According to Sir Leonard Joseph Knowles's lawsuit, Mitchelson had retained him with a $5,000 cashier's check and two $10,000 checks that both bounced. The lawyer had fronted some other expenses, too, for which he expected reimbursement—including bail money for two security men who'd been arrested for using excessive force in serving legal papers on the sheikh at the Paradise Island Hotel. Knowles's resultant $31,260 lien against the Fassi mansion was one of at least eight such recorded judgments and tax liens against Mitchelson—all tying up the Sunset Boulevard estate before Marvin had a chance to cash in on his share of the property. Altogether, the liens against him totaled $323,162, and they all had to be satisfied before the house could be sold.

Marvin Mitchelson, it seemed, was a real deadbeat.

Around the time of the Fassi case, Mitchelson owed $129,835 to the Internal Revenue Service and various state and local tax authorities. He owed at least another $103,858 to settle his long standing problems with the Sari Heller Gallery. Then, there were the matters of $57,942 in unpaid back rent for his office at 1801 Century Park East, and a $4,122 bad check he'd written to his publicist, Sy Presten. (Presten cashed it at Chemical Bank; Chemical then passed it on to Northern Trust Company in Chicago, which got stuck. Confronted about it later, Mitchelson had memory problems.) And, of course, there were the bounced checks and unpaid bail money to Knowles.

Mitchelson invariably tried to pass off his financial peccadilloes as some minor nuisance that no one, least of all he, needed to be concerned with. "You say I'm broke, but that's a relative term," he explained with an earnestness that was seemingly genuine if totally unbelievable. "It's not so much a matter of being broke. It just takes a lot of money to run my life. When you've got an overhead that's $100,00 a month, if you have a slow month, you're broke, right? I'm talking about cash flow. It gets tough, sometimes."

Mitchelson played his deadbeat's role with characteristic panache. His mother, Sonia, died in 1984 in Seattle and was put to eternal rest without the formalities of probate. The story was told about how Marvin owed the Groman Mortuary $7,000 after her funeral. He didn't pay it. After the debt had been ignored long enough, Groman's lawyer was called in. Get the money, the lawyer was instructed.

He confronted Mitchelson with a line that could have come from Henny Youngman: "If you don't pay for this funeral, your mother's *coming back!*"

Marvin paid.

Being Mitchelson meant you could use tortured logic when it served your ends, regardless of whether it landed you in court. There was the time he moved from one building in Century City to another—taking the beautiful antique doors from his old suite with him. He claimed the $7,500 doors belonged to him because, when his old suite was re-decorated, he was told that he could keep anything that the previous tenant left hanging on the walls. "They were doors on hinges, and they were removable." It took a lawsuit to change his mind.

Marvin's house on Sunset Heights Drive had five mortgages on it when he abandoned it to satisfy the judgment obtained by his erstwhile client, Bonnie Grant. Ever the opportunist, Mitchelson moved into a $4,000-a-month Beverly Hills rental on North Alta Drive and within the year had his new place listed in *Los Angeles* magazine's "Gray Line Tour for Non-Tourists." By 1984, he was still living in the house—he just wasn't paying his rent. That prompted another lawsuit. The owners eventually got a judgment against him for $20,008.

There were lawsuits for non-payment filed against Mitchelson by dif-ferent cocounsel in various cases, and a lawsuit filed by an employment agency that said it sent him a secretary and never got its referral fee. And who could explain why a publicity hound like Mitchelson would even stiff his own clipping service? That's what the service claimed he did in 1987. The clipping service sued, too.

At least one bank, frustrated over Mitchelson's chronic bad checks, finally closed out his account and told him to take his business else-where.

"I would *never* trust him with my money," Martha Smilgis ex-claimed. "When they bury Marvin, there's not going to be anything in the bank!"

He ran up a $23,587.67 Diner's Club bill in 1972 that the credit card company had to go to court to collect. And even though Marvin still hung on to at least eighteen credit cards—Neiman Marcus, American Express, Macy's, Nordstrom, you name it—he seemed to take perverse pleasure in taunting his creditors.

Acaldo recalled that "Once, during the Hughes Will case, we stayed at the MGM Grand, and they wouldn't give him credit. Marvin said, 'Who the fuck do they think they are?' So he invited me to the MGM Grand dining room for a sumptuous dinner. Then, Marvin signed the check. I said, 'You're going to get into trouble.' He told me, 'Fuck them. They don't tell Marvin Mitchelson to pay cash!' So he signed the check and left the table to start gambling. Next thing, I heard him paged in the casino. He ignored it. Then, they paged me. I pointed him out to the management, and they made him pay the check.

"But the next day at breakfast, he tried to do the same thing! And the next night, at dinner, when the check came he signed it: 'Fuck you. Marvin Mitchelson.'"

Marvin and Marcella had nightmarish problems with the IRS. They almost invariably filed every federal tax return several *years* late, with the result that huge tax liens against the couple were frequent and enduring. Among these there were some real whoppers: $275,379 for 1978, which the IRS was still trying to collect in 1987; and $109,830 for 1981, also still unpaid in 1987. One case against Marvin and Marcella was resolved by the U.S. Tax Court, which, in 1979, assessed an additional $73,043 in taxes for the year 1973—down from $259,682 that the IRS originally sought.

The money problems showed Mitchelson's childish side. He was still the irresponsible boy-man who, as Maureen Hancock [name changed] put it, squandered a fortune on "expensive champagne, hotels, fine art, women, gifts, and trips to Paris."

And on his own luck. "He likes to gamble; to call somebody's bluff," said Martha Smilgis. "Life isn't exciting otherwise." In Las Vegas, craps was Mitchelson's game. Acaldo said he only played with the black chips. "Never won anything. He always lost as far as I can tell. Liked to impress people and put down a pile of black chips." Smilgis remembered Mitchelson inside the casino at the Sands Hotel during the Khashoggi case, losing $2,000 on two rolls of the dice in two minutes. "He didn't think a thing about it."

Marvin Mitchelson always seemed to be broke. Pamela Rushworth, who had worked for him longer than anyone, first as a nanny to Morgan and then as his office bookkeeper, loaned him money from an inheritance she had. "She was his pocket cash," said a lawyer in Marvin's office. "His ready reserve." Rushworth told of Marvin's making an interest payment only to *re-borrow* the money the same day.

Chopsey Pelter, the brother of an owner of one of the process-serving companies Marvin worked for during college, had been loaning money to him since at least 1964; $70,000 altogether. Pelter told people: "We were like brothers." But the creditor-lender relationship between the two was less than totally amicable; they ended up in court in 1972, arguing over whether Mitchelson was in default on a note.

Paying the $12,258-a-month office rent was a chronic problem for Mitchelson. The landlord used liens and lawsuits to try to get the rent out of him. Steve Landau, who sublet some of Marvin's office space and took referrals from him, came up with a $150,000 loan to keep the rent current.

Acaldo loaned her boss all the money she had, $8,000, and said that while she worked in his office during the 1970s he borrowed another $350,000 from two other people.

Acaldo recalled one of these transactions: "Back in the sixties, there was a guy who used to be a dope pusher. . . . Marvin got his butt in some kind of a jam. . . . He needed one hundred thousand dollars and he needed it fast. And he told his friend. . . . [The friend] walked in there, and without even so much as asking for a note, handed him, in cash, according to Marvin, one hundred thousand dollars to get him out of this mess." A few years later, Marvin's friend killed himself. That was when the friend's mother came to work as Mitchelson's book-keeper—"so she could get her money back!"

Perhaps the strangest transaction, given its source, came from Raoul Lionel Felder, Mitchelson's New York nemesis.

Felder recollected a telephone call from Mitchelson some ten years earlier. "He calls me, agitated. I didn't know him well. I'm surprised. He called me, and he says: '*Shvartze*'s stole my money!'" The term *shvartze* was a Yiddishism, an inside word among Jews denoting a black person. "[He said] he's at the Dorset Hotel. 'Could you send me over some money?'"

Mitchelson said he needed $2,000 in cash, right away. Felder didn't ask why, but he asked himself: "Now, what the hell does anybody need two thousand dollars cash to be delivered over immediately? And he didn't know me [as a friend]." Felder got the money, in hundred-dollar bills, and gave it to his nephew, who worked part-time in the office, to take to Mitchelson. In repayment, Marvin gave the nephew a dirty, crumpled-up check—one he had obviously been saving in his wallet for a long time. The nephew told Felder that Mitchelson's room reeked of men's cologne.

"I put the two grand [check] in the bank, and the check was good." Felder was surprised. "It was so strange. I met somebody from [Roy] Cohn's office in court, and I said, 'You know, I had this strange experience with him.' And he said to me, 'Was the check good?' I said, 'Absolutely, it was good!' And the guy from [Cohn's] office said, 'You're okay, 'cause he did that to somebody in our office, and there was a problem with the check!'"

Mitchelson's financial travails invariably led his creditors back to his only attachable asset. The net result was that, when the Fassi mansion was finally sold for $4,175,000 in April of 1986, Rhoden and Dena made out nicely, but Marvin didn't get to keep even one cent for himself. Instead, checks totaling his share of the profit—exactly $374,846—went right to some of his creditors, including: his office mates Landau and Rushworth for personal loans; the Beverly Hills landlord whom he'd stiffed on back rent for his Alta Drive house; the trustee for Heller Galleries; and Mitchelson's tax lawyer, fifty-two-year-old Eli Blumenfeld. The check to Landau was for six figures; the others were for five.

For their role in the Fassi case, Mitchelson and Rhoden also got a combined 20 percent share of a $1,590,000 Lloyds of London insurance check. That was in reimbursement for the fire damage to the Sunset Boulevard mansion on New Year's Day of 1980.

By Mitchelson's reckoning, he and Rhoden had collected something like $7 million altogether for Dena, against the original default judgment of $81 million. The $7 million was mainly from the sale of the house, and from the insurance payout.

But more important to Mitchelson were the assets that remained to be found. He and Rhoden still had their contingency, and in six years the original $81 million default judgment now had swollen, with interest, to at least $130 million. All Mitchelson had to do was to lay his hands on a sufficiently large corpus of Mohammed al-Fassi's liquid assets—if any remained—and he would, *ipso facto*, satisfy what had up to now been his unquenchable thirst for wealth: His and Rhoden's contingent fee on the unpaid Fassi default judgment now ran to $26 million.

But of course there was a problem. There were always problems, dammit. If Dena made her own separate peace with her ex-husband, just as some of Mitchelson's other clients had done, the possibility of a big payoff might dry up, and there wasn't a thing he could do about that. In fact, Mohammed al-Fassi was said to be angling for a sweetheart settlement with Dena. He still had their children, after all, and being able to see them would be a powerful inducement for her to settle cheaply. If Mohammed's rumored plan succeeded, Mitchelson would lose any prospect of a gigantic payday.

From the moment the sheikh first tried to entice Dena to return to Saudi Arabia, Marvin had been on the scene, playing his usual role as father-protector. When, for instance, a man showed up at Dena's place in the middle of a May night in 1982, saying he'd been sent by Mohammed al-Fassi to bring Dena home, Mitchelson arrived straight away, too. So did officers of the Beverly Hills Police Department. Everybody had a job to do.

To the cops on the scene, this was a simple matter. Dena wanted the man to leave, which he finally did. What was noteworthy to the police was Mitchelson's reaction: He wanted to make a citizen's arrest of the man who purported to represent the sheikh.

Mitchelson put out feelers for a meeting with Mohammed al-Fassi, to see if Mitchelson could come to terms with the Saudi playboy. There were secret meetings with people he knew were close to Mohammed, and when someone reported Mohammed was returning to Florida, Mitchelson considered rushing there. After he had met with Dena in Paris.

"It's just a crazy life," Mitchelson said, his voice curiously frantic, for understandable reasons, and sheepish, because his greed was so obviously showing. He slowed down a little, picking through his vocabulary for just the right words. "When somebody owes you one hundred and thirty million dollars, it's a lot of money. I'm anxious to get him."

23

Richard Hirschfeld had lived an interesting life—first as a flamboyant promoter of high-flying businesses and later as a world traveler whose travels may have been in the service of U.S. intelligence. Hirschfeld himself liked to cultivate an aura of ties to U.S. spy agencies, but when asked directly about intelligence work, his standard reply was "Nobody's ever heard of a Jewish James Bond."

The "Jewish James Bond" moniker was one Hirschfeld advanced playfully even as he insisted it didn't apply to him. A plausible denial. But the truth was that Hirschfeld, trained as a lawyer but restless for much bigger things, showed a willingness to get involved in some wild schemes.

And so it was that, in 1987, Hirschfeld offered his services and his connections to the U.S. Department of Justice in a bizarre scheme to lure an accused assassin out of Iran.

Mitchelson would be the bait.

How the Hirschfeld caper came about was an amazing story of opportunism, revenge, and ordinary bureaucratic infighting. In the midst of it all was Mohammed al-Fassi, a "nut case," as Hirschfeld called him, albeit one bent on clever revenge. The story had its highs and lows and more than its rightful share of intrigue. But no one was more shocked than Marvin when it was finally revealed that the federal government supported a phony plot to pay a hit man $2 million to assassinate the divorce lawyer himself.

The opportunist, of course, was Hirschfeld. He parlayed a talent for self-promotion into lucrative relationships with some of the world's wealthiest and best-known people. He had also been in trouble with the law. In Hirschfeld's wake were three federal securities violations (two settled by Hirschfeld without any admission of wrong-doing); a 1986 conviction for criminal contempt; and, by 1987, when the phony plot to kill Mitchelson started unfolding, a federal criminal grand jury investigation.

Hirschfeld was from coastal Virginia, and it was there, when he was just twenty-seven years old and two years out of the University of Virginia law school, that he began plans for his own bank to be named after himself. But the bank never opened, and Hirschfeld ended up having to pay back a trail of debts. In 1977, after declaring bankruptcy in Nevada (debts: $5 million; assets: $2,000), Hirschfeld started over in California.

Hirschfeld went to work there for Donald Nixon, the former president's brother, who, he said, introduced him to celebrities. Hirschfeld met John Wayne. Around 1979, he also met Muhammad Ali, the legendary former heavyweight champion. They were in London and, as Hirschfeld later related it, Ali hired Hirschfeld as his lawyer because of the mistaken impression that Hirschfeld already represented Wayne.

Ali also was friendly with Mohammed al-Fassi, and that was a connection that worked for Hirschfeld, too. Ali got the two of them together, and Hirschfeld was soon advising Fassi on how and where to invest his money—and on how to get rid of that pesky default judgment that Dena and Mitchelson had against him.

So now he had one very rich client, Fassi, and one beloved one, Ali. Hirschfeld was vague about the other people he represented, but he hardly needed other clients. Having returned to Tidewater Virginia, in 1980, Hirschfeld and Ali had gone into business together.

One of their enterprises was called Champion Sports Management, Inc. The company was going to recruit, train, and promote professional fighters. Hirschfeld was the president; Ali the chairman. The company's CEO was Herbert Muhammad, Ali's longtime manager and the son of Elija Muhammad, the founder of the Black Muslim church.

Within a year of Hirschfeld's trying to take the company public in 1983, he was in trouble with the SEC again, this time for misrepresenting the company's financial position, assets, and ownership in a stock prospectus. He fought the charge but in 1984 was forced to return investors' money and enjoined from fraudulent activity. Then, in 1986, he pleaded guilty to criminal contempt for failing to disclose the injunction in the annual reports for another company he was a director of. That same year the SEC permanently barred him from practicing before it. That was largely a toothless sanction, though, because Hirschfeld had much more important things in store for himself. By 1987, the Jewish James Bond was using his connection to Fassi as an entree into international intrigue.

He'd gauged the potential of his Fassi connection the previous fall in Honolulu, when deposed Philippine president Ferdinand Marcos sought out Hirschfeld because of the latter's relationship with the wealthy Saudi prince. Marcos wanted Fassi to loan him $18 million for weapons purchases, so Marcos could launch an invasion of his homeland and topple the government of Corazon Aquino. Marcos intended to use Fassi's loan to buy Stinger missiles, M-16 rifles, tanks, grenade launchers, and enough ammunition to equip ten thousand soldiers for three months. The loan would be secured by Marcos's hidden gold and a lien on his Swiss bank account.

Marcos bought himself a Stinger, all right, but the missile answered to the name Hirschfeld. Pretending to cooperate with the old man, he instead introduced him to a friend who posed as an arms dealer. Using a bugged briefcase and a tiny pocket recorder, the two of them secretly recorded Marcos—not only as he described his overthrow plot, but also as he revealed the existence of a one thousand-ton stash of gold worth an estimated $14 billion. The whole crazy caper, tapes and all, was later revealed in a hearing before a House Foreign Affairs subcommittee. Hirschfeld and his sidekick, Robert Chastain, were the star witnesses.

Hirschfeld was about as unlikely a James Bond as anyone could find. Slender and fragile looking, he stood no more than five feet, six inches tall. Tieless, tanned to the point of artificiality, and with thinning, carefully trimmed hair, he looked more like someone from the William Morris Agency.

It was hard to know what motivated Hirschfeld to make his "citizen's sting" of Ferdinand Marcos. Maybe it really was, as Hirschfeld insisted, from a concern that not acting might have left him and his sidekick legally vulnerable, and could have led to Philippine deaths. Then again, maybe it was the greed factor. Hirschfeld and Chastain wanted the Philippine agency responsible for recovering Marcos's hidden wealth to pay them a commission if their efforts really led to a gold cache. The agreed-upon commission: 5 percent of the gold.

Hirschfeld had tried, unsuccessfully, to get the Justice Department to participate in his sting. But, instead of cooperation, all he'd received was indifference. A few months after he first met Marcos, though, Hirschfeld was talking to the department again. And this time, the powers that be were much more interested.

The U.S. Marshals Service, an arm of the Justice Department, was responsible for catching federal fugitives. The service arrested about 14,000 of them each year—more than all the other federal law-enforcement agencies combined—but that was still one fugitive too few, as far as U.S. Marshal Herbert Rutherford III was concerned.

Standing six feet, five inches tall and weighing 240 pounds, and with a resonant baritone voice that seemed to originate all the way down in his boots, Rutherford was the chief marshal for Washington and a commanding presence around the federal courthouse there. He was an imposing, powerfully built black man with a huge paw of a hand. When he greeted someone, he didn't so much shake their hand as engulf it.

Somehow—it still was not clear—Rutherford hooked up with the little James Bond. Each sought his separate ends.

Rutherford wanted to capture an accused Iranian assassin, and he had ample reason to believe that Hirschfeld could assist him. Hirschfeld, on the other hand, would get some help from the feds in return—help for a friend, certainly, and maybe for himself, too.

Daoud Salahuddin was the fugitive that Rutherford wanted to capture, but Rutherford refused to call the man by his Black Muslim name. To him, Salahuddin still was David Theodore Belfield, born in 1950 in Roanoke Rapids, North Carolina. In a slick 1980 operation that had been engineered by the government of Iran, an assassin the authorities believed to be Salahuddin gunned down an outspoken critic of the Ayatollah Khomeini. Dressed as a postal delivery man, Salahuddin was said to have shot Ali Akbar Tabatabai on the doorstep of his home just outside Washington, then fled to Montreal and Geneva. Salahuddin was long gone by the time the feds knew where to look.

Hirschfeld, though, spoke elliptically of having excellent connections in the Middle East, particularly in the orthodox Muslim countries where his associations with Ali, who was revered in the Muslim world, provided clout. Hirschfeld had spent enough time in the Persian Gulf region to speak with familiarity about the people and places he knew there. He and Ali even went on a Middle East mission in 1985 in an unsuccessful attempt to free U.S. hostages. Parceling out tantalizing but unverifiable little bites of information, Hirschfeld later came back from the Middle East and said flat out, for instance, that he knew where the Anglican Church envoy Terry Waite was being held prisoner (answer: inside a fortress in Hamadan, Iran).

Hirschfeld told Rutherford he knew where Salahuddin was holed up, too. He spoke guardedly about exactly how he would do it, but Hirschfeld said that with Fassi's help he could lure Salahuddin from what Hirschfeld said was a complacent life in Bandar 'Abbas, Iran. (Fassi himself had been the object of a foiled assassination plot in London in 1983.)

The idea appealed to the U.S. marshal. What Hirschfeld would get in return for his and Fassi's aid was possible government leniency for a friend, Robert Mario Sensi. Sensi, once a CIA operative who recruited spies inside Iran, was facing charges that he embezzled $2.5 million from the Kuwaiti government-owned airline.

Rutherford wrote Hirschfeld a letter on January 14, 1987, advising that he wanted to go forward. It alluded help not just for Sensi, but also for "others participating in this law enforcement endeavor." At the time, Hirschfeld was having his own problems with a federal grand jury in Norfolk investigating his income taxes.

When Rutherford met with an enthusiastic Hirschfeld, what he saw was a cowboy in a Brooks Brothers suit. "I realized his motivations weren't just to help himself, but also to be in an exciting game. I think he was very excited to be at the center of this action."

As planning for the covert operation got underway, Hirschfeld next met with agents of the Federal Bureau of Investigation. He also arranged for Fassi to speak by telephone with Rutherford.

With Hirschfeld directing the action, Fassi and his men were to make contact with Salahuddin, offering him up to $2 million in cash to assassinate Mitchelson. The white-haired divorce lawyer was chosen as the target because Fassi had such a plausible motive for getting rid of him. Fassi was instructed to drive a hard bargain—to make the deal for $1 million if he could—in order to make the plan seem believable to Salahuddin. Hirschfeld, who wouldn't say if he ever met Salahuddin, actually thought the proposed assassin "would probably have shot Mitchelson for ten thousand dollars."

The assassination was to take place in Cairo. Fassi would invite Mitchelson to come there to settle Dena's divorce case; Mitchelson surely wouldn't pass up that opportunity. Fassi's men would arrange a fake passport for Salahuddin. When Mitchelson was in the air and on his way to Cairo, Salahuddin would be told to fly there, too. The Egyptian authorities would cooperate by having police officers disguised as passengers on his plane, and, when it landed in Cairo, Salahuddin would be arrested for extradition to the United States.

Mitchelson was never informed that he was to be the bait in an international plan to arrest an alleged Iranian terrorist. As Hirschfeld later described it, telling him wasn't necessary because "the plan was to arrest Salahuddin the moment he landed. Supposedly, Mitchelson wasn't even going to be touched. Salahuddin wouldn't even get close."

Rutherford was gung ho for going ahead. But FBI officials began having second thoughts. They worried that, even if Salahuddin were captured as planned, someone else might hear of the false scheme and kill Mitchelson to collect Fassi's reward. The plan was called off, and bureaucratic amnesia seemed to set in. Within the Justice Department, the FBI's second guessing of the Salahuddin plan resulted in a turf-carving deal to give the FBI sole jurisdiction over fugitive international terrorists. In response to a Freedom of Information Act request, the department said it no longer had any files on the Hirschfeld-Fassi-Salahuddin affair and acted like the whole thing never even happened.

Rutherford was frustrated. He thought the marshals had a chance to grab Salahuddin. "You know," Rutherford said, "I think we really had a shot at this guy. He'd been over there six, seven years; nobody'd been on his case. As far as he's concerned, he's in fine shape. We had a shot. But, now, he's deep in the woods. He's on to us. I doubt we've got a chance now. We lost our opportunity." Hirschfeld said Salahuddin now was deep under cover in the same Iranian fortress where, Hirschfeld claimed, Terry Waite was once held hostage.

All Mitchelson could do when he heard two years later about the plan to bump him off was to marvel that a mere divorce case, albeit one as big as Fassi's, had put him so close to final jeopardy. "If they screwed up, I'm *dead!*" he screamed. "I mean, they didn't get the hostages out of Iran, either!"

24

Mitchelson had an astounding resiliency. He started the decade of the 1980s with his reputation burnished by *Marvin*, and would end it in disrepute. But the years in between were not unkind. Even as the curtain slowly lowered on his act, Marvin kept up appearances, kept right on winning high-profile cases in the courtroom, kept grinding out the publicity that brought in new clients.

Roxanne Pulitzer's was a case in point. At first, she saw him as her jet-set salvation. During an eighteen-day trial in 1982, her husband won custody of their twin sons and cut her out of his estate in a case that made tabloid headlines with its allegations of cocaine use and kinky sex ("I Slept with a Trumpet"). Peter Pulitzer even accused Roxanne of bedding down with a host of lovers, including the beautiful young wife of another millionaire.

Mitchelson hadn't been Roxanne's trial attorney—he'd never met her, and he wasn't admitted to practice law in Florida anyway—but when he read of the verdict, he let it be known that he was available and that he wanted to handle Roxanne's appeal, gratis. Fine, okay, Roxanne replied. Out of money and facing eviction from the family house, this offer from the master sounded too good to be true.

Mitchelson knew the value of her case. He immediately flew to Palm Beach, checked into a $375-a-night suite at the Breakers, and phoned *People* magazine to come over for an interview. Two weeks later, arm draped protectively over Pulitzer's shoulder, Mitchelson appeared on the magazine's cover. An adoring article about him ran inside.

Roxanne Pulitzer lost all her appeals and could be found two years later posing between the covers of *Playboy*. But, to hear her tell it, Marvin disappeared almost as soon as the *People* piece came out. Without a license to practice in the Florida courts—a technicality she said he'd neglected to tell her about earlier—other lawyers had to be brought into the case. To top it off, she said, Mitchelson billed her $7,000 for his personal expenses. Pulitzer refused to pay.

It wasn't long before Mitchelson was rushing to the aid of another damsel in distress. This time it was Karen Prunczik, wife number four of Broadway mogul David Merrick.

Merrick always prided himself on being the meanest son of a bitch in a city full of them, but by 1983 he was losing his power. In February of that year, the seventy-one-year-old Merrick suffered a stroke that left him partially paralyzed. For a non-stop dealmaker, the diagnosis couldn't have been worse: Merrick was suffering from global aphasia, a syndrome that caused him to transpose the meaning of words. Merrick said "he" when he really meant "she" and "yes" when he really meant "no."

Prunczik was a twenty-six-year-old tap dancer who played the role of Anytime Annie—the girl who only said "no" when she didn't hear the question—in Merrick's big hit, *42nd Street*. She left the show a week before their marriage, but the way things now looked she should have stayed. Prunczik and Merrick separated twice; once, he threw her out for six weeks. By the time of Merrick's stroke, seven months after their wedding, they hadn't had much of a marriage at all.

Three weeks after his stroke, Merrick was in the Rusk Rehabilitation Institute at New York University Medical Center in Manhattan. But within a day he escaped—by rolling his wheelchair down First Avenue in the pouring rain without a coat. By the time the police found him, he'd made it all the way to a Korean noodle factory at 24th Street and Third Avenue. The cops said he was incoherent.

Since he refused to go back to the hospital, Prunczik took him to their Manhattan apartment. That was when she said her husband started exhibiting "severe paranoiac tendencies." Prunczik would later say in court papers that he thought his food was poisoned and wouldn't touch it unless someone else first ate half, and insisted on listening in on a phone extension to see whether others were plotting against him. She also claimed that he threatened to kill himself, and that when she tried to take him to another clinic in La Jolla, California, he flipped out again and ended up being involuntarily held for seventy-two hours at Cedars-Sinai Medical Center in Los Angeles.

Since Merrick was often incoherent and sometimes confused yes with no, it was hard to know who or what he was running from. But Raoul Felder thought he was running from his wife.

The story of how Mitchelson's arch-rival got into the picture as Merrick's divorce lawyer was no less a moonstruck one than the rest of the Merrick-Prunczik saga. Felder had represented Merrick's wife number three, Etan, in *her* bitter divorce from Merrick. But, as Merrick fled from wife number four, he now wanted to remarry number three, thus making Etan number five. This time, Merrick wanted Felder on *his* side.

"He told me, 'You never got paid right in the first divorce,'" Felder recalled. "'I'm going to make it up to you. I want to make some money for you on this one.'"*

As Felder later recounted it, Merrick literally begged somebody—anybody!—to take him away from Prunczik. Finally, Merrick called his best friend, a seventy-six-year-old lawyer named Morton Mitosky. Mitosky had invested in every single one of Merrick's eighty-four Broadway shows. "Get me out of here!" Merrick slurred. In a frenzy of excitement, Mitosky obliged, spiriting Merrick out of Merrick's own apartment and into Etan's. Then, Felder filed for Merrick's divorce.

Prunczik struck back, filing a police report about what she said was Merrick's coerced removal from the apartment (the police called her report unfounded); slapping a writ of habeas corpus against Mitosky to produce Merrick's body ("which he does not have, incidentally," Felder deadpanned); and petitioning the New York Supreme Court for an order restraining Mitosky from acting on Merrick's behalf. At that moment, she told the court, Merrick was making $120,000 per week in profits from *42nd Street* and had a net worth of $50 million.

But Prunczik couldn't play hardball alone against New York's best divorce lawyer. She wanted Marvin Mitchelson. He got the usual panic call, and by Monday, May 2, he had signed on as Prunczik's counsel, replacing another lawyer. There would be a hearing on the conservatorship issue exactly a week later, and Mitchelson was going to be there.

"The next thing we know, she hires Mitchelson and Mitchelson holds a press conference in Merrick's old apartment," Felder recalled. "She still loves Merrick," Mitchelson told the reporters at the time. "She doesn't want a divorce."

Felder and Mitchelson squared off in the courtroom of Judge Hilda Schwartz on Monday morning, May 9. Recalling the action in his nasal brogue, Felder sounded like Walter Winchell going to press. "Mitchelson is not doing well in the case. For one thing, we have a very tough female judge, Hilda Schwartz. And he brought his California style,

---

*An unhappy Felder ultimately received $91,000, which he considered chump change. Felder called Broadway's biggest bad guy "a difficult, impossible man. A terrible human being. A mean guy."

with his atrocious taste in clothing, into court. He looked like he got dressed in a closet!

"Anyway, so he comes to court, and at one point he doesn't stand up when he addresses [Schwartz]. And she says to him: 'Stand up! Don't you stand up in California when you talk to the Court?'

"By the end of the second day, she got him so mixed up he didn't know *what* he was doing. Stand up! Sit down! One time he stood up, she said, 'You don't have to stand up! Sit down!' . . .

"He was badly mauled by the second day. By the end of the second day, he was mixed up whether he should stand up or sit down. She had him going. She was very rough." (Mitchelson acknowledged the experience. "In New York, they all talk at once, and the judges yell at you. They yell at anyone; at everyone!")

"Mitchelson was badly mauled," Felder continued, "and what had happened is that Karen put all her eggs in Mitchelson's basket. She was from [Pittsburgh] or somewhere. Her father was involved in the picture. They came to court. . . . And that was the scene there. I started chopping away and cutting him off and really bouncing him around the courtroom. I think [Karen] was disillusioned by the second day.

"Mitchelson then made a settlement on behalf of Karen. And my sense of things was, it was a very bad settlement for Karen. For one thing, Merrick at that time was alleged to have a $50 million estate. He couldn't talk. He'd had a stroke. So there's an obvious question: How's the man going to persevere in a lawsuit if he can't talk? He can't express himself.

"My strategy, if I were Mitchelson, would be to [have my client] hang in there, resist, and be the Widow Merrick at some point, when she inherits $50 million and gets support until then! Karen had only been married a short period of time. But she still would've been the Widow Merrick.

"So we settled the case. Very unfavorably for her." Mitchelson insisted that Prunczik was satisfied with the settlement.

"The judge is waiting and doesn't know we've settled the case," Felder went on. "The judge is irascible. So we pile into a limousine, I think it was Merrick's limousine. . . . We're up to here"—Felder pointed to his forehead.

"And so Mitchelson decides to tell this joke. The joke is, the Pope decides he wants a woman, and so he goes to the College of Cardinals, and says, 'Listen, I need a woman.' They said, 'Holy Father, this is terrible!' So they go into conference and say 'Okay, we've gotta get you a blind woman, so she can't see you.' He says, 'That's okay with me.' They say, 'We've gotta get you a deaf woman, so she can't recognize your voice.' He says, 'That's okay with me.' They say, 'Everything's okay, Father?'

"He says, 'Yes, there's only one thing.' They say, 'What's that?' He says, 'She's gotta have big tits!'

"He tells this joke! I was just appalled. First of all, Merrick is a glum person. Wanda Richert [the original star of *42nd Street* and a friend of Merrick's] is a born-again Christian. I mean, it was just a disaster.

"Just dead. It was the craziest thing. . . . It was like something out of a Fellini movie. I couldn't believe how he could say something so inappropriate! Then he talked about an automobile accident I think he'd had. Which was not too felicitious in a car packed with people, too."

It was, said Mort Mitosky, "the fastest divorce I've ever seen! It came and went in forty-eight hours!" The settlement Mitchelson quickly got for Prunczik gave her $125,000 in a lump sum, plus $3,000 a month for the next twelve years. "Why did Mrs. Merrick steal away with only a small cherry?" sniped gossip columnist Liz Smith in a piece that seemed planted by Felder.

Mitchelson's fees were taken care of in the settlement, too. For just a few days' work, he earned $100,000, splitting half of it with his regular New York cocounsel, Bernard E. Clair and Anthony R. Daniele.

Mitchelson was grateful, and why wouldn't he be? He'd wrapped up Prunczik's case in forty-eight hours and earned a $100,000 fee besides. Mitchelson told Felder he wanted to see Merrick privately, to thank him. True to his reputation, the meanest man on Broadway said no.

"Then," Felder went on, "[Mitchelson] wrote Merrick a note, something like, 'You're a very fine man. It was a pleasure to meet you.' Something like that."

Felder took the note into the adjacent room, where Merrick was waiting for all the lawyers' haggling to end. Merrick took one look at the note, mumbled "Ugh!" and flung it back at Felder. "Then Mitchelson called me later to get him tickets [from Merrick] for *42nd Street*."

The next night, Mitchelson had a royal celebration. Sheikha Dena al-Fassi was on one arm; Karen Prunczik was on the other.

Merrick remarried Etan six weeks later. By some accounts, she got back a very difficult husband. In 1989, Merrick was described as saying he wanted to kill Etan.

Mitchelson reveled in the quickies like *Merrick*. They brought him lots of what he liked: publicity and money.

But not all of his cases during the 1980s had such double peaks. In some, he had to settle for either publicity, or money, but not both.

The 1984 case of *Montie vs. Eleanor Montana* fell into the first category. It was tailor made for Marvin's press-agentry.

Montie Montana was a seventy-five-year-old rodeo star. His wife, Ellie, was sixty-five. Montie had ridden in fifty straight Rose Bowl parades, and had appeared in cowboy movies with the likes of John

Wayne, Roy Rogers and Dale Evans, Jimmy Stewart, and Gene Autry. He even lassoed President Dwight Eisenhower during Ike's 1953 inaugural parade.

Ellie and Montie had been married twelve years, but just one day after Montie kissed his wife good-bye and sent her off on a vacation, he filed for divorce. "I know a lot about horses and ropes," Montie said, "but very little about women." Nevertheless, his wife accused him of running away with a thirty-six year old.

Montie had a reputed $5 million fortune, and Ellie wanted half of it. But what they *really* argued about was Montie's prize horse, Larry.

"Don't mess with my hat, my horse, or my wife, in that order," Montie drawled.

Ellie Montana ran to Marvin Mitchelson. He asked for a $10,000, cash retainer, so she borrowed the money from a friend and returned with three cashier's checks.

I said I wanted *cash!* Mitchelson told her.

She returned with the money stuffed into a brown manila envelope and gave it to the receptionist.

When Marvin announced to the media that he had the case, Montie was unmoved. "Her attorney wants a lot of publicity, you know? I hear that he's one of those palimony attorneys. Well, you know what a palimony is? A cross between a palomino horse and a pony, as far as I know."

This was Marvin's kind of case. Who could resist the story about a couple trying to negotiate joint custody of a *horse*? And who could resist the awful puns: Montie was horsing around; Ellie was getting the short straw; the couple was locking horns; and so on, *ad nauseam*. Mitchelson got up before dawn and appeared on a New York radio talk show to get his licks in. "I even offered to the court if they would like to take a look at Larry and see which one he prefers," Mitchelson reported cheerfully. "Like a dog might run and come jump on your lap."

"What's the judge's name?' the interviewer asked Mitchelson.

"I think it will probably be a man named Judge Rudder—but I hope he *steers* it the right way!" The case was settled for $137,000, a silver saddle, and a car.

Mitchelson wasn't always a blabbermouth to the media. He could keep a secret when he absolutely had to, because sometimes the promised absence of his brand of hurtful publicity was worth a small fortune to the other side. He was quite happy in those situations to settle instead for the long green.

These were what he called his "quiet settlements," the situations where everyone got what he wanted and no one was soiled with unsavory press coverage.

Yes, stealth settlements were a Mitchelson specialty, too.

As one of Wall Street's savviest corporate raiders, Ronald O. Perelman was also practiced in secrecy. Gambling billions of dollars on a big takeover, Perelman kept his investment plans quiet until he was ready to spring. Then he went right for the corporate heart. Even when his prey escaped, he usually profited. Such was the business of greenmail.

Perelman was one of the richest men in the United States, if not *the* richest, with an estimated worth of $2.9 billion. He owned a slew of household-name companies, from Revlon, Inc., to Marvel Comics, and he and his second wife, TV gossip reporter Claudia Cohen, were fixtures on the New York social scene.

But the story of Ronald Perelman was not all glitter and glitz, for he had crossed paths with Marvin Mitchelson, too.

Perelman was just a thirty-two-year-old employee of his father's Philadelphia manufacturing conglomerate when he first met a vivacious woman named Susan Kasen. He, his wife, Faith, and their four children aged two to seven were vacationing in Barbados. So were Susan Kasen and her family. Within eight months, they were carrying on a torrid affair.

"She was my girlfriend," Perelman bluntly recalled in a deposition after their relationship had soured. "She and I had an illicit relationship during the time of my marriage." But under absolutely no circumstances did he want his wife to find out.

The corporate raider went to extreme, sometimes even comical, lengths to keep his affair a secret from Faith. He used an alias, "Raymond Parson," to buy jewelry for his lover from Bulgari, even though when the bill came he paid it out of his and his wife's joint bank account. New York's most exclusive jeweler invoiced him, using his alias, at an address outside Philadelphia, instructing Perelman to make his check out to a subsidiary called "Danaos, Ltd." The folks at Bulgari were so anxious not to foul things up for their excellent customer that they stupidly listed Perelman's alias right alongside his real name at the top of his ledger sheet, noting: "Buys for girlfriend."

Kasen's relationship with Perelman would later give rise to several lawsuits, including one between Kasen and her former friend, the psychiatrist and author of best-selling diet books, Stuart M. Berger. In that lawsuit, Berger alleged in an affidavit that Kasen was having an affair with another married executive at the same time as her affair with Perelman.

"She was not only torn by the conflicting desires and demands of [the other married man] and Mr. Perelman for her time and affection, but by her own uncertainty as to her true feelings regarding her lovers," Berger related.

"Ms. Kasen did not have much time for uncertainty, however, because it became readily apparent that the desires of Mr. Perelman could not be easily thwarted."

Kasen replied with her own affidavit, calling Berger's affidavit "completely unfounded, scurrilous, and perjurious."

In any case, Berger's description of Perelman's feelings for Kasen were not off the mark. Perelman conceded as much in his own testimony in another case. "I wanted a continuation of the relationship as it then existed, and one of the threats was that it would end and I wanted it to continue."

He was insistent—according to Kasen's testimony, so insistent that she was terrorized by his violent temper. "I was beaten by Ronald Perelman and we have pictures to show it." She described a familiar cycle of anger and reconciliation, in which she sought restraining orders against Perelman, only to make up with him.

This was where Mitchelson came in.

In May of 1982, in the midst of all this extramarital craziness, Kasen telephoned Mitchelson and asked him to get a restraining order protecting her from Perelman. She wanted Mitchelson to come to New York because she knew Roy Cohn handled Perelman's private legal affairs "and I wanted someone equally as strong."

What quickly eventuated, once Mitchelson and Cohn got together, was an agreement that guaranteed Kasen millions of dollars for what Perelman later said were basically sexual services.

Mitchelson's preferred Manhattan hotel back then was the Mayfair Regent, and he and Kasen conducted their negotiations from a suite there. Cohn and Perelman were nearby, at Cohn's townhouse, but as work on the agreement continued Perelman took a room at the Mayfair Regent, too, and urged Cohn to let him make his deal directly with Mitchelson.

"He's a big talker," Mitchelson recalled. "He kept calling, *begging* to see Kasen, so he could arrange the settlement directly with her. Perelman was going *crazy!* Finally, Susan said okay."

Mitchelson exploded. If Perelman were this desperate to see his lover, denying him would bring the negotiations to a conclusion that much faster. "I said *don't* see him! We'd been going back and forth on this thing for days. What really got it settled quick was that he wanted to see her. We drew the whole goddamned thing up in one day," on Friday, May 14, 1982. "Nothing stopped it!"

The agreement was couched in precise legal terms, although Perelman later claimed both Cohn and Mitchelson had said the document was unenforceable. It spoke transparently of the "business relationship" between the two—she owned a little florist shop in Manhattan that sold flowers to Perelman's company. In consideration of that business relationship, Perelman promised to:

—give Kasen $1 million, tax free;

—take out a $1 million insurance policy, with Kasen as the bene-
ficiary;

—buy her a $500,000 apartment of her choice in Manhattan;

—pay off her Mercedes;

—give her a $5,000-a-month tax-free allowance;

—pay her $50,000, tax-free, on May 15 of every year; and

—pay Mitchelson's attorney's fees of $75,000.

"Big case! Big case!" Mitchelson exulted. "And a real good settlement!"

Perelman covered his tracks. So that the money couldn't be traced
back to him, he had his friend and business partner, lawyer Bruce
Slovin, pay Kasen the first $200,000. Berger, the psychiatrist, acted as
an intermediary, picking up the check from Slovin at the Harvard Club
in New York City. A second $300,000 check to Kasen came from
Cohn's law firm. Proceeds of the million-dollar insurance policy were
payable to Kasen through a trust, "so her name did not appear on the
policy," Perelman explained.

But Perelman's personal life was falling apart. His wife, Faith, found
out about his affair with Kasen and hired a team of private investigators
to shadow them, even to France. The private eyes amassed photographs
and evidence for the looming divorce.

Even then, Kasen was trying to break things off with Perelman, too.
One Friday afternoon late in 1982, Faith's investigators secretly watched
as Perelman confronted Kasen in her car outside her florist shop on
East 65th Street. Trying to get her Mercedes door open, Perelman stuck
his hands through the slightly rolled-down car window and shook it so
violently that the window pane snapped off and he fell to the ground.
A crowd had gathered, and one passerby, apparently thinking Kasen was
being attacked, jumped on top of Perelman and attempted to physically
restrain him. Only then did Kasen open the car door, running to Perelman's side and picking pieces of broken glass off of him.

Soon, Ronald and Faith Perelman were divorced. Not much later,
Kasen and Perelman were squabbling again, too. She finally had broken
off their relationship, and now Perelman was refusing to pay her the
rest of the money called for in their agreement.

The scandal spilled into the courts, although nobody ever heard
much about it because Roy Cohn got a court order keeping everything
out of the public record. In a $30 million lawsuit that vividly painted
a picture of Perelman as a woman-beating, abusive tyrant, Kasen demanded the rest of her money, and alleged that Perelman had been
concealing from her the fact that he had venereal herpes disease
throughout virtually the entire course of their relationship. According
to charges levelled by Roy Cohn in another lawsuit, her process server
even emulated Mitchelson's old tactics: Upon being denied entry to Per-

elman's office, the belligerent server loudly threatened to plaster the lawsuit's allegations on signs all over the city.

Cohn claimed Kasen was blackmailing his client. He filed a lawsuit for Perelman declaring the agreement unenforceable and demanding back all the money Kasen had already been paid.

Mitchelson was out of the case by then. But he was getting his legal fee from Perelman in annual installments, and when the next one didn't arrive he found out why.

Cohn and Mitchelson had both countersigned the original document. Now, Cohn was disavowing the whole thing, claiming in a sworn affidavit that the agreement's allusions to the couple's business relationship was just a bunch of lies cooked up to keep their sexual relationship a secret.

"I heard he reneged and I was absolutely astounded!" Mitchelson recalled. "I mean, Roy was the lawyer who helped draft that agreement. It was a classic conflict."

The whole mess was finally settled—secretly, of course—in the summer of 1984, and Marvin eventually got the rest of his money. Kasen didn't do too badly either, picking up cash and property that Mitchelson said was worth at least $2 million, and maybe much more. But she didn't want to talk about it. "What was, was," she said. But "what was" certainly opened up a new opportunity for "what is." The amount she got from Perelman enabled her to close up her shop and pursue things that were much more interesting than flower arranging. Kasen became an avid art collector—she called her pieces "fabulous" and employed a curator and an assistant. She and her new husband, the record executive Robert Summer, had homes in the city and the country, and they traveled all the time.

"I *adore* Marvin," she cooed. "We have a close personal relationship."

For all Cohn's brazen duplicity in the Perelman case, he was rewarded with Mitchelson's continued respect after it was all over: "'God,' I said to myself, 'has Roy got *balls.*'"

The next time Mitchelson saw Ronald Perelman, it was at the 1987 opening-night Broadway performance of one of Marvin's favorite shows, *The Phantom of the Opera*. Perelman was sitting directly behind him, with his second wife; Mitchelson's date was an attractive woman twenty years his junior, Kathleen Markey Perdue.

Her former husband, chicken rancher Frank Perdue, was sixty-four years old when they married in 1985; Kathleen Markey was a mere thirty-seven then. They stayed married three months shy of two years, and Kathleen Perdue walked away with at least $2 million. If the match between the king of poultry and the attractive stockbroker from Salomon Brothers didn't seem to make sense, maybe what was needed was the perspective of Mitchelson's friend, Martha Smilgis, to see that things didn't turn out too badly for Kathleen.

"[Marvin, Kathleen Perdue, Sy Presten, and I] all had breakfast or lunch at the Regency one day, [just as Marvin was] finishing up the touches on her divorce [in 1987]. Kathleen was pretty in that wholesome way. She was not a sexy knockout at all. Wholesomely pretty. Truly wholesome. Naturally blond hair, blue eyes. Not a lot of makeup. Extremely well dressed. . . . Also quite pleasant. Reserved. I liked her.

"I remember asking Marvin how much she got, and he said $2 million. I thought, Wow! Where do I meet this man? . . . I remember tabulating in my mind how much it came to a month. I was thinking to myself: This isn't bad!"

The story was that Frank Perdue had chased Kathleen Markey. But before Kathleen became wife number two, she signed a prenuptial agreement, which Marvin had to get around in order to get an acceptable settlement for Kathleen. Everything was handled very quietly. Mitchelson's name never appeared in the divorce record, and only the barest account of the proceedings could be found in the rural Maryland courthouse where the divorce was filed.

Mitchelson didn't do badly, either. He received $200,000 as his fee.

Frank Perdue was already aware of Mitchelson's winning ways by then. Before he married Kathleen Markey, the chicken man had broken up with a young woman from Dallas—and *she* had hired Mitchelson. Mitchelson told a story of how he flew to Dallas and had a talk with Perdue's lawyers. He explained how his quiet settlements worked. Without filing a single piece of paper, he soon got a $400,000 settlement for the woman, and $100,000 as his fee. Frank Perdue apparently liked the idea of a quiet settlement, too. "Guys like Perdue," Mitchelson explained, "when they settle a case, part of the settlement is, you're not to talk about it."

Dallas had been good to Marvin. In 1983, he worked the same kind of deal with Clint Murchison, the wealthy owner of the Dallas Cowboys football team. Mitchelson was hired by Murchison's mistress. Clint didn't want his wife to know about her, so all Mitchelson had to do for his $150,000 fee was show up at the door and solemnly announce: "We've got a problem." Well, Murchison sure did. Without so much as one piece of paper touching the public record, he paid his mistress off, and Marvin, too. Murchison used his best friend as a conduit for the settlement so as not to arouse suspicion.

Marvin veritably gushed with pleasure when he spoke about the Joan Collins-Peter Holm divorce. The publicity he got rivaled that of *Marvin*, and he envisioned it as a script right out of "L.A. Law."

As divorce cases went, the Collins-Holm imbroglio actually was small time. It was really just about the validity of a prenuptial agreement limiting Holm to 20 percent of Collins's earnings during their thirteen months together. Either the agreement was valid, or it wasn't. Once that issue was decided, the rest of their divorce case would turn into elementary arithmetic.

In other words, Holm was surely going to get something in the way of a settlement from his wife; the only question was how much. His lawyer, Frank Steinschriber, didn't even think it would matter much whether the prenup, as the lawyers called them, was valid or not, because he figured 20 percent of Collins's $5 million in *gross earnings* during the thirteen months the couple was married would just about equal the 50 percent of *net assets* that Holm would otherwise be entitled to under a community-property split.

Mitchelson's fee from the actress reflected the ordinariness of the dispute. All he got was a paltry $15,000 retainer, and all he received for seeing Collins's case through the rest of the way was another $35,000—a fraction of what the Ladies' Man in 1987 could have gotten from any number of his anonymous clients. But the publicity and the attention were something else. They were what Marvin lived for.

As he had once reminded Vicki Morgan, the press has a way of sometimes missing the real story—particularly when the real story gets in the way of a good one. Peter Holm's lawyer saw that, too. "You have to *understand*," he said, "it's a theatrical performance by *all* the parties."

Holm certainly knew something about drama. He once picketed outside Collins's Beverly Hills home. He also barricaded himself inside another house they once shared and reportedly threatened to shoot anyone who tried to make him leave. Still holed up, he invited twenty reporters inside the nearly empty house, served them hors d'oeuvres, and advised them: "If you want to see a gun battle, stay."

Thus did a routine Hollywood break-up between the actress and a Swedish used-to-be singer become the World Series of Splitsville.

Thus was a routine hearing on the prenuptial agreement transmogrified into what the world saw as a major trial.

Mitchelson's star witness at that July 23, 1987, hearing was someone whose testimony never even made it into the hearing record. She called herself Holm's "passion flower," and Mitchelson's calling to the stand the twenty-three-year-old bronzed bombshell who claimed she was Holm's extracurricular lover was either a stroke of genius or the cheapest of cheap tricks. Or maybe it was both.

"Peter Holm was a fool," Mitchelson later said. He didn't comment on the bona fides of his own surprise witness. Romina Danielson dressed in skintight clothes, lustily admitted to having sex with Holm before and after his marriage to Collins (and while twenty-three-year-old Romina herself was married to an eighty-year-old millionaire, Axel Danielson), and was possessed of a driving ambition to be famous. After the second day of what was to have been a two-day hearing, the dark-haired, Italian-born Romina met Mitchelson at the Beverly Hills Hotel and volunteered to take the stand the following day. "She was looking for a little publicity . . . in terms of her acting career." Marvin, of course, was only too happy to oblige.

Joan Collins walked into court the day of Romina's testimony trailing a gaggle of photographers, reporters, and her own bodyguards, and flashing two upraised fingers, in a Churchillian "V" for what was about to take place.

Mitchelson later talked about the events with Corbin Bernsen, the actor who portrayed Arnie Becker on "L.A. Law," for an article in *Rolling Stone.* "After lunch, Holm is almost off the stand," Mitchelson explained, "and I said, 'Do you know Romina Danielson?' I got a yes. 'How long ago did you meet her?' Then I said, 'I suggest that you went to [the Danielson house on] Mulholland Drive,' and I laid out the entire affair, step by step. 'You went to your friend's house in Santa Monica, and you stayed there.' 'No, that's a lie, sir. That's preposterous.' I said, 'I suggest that you then told her that you would marry her and she should have your baby, right? And that you would leave Joan as soon as you could get enough money out of her.' 'Absolutely false!' He's screaming, turning crimson, going crazy.

"So finally I called her up and asked her the very same questions I'd asked him. She described how he called her his passion flower. I asked why he called her his passion flower, and she said it was like pulling one of those flowers out of the ground that open up and become purple and reddish and bluish—incredible detail. . . . She's trembling, I looked down to see if I had the last question, I look up, and she's not on the stand. She had fainted!"

The scene was a classic. Romina swooned melodramatically, gasped for air, and the zipper fell down her skintight bodice. A *very* healthy Romina bared her breasts, and fainted away.

"People are going mad. Reporters are running around. It was the most dramatic scene I have ever seen. . . . She wasn't very well the next morning. The judge struck all her testimony, but the impression lingered. I think we would have won the case without her. But for three days, the Collins thing—I could never have written a script like that. Everything combined was just like ['L.A. Law']. You couldn't duplicate it. It all worked." The next morning, all the newspapers carried a photograph of Mitchelson hovering over a supine Romina, his eyes fixed on her ample bosom.

Marvin's unlikely adversary in the Collins-Holm case was the proprietor of a Sherman Oaks do-it-yourself legal workshop. Holm liked being his own lawyer, and that's what Frank Steinschriber's firm was all about. In fact, it was Holm's penchant for doing his own legal drafting, long before he ever met Steinschriber, that caused the judge to enforce the prenuptial contract.

"Normally," Steinschriber explained, "it would have been void, because it was too vague, they had no counsel, and it just didn't meet all the requirements of California law. But the judge said that since Peter wrote it up, he would be bound by it."

Even though the prenuptial agreement was valid, Holm still got about $1 million from Collins. That came to a little more than $2,500 a day for the thirteen-month outing. Steinschriber ended up getting more in attorney's fees than Mitchelson did.

"That was their 'big victory,'" Steinschriber said derisively. "Who cares?"

Petro-mony divorce cases kept tumbling into the Mitchelson office like so many dominos: The fabulous *Marvin* publicity brought him *Khashoggi*, *Khashoggi* led to *Fassi*, and *Fassi* begat still others.

There was the case of *Edith al-Midani vs. Mouaffack al-Midani*. The secretive Mouaffack was a native of Syria who owned electric and telephone companies in Saudi Arabia; Edith was his Christian wife from Lebanon. The two led a very Khashoggi-ish life, owning, as they did, three jets, a yacht, at least ten hotels, and twenty houses around the world.

Mouaffack also cultivated friends in high places. He bought a sprawling Beverly Hills estate and used it, among other things, to throw a soirée for Nancy and Ronald Reagan when they returned to California from the White House.

Eventually, however, the marriage deteriorated and Edith sued her husband for divorce in California. Mouaffack al-Midani's extensive holdings were hidden under an umbrella of offshore companies and scattered all over the world. So Edith enlisted her brother, Hassan Saade, and a friend of his, California lawyer Evelyn Gruen, to find the companies and document their ties to Midani. According to Saade, the process took years, cost over $20,000 in photocopying fees alone, and required his going through records written variously in French, Arabic, and English.

Hassan Saade said that Edith al-Midani told him her divorce case would be a business proposition: If Hassan could help her get some of Mouaffack's estimated billions in assets, she'd compensate him for his efforts.

By 1986, lawyer Gruen figured she was going to need a big gun for Edith's looming divorce trial, so she left a message for Mitchelson saying she "wanted to discuss a case similar to the Khashoggi matter." That was enough to pique Marvin's interest; he called right back and ultimately signed on to the case. Mitchelson and Gruen would share a 10 percent contingency on the Midani case.

But the prospect of big money sometimes has a way of changing one's perspective, and that is what happened in the case of *Midani vs. Midani*. Family members went at each others' throats. So did lawyers.

Edith al-Midani was awarded an interim $5.5 million judgment against her husband on May 8, 1987. But, according to a lawsuit later filed against his sister by Hassan Saade, Edith paid him $50,000 and then reneged on her commitment to pay him any more.

Mitchelson, meanwhile, had ridden off the reservation, too. On May 15, a week after his and Gruen's client was awarded the $5.5 million interim judgment, he visited City National Bank in Beverly Hills and picked up two checks that were made out to him and Edith al-Midani. Edith signed a $450,000 check over to him (the balance of his and Gruen's 10 percent contingency, minus a $100,000 retainer she previously paid), and he signed a $5,050,000 check over to her. Although he and Gruen had signed their own agreement to split the Midani fees right down the middle, Gruen asserted that Mitchelson never said a word to her about what he *really* intended to do, which, she contended, was to take the entire Midani fee for himself.*

"This was a case of, 'Go screw yourself,'" Gruen muttered. Unsuccessfully seeking an injunction against Mitchelson's spending what she said was her half of the $450,000, she filed a declaration recounting Mitchelson's embarrassing financial situation: "no less than $539,091.35 of state and federal tax liens [and] a plethora of pending litigation [against Mitchelson] . . . the outcome of which no one can predict."

The Midani divorce was terminated by a settlement in 1988, and the record was sealed by a court order. But the lawsuit filed against Edith by her brother, Hassan, intimated that her divorce settlement with Mouaffack was in excess of $20 million. That amount might be a pittance to one of the richest men in the world, but even a 10 percent contingency represented a nice piece of change for Mitchelson.

After paying off the other lawyers around the world who helped him, as well as taking reimbursement for his expenses, Mitchelson would have banked somewhere around $900,000 for his efforts. It was a good thing, too, because by now he had another creditor on his back, and this one wasn't nearly so patient as the IRS.

---

*Mitchelson claimed the $450,000 was needed for expenses, although Gruen argued that his claim was contradicted by his depositing the money in his own general working account rather than in a trust account. Mitchelson subsequently accused Gruen of bad faith, too, claiming she had billed his client separately, thereby pocketing $110,000 "behind everyone's back." He also asserted Midani wanted Mitchelson rather than Gruen as her lead divorce lawyer in the first place. In any event, Gruen never got paid and she was soon off the Midani case altogether.

PART FIVE
A Good Luck Charm

25

Marvin Mitchelson called Nina Iliescu his good luck charm. Nina did the things Marcella didn't, or wouldn't. She chauffeured him to the courthouse in his Rolls, and sat in the courtroom audience to cheer her hero. "She practices witchcraft," Mitchelson once confided to Evelyn Gruen with absolute seriousness. "When I bring her to the courtroom, I have good luck. Things go my way. She casts spells for me."

The two met around 1970. They had the occasional good time together during the 1970s, but for years their relationship was just casual, nothing heavy. Then, in 1983, as Nina later told it, she became deeply involved with Mitchelson as he was helping her to file in Reno what turned out to be an unsuccessful palimony suit against a man she had lived with. (The court dismissed it.) Nina would later say in court papers that she quit her job at Marvin's insistence and started relying on him for the money she needed. She did this, she told a female acquaintance, because "every single, solitary second he would want me around—if not up at the office [then] wait[ing] across the street."

By 1987, Nina was a well-kept fifty-one year old, a platinum-blond beauty with an unlined face and a great figure. "An aging nymphette," Gruen called her with at least as much envy as disdain, "with obvious health in the boob department. She'd wear clingy sweaters, and a woman of her age and build—she was no more than five-feet-two, just a little slip of a thing—should have succumbed to the forces of gravity." Nina also favored lots of showy jewelry, and there was still the trace of a drawl from her native Texas.

Because of the Midani case, Mitchelson made more than his usual quota of trips abroad in 1986 and early 1987. He sometimes invited attractive younger women to join him on European jaunts. By his own reckoning, Mitchelson had been to Paris more than a hundred times. Cathy Mann had been a regular companion of his during the 1970s, of course, but the list of Marvin's consorts was quite eclectic. For one trip to Paris, in the mid-1970s, he invited a young woman who worked part-time for a catering company. Marvin was still on an art-buying binge then, and he told her he wanted her to be his assistant. But soon after she arrived there, the girl fled Paris and flew back to Los Angeles, telling friends a story of how she opened her suitcase and found cocaine rolled up in her underpants. Mitchelson called her a liar and said he sent her home when he learned she had previously tried to kill herself. "She's a wrist slitter," he claimed.

In early April of 1987, Marvin found something in Europe worth taking his good luck charm to. Mitchelson and Nina traveled to the auction of a lifetime.

Sotheby's auction of the Duchess of Windsor jewels took place in a lakefront tent at the Hotel Beau-Rivage in Geneva, on the first Thursday and Friday nights in April. For a romantic like Marvin, the event's lure was irresistible. The Duke and Duchess of Windsor, after all, starred in the love story of the century. It was fitting that this lawyer, having made his fortune on the failed loves of the rich, would be in on the kill when the Duchess's jewels went under the hammer.

It was an auction under the big top, attended by the Sultan of Brunei and Prince Bernhard of the Netherlands and one thousand of the richest invitees in the world. This was where Marvin Mitchelson sought the ultimate validation of his glory. This jewel auction to end all others would begin as a personal celebration of his fame, money, and place in the world. But it would end as an affirmation of just how small and vulnerable he really was.

There would come a time when Mitchelson, quite literally, would profess to be unable to account for Nina Iliescu's presence at the auction, even when confronted with a picture from the auction of an adoring Nina, Marvin at her side, admiring a photograph of the huge diamond, amethyst, and turquoise bib necklace that the auction's official chronicle said he bought *for her*. He had dropped $584,522 on the Cartier bib necklace and $358,255 on a huge Cartier sapphire-and-diamond pendant.

It was comical, the way he feinted and bobbed and weaved as he tried later to evade the questions about his and Nina's attendance at the Sotheby's auction. "I wouldn't know where she is," Mitchelson said, even when faced with the photographic evidence that so obviously showed him and Nina together. "[I wouldn't know] how to find her. Or anything. I haven't been in touch with her for a long time. Incidentally, if you got in touch with her, I think you'd find it very boring, other than the fact that she went to an auction and saw me bid on some jewelry. It isn't one of the better Marvin Mitchelson stories."

Maybe she was bad luck, Marvin's interlocutor suggested. Delicious irony, since Nina was supposed to be his talisman.

"Bad luck was Marvin Mitchelson buying them. One of my mistakes."

Even his detractors had to cut him a little slack over his reluctance to tell the whole truth about his guest at the auction. Although he did not say so, Mitchelson surely surmised, by then, that Nina Iliescu was much more than his mistress. And the realization of her disloyalty must have torn at him.

Linda Acaldo knew Nina by the code name "Cathy."

Internal Revenue Service criminal investigators knew her as their controlled informant.

The Los Angeles Police Department and the State Bar of California also learned all about Nina Iliescu in the course of their own investigation into Marvin's extraordinary career.

Nina was popular, all right. With her consent, the feds had bugged her telephone and also given her a super-sensitive, tiny hidden microphone to secretly record meetings with her paramour. Once, in May of 1989, Acaldo, cooperating with the LAPD and protected by plainclothes sharpshooters, agreed to wear a body wire, a hidden microphone taped to her chest, to meet an anonymous caller who wanted to give up some information about Mitchelson. Elaborate precautions were taken for what turned into a bizarre case: Deputy District Attorney Acaldo's secret caller was none other than Nina Iliescu.

When he was still on top, Marvin used to laugh about how his mistress had filed her first palimony suit fifteen years too late. That was true. But late in 1990, she drew up and filed (but did not serve) another palimony suit—against him. By the time Mitchelson suspected that his mistress had turned against him—well, by then, it was too late to stop her.

Because the Sotheby's auction was for charity, bidders got caught up in the erotic intensity of their own exquisite moment as well as in the excitement of doing something noble for the Pasteur Institute. The leading French medical institution involved in finding a cure for AIDS was the beneficiary of the charity auction. Sotheby's pre-sale estimate for all 306 lots had been $7 million, but ordinary rules obviously didn't apply where the Duchess and her charity were concerned. The jewels fetched $45 million.

Mitchelson bid with customary brio, but since he had no idea what the exchange rate for Swiss francs was, he ended up bidding an unintended fortune. Nina said her man didn't even *know* he had been the successful bidder on the lesser of the two jewels, although he turned his ignorance into a nice recovery by tantalizing the press with hints that he bought the pendant for Joan Collins. Mitchelson didn't dare reveal the truth: that her $50,000 fee to him was peanuts when compared to what he'd paid for the Cartier piece.

That was bad enough, but when Marvin looked back on the folly of what he'd done, he literally concluded that a *sinister force* had urged him to raise his hand. Unbelievable as his excuse was, he favored it over temporary insanity, which was the only other plea he could offer for having bid nearly one million dollars for two treasures that he couldn't possibly pay for.

Mitchelson rationalized his behavior. Long after the auction had ended, he still told of how it wasn't really him, but someone else, *another Marvin*, who was the bad boy that day.

"That was *another* Marvin Mitchelson [bidding for the jewels]. Marvin's sitting there, raising his hand, trying to outbid someone! Counting what he thinks he's going to make next week!" Mitchelson roared with laughter as he continued. "I was competing against someone else! Another guy. Absolutely! I wish I could get that guy! I'd make him pay! If I did, I'd send him the bill! I was going to go to twenty-eight thousand dollars—and I went up to nine-hundred grand! I said, 'Shit, I'll fight that guy.' It's auction fever!"

Without realizing it, Mitchelson's rationalizations of his own conduct at the auction were strikingly similar to insights he gave into the criminal minds of others he once represented.

"There's tremendous self-denial with criminals," he explained. "They're very compartmentalized. And, generally speaking, they have this tendency to look at the part of their personality that did these things as though they're some other person.

"And that's how they think. 'It really isn't me. It's someone [else] out there. I know what he did. But I've separated myself from it.' They rationalize their innocence, their culpability, their degree of guilt.

"I used to like to talk to these people; really fascinating to deal with them and talk with them."

During the auction, he sent a note to the debonair auctioneer, Nicholas Rayner—a man called the Cary Grant of the auction world—asking him to announce that Marvin had purchased the amethyst-and-turquoise necklace in his mother's honor. The necklace soon possessed a checkered history. It had been bought in honor of his mother, admired by his mistress, and worn by Marcella as she posed for *People* sitting directly beneath an almost life-sized portrait of her dead mother-in-law!

"I said, 'I bought it for my mother!'" Mitchelson cried out. "My mother would *kill* me! Skin me alive!"

Mitchelson picked up the jewels he'd just bought and talked his way out of the Sotheby's tent without paying. He returned to Nina's and his hotel room at the Beau-Rivage and cackled at his bravado. When they flew back to the States a few days later, Nina told investigators, Mitchelson shoved the jewels into his pants and casually strolled through Customs without declaring them.

Walking around the downtown Los Angeles courthouse a short while after that, he opened his briefcase and showed the jewels to an astounded Gruen. Although carrying around a million dollars' worth of rocks, he continued to brazenly play the role of the good son honoring his mother.

"My mother, God bless her, never wanted me to spend any money on anything that wasn't necessary," Mitchelson solemnly explained. He was at his cloying best. "I know that her favorite color was amethyst. There was a necklace that the sheikha had in our sheikh [Fassi] case, and I received it as part of our initial fee. And my mother said, 'If you ever buy me anything, Sonny, buy me something with that color.' That's all she ever said! And, you know, I saw this necklace and I got very, very excited about it. And I got to thinking about her. I did a lot of rationalization, to be honest.

"But at the time that I did bid on it, things were looking very, very good for me. I had the al-Midani case, and really I thought it would be settled within days of that. I thought it'd be several million dollars, the biggest fee I ever had. And then I had the judgment on the al-Fassi case. As it happened, we'd been negotiating for some time, ever since we got that big judgment, about what it would take [to settle the case]. We had what I thought was a serious negotiation. And we were to meet in Geneva with the other side on the very day I bought the jewels. There were indications that, while we'd be knocking a lot off of the judgment, they were still going to give me several million dollars. Right now, to satisfy the judgment, the attorney's fees would be about twenty-six million dollars.

"So I was very optimistic about both those things. And, when you're optimistic, discretion is not the better part of valor. I just felt I was riding some million dollar fees, and I found myself raising my hand."

But Sotheby's didn't intend to wait forever for its money. Polite inquiries about payment soon gave way to lawyerly insistence. Watching Mitchelson wiggle and squirm while Sotheby's tried to be paid was akin to observing a resourceful fox being chased by a pack of bloodhounds. Mitchelson considered himself the courthouse's fastest thinker on his feet—"fleetingly fast!"—and he gave a lesson to Sotheby's in the perverse art of outwitting those more honorable than he.

Sotheby's demanded immediate payment; Mitchelson claimed the auctioneers had waived that condition of sale by letting him walk out of the tent with the jewels. Sotheby's sought an assignment of fees from one of his big cases; Mitchelson at first agreed but then disappeared when it came time to sign the required documents. Sotheby's got stipulations of assignments for some of Mitchelson's cases, and still Mitchelson held back. In depositions, he took the Fifth Amendment. Sotheby's demanded the jewels back; he shipped them out of the country. When the U.S. Customs people started poking around, asking why he hadn't declared the jewels, Mitchelson hedged his answers. "I never smuggled anything in my life," he later said. "Never knowingly, anyway."

Marvin seemed to relish the challenge. This was the same old Marvin, living on the edge and daring an adversary to knock him off. "He gets a hard-on, doing things like that," Nina told a friend. "That's what turns him on."

The amazing, if not the brassiest, thing about the Sotheby's affair was that during the more than three years that Mitchelson kept dodging the auctioneers, he earned some of the biggest fees of his career. Any one of them could have paid off the Sotheby's debt in its entirety. One such fee came when the Midani case settled. But he also settled a huge case in Japan, in February of 1989. His client, Joan Shepherd, was a forty-five-year-old expatriate American. She earned one fortune as a singer in Japan and received $40 million more in a divorce settlement negotiated by Mitchelson. She paid him $1.1 million—Mitchelson had first asked for some Hawaii property she owned—but she was so grateful for his good work that she would have paid him $5 million if he'd asked. Mitchelson didn't. Then again, even one million dollars went a lot further for Mitchelson if he didn't have to share it with his many creditors.

Sotheby's finally got a court judgment against its deadbeat client for the full amount he owed. With $173,057 in accumulated interest (mounting at $94,000 a year) as well as over $100,000 in attorneys' fees, the debt to Sotheby's had ballooned to over $1,215,000 by the beginning of 1989. Sotheby's finally located the two pieces at Cartier in London, and had them sold at auction there. But they brought in only $350,000, or slightly more than one third of what Mitchelson bid at the Beau-Rivage auction. Mitchelson had astoundingly overpaid when he bought the jewels. Sotheby's applied its recovery to his debt. It also managed to get, before he could, the $100,000 contingent fee Mitchelson earned as his share of a partial settlement in the highly publicized case of *Marc Christian vs. Rock Hudson.**

Michelson, having grossly overpaid for the jewels, didn't even own them anymore, but he was still stuck with the million-dollar bill. Since he showed no inclination to further pay down his debt, Sotheby's got

---

*Christian was Hudson's alleged homosexual lover, and he sued the actor's estate for his having been exposed to AIDS. As Mitchelson's cocounsel, Rhoden said he did virtually all the work for half the fees in the celebrated case. Knowing Mitchelson's publicity proclivities and fearing a backlash from them, Rhoden banished him from the courtroom for the duration of the six-week trial in 1989. After five years of litigation and a reduced $5.5 million judgment that was still on appeal, Rhoden was, as usual, insolvent. He didn't get to keep his share of the contingent fee he derived from the partial settlement, either. Rhoden's half was split between the IRS and the bank that loaned him his living expenses during the Christian case. Rhoden blamed the Sotheby's mess on the toxic mixture of a publicity-hungry Mitchelson and the world press. "He's going to be hurt for this stupid thing he did," he said with disgust. "The only question is how great the hurt is going to be. But he's got it coming."

a court order on February 16, 1990, allowing its receiver to move right into his offices and start going through his books and records to take any money that could be found.

Mitchelson's entire law practice was to be placed in receivership. A federal judge signed the order at four o'clock on a Friday afternoon. Almost immediately, the federal court receiver, David L. Ray, dispatched uniformed guards to stand an around-the-clock weekend watch outside the 19th floor law office in Century City.

Mitchelson showed up the following morning, a Saturday. What the hell are guards doing here? he demanded to know.

The men told Mitchelson they were there to make sure he took nothing out of his offices. From now on, the federal receiver would even be picking up all of the mail and opening it, to grab any checks that came in.

Mitchelson was incensed, but he also had reason to be worried. Having received, literally, million of dollars in fees during a time he told Sotheby's he could not pay, he couldn't afford to have the receiver gain a true picture of his affairs.

Mitchelson went down to the basement of his building and told one of the parking attendants, in essence: Don't let the guards get anything. The attendant took the order literally. When the federal receiver's guard went down on Monday morning to pick up the mail, all he found was a solitary note in the mailbox. "Dear Mr. Mitchelson," it began. "Your mail is at the parking attendant's counter. Please destroy this message after reading this."

Sotheby's lawyers tried to use the mail-hiding as evidence of bad faith, but any leverage it gave them quickly dried up. Mitchelson soon got the receivership stayed. The guards had to be pulled. By the next day, Mitchelson's secrets were safe again. And Sotheby's *still* couldn't start getting its money until six months later, when all his appeals were finally exhausted. Thereafter, a clerk dutifully appeared in Mitchelson's offices twice a day to open the mail and take any checks that came in. Having been precluded from spending more than $500 on any one expense without Ray's permission, Marvin on at least one occasion was reduced to staying in a suburban Holiday Inn when he traveled.

Sotheby's deserved not to be paid, Marvin intimated, and it sounded like he'd convinced himself he meant it. "They're voracious, greedy people."

26

In the old days, when he was still at the top of his game, Marvin Mitchelson had been able to juggle his different lives effectively enough to keep any unhappy clients, creditors, and regulators at bay.

But by the late 1980s, the cracks in his various public and private façades had deepened to the point that it was no longer possible for him even to maintain appearances. Sotheby's was only one of many burdens.

The drug problem he'd been battling since at least the 1970s became more serious as Mitchelson discovered more potent forms of cocaine. Maybe drug use compounded his other problems, or maybe it was the other way around. But, inevitably, his private battles with drugs, money, women, and unhappy clients gave him unwanted attention. He was hounded by public protectors, from official watchdogs, like the State Bar, to the self-appointed, like CBS's "60 Minutes."

Raoul Felder remembered how, around the time of the *Merrick* case in 1983, one of Mitchelson's cocounsel walked up to him in court and confided that Mitchelson had gone through a detoxification program and was finished with drugs.

"That's how I first found out," Felder explained. "I'm standing next to one of them . . . in court, and I said, 'How's Marvin?' I was just trying to be polite.

"One of them says, 'I can tell you, 'cause you're a friend of Marvin's. He's *finished* with it. He got out of the hospital. He licked it.' I thought he was in the hospital for his *back* or something! The guy told me because he thought I already knew! But that's the first time I knew about the drugs."

In fact, Mitchelson's private demons were as insidious as ever, as the case of Veronica Buss amply proved.

She was the tall, beautiful thirty-five-year-old companion of sports magnate Jerry Buss, the multimillionaire owner of the Los Angeles Lakers, the Kings, and the Forum sports complex. Jerry Buss, then fifty years old and worth an estimated $250 million, prided himself on living the good life of a wealthy Californian. He lived at Pickfair, once the Bel Air mansion of the late film stars Mary Pickford and Douglas Fairbanks; he boasted of dating seventy women regularly, and kept company with a retinue of Playboy bunnies. The statuesque Veronica had been one of them, but whether she and Jerry ever were legally married was in dispute: In the steamy case of *Buss vs. Buss*, each side accused the other of bigamy.

When Veronica moved out of Pickfair in December of 1982, she took only her Rolls-Royce, her 210-pound Great Dane, Lucifer, and "a pair of jeans and a little undershirt. That's it."

Mitchelson pursued his own agenda when Veronica Buss hired him. "Everybody that Marvin knew, that I ever met, had the same feeling—that Marvin, somewhere in his head, thought of himself as this God-like person, sitting on a throne. . . . Marvin was so anxious to publicize this situation," she remarked later. "The sincerity of my heart, my head—he really didn't care where in the hell I was. What he went after was strictly the [Buss] name. He saw his own publicity. Again, Marvin Mitchelson would be [in the] headlines, and be in the news."

Mitchelson's agenda also included acquiring for himself her almost-new Rolls Royce at a distress-sale price. To put some quick money in Veronica's pocket, he offered to buy it for what Buss said was much less than it was worth. Mitchelson would pay her on the installment plan: $1,000 a month, cash. "I needed the money," Veronica recalled. "So I said, Okay. Fine."

Now she had enough money to rent an apartment. But the deal also left her with no way to get to and from her lawyer's office, or anywhere else in far-flung L.A.

"It was just ridiculous!" Veronica recalled. "I was *hitchhiking* to my deposition, which I *had* to do. Back and forth [between Malibu and Century City]. And Hal Rhoden pulled up along side of me one afternoon, after we had been in the deposition, and he said, 'What the hell are you doing?' And I said, 'Hal, I've got to go back to Malibu.' And he said, 'Where's your car?' And I said, 'I sold my car to Marvin.'

"Well, Hal got out of the car and almost threw me, literally, into his car. . . . And when I told him Mitchelson had bought my car, Hal said, 'What?' I mean, I don't think Hal even believed this one. This was kind of a topper with Marvin, even under the circumstances Hal had seen Marvin in, I believe."

Rhoden stormed into Mitchelson's corner office the next morning. "Hal went in there and said, 'Marvin, if you don't give this woman [back] her car. . . I guess he would have taken Marvin to court over it, or something. Which of course Marvin didn't want. And somehow I gave the money back to Marvin. . . . Anyway, I got the car back."

This was around the time of Vicki Morgan's brutal death, and Mitchelson wanted Veronica to be safe. He suggested she move into the Malibu beach house rented by one of his young lawyers, Sharon Thomas.

Not long after that, according to Buss, Mitchelson telephoned her one night when she was alone in the house and told her he needed some papers signed right away. After Mitchelson arrived, she said she witnessed him freebasing cocaine.

Ten years after Acaldo had first seen Mitchelson snort coke, the lawyer had graduated to freebase, which gave a more intense high. Freebasing involved treating cocaine powder with ether and reducing it to a crystalline base, which, when smoked, produced a sharp, pleasurable rush.

Buss said to herself: "This man is my *lawyer*. . . . He was involved in drugs, which no one wants their lawyer to be, any more than you want your doctor, before an operation, to be involved in drugs. . . . Because, anyone on drugs, you're not dealing with a person, you're dealing with a drug-induced situation. And I do believe sincerely that Marvin is not the same man he is when he's on drugs. At least, I pray for his sake he is not."

So, she booted Mitchelson out of the house, and went to bed and cried. "Marvin [was] the man who was supposed to represent me! My God! I was hysterical! I was laying in bed, as a matter of fact, crying, thinking I'd made another wrong decision by hiring this idiot.

"And, about ten minutes later—there was something wrong with the front door of the house, where it really didn't lock—he just walked through the door and came into the house. And, with that, Marvin came back in[to the bedroom], and all of a sudden jumped in my bed. I was wearing, like, a little teddy negligee. The things I sleep in. I was going to bed. I wasn't planning on company.

"He came in and was jumping all around [in bed] and everything. Which, I mean, to my shock, I don't know what the hell he was thinking at the time. And finally I just, we tussled back and forth and then he realized that it was just very serious that he get out of the house, which at that point he did do. Whatever I did, it was definitely to let him know to get the fuck out of the bed. And he got up and [went] out the door." She called him "just an ugly old man. He's not attractive. The thing that he does is, he has people who are vulnerable. You know, I should've just blown his brains all over the ceiling when he did that. But I was just too vulnerable. I couldn't do it. I had my own problems."

Buss told Rhoden about the incident and insisted that Mitchelson have nothing more to do with her case. Marvin stayed away after that, although he nevertheless received the previously agreed-upon contingency when her case settled for what Mitchelson said was "a good deal more than one million dollars." The actual amount of the settlement was sealed. Whatever the amount, it was enough for Veronica to buy some significant chunks of real estate in Los Angeles, Palm Springs, and Arizona, with enough left over for a new Rolls-Royce and a Mercedes-Benz. Mitchelson's fee was at least $120,800, split evenly with Rhoden.

There was one positive development for Mitchelson from the Veronica Buss case, though. When another of Jerry Buss's love interests, a woman who called herself Puppi Buss, filed a palimony suit in 1987 against the sports magnate, it was Marvin who once again was called upon to do the honors.

Among some of the clients Mitchelson became friendly with, his cocaine use was about as much of a secret as his weakness for women.

In 1979, Lydia Criss was the thirty-one-year-old estranged wife of drummer Peter Criss, of the heavy-metal rock group Kiss. Mitchelson was her lawyer, and he relied on all the usual characters—Roy Cohn, publicist Sy Presten, *People* writer Martha Smilgis—to help him orchestrate her settlement. The Criss case was a good window for viewing how Mitchelson worked. Cohn helped by finding another lawyer who could handle part of the case. Smilgis batted out a homer about Lydia's "Million-Dollar Kiss-Off." And Presten, the old-fashioned press agent, arranged for the divorce celebration at Nirvana, where Mitchelson paid for the champagne at $80 a bottle.

"But he sure liked the cocaine," Criss added. "Cocaine and champagne—those were the things that Marvin liked to do. And only the best champagne: Dom Perignon; Tattinger's if he could get it." Lydia said that Mitchelson offered her coke, or asked her for it, just about every time they met.

Mitchelson got Criss a $500,000 settlement, and charged her $75,000 plus $10,000 in expenses—mainly for six nights in a $1,100 suite at the Carlyle Hotel. Later, Lydia filed a malpractice suit against him. The drug allegations were a sexy, but unresolved, part of the litigation, because Mitchelson refused to answer them under oath. Lydia didn't get a dime from him, although she did get a small settlement from another lawyer that Cohn had recommended. Mitchelson gleefully reported how Criss's lawyer later told him: "If I knew you didn't have any insurance, I wouldn't have sued you."

Another prospective client told of how, contemplating divorce in the 1970s, she called Mitchelson. He asked where she lived and when she gave her address, he cheerfully exclaimed, "Oh, my God! We're neighbors!" Mitchelson said he'd be happy to make a house call, and that night he came over and brought cocaine with him. They shared it, and Marvin also drank gin straight from the bottle until he passed out on her sofa. At 6 A.M., she shooed him out of her house: "I've got a daughter. You've got to get out of here!" The prospective client said Marvin told her at the time that he binged on coke for days on end, then crashed and slept.

By 1988, the state and federal investigators who were taking an interest in Mitchelson had heard about his drug problem, too. In March of that year, two investigators for the Los Angeles District Attorney's office interviewed one woman who had been his client in 1981. She told of having been taken by Mitchelson in his Rolls-Royce one evening to a dirty pink stucco house in Hollywood, where a couple in their early-to mid-thirties gave Mitchelson a glass vial of cocaine. Marvin, the woman told the investigators, took the cocaine back to his office, offered her some, snorted it himself, and forced her to have sex on his office floor afterwards. The woman said she felt pressured to give in. She thought that if she didn't, he'd ditch her case. The investigators had heard that from other women, too. But, she continued, at the time of her divorce hearing, Mitchelson nonetheless handed her case over to one of his female associates anyway, telling his client that her judge was a homosexual and that she and the associate were to give the appearance of being lesbians so as to obtain the judge's sympathy. Mitchelson just laughed the whole accusation off: "You deal with a lot of crazies [in the divorce business]!"

LAPD detectives, meanwhile, were following up a similar tip from a woman who wasn't the most reputable witness, but whose story was similar to the others. Nancy Michelle Vincent [name changed] had an extensive criminal record going back to 1976. When the detectives interviewed her, she was doing four years at the California Institute for Women at Frontera for child cruelty and seduction of a female child for purposes of prostitution. Vincent told of how, while operating her "modeling agency" in 1981, she hired Mitchelson to represent her in getting a legal separation from her husband. Marvin wanted his $5,000 fee in cash, and he was anxious enough to get the money that he drove her to her bank himself. On the way there, Vincent told the LAPD detectives, Mitchelson pulled out a vial of coke, offered her some, and snorted some himself. She also described how he suggested that perhaps she might be able to "set him up with a date, with one of the girls from the modeling agency." She never did that.

Even the Internal Revenue Service, whose criminal investigators initially weren't looking for evidence of drug use, couldn't help but run into it. Their undercover informant, Nina Iliescu, said Mitchelson used cocaine and freebase.

The investigators heard many variations on the theme. One of his attractive New York clients told the authorities about how Mitchelson would show up in Manhattan and invite her to go out with him to dinner or to the theater. Mitchelson always promised to discuss her case, she said, but, invariably, that was the one thing he never did. Instead, when they went out, he picked her up in a limousine and then had the driver stop off at an apartment building on the West Side, where Mitchelson got cocaine that he used in the back of the limousine.

Not all of Mitchelson's sources dispensed the drug illegally, though. In Manhattan, he frequently visited a cocaine-prescribing doctor whose office was conveniently situated directly across the street from his favorite hotel, the Regency. Milton Reder was a ninety-year-old Dr. Feelgood who administered as a painkiller what the state director of controlled substances called "a legal hit of cocaine." For $25, Reder dipped cotton swabs in liquid cocaine and shoved them four inches up a patient's nostril, until the swabs pressed against a nerve in the nose. Reder was the state's biggest legal buyer of the drug, and he continued his "treatments" even as state authorities wanted to bring a halt to the practice. Reder was a legal cocaine source to the stars. In addition to Mitchelson, his patients during sixty-eight years in medicine included singer Sonny Bono, comedian David Brenner, and, he claimed, at least one hundred others listed in *Who's Who in America*—from John F. Kennedy to Rudolph Valentino. Reder called his drug "magic." His dark, musty waiting room off Park Avenue made for a surreal scene, with patients sitting quietly on tumble-down furniture, two long swabs hanging out of each nostril.

Mitchelson had been a target of the IRS tax-collectors virtually for two decades. His income tax returns had been audited for the years 1972 through 1979, with resultant back taxes and penalties running into the six figures. But the IRS audits had been sporadic since then, because during the 1980s he sometimes was years late in filing his annual returns. Having once advised a friend that filing a tax return would only give the IRS too much information about the extent of her wealth, he seemed to be taking his own advice. Mitchelson filed his 1982 return years late, for example. He didn't file his 1987 return until early 1990, after becoming the subject of a criminal tax-fraud grand jury investigation. Even then, Mitchelson left unpaid over $250,000 in past-due taxes that his 1987 return said he owed on a gross income of $2.2 million.

It took some time, but Mitchelson's dilatory ways finally caught the eye of the IRS's criminal agents. His file had already been flagged for possible tax-fraud investigation, but the IRS's criminal investigation didn't begin in earnest until Nina Iliescu walked into the Los Angeles field office on January 3, 1989.

The IRS criminal agents were a small, elite unit of the tax agency whose job wasn't so much to collect money as it was to punish tax cheaters. Most of the IRS's 123,000 employees were drones, carrying out the drudgery of examining returns and collecting taxes. Only 4,000 people worked in the Criminal Investigation Division (CID), but they were the highly trained, direct descendants of the agents who, some fifty years before, locked up the nation's number one criminal, Al Capone.

The distinct roles of the civil and criminal sides of the IRS could be illustrated by one simple fact: IRS auditors toted calculators and copies of the revenue code; the agency's criminal agents carried guns and handcuffs.

When the criminal agents went to work on an investigation such as Mitchelson's, they amassed their proof using all the usual tools of a police agency. Sometimes, the agents gathered their evidence through undercover surveillance and, with Department of Justice approval, wiretaps. Always, they subpoenaed bank records and the taxpayer's own records, painstakingly matching every microfilmed bank deposit and check against the income and expenses the taxpayer actually reported.

At an investigation's conclusion, the results of the criminal agents' work were presented to a federal grand jury by a prosecutor, called an assistant United States attorney. The assistant U.S. attorney, an employee of the Justice Department, was responsible for securing the taxpayer's indictment and ultimate conviction. He was the point man in court, but it was the IRS criminal agent who really made the case.

Obtaining a criminal indictment was such a resource-intensive job that only a miniscule number of IRS cases went that way. In 1988, for example, the IRS imposed twenty-three *million* civil penalties against taxpayers, while the number of tax fraud indictments obtained by the Justice Department was one ten-thousandth of that.

But the flip side of that statistic was that, because of its huge investment in every criminal case, the IRS had to choose its targets very carefully. Thus, the criminal agents almost always got their man once they went after him. A criminal tax indictment was about as close to a certain conviction as any indictment could be. To illustrate: During the year 1988, there were 2,769 criminal tax fraud indictments, and 2,491 criminal convictions. A prison term often followed.

Those were the long odds Mitchelson faced.

If some of the criminal agents in the IRS's Los Angeles field office were as rowdy a bunch of urban cowboys as were likely to be found anywhere in any buttoned-down federal agency, that was probably attributable to their city's breezy style.

The L.A. field office was a freewheeling outpost. From 1987 to 1989, it was also the focus of several widely publicized private and congressional investigations of alleged misconduct.

The ambience of the CID's squad room in Woodland Hills said it all. This was the place where agents, armed with automatic weapons, cut the occasional boredom with their own quick-draw contests. Prominently displayed on one desk was this sign: "MY WIFE, YES. MY DOG, MAYBE. BUT MY GUN, NEVER!"

The IRS criminal agents on the Mitchelson case believed that evidence of Mitchelson's cocaine habit could be a significant part of the IRS's case. This was a financial case, true, but knowing what Mitchelson spent on drugs might indicate how much hidden income he had.

They decided to put Mitchelson under occasional surveillance, not only to detect the celebrity lawyer's cocaine sources but also to test Nina's veracity. She had been telling the agents intimate details of her relationship with Marvin. Mindful that she could be lying, the agents wanted to verify that she and Marvin really had a relationship.

On five different nights during the fall of 1989, teams of IRS agents in two unmarked cars—the IRS favored dark blue Fords—trailed Mitchelson from his Century City office building. The agents observed him visiting their informant and going to the homes of known or suspected cocaine dealers.

One of Mitchelson's stops one evening was at the Studio City home of a hairdresser who lived near Nina in a home that had great views of the Valley. He had been arrested in 1982 and 1984 on drug charges, and both times the inventory of drugs he possessed (with the intent to sell them, the charges said) included between $40,000 and $50,000 worth of cocaine. (At the time of his second arrest, the cops reported that he told them: "I've got to make money. . . . I never thought of myself as a criminal just because I sell cocaine.") According to Nina, the hairdresser, although only recently off of probation, still discreetly took care of his favored clients from a stash he kept in a desk at the top of his stairs.

During another surveillance, the agents followed Mitchelson to an apartment building in West Hollywood. Why did he go there? The agents didn't know, so they pressed Nina. She reluctantly identified the building as a place where she had accompanied Mitchelson when he used crack cocaine.

The IRS's surveillance efforts had, indeed, revealed a hidden side of the celebrity lawyer's life. One agent jokingly called the tailing "the most cost-efficient surveillance in the history of the federal government," but the reality was that Mitchelson's habit was probably only costing him about $25,000 a year. That hardly pointed to much hidden income. On the other hand, the agents had a hunch, nothing more, that the hairdresser might know much more about Mitchelson, and that he could be induced to reveal what he knew. Their plan was to have the hairdresser arrested again by the Los Angeles Sheriff's Department for drug dealing, then offer him a deal in exchange for his testimony against Mitchelson.

The key to this plan was Nina. Having been burned once, the hairdresser wouldn't be foolish enough to sell to someone he didn't know, so Nina would have to make some undercover cocaine buys from him. The sheriff's department was willing to set up the drug buys, but Nina wavered. Finally, she said no. Even though she was informing on her paramour, she still had her limits.

But that didn't preclude Nina's concealing a hidden microphone that secretly transmitted her conversations with the man she referred to as "M3." Three times, the agency's wired informant met her lover at favored haunts. But Mitchelson disappointed the agents who sat listening outside. He already knew he was under federal investigation, even if he didn't yet realize his mistress was cooperating. He also knew that the investigation encompassed not only criminal tax violations but also Customs violations. The agents figured he might try to induce Nina to testify falsely, or to interfere with her testimony in some other way. But

Mitchelson was cautious, even with Nina, and his statements were laden with ambiguity.

The taping produced its share of comedy, too. It was outside a Studio City restaurant, for example, that the three agents in an IRS car eavesdropped on what became a triple-X–rated conversation between Mitchelson and his girlfriend. Two agents laughed uproariously as Mitchelson suddenly and, despite Nina's embarrassed protests, persistently began whispering *very* explicit descriptions of some imagined sex acts. As his two compatriots guffawed irreverently, the third agent solemnly said he couldn't believe what he was hearing. "He's a sick man," the stunned agent muttered.

It was hard to reconcile this tortured, scheming, drug-abusing side of Mitchelson with the polished façade that the public saw: that of a skillful lawyer who was always in control, whether in the courtroom or in the media. The truth was, his two worlds *couldn't* be reconciled. Marvin Mitchelson continued to exhibit an amazing talent for walling off his various lives. He demeaned the complainants against him as "twenty-five disgruntled clients out of five thousand." Even as his world crumbled, he continued to attract his quota of celebrity clients.

In court, on a familiar stage and playing his familiar role, Mitchelson still could be every inch the tireless, resourceful advocate he was in *Douglas* nearly thirty years before. In the midst of this crisis, he did what he had always done best, and what had gotten him this far.

What he couldn't do, though, was to turn down the crescendo of complaints that kept coming into the State Bar of California from the ordinary clients who felt they'd been cheated or otherwise harmed by him.

27

Marvin Mitchelson couldn't possibly have seen the trouble ahead when he first met the woman who called herself Kristen Barrett-Whitney. With a kittenish voice that betokened vulnerability, over the telephone she might have sounded just like a person he would love to meet.

Things are often not as they seem, and that was particularly true in Barrett-Whitney's case. She was an overweight woman, thirty-five years old, who lived on Social Security and Medicare payments because of disabling multiple sclerosis.

Barrett-Whitney was also a woman who used a number of

names—living in Chicago, she once called herself Barbara Anderene Burke; her cleaning lady also knew her as Stephanie Spaulding and Allison Hamilton; and Mitchelson eventually cataloged twelve aliases for her, including Barbara Gryka and Joyanna. Later, Mitchelson would call her "an experienced extortionist, a conniving con artist, a psychopathic liar and a highly sophisticated professional plaintiff" who used lawsuits to blackmail wealthy professionals. Mitchelson had been hired to file a palimony suit for her. To hear him tell it, he became one of her victims. Barrett-Whitney, of course, told a far different story.

Barrett-Whitney was not new to the Los Angeles District Attorney's office. In 1985, she went to them and revealed the criminal past of a former boyfriend.

Actually, whether Chase Revel was *really* Barrett-Whitney's former boyfriend was one of many facts in dispute about their relationship. She said he abused her. Revel insisted she was merely his housekeeper for a year, and he claimed she had stolen from him. Who to believe?

Revel used aliases, too. He answered to the name of Jacques Victor Baron, but that turned out to be just another *nom de plume*. The man who called himself Chase Revel and lived a millionaire's life in California as the publisher of *Entrepreneur* magazine was really a convicted swindler and bank robber whose real name was John Leonard Burke.

If nothing else, Revel's criminal history revealed his amazing entrepreneurial bent. Twenty years earlier, he'd robbed banks in Houston by hiring other people to do the jobs for him. Revel, then using the alias Charles Hudson, went to the Texas Employment Commission and told people there that he was an electrical contractor with jobs wiring banks. He needed four men with cars, and he would pay them $2 an hour.

Each of his brand-new employees was given a sealed envelope and told to present it, along with a bag for the "payroll," to a specific teller at a specific bank. Inside each envelope was a note—a ransom note that falsely said the teller's children were being held hostage.

Revel had worked such a con on his unsuspecting new hires that, even after they visited the banks, the four didn't know what they had done. One of the four left empty-handed, because the teller he was supposed to see wasn't there. Two were arrested within minutes. And the fourth actually delivered $11,000 in cash in Revel.

However, his capital-raising savvy didn't extend to getaways. Soon, he was arrested not only for the Houston robberies, but for a $5,000 bank job two weeks earlier in Las Vegas. Released after four years in prison, he settled in Los Angeles, where, under the name Rio Sabor, he ran an art gallery and, as Jacques Victor Baron, he operated a mail-order swindle for which he was arrested again and put on probation.

Barrett-Whitney revealed Revel's criminal past to the D.A.'s office, claiming she had been jilted and then beaten by her live-in lover. Revel contended that she was just blackmailing him; for proof, he pointed to

her palimony case against him. But her motivation didn't matter to the
D.A. Barrett-Whitney did, indeed, deliver some incriminating evidence: that Revel was an ex-felon who kept a handgun at his house.
Being an ex-felon with a gun was enough to get him busted in August
of 1986.

By then, Barrett-Whitney had already made her mark against her palimony lawyer, too. Her accusation of rape against Marvin was detailed
and graphic: Mitchelson, she said, feigned a heart attack in his office
bathroom and then jumped on top of her when she tried to help him.
She also claimed he coerced her to masturbate him twice, once while
he was driving her in his Rolls-Royce to the downtown courthouse, and
again on the way back. After they returned to his office that afternoon,
she said he made her perform fellatio in the bathroom.

When she made these charges to the LAPD more than two months
after the alleged attack, on January 31, 1986, the investigating detective
took her seriously enough to have Barrett-Whitney immediately telephone Mitchelson in an effort to extract an incriminating statement.

The resultant tape recording showed him making some suspicious
responses to Barrett-Whitney. But it didn't prove she'd been raped. Because the alleged incident had taken place more than two months earlier, there wasn't any physical evidence.

All the cops could do was keep trying to get Mitchelson to incrimi-
nate himself. In early February, Barrett-Whitney, once again wired for
sound by the LAPD, visited Mitchelson's office and tried all over again
to induce Mitchelson to give himself away.

But Mitchelson smelled the set-up.

"You think I'm going to sit here and talk to you about an accusation?
You're mistaken! And I don't want to get angry, but every time you do
that, how do I know you're not tape recorded?"

"I'm not," Barrett-Whitney lied. There was an LAPD detective hiding in the 19th floor men's room, taping everything.

"You say you're not," Mitchelson pressed back. "How do I know
you're not? You want me to check you for a tape recoding? You don't
want me to do that, do you?"

"I don't ever want you to touch me again."

"Yeah, okay. Okay." Mitchelson fell back and regrouped. "Well, I
didn't touch you, I'm *not* touching you, and I told you that if you want
to talk about law, I'll talk to you about law. I will *not* be in the position
where I'm going to sit here and deny something, and you're going to
accuse me of something. I'm not going to do it."

"I'm not accusing you. I'm just making—"

"Okay, okay," Mitchelson replied impatiently. "You want to say anything, say anything you want for the tape. Say it! You want to say something for your tape recorder?"

Barrett-Whitney lied again: "I'm *not* being tape recorded." But soon she did say something else for the tape: "Why did I have to be sexually assaulted by you?"

Mitchelson grew irate. "Look, I never sexually assaulted you. Now, the conversation is over! Okay? It's *over!*"

"Do you realize how strong I am, Mr. Mitchelson?"

"It's over! It's *over!*"

Barrett-Whitney said Mitchelson's anger was making her upset, which prompted him to reply: "I think you're more clever than you say you are." And Barrett-Whitney proved him right—or was it wrong?—by breaking down, sobbing uncontrollably right there in his office.

He had other clients waiting, but the woman would not leave without the admission she came for. The glibness that invariably carried Mitchelson through tough courtroom arguments counted for little now as he argued one-on-one against a woman who seemed determined to bring him down. In exasperation, he finally summoned one of his secretaries, telling her he and his client were having a disagreement about fees and would the secretary *puhleeze* get her the hell out of there.

Barrett-Whitney still wouldn't be budged.

"Look," an agitated Mitchelson finally told his secretary, "she's alleging that I sexually assaulted her. And I'm denying it completely. And that's all I can say." Then, to Barrett-Whitney: "Do I have to raise my voice and tell you that you're a liar?"

"You can say whatever you want. I know I'm not a liar."

"I'm telling you, you're a liar! I never sexually assaulted you in my life! Look me in the eye. Never did I sexually assault you."

"Yes, you did—"

"Get out of this office right now! Get out! Get out! Do what you want, but don't come back here!"

"—And I will look you straight in the eye because I know the truth!"

Mitchelson didn't yet know it, of course, but as Kristin Barrett-Whitney walked out of his office that day, she had his reputation—indeed, his very existence as a lawyer—in her hands.

Barrett-Whitney made Mitchelson her private obsession. "He has destroyed my life," she said. "I live to fight this case so that he will never, ever hurt another person. It keeps me alive."

She was, said a reporter who spoke to her frequently and at great length, "the prototype of the woman scorned." She became Mitchelson's Client From Hell, suffering, she said, from Post-Traumatic Stress Disorder that kept her fixated on Marvin to the apparent exclusion of just about everything else. No matter what she did, she couldn't erase "the smell of Mr. Mitchelson."

One of the detectives on her case likened Barrett-Whitney to a memory bank that "just keeps playing everything [about the alleged rape] back again and again, to make sure she doesn't forget any of it." But a reporter who frequently spoke with her had a different perspective: "She manipulates people into becoming very concerned about her, and she's unrelenting."

That was probably the most amazing thing about Barrett-Whitney. She frequently spoke of her own weakness and vulnerability, but her ability to work the phones—using her soft, unthreatening voice and manner to build astounding credibility and support—showed her to be a savvy operator and a gifted talker. The first LAPD detective on her case, Robert Kestler, remained a true believer in her story even after he was reassigned to another case and replaced by a second detective, Steven Laird. "I'd love to see Mitchelson swing by the balls," Kestler grumbled. "Sumbitch is guilty."

But Kestler was by no means her only credible adherent. She also had support from the bodyguard she hired, the two psychotherapists she went to after Mitchelson's alleged attack, and some influential lawyers.

Her search for a lawyer to help her press the rape charges showed characteristic tenacity. She flew to New York and consulted with at least one well-known lawyer there who did not take her case.

Barrett-Whitney found an article in *Town and Country* magazine about the nation's best lawyers and simply started telephoning them. One of the lawyers she called was Edward Bennett Williams. The great lawyer actually thought there was enough to her story to warrant referring her to an associate in California.

Pierce O'Donnell had been a lawyer in Williams's Washington, D.C., firm from 1975 to 1978, but by 1982 he headed his own small Los Angeles firm with blue-chip clients.

The thirty-nine-year-old Ivy Leaguer genuinely believed Barrett-Whitney. But he could not have been unaware of the publicity her case would generate, and apparently learned quickly to enjoy it. One reporter who worked on the story early said O'Donnell "had an orgasm" when the national press started calling. He also saw the book and screenplay possibilities in Barrett-Whitney's story.

O'Donnell took Barrett-Whitney's case and represented her, *pro bono*, for the better part of two years. O'Donnell used all his connections, and all his skills, in an effort to get Mitchelson prosecuted. He presented the case to the LAPD, the Los Angeles district attorney, the state attorney general, the State Bar, and the Los Angeles County grand jury, each time obtaining extensive coverage of her rape allegations in all the local media. The National Organization for Women (NOW) even weighed in. NOW raised, in the recollection of its California state coordinator, Shireen Miles, "as much hell as possible."

The publicity hurt more people than just Mitchelson. It stung particularly hard within the office of Los Angeles District Attorney Ira Reiner, who was then preparing for what would be an unsuccessful bid for the state attorney general's job. The publicity kicked up by O'Donnell implied that the office's failure to prosecute was the result of Mitchelson's receiving preferential treatment.

"It was unbelievable that this case was receiving as much publicity as it was," recalled Gilbert Garcetti, Reiner's chief deputy at the time. "This was *not* a close case. It simply wasn't close, in terms of a criminal filing. I personally had respect for O'Donnell; I can't speak for others. But there was always a question in our mind: What magic spell has [Barrett-Whitney] spread over Pierce O'Donnell? Because, as an experienced trial lawyer, he knew what our burden of proof was. He knew what we had to establish. How could he honestly think that we could ever get a conviction? The best we could get would be a hung jury, and we were convinced it would be a not guilty."

The D.A.'s office wasn't lacking for reasons why it would not want to take on a potentially losing case. The office had already been embarrassed by dismissals or outright losses in some of its most highly publicized cases, including the *Twilight Zone* manslaughter trial against director John Landis, a campaign-finance misconduct case against Rep. Bobbi Fielder, and the McMartin and Northridge schoolchildren molestation cases. Nobody thought they wanted another disaster.*

Acaldo's presence in the D.A.'s office complicated things, too. As a public prosecutor, Mitchelson's former secretary confronted an ethical dilemma when she read the newspaper reports that her former boss was under investigation for rape.

"This may not be important, it may mean nothing . . . ," she remembered telling her supervisor. "I'm not going to sit here and say I used to be Marvin Mitchelson's secretary, because it wasn't just that. There was more to it than that, okay? I did pick up and carry his cocaine years ago. And I was his lover for four years. And I think that the office should know that. Because I don't think, in my history with Marvin, that I could prosecute Marvin. And, that being the case, I think, ethically, the office has to bow out and let the [state] attorney general take it. . . . I just couldn't let them go forward without at least letting them know.

"I never saw this office move so fast!" Acaldo continued. Almost immediately after she spoke up, Stephen Sitkoff, the deputy district attorney overseeing sex-crime prosecutions, called her in for a formal, tape-recorded interview. Sitkoff's boss, Ron Ross, was also there, along with John Baker, a senior investigator from the D.A.'s office.

---

*The D.A.'s office also found itself in an untenable position regarding the ex-felon-with-a-gun case against Revel. Barrett-Whitney couldn't be a credible witness against Revel if the D.A. had already dismissed her story about the Mitchelson rapes. Thus, a trial against Revel had to be avoided. Over objections from some within the D.A.'s office, Revel got off with probation after copping a plea to the firearm charge. The D.A. dropped a related bomb-making charge.

For thirty-six minutes, the three of them prodded Acaldo for details of the affair and her role as drug courier. She was her usual loquacious self, cheerfully rambling on at great and entertaining lengths, mainly about Mitchelson's drug binges and philandering. Much of the time, they sounded like four good old boys swapping tales.

Ross was dumbfounded by Acaldo's description of Marvin's drug use. "It's amazing that he hasn't killed himself yet." Sitkoff tried to act like the wizened one: "Those kind of guys just linger." The D.A.'s office ultimately decided Acaldo's presence didn't create a conflict of interest.

No lawyer could have done a better job for his client than Pierce O'Donnell did for Barrett-Whitney. He even located and referred to the authorities two of the other former clients of Mitchelson's who alleged that they, too, were victims of his improper sexual advances. Some of those former clients had stories that were stunningly similar to hers. One such woman, Patricia French, actually had filed a suit against Mitchelson in 1983 alleging that she had been raped by him in 1981, when she was thirty-six years old—and Mitchelson's alleged *modus operandi*, as outlined in a lengthy deposition taken more than two years earlier, was similar to Barrett-Whitney's story.

But in spite of everything O'Donnell did for Barrett-Whitney, he still couldn't get the authorities to prosecute. That was because her obsession cut two ways. It made believers out of some, but it created skeptics, too. Invariably, even some of her supporters within the various agencies that considered her charges wondered about the reasons for her vendetta.

Frustrated and bitter, Mitchelson's accuser turned against others who she hired to help her and sometimes even sued *them*, too. She filed (but did not serve) a malpractice lawsuit against one of her psychotherapists, Jacqueline Bouhoutsos, and made noises about doing the same to O'Donnell.* She fired O'Donnell after she had a falling out with him, and later filed (but did not serve) the threatened malpractice suit against him. Barrett-Whitney also threatened suicide more than once. Steve Laird, the LAPD detective who'd been on her case almost from the start, once became so concerned about her apocalyptic threats that he got inside her apartment to see if she really was dead.

On a Monday morning, the day after Easter in 1988, Barrett-Whitney left a message for Laird. She wanted to talk to the detective before she killed herself. When Laird returned the call, she told him she'd

---

*The California Board of Psychology filed disciplinary charges against Bouhoutsos in July 1991, alleging gross negligence and fraud in her treatment of Barrett-Whitney. The charges were pending at year's end.

decided to kill Reiner and Mitchelson instead, "and then you will have to kill me or send me to prison to die." (The next day she said she was just mad and didn't really mean it.) It was Mitchelson's turn to hire a bodyguard.

Even O'Donnell came to view his former client warily. "She's got serious emotional problems," he said.

Ultimately, the judgment of the skeptics received support when Barrett-Whitney damaged her credibility with the LAPD by filing yet another rape allegation that the police this time concluded was unfounded.

Barrett-Whitney's new rape complaint was against a slightly built twenty-seven-year-old Hispanic tile setter whom she befriended. She went to the police in June of 1989 and accused the man of raping and sodomizing her a month earlier. But according to statements made to the LAPD's investigators, the man actually had lived with her for a short time and they had been occasional lovers, at Barrett-Whitney's apartment and at the Bel Air Sands Hotel. Barrett-Whitney even took her young friend to her doctor for an AIDS test, and put his name on her mailbox. When she found out the LAPD didn't believe her, Barrett-Whitney wrote Laird a note implying that she intended to commit suicide.

In spite of everything, Laird still found himself gripped by the undeniable tenacity of this woman who wouldn't rest until Mitchelson fell.

"Kristin," Laird recalled telling her, "you know, if you're standing there with a candle, and there's a million-candle-power light shining back at you, your candle cannot be seen. But if it's totally dark, and yours is the only light, then everybody knows whose it is. And you were there when it was dark, and you were the only light, and nobody will ever take that away from you."

28

Aided by his resourceful criminal lawyer, Howard Weitzman, Mitchelson managed to rebut the rape charges in each of the various investigations that Barrett-Whitney and her lawyer pressed. Surely, the worst was behind him.

From its interviews, the LAPD had concluded that Mitchelson was, indeed, having sex with some of his clients. French and Barrett-Whitney alleged rape, but the rest "just finally gave in," a detective said, "because it was easier than resisting. Marvin said, 'Give it up. Give it up. And if you don't give it up, I'm too busy to bother with you.'"

As the rape investigations were being closed, Mitchelson also prevailed in a non-binding arbitration of Patricia French's $6.5 million rape suit against him. French's lawyer was a seventy-one year old named Daye Shinn. He'd had his own problems with the State Bar.* When Shinn, working on a super-sized 50 percent contingency, tried the case before a jury the following year, French again came up a loser.

Mitchelson was on his best behavior during that trial, a well-pressed and glib counterpoint to the pitiable Pat French. Prohibited by the judge from alluding either to Mitchelson's cocaine use or to any allegations by others of sexual misconduct by Mitchelson, French could do little more than sob on the stand and stick to her story of how Mitchelson forced her to drive him to Tony Curtis's house after raping her three times in thirteen minutes. A gag order kept her from talking to reporters or posing for photographs. Harold Rhoden, defending his old friend, tried to disprove her allegations by summoning to the stand three doctors, one of whom laughably confessed that his clinical judgment about the physiological impossibility of her story came from personal experience, fraternity parties, and talking to friends. The crusty, com-

---

*Shinn received a private reproval by the Bar in 1968 for stopping payment on a $500 check he had given to former attorneys for a client. He was suspended in 1987, and charged again in 1989, both times for misusing clients' funds. A hearing panel recommended disbarment for the final offense, which involved $90,000 in client funds. The disbarment recommendation was still awaiting final action by the California Supreme Court as of February 1992. Shinn was also the defense attorney for Susan Atkins, one of Charles Manson's codefendants, and he was indicted in 1973 on perjury charges stemming from that case. Shinn was alleged to have violated a court gag order by leaking testimony to newspaper reporter William Farr, and then lying about it under oath. Farr spent 46 days in jail for contempt for refusing to reveal his source. The charges against Shinn were later dismissed for lack of proof.

bative Rhoden was back in his element. He pointed out how French's aged doctor, writing up his notes after examining her following the alleged rape, confused her vaginal muscles with ones from her jaw and cheek. And he had a field day with her assertion of Mitchelson's speedy comings and goings.

"All I know is, say anything you want about Marvin Mitchelson, the guy is not a rapist!" Rhoden said a few weeks before the start of the trial. "Her story of the rape, if you were to hear it, you wouldn't ask why. You would conclude she's either mentally ill, or a liar, or both. But there was no rape. . . .That's what the judge concluded. He didn't believe her. . . .

"In Mitchelson's case, this woman claims he had three orgasms over a period of about twenty minutes. She claimed he raped her first by sodomizing her, and had an orgasm in her rectum. He didn't take her pants off, mind you, he just pulled them down. And using physical force, he inserts his penis into her rectum and has an orgasm. Now, I want to suggest to you, this would be very difficult physically to do. . . . She's a big, powerful lady. . . . This is Big Pat. This is Patricia French.

"Then she claims he takes her out of the bathroom, where the first act took place, right into his office and he immediately removes all of her clothes, by force against her will. Nothing was torn. No buttons were torn. Her stockings were removed. They weren't ripped off or pulled off. He's taken them off by force. And she objects to all this. And he completely removes all of her clothes without as much as a rip. Okay? Then he has sexual intercourse with her orally, and has a second orgasm in her mouth. Then he has a third orgasm in her vagina. Bam bam bam!

"Now, I could easily understand Mitchelson *not* wanting to deny this! Comes three times in twenty minutes? It may not be a world's record, but it's not going to be far from it! Look what this kind of publicity has done to certain celebrities!"

French, attractive in a Barbie doll way, once did some acting (a walk-on in *The Nutty Professor*), hosted a Christian radio show, and ran a charm school ("To Help Every Woman Become a Model Lady and Develop Her Maximum Poise"). Mitchelson was hired to represent her in a palimony suit against charismatic preacher and TV evangelist William S. McBirnie. (Another lawyer ultimately got her a $50,000 settlement.) When Mitchelson told her to summarize the story of her relationship with McBirnie, she turned in a steamy account of her claimed sexual escapades with the evangelist.

French had such a propensity for the written word that, for months after the alleged rape, she continued to send Mitchelson a slew of adulatory Mailgrams that hardly sounded as if they'd been written by a rape victim.

"You can see from the Mailgrams that what she wanted was for Mit-

chelson to blackmail the minister!" Rhoden thundered. "'Here we are
having sex, the minister and me, while the choir is practicing.' This
isn't evidence that would entitle her to money under *Marvin*—evidence
of promises he made. This is evidence that would be used to blackmail!
You can't miss it! And then she made it clear in the last Mailgram that
she wrote, that if Mitchelson didn't file that complaint against the minister, she was not going to like what she would have to do.

"One year and nine months later, he's contacted by the press: 'You've
been charged with rape.' Who? What? He didn't even see it. This lady
and/or her lawyer held a little press conference and that's how the press
got it. And then Mitchelson read what he had been charged with."

French claimed she hadn't filed the rape charge earlier because she
didn't know she had a cause of action against Mitchelson.

"A guy rapes her but keeps *secret* from her the fact that he did it!
How can you *rape* somebody and keep it secret from them?"

Acaldo appeared at the trial to testify that Mitchelson had once affirmed French's allegations. That supposedly occurred when Acaldo
mentioned to him a news item about Mitchelson's alleged rape that
she'd seen in the *Salem* (Oregon) *Statesman*: "You knew I was guilty.
You know me so well," she quoted him as saying. Rhoden was smart
enough not to cross-examine her.

Called to the stand by French's lawyer, Mitchelson took the same
position as he had with Barrett-Whitney: that he only ever shook her
hand, nothing more. "Nor did I want to."

Rhoden used the first hour of his closing argument to lambaste
French for her rape charges, and in doing so he painted a different
picture from his client's. "Maybe there could have been a consensual
act of intercourse, and maybe when she's not invited into Tony Curtis's
house, the loneliness might have made her mind snap," Rhoden suggested to the jurors. He only spent a few minutes rebutting all the other
fraud counts, but that was time enough. It only took the jurors three
and a half hours to absolve Mitchelson of every charge.

But another such trial loomed.

In a sense, the complaint filed against Mitchelson by his former client, Felicia MacDonald, was another legacy of Roy Cohn's, for it was
Mitchelson's pit-bull friend who referred her to him.

The tangled case of *Felicia MacDonald vs. Robert MacDonald* was
also a microcosm of the way Mitchelson ran his law practice in the
1980s. She was his typical client, an attractive-but-inevitably-aging
blond princess with a $462,400-a-year lifestyle. According to Mitchel-
son, Felicia was paranoid about the CIA people she thought were surely
following her and tapping her phone. An associate in Mitchelson's office said there was one nasty confrontation with an elevator repairman,
whom Felicia accused of working "undercover." Mitchelson claimed

she drove him crazy, pestering him at one point to change the labels on her files to "Cohen" to foil the spies. Finally, an exasperated Mitchelson said he tried to reassure her by having her talk to Max Hugel, an acquaintance of Cohn's who was ex-CIA. Hugel was supposed to reassure Felicia that the CIA couldn't possibly be out to get her.

Felicia was a characteristic client in other ways, as well. She became Mitchelson's occasional sex partner, discussing their relationship in court testimony and later telling the LAPD during its rape investigation that he pushed her into having sex four times with him. She testified he once greeted her clad only in a black robe and a barrister's wig. And Mitchelson did what she said was a lousy job on her case.

After Felicia turned down a $1 million settlement offer, Mitchelson, saying he had a neck injury, opted out of her divorce trial at the last minute in March of 1984 and dispatched two young associates to take his place. They got Felicia a $3.7 million judgment, but she claimed Mitchelson failed to protect her half of her husband's estimated $8 million fortune, so that she wound up with only $232,000.

Felicia blamed Marvin for her predicament and instructed her new lawyer, Stephen A. Kolodny, to file a $6 million lawsuit against Mitchelson. Felicia's complaint accused him of causing her "extreme anguish, extreme upset, an almost devastating feeling of abandonment, depression as to the future of her case, and physical pain and discomfort."

Mitchelson said this of Felicia: "She's a ball breaker—one of the original ball breakers!" He was screaming. "This lady is absolutely out of it! She led the good life and she can't accept that it's no longer there!"

MacDonald's track record with her new lawyer turned out not to be much better. After advancing her substantial amounts of money for a while, Kolodny bailed out, and later sued her for $199,118.54 in legal fees and expenses he claimed she owed him.

"It was like Peyton Place," laughed Michael Krycler, the forensic accountant on the case who said he never received his $31,000 in fees from Mitchelson or anybody else, either.

Kristin Barrett-Whitney still vowed that she would "be the one to get Marvin Mitchelson." So it shouldn't have been a surprise when she materialized in the courtroom on the first day of the trial of Felicia MacDonald's case.

Mitchelson was frantic when he saw her, though, summoning a bailiff and asking that she be immediately searched for a weapon. The judge ordered everyone out into the hallway, and then a female marshal patted down Barrett-Whitney and went through her purse. There was no weapon, just a newspaper clipping announcing the start of the trial.

After that incident, Barrett-Whitney figured she needed some moral support. She called Steve Laird, the LAPD detective, and he ambled over to the courtroom to reassure the guards that she wouldn't harm anyone. That evening, Barrett-Whitney telephoned French and asked her to come to court with her the following morning. For the next two days, the two of them, French and Barrett-Whitney, sat in the courtroom as silent witnesses against the man they claimed had abused them. Marshals eyed them constantly.

Barrett-Whitney told French they should give some flowers to Mac-Donald, to show their solidarity with her. French was aghast. "Of all things! Don't you know what they do in Mafia pictures? They smuggle *guns* in, inside a bouquet of flowers! And they *already* think we're going to shoot Mitchelson!"

The two women resolutely bought the flowers anyway. Barrett-Whitney split the cost with French, but then needed a $10 loan for lunch. That irritated French, but not so much as Barrett-Whitney's thrusting the flowers to her as they returned to the courtroom. She didn't want to be searched again.

French ditched the flowers on the back bench. "Leave them there! The bailiff can search them!"

With her cascading California blond hair tied back and wearing pearl earrings, Felicia still had the demure look of a forty-eight year old to whom life had been very kind. She was petite and slim, with Waspish good looks and that self assurance that the upper class seems born to. One look at her explained the initial attraction.

"He sold me out," she said of Mitchelson when she took the stand. She described accompanying him to New York, staying in an adjacent room at the Mayfair Regent Hotel until a sobbing Mitchelson begged her to come into his room because of the hallucinations he was having: He heard knocking sounds outside his door and thought horses were stampeding through. She told about taking Mitchelson to Dr. Reder for his cocaine treatments. She said she consoled him when his mother died, and was his confidante when Marvin got "his girlfriend" pregnant. "He did and he didn't" want her to keep the baby, Felicia explained.

"I was there for him; he wasn't there for me," Felicia complained.

Mitchelson expected to do better defending this case than he'd done handling her divorce. He took the stand in July of 1989 to indignantly deny that he'd ever done anything wrong.

"It's a vicious, rotten lie!" he boomed to the jury. Having failed, in a sealed motion, to exclude any reference to their sexual relationship, Mitchelson scripted an artful denial. "There was no affair. There was no solicitation for sex. She has the wrong person." Mitchelson later laughed about that part of his testimony. "I told the court, 'She's got me mixed up'" with someone else.

But what iced the verdict was his own closing argument. Mitchelson proved he still had the old magic. His white mane gave him that aura of unimpeachable dignity that the best trial lawyers have, but it was his method-acting ability that carried his story to the cheap seats. In court, Mitchelson fancied himself to be another Olivier. Arguing to a jury, Mitchelson said, was like playing *Henry V*. Mitchelson had recently seen actor Kenneth Branagh, the "new Olivier," play that role. "There's a couple of speeches he gives that remind me of myself, because of the fervor and the fire and the passion. Marvin at his *best!* . . . Vintage *me!*

"You'll get a different Marvin in the courtroom than you will talking to me. There's a role. Suddenly, there's a stage! It's like being in the theater. It's performing. And it's emanating from within yourself, everything you want to do. . . .

"It's a different Marvin Mitchelson. It's a different compartment. Something happens. I'm in my element. I believe in myself, and I believe in my cause. . . . It's theater. But it's the *human* theater, for keeps. That's the difference. Because people's lives, property, fortunes, and relationships are at stake, when you're arguing in court.

"There's something different about representing people, and pleading for them. I like to plead for people. I like to plead for the cause of the client, and I like to see the point of view of the client and plead for it. And so I step into their place. And that's what gives me the compassion to do it, really."

There was only one difference this time. It was his own skin he was saving.

Mitchelson's closing argument had something for everyone. He invoked the dead to maximum dramatic effect, turning on the tears about Sonia and defending the honor of his friend, Roy Cohn, who was dead of AIDS. And he pointed out that even the best lawyer in the world couldn't get blood out of a turnip: For God's sake, he told the jury, her ex-husband *went to jail* for not paying her. How could any lawyer, even Mitchelson, have changed that?

Finally, he begged: "I *beseech* you not to award a penny in damages against a lawyer who tried to help this lady and still hasn't been paid for it!"

The jury bought it, finding that although Mitchelson failed to use proper "care and skill" in handling her case, he did not commit malpractice and no harm resulted. Afterward, there was some commotion in the hallway outside as the two litigants tried to upstage each other in front of the assembled reporters and television cameras. It was the only skirmish of the trial that Felicia won. "I was too nice," she told the press. "I should have told them about his cocaine habit."

Out in Woodland Hills, the IRS agents who were quietly compiling their case against Marvin taped Felicia's quote to a filing cabinet when they read it the next day in the *Los Angeles Herald Examiner*.

Hal Rhoden would have kept Mitchelson quiet. He would *never* have risked letting him make his own closing argument.

But Rhoden was dead now, too.

Mitchelson hadn't seen Rhoden since their big win in the Patricia French rape trial. Two weeks after winning that trial, Rhoden flew his private airplane—a single-engine Trinidad TB-21 that was his pride and joy as well as a frequent source of collateral—to Sacramento. He was taking an instrument-flying refresher course. Rhoden's wife, daughter, and mother-in-law flew along, and the four of them had almost made it back to the Van Nuys airport when Rhoden's engine conked out.

"I have, ah, engine trouble," Rhoden radioed to the Van Nuys tower. "I'm not gonna have enough power to make it. . . . I've got to get the hell outta here!"

The controller calmly answered as Rhoden's plane dropped from the sky. "Trinidad Eight Lima Romeo, Van Nuys Tower. How do you read me?"

"I hear you loud and clear," Rhoden called back. "I could use a little help, or I'm on my own."

He was always on his own.

Rhoden saw the Sierra Highway and banked to put himself down on it. He probably would have made it, too, if it hadn't been for a power line in the shadows. Rhoden's left wing clipped it and his plane cartwheeled to the ground at 130 miles per hour. Everybody was killed.

Two days passed before authorities revealed the identity of the pilot. But a private investigator working for the Rock Hudson estate learned who it was almost immediately, from some police sources, and he passed the word around. In the heartless world of litigation, this was good news for the Hudson estate; nobody knew the *Christian* case like Rhoden.

Mitchelson allowed as how he didn't mind not having said "goodbye." Mitchelson thought Rhoden already had heard anything he would have said. But that rang hollow. As strange as their relationship was, the older Rhoden was as much Mitchelson's only remaining parent as his last real friend. One by one, every important man in Mitchelson's life had died unexpectedly: Herbert Mitchelson, Bob Landry, Roy Cohn. Now, Rhoden. They were all gone.

There was a dispute between Hal's and Sheila's families about what kind of funeral to have, and in the end there was none, just a memorial service. Mitchelson spoke.

"I talked about his wonderful sense of humor and his good qualities in relation to his sense of humor," Marvin recalled right after the service. "That got me by. I pointed out that Hal was very direct; always got right to the point.

"I said that once, in the early sixties, we were working on a case together involving a magician we represented who was married to a singer who was pretty friendly with Johnny Carson. So we took his deposition. Hal started out the questioning and the first thing he asked Johnny Carson was, 'Did you ever take a shower with Nancy?' And he gave us a *look*. And I said, 'We didn't get very much out of Carson the rest of the day! . . .'

"And then I talked about the *Hughes* case. How we thought we were going to win it. How we'd divide up the casinos every night. I'd take the Desert Inn and he'd get the Sands!

"And then I talked about the wonderful job he did in *Marc Christian*. And the *French* case last month. And how I felt about him.

"He was, you know, a real lawyer. A legal lawyer."

Mitchelson gave Marc Christian a ride home from the service. Tashi Grady said she'd had a premonition about Hal's death a few weeks earlier. Mitchelson hired William Glucksman, a lawyer who rented office space from him, to take Rhoden's place as his defense lawyer.

"Marvin must be sick," mused Maureen Hancock [name changed]. "Poor Hal's dead."

29

Kristin Barrett-Whitney's presence at Mitchelson's trial was part of her campaign of vengeance. She had, indeed, succeeded in hurting him. His law practice suffered, and Mitchelson's telephone, which rang less often, became a metaphor for what his presence sometimes created: an awkward silence.

Mitchelson kept a dartboard on a bookshelf in his office, and Barrett-Whitney's photograph was in the bull's-eye. Also inside the target were pictures of Acaldo, French, and Carrie Leigh, whom Mitchelson once represented in a 1988 palimony suit against *Playboy*'s Hugh Hefner. Leigh was another ex-client who accused him of supplying her with illegal drugs. But according to Mitchelson, his real troubles began when Hefner decided to look into Mitchelson's problems in retaliation for his having filed the palimony suit. Mitchelson thought all the negative publicity started with that public feud. Whenever a reporter called to check out a negative story, he cursed Hefner all over again.

Marvin Mitchelson was damaged goods in a market that demanded perfection of its media stars but didn't stay interested in them unless it found the flaws. Maybe that made it inevitable that the national television program that once so adored him would come knocking to do a story about his travails.

Mitchelson knew what "60 Minutes" could do to his reputation. Where he once courted and fawned over the television press, now he stonewalled. He also thought the CBS show owed him a break. He was featured on "60 Minutes" the very first time it reached number one in the Nielsen Ratings system. But the fact that he thought that entitled him to special consideration meant that Mitchelson knew little about the rules of the high-stakes game he played.

Chuck Lewis was a thirty-four-year-old producer for "60 Minutes" with the long pedigree of an ambitious overachiever—Eagle Scout, high school student-body president—and the hunger to make his mark. He'd found his way into television, working as an off-camera reporter on what he called "bust your ass, get threatened with lawsuits" stories.

A stocky, soft-featured man with vivid green eyes and an expressive smile, Lewis's diffidence made for a deceptive first impression. He had been an investigative producer for ABC News in Washington for seven years, and, after that, for CBS. Lewis had been one of Mike Wallace's producers at "60," as the insiders at CBS called it, since 1984.

On any television news show, but particularly on the ones such as "60 Minutes," the producer's job is the most essential and also the most thankless. It is the producer who thoroughly researches a story long before the on-camera star steps in, and who supervises the editing of the raw tape into the finished piece long after the correspondent is gone. By the time Wallace arrived to tape his interviews, a producer had done all the necessary leg work, pre-screening every interview prospect and providing the network "talent" with detailed memoranda about the story and even a list of questions to ask. Wallace admired the care this producer took in weaving his pieces. Lewis likened his job to feeding meat to a shark.

In early 1988, Lewis was finishing an exposé for "60 Minutes" about flaws in the California victims-compensation agency. It gave out about $60 million a year to 25,000 crime victims in the state.

"We just got the strangest claim for money from a victim," a source within the agency told Lewis while he was researching that piece. "This person, Marvin Mitchelson, apparently *raped* this woman."*

Lewis tried to act nonchalant—he was practiced in that—but, in truth, the producer nearly fell off his chair. He phoned an assistant back at CBS, quickly had her search a computer database of newspaper stories, and soon learned that not all of the important news in the world reaches Washington. The assistant pulled up almost two years' worth of stories about the controversy surrounding Mitchelson's alleged rapes.

It said something about "60 Minutes"—indeed, about the hot medium of television—that such a story that had already been widely reported in the Los Angeles media was nevertheless viewed as good copy by "60 Minutes." But it also said something about the complacent hometown media, particularly the *Los Angeles Times*, that an outsider like Lewis could swoop in and reveal important evidence that had been sitting in the investigative files for nearly two years. Lewis gave his project a secret name, "Project M," so as not to arouse suspicion around his office. Then, he typed out a one-paragraph memo proposing his story. These memos were called "blue sheets" at the show, although they weren't blue and Lewis didn't know the origin of the name. Getting a blue sheet approved essentially meant that there was a budget to do the piece. It was also a producer's territorial claim, a warning to other producers that a story was in progress and they were not to infringe. Don Hewitt, the show's founder and executive producer, gave Lewis a big "attaboy" when he read the March 30 memo. It talked about the rape allegations and lawsuits against Mitchelson and the grand jury investigation that was then going on.

Barrett-Whitney was deeply involved in assisting Lewis as he researched the piece during the Spring of 1988. She provided thousands of pages of documents, served as a kind of institutional memory about the whole case, and helped Lewis round up other alleged victims to be interviewed. When the piece aired on June 26, both she and French were interviewed by Wallace on camera. Nevertheless, Lewis was well aware from the outset that a piece based *only* on the credibility of a few alleged victims wouldn't hold up.

He needed corroboration, and, as far as he and "60 Minutes" were concerned, he found it when he learned that the D.A.'s office had interviewed one of its own prosecutors—Acaldo—nearly two years earlier about the rape allegations, and that she had essentially affirmed their plausibility. Acaldo's name had never surfaced.

Lewis was aided by a "Deep Throat"—not Acaldo—within the D.A.'s office, and by another within the LAPD who met Lewis at the Code Seven Bar across the street from police headquarters. From those two sources, Lewis also learned that Barrett-Whitney and French weren't the only rape complainants. In fact, the district attorney's office had closed its investigation of Mitchelson despite having at least five other unrevealed reports in its files from women, including ex-clients, who claimed they were victims of Mitchelson's improper sexual advances or physical assaults.

One of his two Deep Throats let Lewis read these investigative reports. That told him where and how the new victims could be reached. One of them, Marguerite Alvarez of Carmel, California, agreed to appear on camera in the "60 Minutes" piece, restating her 1986 complaint to the D.A.'s office that Mitchelson made what she thought was a sexual advance to her while taking a bubble bath in his office Jacuzzi, and that he later pushed her down on the bed in her Los Angeles hotel room and fondled her. Another complainant to the D.A.'s office, a woman who said she was a former babysitter of Mitchelson's son, also agreed to be videotaped. Disguised by a Hollywood makeup artist, she described how Mitchelson allegedly tried to rape her ten years earlier. (Hewitt later thought the piece was harder and slicker without the babysitter interview and ordered it taken out.)

But there was still another reason why Lewis considered this story so credible: He had learned that the State Bar had begun its own investigation of the rape allegations. Even though that was important, the last thing he wanted was to stir the Bar to move quickly. Lewis hoped to reveal the Bar's investigation himself, rather than letting the bureaucrats steal his glory. Wanting to beat the Bar to the headlines, Lewis wisely decided not to inquire further about that investigation.

On April 21, three weeks after turning in his blue sheet, Lewis followed up with a second memo, this one to Wallace. It was an instruction package to the correspondent, describing how Lewis's reporting was falling into place and containing a sharply worded conclusion that was intended to grab attention. What was noteworthy to Lewis was what he called the widespread belief among credible sources that Mitchelson had committed rapes. Lewis thought some hard questions needed to be asked.

As Mike Wallace flew to Los Angeles early in May for the interviews Lewis had arranged, he carried with him a May 1 memorandum breaking the evidence into five parts—LAPD, state attorney general, district attorney, private attorneys, and the victims themselves—and elaborately choreographing how each would be approached during the ensuing interviews. Putting together a story like this was like playing a chess game. Lewis not only had to get the story, he also had to use the weight of his evidence to overcome any skepticism Wallace might still have about the motives of Barrett-Whitney and French.

Their "spine" interview—the very first one, to acquaint Wallace with the story as much as to lay the foundation for interviews that followed—would be with Barrett-Whitney's lawyer, Pierce O'Donnell. Having first met and interviewed him two weeks earlier, Lewis considered O'Donnell a solid player in the drama, and he was impressed by the anger that came through when O'Donnell talked about the case. O'Donnell had spoken to Lewis for four and a half hours that first day, in the impressive, oak-paneled conference room of the big downtown law firm he was by then working for. Lewis's personal notes from that meeting described all the horrendous things O'Donnell thought Barrett-Whitney had endured in her life: a bad marriage; a psychiatrist who she said turned their hourly therapy sessions into perverted sexual gratification sessions; alleged sexual abuse by a dentist; the common-law marriage with Chase Revel, who Barrett-Whitney then discovered was really a convicted bank robber using an alias; and, finally, suffering from multiple sclerosis, then meeting up with Marvin Mitchelson.

Wallace taped his interview with O'Donnell on Wednesday, May 4. By lunchtime on Thursday, he and Lewis also had in the can their four separate taped interviews with the alleged rape victims. Other interviews were scheduled for late that afternoon and the following day, but the duo still hadn't lined up Mitchelson for an interview.

It wasn't for lack of trying. Although Mitchelson had said from the outset that he would appear on camera to rebut the women, CBS's efforts to nail down an on-the-record interview with him had been unavailing. Wallace even telephoned Mitchelson various times from Russia and London, while reporting other stories, and on another occasion reached Mitchelson in Paris. Each time, Mitchelson would proclaim his innocence, complain about the unfairness of the situation, and say he probably would go on the show "and I'll get back to you." This went on week after week. Still, no interview.

Now, on the spur of the moment, Wallace decided to telephone Mitchelson again. He called from the lobby of the Beverly Hilton Hotel, and, after a few moments, a friendly Mitchelson came on the line. Wallace explained that he and Lewis were doing their interviews, and Mitchelson let out a long sigh. He agreed to talk to him, without the cameras.

Roz Karson, an associate producer from the Los Angeles bureau who was helping with the interviews, worried about this. She thought—correctly, it turned out—that Mitchelson would make an emotional appeal for "60 Minutes" to drop the story, and she also feared that Mitchelson might be successful.

Mike Wallace had his own ideas, though. Cameras or not, he wanted to get something usable from this visit with Mitchelson. Lewis said Wallace suggested over lunch that Lewis carry a hidden tape recorder into the meeting. Wallace was already seventy years old, but at times like this he acted like the kid among the crew. Lewis had misgivings about the secret taping, but Wallace really wanted to give it a shot.

Wallace instructed Lewis to go to the hotel garage, where the crew was loading up its gear, and fetch a tape recorder from the sound man. Lewis tried to stuff it into his sportcoat pocket, but the pocket bulged. The sound man suggested he wrap the recorder up inside a newspaper and shove the works inside a raincoat pocket, which he could then casually sling over his arm.

Lewis still worried that they risked botching the whole story if the gimmick backfired. Ultimately, he won the point after CBS lawyers advised them that California law required Mitchelson's permission to be taped.

Lewis had been hearing all kinds of colorful descriptions of Mitchelson's office, but none of them had prepared him for what he saw. With its showy abundance of red tones and stained glass, this was unlike any law office he had ever seen, anywhere.

Marvin walked into the reception area and warmly shook their hands. He had on a suit, but his shirt was open and he wasn't wearing a tie. He reminded Lewis of a gambler in Atlantic City. Mitchelson, he thought, had that smooth, slick way with people. About fifteen minutes later, Mitchelson came out again and led them down the hallway to his corner office for a meeting that would consume the next fifty minutes.

Sitting behind his desk in his famous Valentino chair, he smoked what was left of a cigar. Wallace and Lewis sat opposite him, and Wallace spoke in almost sorrowful terms: "Marvin, I'm sorry to be coming to you under these current circumstances."

"Oh, Mike, I am, too."

Wallace acted appropriately diffident, playing for effect. "Well, anyway, we, y'know, we, uh, you know how we got on the story. Y'know, we got a tip, you know, out of left field."

Mitchelson point blank told the two men he knew their tip came from Barrett-Whitney or Hugh Hefner. He was absolutely convinced it had, and he was stunned when Wallace said it hadn't.

Mitchelson expressed surprise and disappointment that work on the piece about him was already so far along. "You've already interviewed so many people." Mitchelson seemed to be saying that if they'd just talked to him first, he'd have been able to tell them what a stupid story it was. He was upset that Wallace and Lewis were so invested in it already.

Wallace said that their purpose in meeting with him was to persuade him to appear on camera. Mitchelson replied that the charges were proposterous—"*outrageous!* I can't believe this is happening to me!"—and he generally denied the allegations with great vehemence.

Lewis, watching and listening but not saying a word, was intrigued. He thought: Here's this world-famous attorney, giving it his all to persuade us our project is unfair and wrongheaded. It's like we are the jury. It's a bizarre situation. Here is Marvin Mitchelson trying to convince me, just like he's convinced judges and lawyers. He's trying to talk his way out of it.

Wallace replied in tones that were warm but also intended to be firm. He gave Mitchelson a sense of the breadth of Lewis's investigative efforts. In effect, what he was doing was rebutting Mitchelson's contention that "60 Minutes" was just relying on a few wackos. Then he nodded toward Lewis: "Look, this guy [Lewis] is not a raving lunatic. He's a very solid guy. He never—he's very copious. He's anal compulsive on his notes. And this is not a guy who would go off the deep end, Marvin. I believe what he tells me. He's done all this diligent work and I've seen all the women, Marvin."

Mitchelson answered: "I've been practicing law for thirty years, and I have had five thousand clients. So what if you found four women? Divorce litigation is very emotional, very intense, and the women are often very distraught!"

Wallace described the stories told by each of the four people they'd interviewed, including the babysitter's.

Mitchelson didn't deny the sitter's story. He just stared back at the two of them, dumbfounded. As his emotions built, he started sobbing. Tears ran down his cheeks. His shoulders heaved. His face became red and twisted.

"Mike, please, *please* don't do this story. I don't want to beg, but if I have to, I will. I've been married for twenty-eight years. My son is twenty-three years old, a fine boy. Think what a story like this will do to them." Mitchelson's emotionalism was ripping at them. "How can you do this to me?"

At this point, Lewis thought Mitchelson was capable of killing himself. He actually worried that if that happened now he, Lewis, would be to blame.

There was a moment of awkward silence. Then Wallace looked at Lewis and asked, very softly and deliberately: "Chuck, what do you think of this?"

Lewis was caught completely off guard. He'd been watching this intense conversation for so long that he forgot he was a participant in it, too. Lewis felt like a napping outfielder who suddenly had to catch a fly ball. He looked directly at Mitchelson and replied evasively but diplomatically, "Well, you're making some very interesting points, and we'll certainly take them into consideration." It sounded like he was from the State Department.

Marvin pleaded again. "I've got ten great stories. I can give you one or several of them. But can't you just pass on this one?"

Wallace replied firmly: "Marvin, we don't trade stories."

Then, almost as quickly as he'd lost his composure, Mitchelson regained it. He apologized, and said with a grin, "Wanna see my bathroom?" He gave them a tour. Lewis made a mental note of the erotic wallpaper with its bare-breasted women and the bathtub that some of Mitchelson's alleged victims had described. On their way out, going from the bathroom to the door of his office, Mitchelson laughed. "Too bad these allegations don't involve beautiful women, like Joan Collins. Think what that would do for my image!"

Wallace and Lewis stepped into the elevator on Mitchelson's floor. Too drained to chit-chat, they said nothing and looked straight ahead as the doors to the nineteenth floor closed in front of them. Finally, still staring ahead, Wallace spoke.

"Well, do you believe him?"

"No. Do you?"

"No."

They didn't say anything else the rest of the way down.

Mitchelson never did respond on camera to the allegations. He was in Japan, finishing the Joan Shepherd divorce case and sobbing to her about the rape charges the night the segment aired. Although "60 Minutes" originally intended to keep the lid on its story until the fall season, ABC's competing program, "20/20," got wind of the impending scoop. A "20/20" producer started putting his own piece together, using some of the same alleged victims that Lewis had already interviewed, as well as some that he hadn't. CBS then started rushing Lewis's piece to broadcast during the rerun season.

There were a few last-minute preparations to take care of. Wallace leaked word of the piece to Liz Smith, his friend who was the gossip columnist at the *New York Daily News*. She closed her column on Friday, June 24, with a chatty item about how that coming Sunday's show would play "some real hard ball via a controversial segment on lawyer Marvin Mitchelson. . . . When investigators Mike Wallace and Charles Lewis went to see Mitchelson in his offices last May, they claim, he wept and begged them not to go on with it. He promised them other, better stories if only they'd lay off, they say. But these '60 Minutes' guys are doing the piece anyway, without his cooperation and participation."

Lewis, meanwhile, telephoned the State Bar to learn the status of its investigation. He'd been afraid to do that earlier, fearing it would prompt the Bar to beat him to the punch. And his concern turned out to be well founded. The State Bar rushed out its own complaint against Mitchelson that very Friday afternoon alleging improprieties in his handling of some cases. That deprived Lewis of a scoop, but it further turned up the heat on Mitchelson.

Fallout from the broadcast continued two days afterward on the "Phil Donahue Show." Donahue brought out some more of Mitchelson's disgruntled clients—three women who claimed he'd botched their cases or cheated them out of their money.

Marvin wouldn't appear on Donahue's show, either, particularly not with the women he later referred to as "those three dogs."

One of the women on the show announced on the air that Mitchelson had sexually assaulted her, too, in his New York City hotel room in 1982. Later, Mitchelson screamed: "She claims I raped her! She weighs about three hundred and forty pounds! I mean, Jesus! I don't even *know* the woman!"

The ubiquitous Raoul Felder also was a guest on Donahue's show that day, as was one of his clients. But, given the state of Felder's relationship with Mitchelson, the position he staked out was surprising.

Felder actually tried to defend Marvin. He told viewers that Mitchelson was the object of "a lot of professional jealousy." And he reminded everybody that, like him or not, Mitchelson had established an important principle in *Marvin.* Privately, Felder said he thought "60 Minutes" had "killed" Mitchelson by getting earlier film clips of him in his bubble-filled tub and mingling them with the rape charges.

That evening, one of Mitchelson's New York cocounsel "comes up here, and I walk with him out into an anteroom, and he says, 'I have a message for you from Marvin.' And he says 'It's two words.'

"I say, 'Listen, lay off.' I'm not interested in all his craziness and all this business.' Because of what I'd said on the show [defending Mitchelson], I was taking flak.

"He says, 'Two words. Don't you want to know?'

"I said, 'No, I *don't* want to know.'

"He says, 'Well, I'll tell you what the two words are. They're: Thank you.'

"'Well,' I said, 'Why didn't he just call me?'

"He says, 'At this point, he's afraid of the telephones.'"

Marvin was convinced his phone was bugged.

As Mitchelson later described it, he was in "a state of shock" when Wallace and Lewis visited him. He also claimed they used secret tape recordings and trick photography and violated an agreement that their conversation be off the record.

He rambled on about how he wanted to sue everybody who ran stories about the rape allegations, except he couldn't because it was impractical and besides the press made his career and it's like what Harry Truman said, if you can't stand the heat get out of the kitchen, right? He railed at Steve Sitkoff, the deputy district attorney who was quoted in the *Los Angeles Times* as saying one of Mitchelson's expensive suits was "frayed."

"That schmuck D.A. who thinks my clothes aren't good," Mitchelson called him. "That guy loved to be quoted! That's the only chance he'll ever have to read his name! It's incredible! I think his name is Sitkoff. You know what I mean? He wants to jump on the bandwagon. He wants to say something. Fine. He said it. Don't think I don't remember.

"Look, I'm happy to show you my wardrobe. You tell me if you think my suits are threadbare."

Sometimes, Mitchelson wondered whether he'd have all these problems if his mother were still alive to keep her Sonny on the straight and narrow.

"I'd like to think I wouldn't, because I loved her so much. . . ," he would say, starting to sob. "But I haven't done any of these criminal-type allegations that have been made against me. . . . I didn't do it! So what could my mother have prevented?"

30

The State Bar of California fully expected Marvin Mitchelson to resist its charges with all of his considerable legal prowess. Despite that appraisal, though, the Bar installed at the head of its case a lawyer without much experience for the formidable task at hand. If fate owed Mitchelson a break, he got one here.

Victoria Regina Molloy was a thirty-two year old who made no secret of her disdain for Mitchelson. She had red frizzy hair and still spoke with the trace of an accent from her native Virginia, but the thing you noticed first about Molloy was her formidable size.

"I don't give up. I'm stubborn," Molloy once said of herself. "Like a mule. I think that, in their own way, Marvin and his attorneys have tried to swat us away, and tried to intimidate us away. They haven't tried bribery or flattery yet. I'm waiting."

Molloy knew about Mitchelson's reputation long before she ever became trial counsel for the Bar. She had read the opinions in *Marvin* during law school, "the minute they came down."

Aside from the American Bar Association, the State Bar of California was the world's largest assemblage of lawyers. All 115,000 lawyers in the state—one sixth of the national total—were required to be members. The State Bar was the private, state-chartered body whose job it was to protect the public from unscrupulous conduct by lawyers, so it was hardly surprising that the Bar became a repository by the early 1980s for client complaints about Mitchelson.

The Bar treated Mitchelson just as it did virtually every other complained-about lawyer then—which was to say, the Bar did absolutely nothing. Until a few years ago, the state was only slightly more likely to disbar a lawyer than to send a murderer to Death Row.

Part of the Bar's lassitude came from its own split personality. The lawyers' group functioned like a trade association, but it also was supposed to seek out and vigorously punish the malefactors in its midst. The Bar's critics, including some influential ones in the state legislature, considered the idea of lawyers regulating other lawyers as foxes guarding the henhouse.

By 1985, the State Bar's failure to carry out its enforcement role had become scandalous. The *San Francisco Examiner* revealed the extent of its inaction in a six-part investigative series written by the paper's California Supreme Court reporter, K. Connie Kang, and an investigative editor, James A. Finefrock. They showed that the disciplinary machinery had broken down. Convicted criminals practiced law in the state: Among those the reporters discovered were a bagman in a bribery scheme, an attorney who burglarized a client's market, a drug smuggler, an embezzler, a cop-impersonator, a Nixon dirty-trickster, and a child molester.

The California Bar was like a black hole: Complaints went in but nothing came out. There were 8,932 complaints made against lawyers the year before the *Examiner* series ran, but only eleven lawyers were disbarred. Charges often were filed in secret, leaving new clients without a warning that they might be cheated.

The Bar's own trial lawyers went on strike. Important legislators, particularly State Senator Robert Presley, were so disgusted by the State Bar's disciplinary system that they threatened to take it away from the lawyers altogether and give the chore to independent prosecutors, with cases resolved publicly in front of an independent state court. Presley got a law passed that required continual independent monitoring of the State Bar's disciplinary process.

Robert Fellmeth, the director of the Center for Public Interest Law at the University of San Diego and one of the original three Nader's Raiders some twenty years earlier, was put in charge of the Presley-mandated monitoring program. What he found was "a complete and utter travesty. They had a room full of complaints. It was called the Red Room, but people there also called it the TNT Room—like, any more cases and it'll blow up! The room was filled with meritorious complaints that were going nowhere. You had a system in shambles. It wasn't operating." The Bar had to make bold changes or risk losing its franchise. Salaries were raised, more lawyers were hired, and the State Bar began to clear its backlog and aggressively investigate citizen complaints.

By 1988, the Bar had accumulated four boxes of files about Mitchelson. Now, it took action. Molloy was put in charge of the investigation.

The early complaints to the Bar weren't about rape or sexual abuse. They were simply from clients who claimed Mitchelson had fleeced them. But with Barrett-Whitney, the Bar started hearing allegations about sex. Investigating those allegations further, Molloy perceived in them the same flaws that other investigators had seen.

Sure, she readily conceded, "there are a number of people who say he touched them, or he made a pass, or whatever, or they just felt that he was pushing for a relationship that they weren't interested in. And I've heard from a number of people who say, 'Yeah, I willingly went to bed with him. I wish I hadn't now, but I did.' . . . A number of former clients have said [that]. . . . We've heard from a number of people that [he has a] there's-no-harm-in-asking kind of philosophy."

But as Molloy saw it, no one else was claiming rape. Moreover, the rape complaints of Barrett-Whitney and French were "credibility cases," and the credibility of the complainants was lacking.

Molloy thus agreed with the D.A.'s decision not to prosecute. She dismissed those who thought that the prosecutors had purposely trashed their investigation. "There are enough problems in that case, from a prosecution standpoint, that I would seriously doubt that anybody had to cover it up," Molloy explained. "Some of the most obvious problems with Kristin's case are that she did not immediately report it, spent the whole day with him, there's no physical evidence, there's no witnesses, not to mention her previous cases against the psychiatrist and the dentist. Those are some real big problems. And I think any D.A. would have to seriously question whether they could sell that case to twelve people. Especially against somebody who's a media star.

"Patricia French's problem with the D.A.'s office was that she didn't complain until after the statute of limitations ran. There was nothing they could do about her case. She complained, I think, five years after the incident. It was too late to do anything. I don't know that they even made an assessment of Patricia French's case, because they obviously didn't have any means to do anything about it."

The State Bar's charges against Mitchelson thus weren't about rape. Rather, the Bar alleged more mundane, but more easily proven, financial and professional misdeeds.

The charges were filed in multiple complaints. The first one—from June 24, the Friday before the "60 Minutes" broadcast—accused Mitchelson of filing two frivolous appeals, for which the California courts had already fined him $40,000; failing to return unearned portions of retainers he'd been paid; and failing to place client retainers in a trust account. The clients he'd allegedly injured included actress Julie Newmar and Eleanor Revson, the sister-in-law of the founder of Revlon cosmetics.

Another complaint against him was filed a little over four months later. This one accused Mitchelson of charging unconscionable fees in a variety of specified cases, as well as illegal contingent fees and unfair and unreasonable contingent fees in two cases. The Bar also asserted that he failed to represent adequately some of his clients, and that he also failed to adequately supervise some of his associates.

Later that month, on November 30, the Bar weighed in with still a third complaint that was potentially the most serious of all the charges.

In more fallout from the Sotheby's imbroglio, the Bar charged that, by not paying for the jewels, Mitchelson had committed an act of moral turpitude. Molloy started saying she was going to go for disbarment.*

If you asked Victoria Molloy why the Bar had become so interested in Marvin Mitchelson after ignoring his alleged misdeeds for so many years, she would patiently reply that only recently had the Bar discerned a pattern of misconduct. "An isolated event, here and there, probably would not have been viewed seriously. When we saw a pattern emerging, we decided to go back and take a look at those old cases."

But Fellmeth said there was more to it than that. He pointed to the "symbolic importance" of the proceeding against Mitchelson. The Bar could prove itself by showing it was not afraid to go after a well-known lawyer. In a twist on Mitchelson's own tactics, now it was the lawyers' group that was plainly riding Mitchelson for all the good publicity it could get. Going against Mitchelson made business sense for the State Bar, the case being a visible manifestation of how well it was doing its job.

Mitchelson variously called the Bar's allegations against him "crap," "ridiculous," "pieces of shit," and "chickenshit." He hired the best lawyer he could get and then dug in for the scrappy, Roy Cohn–style of defense he always mounted when litigation threatened his livelihood.

Mitchelson's defensive strategy was always the same: first, deny; then, delay. He put off scheduled depositions so many times that the Bar finally started trying to schedule them at night, when, its attorneys wrongly presumed, Mitchelson wouldn't have so many conflicts.

Arthur Margolis was Mitchelson's lawyer in the State Bar matter. He had formerly worked as a trial lawyer for the State Bar; in fact, he had been Victoria Molloy's supervisor there. Margolis claimed the Bar was pursuing a vendetta against Mitchelson to get publicity. "I've never seen anything like it!"

To hear Molloy talk about Mitchelson and the case against him was to see the plausibility of Margolis's point. "Maybe this is wrong," she explained, describing her first meeting with Marvin, "but . . . based on his letters that I had read, [and] based on the interviews I had done with countless people—people who are complaining witnesses— . . .I already had an impression of him in my mind, and he just affirmed it. [He's] a man who sees himself as indestructible. And the State Bar is

---

*Before Rhoden's death, the crusty lawyer represented his friend in this part of the Bar proceeding. The way he figured it, the Bar wasn't kidding about disbarment. "The people in the Bar who are after his ass, they don't want a suspension; they want him disbarred. It's a close question. It's gonna be awfully close. I'm gonna do everything I can to save his ticket for him. But it is a close question." Rhoden had facetiously asked the Bar's lawyers once whether they'd settle for a public hanging of Mitchelson at high noon instead of disbarment.

like a fly buzzing around his head, and he's just trying to swat us away."

The Bar's chief prosecutor on the Mitchelson case sounded as angry as any of Mitchelson's alleged victims. She criticized him for being, in essence, a bait-and-switch artist; for using publicity to lure in ordinary clients and then failing to serve them. "He's a user," she snorted. "He's a user of people; he's a user of opportunities. He's in a service industry, and he doesn't feel that he has to serve anyone."

Behind his back, Molloy also lambasted Mitchelson about his cocaine habit and laughed that she'd hate to see "the inside of his nose." She speculated that he might have been on cocaine during his depositions with the State Bar. His office furniture was "tacky"—"like he is." His clothes were no good. She called him a liar; claimed he didn't respect her because he "doesn't respect himself." She alluded to having heard "stories we can hardly believe," but explained another time that "once you realize what he's doing, nothing surprises you."

Molloy thought she had Marvin Mitchelson all figured out.

"It constantly amazes me," Molloy mused. "I see this with attorneys all the time, who have that golden opportunity and just throw it away.

"If he had just used that break with Pamela Mason and run with it, and not been afraid of the hard work, not been afraid to take on cases and do whatever he had to do to make himself competent. If he had taken all the breaks he got from the media—instead of just using them as an opportunity to get money—but rather to build a base for himself. He has an opportunity that so few attorneys have, to really get the big cases, to make the big bucks. He threw it all away. He threw it all away for greed.

"I see that with attorneys and it constantly amazes me. There are young attorneys who would kill for a tenth of the business Marvin Mitchelson can bring in. And he throws it all away. He squanders more than money. He squanders his success, and his opportunities for success. He's just one of those live-for-today kind of people. I guess that I see him as having no self-respect because he didn't do what I think someone with any pride and self-esteem would do, and that is to make something of the opportunity that fell into his lap.

"The golden goose laid an egg right in front of him, and he stepped on it. I find that incredible!"

For all Molloy's tough talk, though, the State Bar's case was really just limping along. Partly, this was a result of Mitchelson's defensive strategy. But the Bar's problem also resulted from its having saddled itself with a case that was inherently unmanageable.

One year passed, then eighteen months. Still, the charges hung around, unresolved. "If they've got some little guy who didn't return a client's phone call, they slam him," commented Ted Cohen, Mitchelson's old law-school classmate who represented clients facing Bar discipline. "But if it's a big guy, they just take their time. These [Bar] guys couldn't function as prosecutors. For them to develop a big case and put it on, it's like they're trying to build a hydrogen bomb."

The Bar began looking for a way out of the morass. But after having ballyhooed its case against Mitchelson, it couldn't possibly drop it without horrendous damage to its own already-less-than-lustrous reputation.

Then the State Bar's lawyers learned about the IRS's criminal investigation. This was a promising development. Maybe the IRS, with its informant, its superior financial-analysis capabilities, and the power of the grand jury behind it, would share some of its evidence. But the answer turned out to be no; there were strict judicial rules against that.

So the Bar settled for the second-best alternative. By December of 1989, there was every indication that the Bar would simply wait for the IRS to finish its criminal investigation of Mitchelson. After all, if Mitchelson pleaded guilty to or was convicted of even one felony count of tax evasion, the Bar could lift his ticket immediately. Why push its own lesser case? The Bar could simply request a long continuance and settle in to await Mitchelson's indictment.

At 1:35 in the afternoon on Monday, January 8, 1990, IRS Special Agents James L. Wilson and Robert Sterling strolled unannounced into Mitchelson's Century City office and asked to see him. They were there to serve a grand-jury subpoena.

The existence of the IRS's grand-jury investigation was no longer a secret to Mitchelson. He had known about it since the previous September, when the IRS began serving subpoenas on his clients, accountant, and banks. The subpoenas were worrying some of his clients, too: It turned out that one high-profile starlet, claiming she was no longer an American resident, hadn't filed a federal tax return since 1982.

In December, the agents stalked out Tashi Grady's house and slapped a subpoena on her, too.

Every one of those moves was thoroughly scripted. Now, the two agents were to subpoena Mitchelson himself.

His trusted assistant, Janet Casey, said her boss wasn't in.

"Well, you don't mind if I sit down right here and wait, do you?" Wilson replied amiably. He intended to park himself on the Tiffany sofa in the waiting area, with or without Casey's accommodation.

Half an hour later, Marvin strode through the door. He had obviously been tipped off by Casey about the agents. He walked right toward them and turned on the old Mitchelson charm. "How are you guys?" He took them back into his office and told them to wait while he telephoned Roger M. Olsen, one of the criminal tax lawyers he had recently hired.

Olsen got on the line and told Mitchelson to give the phone to Wilson. "I should've suspected it was you," Olsen said sourly. "What do you want?"

"We're here to serve a subpoena on Marvin Mitchelson."

Olsen said, "Is that all you're doing?" Olsen seemed to want an assurance that Mitchelson wasn't going to be arrested.

"For now, yeah."

"Okay," Olsen replied. "We'll accept the subpoena."

Still as affable as when he first saw the two agents, Mitchelson took the subpoena, then shook hands with Wilson and Sterling. Walking the two men back to the outer door of his office, he zinged them: "Tell your wives they'll never have to worry. I'll *never* represent them"

Mitchelson's apparent placidity, given what was happening to him, was a frequent source of amazement to his acquaintances. But his calm on this particular day was extraordinary, because Mitchelson had much more on his mind than just a grand-jury subpoena. Later that evening, he was to secretly meet a man named Mike Williams. The man promised he could solve all of Mitchelson's problems.

Two weeks earlier, Mitchelson had received a foreboding letter from Williams. The stranger said he had an inside track on the Bar's case against Mitchelson, and that he could thus help Mitchelson in ways that his lawyer "can only dream of." Williams promised to contact Mitchelson on the day after Christmas, and warned him to keep their dealings secret.

Mitchelson received a second letter from Williams exactly a week later, instructing him to call an answering service to arrange a meeting. He did. On the evening of the day that Wilson served his subpoena, Mitchelson found out that Mike Williams was for real.

They met in Mitchelson's office. Williams said he was an ex-Dallas police officer. He wanted money, although he did not say how much. In a third and final letter mailed three days after their meeting, Williams promised that he could deliver information about "highly illegal" measures used against Mitchelson "by various agencies." The stranger told him that this information could enable Mitchelson to get the entire investigation halted.

By now, Mitchelson had alerted his lawyers, Olsen and Margolis, about this strange development. Olsen, in turn, notified George Newhouse, the assistant United States attorney who was preparing the tax evasion case against Mitchelson. Newhouse told Olsen he wanted to arrange a sting, with Olsen as the bait.

Olsen summoned Williams to his office for a meeting on Tuesday, January 16. When he arrived, Olsen introduced him to Steve Walsh, a "law clerk" from his office who was, in reality, an undercover agent from the IRS. Walsh used a hidden microphone to secretly record everything Williams said during the meeting. More agents hid outside.

Olsen said he was considering hiring Williams. His visitor replied that he wanted $25,000 in exchange for providing specifics about the

State Bar's illegal conduct against Mitchelson. It was obvious that Williams had access to at least some of the State Bar's prosecutorial documents, and he boasted that he'd sold such information before. Williams said his information would show that the State Bar's charges were trumped up for their publicity value.

The impostor law clerk in Olsen's office questioned Williams further. He definitely knew about the IRS's criminal investigation, too. Could Williams get the grand jury transcripts? Affirmative, Williams replied. But that tipped the agents off that Williams was bluffing; there were no transcripts yet.

At first, Newhouse presumed that Williams was just someone who had an inside source at the State Bar and was playing that for all it was worth. But the IRS agents had followed Williams to his car, a 1988 BMW, and traced his license plate. The car was registered to someone named Thomas Scott Molloy—and Mike Williams and Thomas Molloy were one and the same.

Victoria Molloy's brother was the shadowy character who was trying to sell his covert services to Mitchelson for $25,000. He had filched at least two documents relating to Mitchelson from his sister's home, where he was also living.

Mitchelson thus generated still more business for the Los Angeles district attorney. This time, Thomas Molloy was under investigation. (The D.A. concluded that no laws had been broken.)

The authorities simultaneously confronted Victoria Molloy and her brother during separate interviews late on a Friday afternoon. Victoria, reduced to tears by the questions from investigators from the D.A.'s office, denied complicity and said she was shocked. Molloy was in an untenable situation, yet she didn't see that, and steadfastly tried to remain as the chief prosecutor on Mitchelson's case. Even more surprisingly, the Bar let her do so for more than two months, until she finally quit the case under pressure from Mitchelson's lawyers.

Thomas Molloy, meanwhile, tried to talk his way out of trouble. Confronted that day, he claimed he was simply helping his "friend," Steve Walsh, investigate Mitchelson's case. "It was a total business deal between me and Walsh."

The IRS agent, who was present but had not yet revealed his real purpose, then pulled out a business card embossed in gold with an IRS lawman's badge. He slid it across the table to Thomas Molloy. The card carried Walsh's name and, below it, the title: Special Agent.

Thomas Molloy, already on probation in Texas for kidnapping, was stunned. "Am I under arrest?"

The State Bar couldn't get rid of the Mitchelson case fast enough after that. It shelved the Sotheby's count and settled every other charge, dismissing seven of the counts outright and accepting his admission to six other counts of failing to adequately supervise his staff, failing to pay refunds promptly, and failing to communicate with clients.*

But Molloy's machinations gave Marvin Mitchelson an edge he would never otherwise have enjoyed. Instead of punishing Mitchelson for his admissions of wrongdoing, the Bar Court judge hearing the case gave Mitchelson more time to investigate whether the Bar used illegal tactics in making its case against him.

Mitchelson claimed Thomas Molloy was part of a Bar plot to infiltrate his defense team. "It's gotta be a vicious attempt to get Marvin Mitchelson," the white-haired lawyer insisted. If he could prove that, the entire Bar case could be dismissed and there would be no punishment.

Score another point for Mitchelson.

31

There was a tight knot of dark-suited people milling and murmuring self-consciously in the thirteenth floor hallway of the federal building in downtown Los Angeles. It could have been a wake for Marvin Mitchelson.

This was the last Wednesday in November, 1990. Tashi Grady stood there with her lawyer. Roger Olsen, who was Mitchelson's criminal tax lawyer, was there with a second attorney for himself. An employee of Marvin's accountant also waited. All were there under subpoena or the threat of same. One at a time, they were summoned into the grand jury room to tell what they knew about the affairs of Marvin Mitchelson.

Mitchelson had not been called, for he was the grand jury's target. But the lawyers and witnesses who were there constituted his spiritual presence. The grand jurors were curious. Being only human, they particularly wanted to hear from Tashi Grady. But now that Tashi was before them she was surprising even her lawyer—or so he later said—by taking the Fifth Amendment.

Tashi refused to talk.

---

*In March of 1990, the State Bar gave Mitchelson another wake-up call, filing eight more charges of trust-account violations, writing bad checks, and keeping inadequate records. The new proceeding didn't move any faster than the earlier one, though, and Mitchelson started trying all over again to get the charges dismissed.

The government granted her immunity from prosecution. That meant her testimony couldn't lead to prosecution against her for any possible criminal acts she might describe.

Tashi Grady returned to the grand jury six days before Christmas of 1990 to tell all that she said she knew. She looked great as she cooly walked into the grand jury room. Under questioning by Assistant U.S. Attorney George Newhouse, she acknowledged a close relationship with Mitchelson during 1985 and 1986. And, no, she said demurely, she didn't know anything about Mitchelson's cocaine use.

Two years into its investigation, the IRS had already returned 107 subpoenas (out of an eventual 135) to the grand jury and documented about $1.5 million in income received by Mitchelson but not reported to the IRS.

Mitchelson's unfortunate case became a legacy to every lawyer in the state. The rape allegations brought a flood of complaints about sexual misconduct by other lawyers—so much so that the State Bar was forced by the legislature to adopt a rule regulating lawyer-client sex. And the IRS targeted other high-paid lawyers in the state for criminal investigation, in a program dubbed Project Esquire, after realizing how easy it was for lawyers like Mitchelson to conceal their true income.

Mitchelson's accountant said that his client lived in fear of an imminent indictment. Maybe that was true. But Mitchelson also acted like he could cheat the inevitable.

Martha Smilgis had seen that when she went along with Mitchelson on what would be his last visit to Roy Cohn. Marvin hired a limousine to drive him up to Cohn's Connecticut cottage.

"We sat down in the living room, and it really smelled sort of like a sick home. You could really get a feeling of illness. . . .

"There was a beautiful, beautiful light," Smilgis remembered, "which made it even weirder. It was sort of spiritual light, you know? That kind of desert light; that slight, tinted, rarefied light.

"And Roy came in, and he looked like he was dead." Smilgis didn't kiss him; Mitchelson shook his hand and hugged him. "He was a *corpse*. He was drinking, I guess, this AZT, because every hour or three hours he had to have this little cup of stuff. He was very thin, but he had been on this drug from NIH. He was at NIH and he had come out and they were keeping him alive, is what it was, with AZT; very experimental."

The odd thing about that day was how no one ever mentioned the imminent death that hung all around them. They made small talk and rode the limousine to lunch and kibbitzed about each other's dietary habits. But there were no last words, no acknowledgement that Cohn was dying of AIDS. All there was, Smilgis recalled later, was "a great sense of relief" when the two of them piled back into the limousine for what turned into a subdued trip back to Manhattan.

Now, that same desperate pall hung about Mitchelson. But he dared not acknowledge it, lest that bring him down. This gifted, flawed, strange genius of a man knew how to defend himself against reality. That was what he had been doing for his entire life. That was how he survived.

POSTSCRIPT

Linda Acaldo was still working as a prosecutor for the Los Angeles district attorney's office at the beginning of 1992.

Kristin Barrett-Whitney lost her lawsuit against Mitchelson after an eleven-day trial in Santa Monica in November of 1991. The jury's rejection of her claim of sexual battery, after listening to an impassioned closing argument from Mitchelson himself, came almost five years to the day after she filed her suit. The court witnessed Barrett-Whitney's tearful accounts about how various men—Mitchelson, her husband, a dentist, and a psychotherapist—had abused her: "I've just had a lot of sad things in my life." The jurors also heard an expert psychiatric witness for the defense claim that Barrett-Whitney suffered from personality disorders marked by manipulation, deception, and lies. Mitchelson compared her accusation and its aftermath to "going through hell." But right after the verdict was in, he just deadpanned: "I told ya I didn't do it."

Richard Hirschfeld was convicted in March of 1991 of two criminal counts of tax and securities conspiracy, and another of filing a false tax return. A federal judge ordered Hirschfeld held without bond pending his appeal, and eight months later he was still in jail.

Thomas Molloy was arrested for kidnapping and raping a woman at gunpoint in Texas several months after his attempt to sell State Bar records to Mitchelson went awry. He was convicted at trial and sentenced to eighty-five years in prison on the rape charge. He pleaded guilty to the kidnapping and was sentenced to twenty years. His probation for two earlier kidnapping and theft-of-service convictions also was revoked and he received two additional ten-year concurrent prison sentences for them. He was in prison at year's end.

Victoria Molloy was still an attorney for the State Bar of California at the beginning of 1992.

Marvin Pancoast died in prison in December of 1991. He had AIDS.

ACKNOWLEDGMENTS

I owe much to many.

To paraphrase Harold Rhoden: If it had not been for my editor, Tom Dunne, this book would still have been written, but I don't know how. Tom saw clearly its potential and supported me through some difficult times in completing it. And he assigned to my book an exceptional editorial assistant, Patty Rosati, whose commitment to the project was total. Thank you, Tom and Patty.

Lotte Meister, associate general counsel of St. Martin's Press, spent the better part of four months checking and challenging every aspect of this manuscript. The book is better for all her painstaking work, and I owe her a world of thanks.

Jane Dystel, my agent, gave me the idea for this book and went to bat for me more than once to make sure that it was published well. Thank you, Jane.

I think the greatest honor in journalism is to have the respect of one's peers, and I was privileged during my research to have the assistance of two journalists for whom I came to have enormous respect: Chuck Lewis, formerly of "60 Minutes," and Jonathan Beaty of *Time*. Both spent many hours helping me, and entrusted me with research materials they had gathered. I am indebted to them.

Several other journalists also provided assistance: Fred Bernstein, whose book, *The Jewish Mother's Hall of Fame*, featured a chapter about Sonia Mitchelson; Martha Smilgis of *Time*; Robin Groom and John Mintz of the *Washington Post*; David Margolick of the *New York Times*; and Patricia Morrisroe, who profiled Mitchelson for *New York* magazine.

Michael John Seeley and Allison Porter were my principal researchers; they were with me from the start and stayed with me throughout. Allison, a paralegal who previously worked as my researcher on *The Litigators*, summarized court documents and assumed the principal burden of finding and doing initial interviews of Mitchelson's boyhood chums as well as women who claimed to have been sexual victims. John covered trials and State Bar proceedings in Los Angeles for me, and obtained documents from the California courts. Collecting so much Mitchelsonia was not easy: One day, as he left the courthouse document room, John looked back and witnessed a clerk pretending to strangle him. I am also grateful for the research assistance of Laura Harris, an architectural historian, who traced the Mitchelson family's background at the Library of Congress and the National Archives, and who also researched the Supreme Court's files on the *Douglas* case; for the assistance of Dr. Maureen Jung, an archivist, who researched the *Douglas* case at the California State Archives in Sacramento; and, of course, for the help of my wife, Susan Raleigh Jenkins, an attorney, who organized and indexed materials relating to the Mormon Will, *Marvin vs. Marvin*, and Vicki Morgan cases.

Lynn M. Ecklund of the Seek Information Service, Glendale, California, got me the otherwise-unobtainable contents of many *Los Angeles Times* morgue files. David Martin, an exceptional editor who also happens to be my close friend, read the rough manuscript and also re-checked every tape-recorded quote for accuracy. It says something that, despite two solid weeks of twelve-hour days doing this, he is *still* my friend.

Early on, before I really knew the direction this book was headed, I received help and guidance that gave me confidence to continue this project. Although he did not wish to be interviewed about the Vicki Morgan case, Michael Dave nonetheless provided public documents and spent one Friday night around his pool explaining them to me. Chuck Meyer of Goldman & Kagon had Bekins retrieve the entire *Marvin vs. Marvin* transcript from his firm's dead files and then helped me make sense of it. Ted Cohen provided hospitality and introductions. Frank Steinschriber provided his correspondence, clippings, and all the depositions from the Joan Collins divorce case. Susie Magee helped me unravel the Fassi transactions and was a charming dinner companion. Linda Acaldo gave up an entire Saturday to sit at her kitchen table and provide me with extensive recollections about her Mitchelson years. After Laura Harris, who was doing my Supreme Court and National Archives research, had tried every possible way of obtaining a transcript of Mitchelson's oral arguments in *Douglas* and concluded that none existed, Judge Jack Goertzen of Los Angeles one day offhandedly asked me whether it would help if he gave me his *tape recordings* of the arguments. I was positively stunned at my good fortune. Having those tapes brought that section of the book to life for me.

The California State Archives turned out to be the veritable mother lode of information about the *Douglas* case. I wish, particularly, to thank the clerical staff there who helped: Mary Lewin, Leslie Laurance,

Rita Rowell, Janette Martin, and their supervisor, Melodi Anderson.

Marion Mitchelson Gartler and May Mitchelson Albert provided photos and letters which could not be reproduced, but which aided me greatly in understanding Marvin Mitchelson's early life. Bill Hooper of the Time, Inc. archives supplied extensive background information about Bob Landry, who was one of Marvin's friends from the early days.

Harold Rhoden spent a great deal of time with me early in my research, at a time when Mitchelson still was saying little or nothing to me. Hal Rhoden was one of the straightest shooters I ever met, and his early help meant a lot. The legal profession lost one of its genuine characters when he was killed in a plane crash in 1989.

Paul Cohen, a private investigator, supplied documents and background on the *Christian* case. He also was the first person to tell me that Harold Rhoden's plane had crashed, before any word of it reached the media.

Bob Arbogast gave me Mitchelson's elementary-school newspapers. Don Llorente of the National Transportation Safety Board was a valued resource for background on the Rhoden plane crash. Eric Rhoden used his late father's Rolodex to help us locate a crucial interview subject who otherwise never would have been found. Joan Glanz Rimmon provided a complete family tree, listing over 3,100 names, for the Mitchelsons. Ken Allen and Mitch Tropin served as confidants and all-around reality testers.

Some who granted interviews or provided documents and other materials are not mentioned in the book despite their contributions. Thanks to Mike Brenner, Abigail Freed, Anthony Glassman, Jack Goehring, Ralph Howe, Tom Kennedy, Ben Norman, Maria Ramsey, and Bob Wian.

Many other people who assisted me did so on the condition that their names not appear in this book, and by honoring their request I cannot list them here. But they know who they are, and I owe special thanks to them.

Thank you, also, to the staff of the Wilshire Royale Hotel in Los Angeles.

Thanks, finally, to my wife, Susan, for understanding the importance to me of this solitary pursuit, and to our children, Jenny, Christina, and Greg. I love you guys. And thanks to my mother, Shirley. Without *her*, this book really wouldn't have been written.

NOTES ON SOURCES

I conducted fifty-one interviews with Marvin Mitchelson for this book. Many were done over the phone, usually on evenings or weekends, an hour or two at a stretch. Lengthier tape-recorded sessions with Mitchelson took place in Los Angeles: We spent the better parts of three days and evenings together, from February 21 through February 23, 1990, in conversations that occurred in Mitchelson's office, home, and automobile, and at various restaurants. With the exception of the restaurants, where we were joined variously by Morgan Mitchelson, Marcella Mitchelson, and Tashi Grady, Mitchelson and I always talked alone. On March 16, 1991 the two of us spent the afternoon and evening at Mitchelson's home, going over various things, including allegations I had received concerning drug use, that I hoped to obtain his clarification of or comment on. This session was also tape recorded.

Altogether, over 1,000 interviews were conducted for this book during more than three years of research. Among 104 key sources, some were interviewed dozens of times; one source was interviewed 154 times. I used many of my interviews with key sources to clarify or affirm information already obtained elsewhere.

As valuable as these interviews were, they alone could not provide the full context for Mitchelson's life. Thus, some of my most important sources were documents gathered and examined during the course of research for this book. Altogether, thirty-two thousand pages of material were amassed from legal and investigative sources. In some cases, I was also given access to contemporaneous writings about, and tape recordings of, Marvin Mitchelson that were made by third parties.

The names of Mitchelson's alleged sexual victims who have come forward to the LAPD or the Los Angeles District Attorney are known to me. But I have here used the names only of those who, by publicly identifying themselves, indicated that they wanted their names revealed.

The names of the rest have been withheld. If described at all, they are identified by a pseudonym.

If a name has been changed to protect someone's identity, the bracketed phrase "name changed" denotes this.

Some of those whom I attempted to interview refused to talk to me. They include: Catherine Mann; Morgan Mason; Pamela Mason; James Bascue, chief trial counsel of the California State Bar; Ira Reiner, Los Angeles district attorney; Yvonne Renfrew, attorney for Kristin Barrett-Whitney in her rape trial against Mitchelson; Adrienne Rhoden Armstrong; Ronald Perelman; Frank Perdue; Kathleen Perdue; Jacqueline Bouhoutsos; Felicia MacDonald; and Doreen Landry Millichip, the widow of Bob Landry.

Timmie R. White, the attorney for Thomas Scott Molloy, and Susan Kasen, who was involved in litigation with Perelman, spoke only briefly and non-substantively to me.

Michael Dave helped considerably by producing documents, but declined to substantively discuss his representation of Vicki Morgan.

Despite considerable effort, neither Bennie Will Meyes nor William Douglas, the two principals in *Douglas vs. California*, could be located. Joe Carr, Burton Marks, and Bill James, three lawyers who also played roles in the *Douglas* case, died before I began my research. Clint Murchison also died before my research began.

Biographical information about lawyers was provided by the California State Bar.

Where someone's age is listed, it is that person's age at the time the events being described were taking place.

Where a person is said to have "thought" or "believed" something, such an attribution is based on a comment by the person himself, either to me or to someone I subsequently interviewed.

Divorce being Mitchelson's business, some of his female clients currently use last names different from when he represented them. In this book, however, they retain the surname they used when Mitchelson represented them. There is a practical reason for this: Their litigation was conducted under that surname, and that is how it is still indexed at the courthouse.

No one who was interviewed received payment; no person received any assurances as to how he or she would be portrayed or how his or her comments would be used; and no one who was interviewed reviewed the manuscript before publication.

In the interests of brevity (and in some cases to preserve confidentiality), I have not included in these notes my sources for every passage in the book. Similarly, I have not always included every source for the passages that are listed.

In the notes that follow, AI stands for Author's Interview and MM stands for Marvin Mitchelson. Where others performed research or conducted interviews, their initials are used: LH stands for Laura Harris, AP stands for Allison Porter, and MJS stands for Michael John Seeley.

PART ONE: I WANTED TO BE FAMOUS . . .

Chapter One (pages 3–6)

p. 3 **Scene at Noa Noa:** The Author was present, February 23, 1990.

p. 3. **Met Tashi at a Paramount screening:** AI with Martha Smilgis, September 6, 1989.

p. 4. **Aaron Spelling, Morgan Brittany:** As to basic biographical information and production information, AI with Bret Garwood, historian of Spelling Entertainment, December 5, 1991.

p. 4. **"I'll be seeing you . . .":** The song was written by Irving Kabal and Sammy Fain.

p. 5. **"I like publicity":** "Divorce, American Style," *Rolling Stone*, July 14, 1988, by Corbin Bernsen.

p. 5. **Scene on Hollywood Boulevard:** The Author was present, February 23, 1990.

p. 5. **Felder's income:** "The Plaintiff's Attorneys' Great Honey Rush," *Forbes*, October 16, 1989.

p. 6. **Weitzman's representation of DeLorean:** General background came from the chapter on Weitzman in *The Trial Lawyers* (St. Martin's Press, 1988) by Emily Couric.

Chapter Two (Pages 7–13)

p. 7. **Description of Barrett-Whitney:** "The Trials of Marvin Mitchelson," *Los Angeles Times Magazine*, October 8, 1988, by Ann Louise Bardach.

p. 7. **"Crazies":** AI with MM, February 21, 1990.

p. 7. **Clients feel like they're falling in love:** "The Pulitzer Fight Goes On," *People*, January 24, 1983, by Eric Levin.

p. 7. **Barrett-Whitney's report of rape:** LAPD investigative report, January 31, 1986.

p. 7. **Made "the hair on the back of my neck stand up":** "Divorce Lawyer," CBS's "60 Minutes," June 26, 1988.

pp. 7–8. **Conversations between Barrett-Whitney and Mitchelson:** LAPD transcript.

p. 8. **Mitchelson's characterizations of Barrett-Whitney:** "Lawyer Is Accused in a TV Broadcast of Raping Two Women," *New York Times*, June 27, 1988, by the Associated Press.

p. 8. **Begged Wallace not to run the piece:** "60 Minutes," June 26, 1988.

p. 8. **"Sensitive-male" image, scene at Le Cirque:** "The Prince of Palimony," *New York* magazine, January 10, 1983, by Patricia Morrisroe.

p. 9. **"Something regal about her":** "Divorce, Mitchelson Style," *New York Times*, January 6, 1980, by Pamela G. Hollie.

p. 9. **Had worn her visage. . . :** "Meet Mr. Palimony," *National Law Journal*, October 11, 1982, by James S. Granelli.

p. 9. **Venus set into the ceiling above his desk:** "Divorce, Mitchelson Style."

p. 9. **Favorite possession in the world:** "My Favorite Things," *Los Angeles Magazine*, April 1983, by Laura Meyers.

p. 9. **Once in that tub, phones turned off. . . :** "Heaven on Earth: The Law, Mom and Venus Above," *Washington Post*, October 20, 1982, by Henry Allen.

p. 10. **Description of Mitchelson bathing, conducting:** "Heaven on Earth."

p. 10. **"Ungrateful Heart":** AI with MM, March 16, 1991.

p. 10. **French retains Mitchelson; he invites her to see bathroom:** "60 Minutes," June 26, 1988.

p. 10. **"I stepped just a tiny bit inside . . .":** "60 Minutes," June 26, 1988.

pp. 10–11. **Barrett-Whitney presses for investigation; complaints about obstruction of justice:** "Grand Juror Who Pressed for Probe of Mitchelson Quits," *Los Angeles Times*, June 11, 1987, by Ted Rohrlich.

p. 11. **Fined for bringing frivolous appeals:** "Trials of Marvin Mitchelson: Lawyer of the Famous Now Defends Himself," *New York Times*, July 3, 1988, by David Margolick.

p. 11. **Said were prohibited:** *Made in Heaven, Settled in Court* (J.P. Tarcher, 1976), by Marvin Mitchelson. The passage in question appears on page 176 of Mitchelson's book.

p. 11. **Back taxes:** "Trials of Marvin Mitchelson: Lawyer of the Famous Now Defends Himself."

p. 11. **Threatening disbarment:** AI with Victoria Molloy, chief counsel in the California Bar's case against Mitchelson, March 30, 1989.

p. 11. **Hospitalized for drug detoxification:** "The Trials of Marvin Mitchelson," *Los Angeles Times Magazine*. Mitchelson denied to the *Los Angeles Times* that he was ever a patient at Beverly Glen. He refused to discuss the matter with the Author. AI with MM, March 16, 1991.

p. 12. **"Maybe I'm a sleepwalker!":** AI with MM, January 6, 1990.

p. 12. **Miramontez case:** "The Dukes of Divorce," *Us* magazine, May 2, 1988, by Cree McCree.

p. 12. **$5 million house:** Mitchelson valued his mansion, with its three acres of grounds, at between $5 million and $8 million. (AI with MM, March 16, 1991.)

p. 12. **Rolls-Royce in mother's name:** Verified through the California Department of Motor Vehicles on September 24, 1991. The Rolls registered to Sonia was a 1977 model. A 1971 Rolls-Royce was registered to Marcella Mitchelson.

p. 12. **"What if it isn't in my name?":** AI with MM, December 5, 1989.

p. 12. **C.I. (controlled informant) goes to the IRS:** Confidential source.

p. 12. **C.I.'s motivation for going to the authorities:** Confidential source.

p. 13. **"I'm not as happy":** AI with MM, February 21, 1990.

p. 13. **"You know something?":** AI with MM, February 23, 1990.

PART TWO: SONNY

Chapter Three (Pages 17–24)

Except as noted below, the sources for this chapter were AIs with May Mitchelson Albert (July 16, 1989; August 28, 1989; and January 4, 1990), Marion Mitchelson Gartler (July 16, 1989), and Bob Arbogast (September 29, 1989).

General background information on the Mitchelson family's early years came from a book written by Sonia in 1981 that was privately published by her family the following year; from old letters and photographs provided by May Mitchelson Albert; and from old Detroit and Los Angeles city directories researched by Laura Harris at the Library of Congress.

p. 19. **Fired from Bob's Big Boy:** AI with MM, September 12, 1989.

p. 20. **Five feet ten, 180 pounds:** Mitchelson's driver's license data. The license lists his eyes as brown.

p. 23. **Hospital corpsman aboard the U.S.S. Shanghai:** Verified by LH from the ship's roster, at the National Archives in Washington.

p. 23. **"Well done":** Letter from Herbert Mitchelson to Marvin, May 11, 1947.

p. 24. **Date and place of Herbert Michelson's death:** From his death certificate.

p. 24. **"So I tried to prove myself to my mother":** AI with MM, June 21, 1989.

Chapter Four (Pages 24–27)

p. 24. **"It was time to come home":** AI with MM, February 21, 1990.

p. 25. **Amorous situation with female tenant:** AI with MM, January 19, 1990.

p. 25. **Sonia fretted about Sonny; wanted to keep him in line; worried about the Hollywood types:** AI with Marion Mitchelson Gartler, July 16, 1989.

p. 25. **Sal Mineo was a tenant.** Mineo was murdered in a garage at the Holloway Drive apartments. Sonia Mitchelson telephoned Marvin, who lived nearby, and they both identified the body for the police. AIs with MM, December 5, 1989 and January 6, 1990.

p. 26. **Mother locked Marvin out:** Notes of Fred Bernstein's interviews with Sonia in July 1983, from AI with Bernstein, February 6, 1990.

p. 26. **She chided him in a letter:** Letter from Sonia Mitchelson to Marvin, April 28, 1979. This letter was also quoted, in part, in *The Jewish Mothers' Hall of Fame* (Doubleday, 1986), by Fred A. Bernstein.

p. 26. **"I stuck the meat knife into something":** AI with May Mitchelson Albert, July 16, 1989.

p. 26. **Other abortive tries at college:** AI with MM, April 29, 1990.

p. 26. **"I was devastated":** "The Prince of Palimony," *New York* magazine, January 10, 1983, by Patricia Morrisroe.

p. 27. **Considers various vocations, finally decides upon law:** AI with MM, February 21, 1990.

p. 27. **"With Marvin's big mouth . . .":** AI with May Mitchelson Albert, July 16, 1989.

Chapter Five (Pages 27–33)

p. 27. **Mitchelson on probation at UCLA Law School:** AI with MM, November 27, 1991.

p. 27. **Southwestern's ambience:** AI with Cynthia Peters, assistant director, public information, August 26, 1991. Also, various articles on the law school's history appeared in 1990 editions of the school's publication, *Southwestern Law.*

p. 27. **Southwestern's accreditation:** The law school did not receive ABA accreditation until 1970.

p. 27. **"Southwestern was the one place . . .":** AI with Ted Cohen, March 30, 1989.

p. 28. **Background of Bob Landry:** Various articles, clippings, and radio scripts supplied to AP by Bill Hooper of the Time, Inc. archives. Also, AI with former *Life* photographer Mark Kaufman, September 23, 1989.

p. 28. **Private weightlifting program:** AI with MM, February 18, 1990.

p. 29. **Underwear in a plastic grocery bag:** Confidential source.

p. 29. **Had a big car; everybody thought he was rich; other recollections:** AI with Cohen, March 30, 1989.

p. 29. **Working as a process server:** *Made in Heaven, Settled in Court* (J.P. Tarcher, 1976), by Marvin Mitchelson.

p. 30. "**Mailboxer**": AI with Cohen, March 30, 1989.

p. 30. **Chased while serving subpoena:** "Man Found Guilty in Battery Case," *Los Angeles Times*, December 30, 1955.

p. 30. "**I'll tell ya . . .**": AI with Mack Marks, August 8, 1989.

pp. 30–31. **Serving subpoena on Joan Collins:** *Past Imperfect: An Auto-biography* (Berkley Books, 1985), by Joan Collins.

p. 31. **One of Sonia's relations was nonplussed:** Letter of Sonia Mit-chelson to Marion, May 12, 1983.

p. 31. **Sonia overdoses; is offended at intimation that she intended it:** Letter of Sonia Mitchelson to Marion, May 12, 1983. This portion of the eight-page letter is reproduced in *The Jewish Mothers' Hall of Fame.*

p. 32. **Pain in shoulder; Sonia nurses Marvin; takes Bar results from mail; gives him the happy news:** Letter of Sonia Mitchelson to Mar-ion, May 12, 1983.

p. 32. **Sets Marvin up in law practice, furnished his office:** Letter of Sonia Mitchelson to Marion, May 12, 1983.

p. 32. **Kept right on living . . . with Sonia:** Notes of Fred Bernstein's interviews with Sonia in July 1983, from AI with Bernstein, February 6, 1990. Sonia told Bernstein: "I had to be a father and a mother. [Marvin] didn't move out until he was a lawyer. He lived at home until he was at least thirty. He moved out when I married Ben [Knoppow], in August 1960. He married in December 1960."

p. 33. **Photograph on courthouse steps:** The family photo was provided by May Mitchelson Albert.

Chapter Six (Pages 33–46)

Except as noted in the page citations below, the sources for this chap-ter were various documents, including trial transcripts and judicial deci-sions, from the case of *People of the State of California vs. Bennie Will Meyes and William Douglas* (Docket No. 208300, Superior Court of California, Los Angeles; 18 Cal.Rptr. 322 and 198 Cal.App.2d 484). A related case involving the same two defendants ultimately was decided by the U.S. Supreme Court.

Meyes and Douglas were arrested for murder on October 24, 1958. Their first trial ended in a hung jury. Upon retrial, on June 23, 1959, Meyes was found guilty of second degree murder; Douglas was found not guilty. Transcripts of both trials were obtained from the California State Archives in Sacramento. Maureen Jung served as my researcher there. She read the extensive trial transcripts, prepared an index of the proceedings, and supervised the copying of thousands of pages of the transcript. (I found it nothing short of amazing that the original tran-scripts had been preserved, for they were made years before anyone could have known of their ultimate importance. Kudos to the state archives.)

Laura Harris served as my researcher at the Supreme Court and the National Archives in Washington, D.C. The Supreme Court still had in its files the original indictments and all the minute entries of the California trial court, which together constituted a kind of blueprint for reconstructing the early phases of the case. At the National Archives, we found the rest of the Supreme Court's records, including the Court's chronological correspondence file; the original copy of the trial-court record; and various *habeas corpus* motions filed by Douglas, who became an accomplished jailhouse lawyer and whose unavailing pleadings nonetheless shed light on how he viewed the criminal proceedings.

p. 33. **First bad check case:** "Divorce, American Style," *Rolling Stone,* July 14, 1988 by Corbin Bernsen; *Made in Heaven, Settled in Court* (J.P. Tarcher, 1976), by Marvin Mitchelson.

p. 33. **75-year-old client:** *Made in Heaven, Settled in Court.*

p. 34. **"Acting for real":** "Divorce, American Style."

p. 34. **"I'm different people":** AI with MM, February 21, 1990.

p. 34. **"No one knows me too long":** AI with MM, December 5, 1989.

p. 34. **"It's lonely":** AI with MM, December 5, 1989.

p. 34. **"Help my boy"; how Mitchelson got the case:** AI with MM, October 19, 1989; also *Made in Heaven, Settled in Court.*

p. 35. **Killing of Detective Gene Nash:** Bitterolf, long since retired from the LAPD, described the shooting during an interview with the Author on February 17, 1991.

pp. 35–36. **Nash was shot in chest, abdomen, etc.:** "Eight Rounded Up in Fatal Shooting of Policeman," *Los Angeles Times,* October 21, 1958.

p. 36. **Nash died before his widow arrived:** "Eight Rounded Up."

p. 37. **Douglas said he was told to confess:** "Tribune Gets First Interview with Benny (sic) Meyes, 'Cop Killer' Facing Death Charge," *Los Angeles Tribune,* November 28, 1958, by Almena Loma.

p. 37. **Tough, emotional case:** AI with Paul Breckenridge, November 30, 1989.

p. 37. **Description of Joseph Carr:** AI with Breckenridge, November 30, 1989.

p. 38. **California law regarding accessories in homicides:** *Made in Heaven, Settled in Court.*

p. 38. **Jury deadlocked 10–2 in first trial:** AI with MM, October 19, 1989.

p. 46. **Mitchelson boasts about victory:** AI with MM, February 21, 1990.

Chapter Seven (Pages 46–48)

p. 46. Landry married again: AI with former *Life* photographer Mark Kaufman, September 23, 1989.

p. 46. Gushing *Los Angeles Times* article: "Bachelor's First Love, Antiques, Keeps Conversation Astir," ran on May 12, 1959, by Dewey Linze. A similar story was rerun in the *Los Angeles Times* on July 27, 1961, by Doug Maldin.

p. 47. Mitchelson joined Landry in Naples: AI with MM, October 19, 1989.

p. 47. Sonia didn't approve; other girls were standing in line: AI with May Mitchelson Albert, July 16, 1989.

p. 47. Marvin always was kind of a screwball": AI with Mack Marks, August 8, 1989.

p. 47. Wedding of Marvin and Marcella: "Beverly Hills Attorney Weds Italian Actress," *Los Angeles Times*, December 19, 1960.

p. 48. Description of Bob Landry's funeral: AI with MM, February 18, 1990; AI with Kaufman, September 23, 1989.

p. 48. Mitchelson's fear of dying: AI with MM, February 23, 1990.

Chapter Eight (Pages 48–61)

p. 48. Lawsuit against Kennedy: "Kennedy Sued by Four Delegates," *Los Angeles Times*, October 27, 1960. The lawsuit was still generating articles in the *Los Angeles Times* and the *Los Angeles Herald-Examiner* nearly two years later.

p. 49. Florence and Beverly Aadland: "Mother Ties Beverly to Three Film Georges," *Los Angeles Herald-Examiner*, April 19, 1960, as well other stories from the Los Angeles newspapers. The case generated extensive coverage.

p. 49. Had trouble controlling Aadland: *Made in Heaven, Settled in Court* (J.P. Tarcher, 1976), by Marvin Mitchelson.

p. 49. *Douglas* case: Following the not-guilty verdict for Douglas (see Chapter Seven), he and Meyes were indicted on August 11, 1959, this time on charges of robbery, assault with intent to commit murder, and assault with a deadly weapon. It was this second case, *People of the State of California vs. William Douglas and Bennie Will Meyes* (Docket No. 218196, Superior Court of California, Los Angeles County; 187 Cal.App.2d 802, 10 Cal.Rptr. 188) that ultimately went to the U.S. Supreme Court. The case was argued during the Court's October 1961 term, and then was reargued during the October 1962 term. (*Douglas et al. vs. California*, 372 U.S. 353, decided March 18, 1963.)

Few law review articles have been written about *Douglas*, and none that was written was used as a source for this book. The several

more-or-less contemporaneous accounts of the opinion and its impli-
cations are nonetheless listed here for those who wish to do more
reading on the subject: "Due Process in State Criminal Proceedings,"
77 Harv.L.Rev. 103 (1963); "The Fourteenth Amendment and Pro-
cedural Rights of the Indigents in State Appellate Courts," 8 St.
Louis L.Jour. 125 (1963); and "Right to Counsel in Criminal Post-
Conviction Review Proceedings," 51 Cal.L.Rev. 970 (1963).

Except as noted in the page citations below, the sources for the
remainder of this chapter were the above-cited judicial opinions in
the *Douglas* case, various documents stored at the Supreme Court
and the National Archives relating to it, and audio tape recordings of
the two Supreme Court oral arguments. Laura Harris did this part of
the document research. Judge Jack Goertzen provided the tapes.

p. 49. Mitchelson was broke after the second murder trial: AI with
MM, October 19, 1988.

p. 50. Atkins considered the defendants ugly and loathsome: AI with
Norman R. Atkins, December 4, 1989.

p. 51. Sent to Folsom and San Quentin: Places of incarceration were
obtained from Bennie Will Meyes's Notice of Motion to Annul, Va-
cate and Set Aside the Judgment, Docket No. 208300, filed February
23, 1967, obtained from the California State Archives, Sacramento.

p. 51. Description of Burton Marks: AI with Jack Goertzen, September
25, 1989.

p. 52. Mitchelson's views on appellate law: *Made in Heaven, Settled
in Court.*

p. 52. *Betts vs. Brady* as existing precedent: *Gideon's Trumpet* (Vintage
Books, 1964), by Anthony Lewis.

p. 52. Supreme Court scene: *Gideon's Trumpet.*

p. 53. Goertzen's thoughts on defending the *status quo:* AI with Jack
Goertzen, September 25, 1989.

p. 54. As Goertzen later explained it: AI with Jack Goertzen, September 25, 1989.

p. 59. *Gideon* case: *Gideon's Trumpet.*

p. 61. Douglas and Meyes convicted at retrial: AI with MM, December 7, 1991. Mitchelson represented Douglas at the retrial; Burton
Marks represented Meyes. Joe Carr was the prosecutor. According to
Mitchelson, the retrial lasted only two days and was confined to their
rearguing the trial record; no live witnesses were called.

p. 61. Discharged from San Quentin, Folsom: Dates of incarceration
in the state prison system were provided to MJS by the California
Department of Corrections.

p. 61. Result announced by Justice Black in *Gideon:* *Gideon's
Trumpet.*

p. 61. **Goertzen felt robbed of greatness:** AI with Jack Goertzen, September 25, 1989.

PART THREE: TICKET TO RIDE

Chapter Nine (Pages 65–69)

p. 65. **Beverly Hills during the 1960s:** "Street of Gold: It Was Luxury They Wanted in the Eighties; Rodeo Drive Had it," *Wall Street Journal*, December 22, 1989, by Kathleen A. Hughes.

p. 65. **"These were the guys":** AI with Carey Caruso (son of Paul Caruso), June 29, 1989.

p. 65. **Paul Caruso's story:** AI with Paul Caruso, May 17, 1989.

p. 66. **Pamela Mason hires, then fires Paul Caruso:** AI with Caruso, May 17, 1989.

p. 66. **Various accounts of why Caruso was fired:** "Divorce, American Style," *Rolling Stone*, July 14, 1988; AI with MM, February 23, 1990.

p. 67. **Pamela's problems against Jake Ehrlich:** *Made in Heaven, Settled in Court*.

p. 67. **Mitchelson boasts about *Douglas* at Pamela's party:** AI with MM, October 19, 1989.

p. 67. **"He didn't seem the standard Hollywood slick talker":** *Marriage Is the First Step Toward Divorce.* (Paul S. Eriksson, Inc., 1968), by Pamela Mason with Vi Wolfson.

p. 67. **"Mrs. Chatterly":** "Pamela Mason Speaks Her Mind," *Los Angeles Herald-Examiner*, July 29, 1984.

p. 67. **Mitchelson a guest on Pamela's talk show:** *Made in Heaven, Settled in Court*.

p. 67. **"All to mother":** *Made in Heaven, Settled in Court*.

p. 68. **Subpoenaed forty of the Masons's friends:** *Made in Heaven, Settled in Court*.

p. 68. **Prepared to disclose sexual matters:** "The Trials of Marvin Mitchelson," *Los Angeles Times Magazine*, October 8, 1988, by Ann Louise Bardach.

p. 68. **Mason divorce settlement:** "Pamela Wins Divorce; Splits Millions," *Los Angeles Herald-Examiner*, August 31, 1964, and other Los Angeles newspaper articles.

p. 68. **James Mason:** The actor died on July 27, 1984, in Switzerland.

p. 68. **Masons sue Loretta Young:** "Pamela Mason, Child Press $138,500 Suit," *Santa Monica Evening Outlook*, April 8, 1965, and other Los Angeles newspaper articles.

p. 68. **Pamela's friends delighted with Mitchelson:** *Marriage Is the First Step Toward Divorce.*

p. 68. **"I am the one who discovered Marvin Mitchelson":** "Pamela Mason Speaks Her Mind."

p. 69. **"That's when I first heard . . .", etc.:** AI with Paul Caruso, May 17, 1989.

p. 69. **Mitchelson's response to Caruso:** AI with MM, February 23, 1990.

Chapter Ten (Pages 70–78)

p. 70. **Size and terms of Mitchelson's retainers; allegations of clients:** Derived from various lawsuits filed in Los Angeles Superior Court against Mitchelson by former clients; the Statement of Decision of a fee arbitration panel of the Los Angeles County Bar Association *(Rosenberg vs. Mitchelson,* Case No. P-721-87-M, September 1, 1988); and the State Bar proceedings against Mitchelson.

p. 70. **Various McIsaac comments:** AI with Hugh McIsaac, October 3, 1989.

p. 71. **Weitzman's comments about his cases:** From Weitzman's speech to the American Bar Association, August 5, 1989.

p. 71. **Felder and Mitchelson considered bicoastal collaboration, planned kickoff party at "21":** AI with Raoul Felder, May 9, 1989.

p. 71. **Felder paid $4,000-a-month to Rubenstein:** AI with Raoul Felder, May 9, 1989.

p. 71. **Rubenstein's other clients:** "Hollywood's Most Secret Agent" (Michael Ovitz), *New York Times Magazine,* July 9, 1989, by L.J. Davis; "Image Makers in Takeover Land," *New York Times Magazine,* September 24, 1989, by L.J. Davis.

p. 71. **Sy Presten's** *modus operandi:* AI with Presten, April 28, 1989.

p. 72. **What Mitchelson paid Presten:** Confidential source.

p. 72. **Presten's comments on getting publicity:** AI with Presten, April 28, 1989.

p. 73. **Felder-Mitchelson collaboration collapses:** AI with MM, January 30, 1990. Felder did not dispute that Mitchelson pulled out of the collaboration, but contended that by then he had soured on the partnership, too. (AI with Felder, November 12, 1991.) Felder stated: "I didn't pursue it. [Mitchelson] wasn't talking substance, just about the party at '21.' I just let it die. I didn't want to get involved."

p. 73: **"I think he was envious of me,"** etc.: AI with MM, January 30, 1990. Mitchelson made similar comments during an interview with the Author on February 21, 1990.

p. 73: **"I think I took advantage. . . . I've paid my dues":** AI with MM, February 21, 1990.

p. 73. **Mitchelson said he tried too hard:** AI with MM, February 21, 1990.

p. 73. **Felder organizes bicoastal practice anyway, holds big party:** "Trajectories of Two Famous Divorce Lawyers Intersect in Tyson-Givens Case," *New York Times*, October 14, 1988, by David Margolick.

p. 74. **Mitchelson's wild-and-wooly press conference:** "Felder in Corner," *National Law Journal*, October 24, 1988.

p. 74. **"By the lawyer's clock":** "Trajectories of Two Famous Divorce Lawyers Intersect in Tyson-Givens Case."

p. 74. **"He had some problems. . . . Very sad call.":** AI with Felder, May 9, 1989.

p. 75. **Mitchelson sued Tyson again (footnote):** "Mike Tyson Sued for $11 Million in 'Palimony' Suit," Reuters, October 1, 1991, by Michael Miller.

p. 75. **Felder's hat trick:** "Trajectories of Two Famous Divorce Lawyers Intersect in Tyson-Givens Case."

p. 75. **Weitzman claimed victory, etc.:** From Weitzman's speech to the American Bar Association, August 5, 1989.

p. 76. **"The best press agent I ever had":** AI with MM, February 23, 1990.

p. 76. **"If I lose this case":** AI with Joanna Winograde, May 19, 1989.

p. 76. **Patti Corman case:** AIs with Corman (née Lear), April 1 and April 7, 1989.

p. 76. **Beatles lawsuit.** Various clippings from the *Los Angeles Times* and *Los Angeles Herald-Examiner*. The suit was settled in 1965.

p. 78. **Minichiello case:** Various newspaper and magazine articles, particularly "Minichiello Is Defended By Citizens' Group and People in Father's Province, *New York Times*, November 3, 1969 by Robert C. Doty; "Return of the Native," *Time*, November 14, 1969; "Anatomy of a Skyjacker," *Time*, December 5, 1969; and a letter from Mitchelson to the Rome *Daily American*, December 16, 1969.

Chapter Eleven (Pages 79–84)

p. 79. **Lerner's eight marriages:** "When the Rich and Famous Split, Big Money Flies," *People*, January 24, 1983.

p. 79. **Lerner wrote *Gigi* for Micheline:** *Made in Heaven, Settled in Court*.

p. 79. **New York divorce laws didn't favor Micheline:** *Made in Heaven, Settled in Court*.

p. 79. **Background of Roy Cohn; friendship with Schine; law practice at Saxe, Bacon & Bolan:** *Citizen Cohn* (Bantam Books, 1988), by Nicholas von Hoffman.

p. 80. **Cohn's litigation style:** "Roy Cohn's Tips to Men on the Divorce Game," *People*, January 24, 1983, by Eric Levin.

p. 81. **How Mitchelson got Micheline's case:** *Made in Heaven, Settled in Court.*

p. 81. **Cohn played by his own set of rules:** *Citizen Cohn.*

p. 81. **"He was a stand-up guy,"** etc.: AIs with MM, February 10 and February 11, 1990.

p. 81. **Jake La Motta story, Cohn's practical joke:** AI with MM, January 19, 1990.

p. 82. **Hero worship of Cohn:** AI with Linda Acaldo, April 1, 1989.

p. 82. **Cohn derided Mitchelson:** "The Prince of Palimony," *New York*, January 10, 1983; "Roy Cohn's Tips to Men on the Divorce Game."

p. 82. **I'm not sure Roy kissed up to anybody . . .":** AI with Martha Smilgis, September 13, 1989.

p. 82. **Animosity between Cohn and Nizer:** *Citizen Cohn.*

p. 82. **Nizer and Lerner accused of trying to drive Micheline insane by their conduct in the case:** *Made in Heaven, Settled in Court.*

p. 82. **Contempt of court hearing; Cohn mocks Lerner:** *Made in Heaven, Settled in Court.*

p. 83. **Both sides hired detectives:** *Made in Heaven, Settled in Court.*

p. 83. **Cohn professed hatred of homosexuals; placed a tap on Lerner's telephone:** *Citizen Cohn.*

p. 83. **Harvey Mann's comments:** Citizen Cohn.

p. 83. **"Grill Lerner's Wife on Diary":** *New York Daily News*, March 6, 1965.

p. 83. **Questioning of Micheline:** *Made in Heaven, Settled in Court.*

p. 84. **Terms of the Lerner settlement:** "Lerner Will Line Out a Million to Shed His Fighting Fair Lady," *New York Daily News*, date unavailable; also *Made in Heaven, Settled in Court.*

p. 84. **Lerner's last poignant gesture:** *Made in Heaven, Settled in Court.*

p. 84. **Alan J. Lerner:** The composer died in 1986.

Chapter Twelve (Pages 84–86)

p. 84. **Steinberg represented a Manson trial witness:** *Helter Skelter* (Norton, 1974), by Vincent Bugliosi with Curt Gentry.

p. 86. **"Jane and Sam fought. . . . [Mitchelson] was a read go-getter.":** AI with Robert K. Steinberg, September 29, 1989.

Chapter Thirteen (Pages 86–92)

p. 86. **Stolkin divorce case:** Various British and American newspaper clippings, including "When We Made Love in Palm Springs," *Lon-*

don Daily Mirror, November 4, 1971, by Alan Gordon, and "Stolkin—The Man Who Made and Lost Millions," *London Evening
Standard*, November 3, 1971, by Leo Armati.

p. 86. **Stolkin thought he was broke:** AI with MM, December 5, 1989.

p. 87. **Acaldo meets Perlman:** AI with Linda Acaldo, April 1, 1989.

p. 87. **Mitchelson's fee arrangements with Bonnie Grant:** From documents in *Grant vs. Mitchelson* (Docket No. C 103138, Superior
Court of California, Los Angeles County).

p. 88. **Acaldo describes affair with Mitchelson, abortion, Mitchelson
with Grant on speaker phone:** AI with Acaldo, April 1, 1989.

p. 89. **Acaldo transporting cocaine:** AI with Acaldo, April 1, 1989.

p. 89. **Acaldo sees Perlman cutting down cocaine:** AI with Acaldo,
May 15, 1989.

p. 89. **Estimated cost of Mitchelson's cocaine habit:** AI with Acaldo,
April 1, 1989.

p. 89. **Alcoholics Anonymous:** Confidential source.

p. 89. **Abused Percodan, cocaine:** AI with Acaldo, April 1, 1989.

p. 89. **Mitchelson's celebrity drug connection:** AI with Acaldo, April
1, 1989.

p. 89. **Mitchelson's clandestine cocaine use:** Audio tape recording of
Acaldo being interviewed by Deputy L.A. District Attorneys Ron
Ross and Stephen Sitkoff, August 5, 1986.

p. 90. **Cocaine habit reported to cost $30,000 a month:** LAPD report.

p. 90. **Acaldo finally refused to act as courier:** AI with Acaldo, April
1, 1989.

p. 90. **Acaldo smashes antique inkwell:** Audio tape of Acaldo's interview with Deputy D.A.s Ross and Sitkoff, August 5, 1986; AI with
Acaldo, April 1, 1989.

p. 91. **Circumstances of Bruce Perlman's death:** From death certificate
and AI with attending physician, Dr. John McAvoy, September 6,
1989.

p. 91. **"He didn't die from drugs. . . . That's all I can tell you about
him.":** AI with MM, December 5, 1989.

p. 91. **Description of Martin Klass:** AI with Acaldo, June 1, 1989; AI
with Paul Caruso, May 17, 1989.

p. 92. **Circumstances of Klass's death:** From death certificate.

p. 92. **Some suspected AIDS:** AI with Acaldo, May 15, 1989; AI with
confidential source.

Chapter Fourteen (Pages 92–96)

p. 92. **"These are pathetic people. . . . It is very lucrative, though.":**
"Dr. Estranged Love," *GQ*, May 1987, by Loren Feldman.

p. 93. **"I have a very simple expression":** AI with Raoul Felder, May
9, 1989.

p. 93. **Joan Shepherd's observations about Mitchelson:** AI with Shepherd, December 29, 1989.

p. 93. **Shepherd's $40 million divorce settlement:** AIs with MM, June 20 and September 12, 1989; "Celebrity Divorce Settlements: Pairs Who Trump the Trumps," *San Jose Mercury*, February 16, 1990, by the *New York Daily News*.

p. 93. **"The thing that he does is . . ."** AI with Veronica Buss, October 1, 1989.

p. 93. **Marvin's affairs just "part of the show . . . one by one in his mind.":** AI with Martha Smilgis, September 13, 1989.

p. 94. **Did things for shock value:** AI with Smilgis, September 27, 1989.

p. 94. **Mitchelson's mother and father figures:** AI with Smilgis, September 13, 1989.

p. 95. **Sonia only wanted to see her son's best side:** AI with May Mitchelson Albert, July 16, 1989.

p. 96. **Refused to listen to criticism of him:** AI with May Mitchelson Albert, July 16, 1989.

p. 96. **$25,000 lawsuit:** The suit is on file in Superior Court, Los Angeles.

p. 96. **"It's in the Italian blood":** AI with MM, March 18, 1990.

p. 96. **Some wondered even about that:** AI with Smilgis, September 13, 1989.

Chapter Fifteen (Pages 97–101)

p. 97. **Cathy Mann's travels as New York Summer Festival Queen:** "Full of 'Rumors,' Politics, Baby," *Des Moines Register*, January 31, 1989, by Marie McCartan.

p. 97. **How Mann met Mitchelson:** AI with MM, January 19, 1990.

p. 97. **Incident in London:** AI with Linda Acaldo, April 1, 1989.

p. 97. **"Knowing laugh":** AI with MM, March 18, 1990.

p. 98. **Incident at Stefanino's:** AI with MM, October 28, 1991; AI with Nikki Blair, October 28, 1991; also described in "The Trials of Marvin Mitchelson," *Los Angeles Times Magazine*, October 8, 1988, by Ann Louise Bardach.

p. 98. **Incident at Century Plaza Hotel:** AIs with Acaldo, February 24 and April 1, 1989.

p. 98. **"She'd always go after the woman.":** AI with MM, March 18, 1990.

p. 98. **Mitchelson's divorce petitions:** Both petitions are on file in Superior Court in Los Angeles. Barens called the first divorce petition "just for show, not go; . . . part of the craziness between [Marvin and Marcella]. . . . They were constantly in very tumultuous fights." (AI with Barens, December 6, 1991.) Rhoden refused to discuss the second divorce petition, citing the attorney-client privilege. (AI with Rhoden, May 18, 1989.)

p. 98. Cathy phoned Rhoden for reassurance: Audio tape recording of Acaldo being interviewed by Deputy L.A. District Attorneys Ron Ross and Stephen Sitkoff, August 5, 1986; affirmed in AI with MM, December 5, 1989.

p. 99. Mitchelson, under pressure, devises ruse to fool process server: AI with Acaldo, February 24, 1989; also described in Acaldo's interview with the deputy D.A.s, August 5, 1986; affirmed in AI with MM, December 5, 1989.

p. 100. Mitchelson's greatest dread: AI with MM, February 23, 1990.

p. 100. "I liked Cathy Mann very, very much. . . . I liked other people.": AI with MM, December 5, 1989.

p. 100. Rhoden derided Mitchelson's marriage: AI with Harold Rhoden, May 18, 1989.

p. 100. "It's not lovey-dovey": AI with Sy Presten, September 13, 1989.

p. 100. "Marriage of convenience": AI with Victoria Molloy, February 22, 1989.

p. 101. Had to fend off an unbelieving Marcella: AI with Evelyn Gruen, September 29, 1989.

p. 101. "There's no open marriage": AI with MM, February 23, 1990.

p. 101 Mitchelson used Bobby Hall: AI with Acaldo, April 1, 1989.

p. 101. Hall's murder: "Two Suspects Arrested in Slaying of Detective," *Los Angeles Times*, September 12, 1976, by Bill Hazlett and Bill Farr; "Suspect Reportedly Admitted Hall Killing," *Los Angeles Times*, September 14, 1976, by Bill Hazlett and Bill Farr.

p. 101. Acaldo couldn't believe Mitchelson was taping: AI with Acaldo, April 1, 1989.

p. 101. Marvin had so little credibility: AI with MM, February 10, 1990.

p. 101. Mitchelson's was far from the model family: AI with Tashi Grady, May 10, 1990; AI with May Mitchelson Albert, July 16, 1989; AI with MM, February 23, 1990.

Chapter Sixteen (Pages 102–114)

p. 102. Rhoden had known Mitchelson since 1962: AI with Harold Rhoden, May 18, 1989.

p. 102. Rhoden's war record: Flap copy for *High Stakes* (Crown, 1980), by Harold Rhoden.

p. 103. "Marvin can't do it without people like Hal": AI with Martha Smilgis, September 6, 1989.

p. 103. "They had a working relationship": AI with Veronica Buss, October 1, 1989.

p. 103. **"Marvin made Hal"**: AI with Michael Krycler, January 6, 1990.

p. 103. **Rhoden's comments on his relationship with Mitchelson**: AI with Rhoden, May 18, 1989.

p. 105. **"People are afraid of libel suits"**: AI with Rhoden, March 23, 1989.

p. 105. **Incident with Steve Landau**: Occurred in Mitchelson's office on February 21, 1990, in the Author's presence.

p. 105. **Paternity suit**: "Mitchelson Named in Paternity Suit," *Los Angeles Times*, March 24, 1982, by Myrna Oliver; "Test Rules Out Mitchelson as Father of Boy," *Los Angeles Times*, April 3, 1982, by Myrna Oliver.

p. 106. **Fight with Steve Landau**: AIs with two witnesses to the fight; AI with MM, February 21, 1990.

p. 106. **Mitchelson as hypochondriac**: AI with Martha Smilgis, September 13, 1989; AI with Linda Acaldo, April 1, 1989.

p. 106. **Had EKG; worried about early death**: AI with MM, January 6, 1990.

p. 106. **Represented Barbara McNair**: "Heroin Rap a Frameup: Barbara," *New York Post*, October 20, 1972; AI with Acaldo, April 1, 1989.

p. 106. **Rick Manzie's background**: "Underworld Link Hinted in Death of Star's Mate," *Las Vegas Sun*, December 16, 1976 by Sharon Spigelmyer; "Heavies Hunted in Manzie Death," *Las Vegas Sun*, December 17, 1976; "New Twist in McNair Hubby Murder," *Valley Times* (Las Vegas), March 4, 1977, by George Kenney.

p. 107. **Mitchelson shoots his desk**: AI with Acaldo, April 1, 1989; AI with MM, January 30, 1990.

p. 108. **Mitchelson's vanity**: AI with Smilgis, September 13, 1989; AI with Acaldo, April 1, 1989.

p. 108. **"Never believe anything. . . . [H]e was in thongs!"**: AI with Acaldo, April 1, 1989.

p. 109. **Mother Butler pie incident**: AI with Victoria Molloy, March 30, 1990.

p. 109. **Hollywood "fake," Mitchelson "lonely"**: AI with May Mitchelson Albert, July 16, 1989.

p. 110. **"I don't think he's happy"**: AI with Rhoden, May 18, 1989.

p. 110. **Liked to gamble, call people's bluff**: AI with Smilgis, September 6, 1989.

p. 110. **Mitchelson living on the edge**: AI with MM, December 5, 1989.

p. 110. **"It's the kind of life he's chosen for himself. . . . [His strength] is incredible"**: AI with Rhoden, May 18, 1989.

p. 111. **Acaldo gave vivid accounts**: AI with Acaldo, April 1, 1989.

p. 111. **Incident at Mitchelson's mansion:** Document obtained from confidential source.

p. 111. **Sexual adventures:** LAPD investigative reports.

p. 112. **Meets "women" at Studio 54:** AI with MM, January 19, 1990.

p. 112. **Comments of Tom Rusk:** AIs with Rusk, January 21 and January 27, 1990.

Chapter Seventeen (Pages 115–122)

p. 115. **Forrest Landers case:** Derived from various documents on file in the case of *People of the State of California vs. Forrest Earl Landers* (Docket No. A 115251, Superior Court of California, Los Angeles County), including the original felony complaint, the district attorney's subsequent recommendation to dismiss the case, a probation report, and letters from the Bank of America and Mitchelson.

pp. 115–116. **Paul Caruso's commitments about the Landers case:** AI with Caruso, May 17, 1989.

p. 116. **Money problems:** Harold Rhoden wrote in *High Stakes* that Mitchelson in 1976 earned $200,000 a year and spent more than that. "Because Marvin never paid his restaurant or laundry bills until legal action was threatened, or his office rent until eviction day, there wasn't one credit card company that would trust him with its plastic. To know Marvin was to know that accepting a lunch invitation from him meant picking up the check." Despite what Rhoden said, Mitchelson did own a number of credit cards.

p. 116. **Tangled finances:** Audio tape recording of Acaldo being interviewed by deputy district attorneys, August 5, 1986.

p. 116. **Mitchelson wrote bad checks:** AI with Acaldo, April 1, 1989.

p. 117. **Mitchelson's angry denial (footnote):** AI with MM, December 5, 1989.

p. 118. **"Marvin would get a large settlement":** "The Trials of Marvin Mitchelson," *Los Angeles Times Magazine*, October 8, 1988, by Ann Louise Bardach.

p. 118. **He'd often "spend the whole thing":** Audio tape recording of Acaldo being interviewed by deputy district attorneys, August 5, 1986.

p. 118. **"They're investing in Marvin Mitchelson":** "The Trials of Marvin Mitchelson."

p. 118. **27-room turreted castle:** AI with MM, March 16, 1991.

p. 118. **Planned to encircle the castle with a moat:** AI with Evelyn Gruen, October 3, 1989.

p. 118. **Frank Heller's art-investment scheme:** Derived from documents and depositions on file in *People of the State of California vs. Frank Raymond Heller* (Docket No. A 393024, Superior Court of California, Los Angeles County), and *C. Douglas Wickle, as Trustee*

*in the Matter of Sari Heller Gallery, Ltd., a Corporation, Bankrupt,
vs. Marvin Mitchelson, etc., et al.* (Docket No. C 166396, Superior
Court of California, Los Angeles County); and from AI with Richard
Moss, November 28, 1989.

p. 120. Bonnie Grant's dissatisfaction: From documents in *Grant vs.
Mitchelson* (Docket No. C 103138, Superior Court of California, Los
Angeles County).

p. 120. "Total revenge;" Grant wanted Mitchelson to marry her: AI
with MM, December 5, 1989.

p. 120. Grant's comment: AI with Bonnie Grant, November 20, 1989.

p. 121. "Amicable settlement": "The Trials of Marvin Mitchelson."

p. 121. Grant foreclosed: AI with MM, December 5, 1989; also, "The
Trials of Marvin Mitchelson."

p. 122. Mitchelson boasted of selling paintings at auction: AI with
MM, December 5, 1989.

Chapter Eighteen (Pages 122–132)

Mormon Will case: Except as noted in the citations below, descriptions
of the events leading up to the Mormon Will trial, conversations between (and motivations of) Rhoden and Mitchelson, and the trial itself,
came from *High Stakes* (Crown, 1980), by Harold Rhoden.

Litton litigation: Except as noted in the citations below, the various
events, lawsuits, and countersuits surrounding Emmett T. Steele's ef-
forts to claim an interest in Litton were derived from documents in
*Emmett T. Steele vs. Litton Industries, Inc., Charles B. Thornton, Roy
L. Ash, Hugh W. Jamieson, et al.* (Docket No. 732883, Superior Court
of California, Los Angeles County); *Charles B. Thornton vs. Noah Die-
trich, Emmett T. Steele, Harold Rhoden, et al.* (Docket No. 810297,
Superior Court of California, Los Angeles County); *Noah Dietrich vs.
Joseph A. Hall, Charles B. Thornton, and Litton Industries, Inc.*
(Docket No. 882073, Superior Court of California, Los Angeles
County); and *Arthur J. Crowley vs. Kathryn M. Steele, as Executrix of
the Estate of Emmett T. Steele, and Harold Rhoden, et al.* (Docket
No C 47481, Superior Court of California, Los Angeles County). The
longevity of two of the cases was amazing: *Steele vs. Litton* spanned the
years from 1959 to 1973; and *Crowley vs. Steele* lasted from 1973 to
1988.

p. 122. Rhoden's will: Filed in the Los Angeles County clerk's office,
July 13, 1989. Mitchelson was the subscribing witness.

p. 123. Dietrich was one of Steele's main witnesses: "Thornton Sued
Again in Lengthy Legal Feud," *Los Angeles Times*, January 20, 1967,
by Rudy Villasenor.

p. 124. Crowley claimed Rhoden turned his client against him; antici-

pated early settlement; apology had to be in writing: AI with Arthur Crowley, September 28, 1989.

p. 124. **Rhoden asked Crowley back in; Crowley refused:** AI with Crowley, September 28, 1989.

p. 125. **Mitchelson makes a $75,000 loan:** Mitchelson filed his creditor's claim on January 25, 1972, in *Estate of Emmett T. Steele* (Case No. 575951, Superior Court of California, Los Angeles County) for "a contingency fee, minimum of $575,000 and a maximum of 10 percent of the gross recovery," and it was later approved as presented.

p. 125. **Mitchelson recalled only earning. . . :** AI with MM, March 16, 1991.

p. 126. **Landmark court case that outlawed irrevocable contingent-fee agreements:** *Fracasse vs. Brent*, 100 Cal.Rptr. 385, 6 Cal.3d 784, 494 P.2d 9 (1972).

p. 127. **"He knew what I thought of him":** AI with Crowley, September 28, 1989.

p. 127. **Dietrich appointed Rhoden:** AI with Rhoden, May 18, 1989.

p. 127. **Mormon Will was one of 35 "lost" Hughes wills:** "The First Admission that a Hughes Will Is Fake," *Philadelphia Inquirer*, December 21, 1983.

p. 127. **Marvin advanced another $300,000. . . :** "Where There's a Will . . ." (profile of Rhoden), *National Law Journal*, January 5, 1981, by Marlene Adler Marks. Mitchelson, in an interview with the Author on March 16, 1991, estimated his total outlays for the Hughes Will case at between $300,000 and $500,000. See also *High Stakes*, in which Rhoden tells of Mitchelson's investing $250,000 by the close of the trial. According to *High Stakes*, Mitchelson also continued to pay Acaldo's salary and expenses while she was in Las Vegas working for Rhoden.

p. 128. **Seymour Lazar brought in over Rhoden's objections:** AI with Rhoden, May 18, 1989.

p. 129. **Crowley didn't believe in the Mormon Will, either:** AI with Crowley, September 28, 1989.

p. 129. **Mel Torme's divorce from Jan Scott:** *It Wasn't All Velvet* (Viking, 1988), by Mel Torme.

p. 129. **Tap on Jan's telephone; Torme was inconsolable as he listened:** AI with Acaldo, April 1, 1989.

p. 130. **Mitchelson's slip-up:** AI with Crowley, September 28, 1989. See also documents in the divorce case of *Thora Janette Torme vs. Melvin Howard Torme* (Docket No. D 903620, Superior Court of California, Los Angeles County).

p. 130. **Not asking for immunity for Mitchelson:** AI with Crowley, September 28, 1989.

p. 130. **Crowley savored trampling on the Mormon Will case:** AI with Crowley, September 28, 1989.

p. 131. **Dummar flunks lie detector on television:** "The First Admission that a Hughes Will Is Fake."

p. 131. **Rhoden lost house, office, plane:** "Where There's a Will . . ."

p. 131. **Mitchelson denied affair with Acaldo:** AI with MM, June 1, 1989.

p. 131. **"She's very mad at Marvin Mitchelson. . . . [S]he sure does hate him now":** AI with Rhoden, May 18, 1989.

PART FOUR: THE PRINCE OF PALIMONY

Chapter Nineteen (Pages 135–146)

Marvin vs. Marvin: Except as noted in the citations below, descriptions of the *Marvin* case were derived from the trial transcript in *Michelle Marvin, aka Michelle Triola vs. Lee Marvin* (Docket No. C 23303, Superior Court of California, Los Angeles County); from related public documents obtained from the court record and as well as from the law firm of Goldman & Kagon, which represented Lee Marvin; and from Mitchelson's books, *Made in Heaven, Settled in Court* and *Living Together* (Simon and Schuster, 1980). The landmark opinion of the California Supreme Court in *Marvin vs. Marvin*, allowing palimony claims for the first time, appears at 557 P.2d 106, 134 Cal.Rptr. 815 (1976). It was this opinion that allowed Michelle Marvin's complaint to eventually come to trial.

p. 135. **Michelle was a tenant there, too:** AI with MM, June 1, 1989.

p. 135. **Sonia worried:** AI with Marion Mitchelson Gartler, July 16, 1989.

p. 137. **Michelle filed her first lawsuit against Lee:** AI with MM, May 13, 1990.

p. 137. **"Michelle was an old-timer. . . . He was only going to pay if she left him alone":** AI with David Kagon, May 19, 1989.

p. 138. **Family law had been steadily and quietly evolving:** The precursor cases to *Marvin* actually stretched quite far back in California. See, for example, *Trutalli vs. Meraviglia*, 12 P.2d 430 (1932), and *Vallera vs. Vallera*, 21 C.2d 681 (1943).

p. 138. **Initially wanted reinstatement of $1,000-a-month support:** AI with Kagon, May 19, 1989.

p. 138. *In re the Marriage of Cary:* 109 Cal.Rptr. 862, 34 Cal.App.3d 345 (1973).

p. 139. **"I couldn't be happier":** "Suit Dismissed in Lee Marvin Case," *Los Angeles Times,* December 6, 1973, by Myrna Oliver.

p. 139. **"I actually never have been so happy":** "Court Rejects Property

Split for Unmarrieds," *Los Angeles Times*, July 25, 1975, by Myrna Oliver.

p. 139. **Mitchelson bankrolled the case:** "$6.50 an Hour? Mitchelson seeks a raise," *Time*, May 7, 1979. The magazine said he had a one-third contingency.

p. 139. **Kagon's comments:** AI with Kagon, May 19, 1989.

p. 139. **Woldman drafted the original complaint; Brown drafted the appeal brief and argued it:** "Mitchelson Unmasked," *American Lawyer*, September 1988, by Amy Dockser and Gay Jervey.

p. 139. **Handed out T-shirts that said, "It's Michelle's Money, Too!":** The Prince of Palimony," *New York* magazine, January 10, 1983, by Patricia Morrisroe.

p. 139. **Coined "palimony" during *Newsweek* interviews:** "Divorce, American Style," *Rolling Stone*, July 14, 1988, by Corbin Bernsen.

p. 140. **Rhoden was still working for Mitchelson:** "Where There's a Will . . ." (profile of Rhoden), *National Law Journal*, January 5, 1981, by Marlene Adler Marks.

p. 140. **Saw trials as great theater:** "Divorce, American Style."

p. 140. **"Three ring circus in a fishbowl":** "Mitchelson Unmasked."

p. 140. **"Publicity is good for business.":** "'Til Millions Do Them Part: Hollywood Divorce Lawyer Marvin Mitchelson Is on the Woman's Side," *Washington Post*, February 9, 1979, by Ellen Farley and William K. Knoedelseder, Jr.

p. 140. **Side with the better script will win:** AI with Kagon, May 19, 1989.

p. 140. **Mitchelson opted for a bench trial:** AI with MM, December 5, 1989.

p. 142. **Mitchelson attacked Doughty:** "*Marvin* Trial Judge Admits Actor's Secret Testimony," *New York Times*, February 21, 1979.

p. 142. **Doughty sued Mitchelson:** *Mervin Richard Doughty vs. Marvin Mitchelson, Michelle Triola Marvin, et al.* (Docket No. WEC 058770, Superior Court of California, Los Angeles County.)

p. 144. **"I warned him":** AI with Harold Rhoden, May 18, 1989.

p. 144. **There was a rumor sweeping the courthouse:** "The Dukes of Divorce," *Us* magazine, May 2, 1988, by Cree McCree.

p. 145. **Expenses estimated at $100,000; but Mitchelson estimated he'd made millions through publicity:** "Palimony Pays for 'Third Marvin', Their Attorney," *Los Angeles Times*, January 30, 1986.

p. 145. **Lee Marvin balked, had his lawyers appeal:** AI with Kagon, May 19, 1989; also, "Marvin to Reenter Case," *Los Angeles Times*, May 24, 1979.

p. 146. **Lee was back in Tucson:** "The Split Decision: $104,000 to Michelle Marvin, but Spoils Go to Many 'Victors,'" *Washington Post*, April 19, 1979, by William Knoedelseder and Ellen Farley.

p. 146. **Michelle's new partner; Mitchelson drew up palimony**

agreement: AIs with Marilyn Boettcher (Malibu neighbor), December 8, 1989, and Tashi Grady, January 12, 1990.

p. 146. Michelle arrested for shoplifting: "Michelle Marvin Pleads Innocent to Shoplifting," *Los Angeles Times*, September 30, 1980; "Michelle Marvin: Now She Has a Written Contract," *Los Angeles Times*, October 3, 1983.

p. 146. Paul Caruso comments: AI with Paul Caruso, May 17, 1989.

p. 146. Forty states now recognized palimony: "Divorce Lawyer," CBS's "60 Minutes," June 26, 1988.

p. 146. Highest palimony verdict for Felder: "Dr. Estranged Love," *GQ*, May 1987, by Loren Feldman. Although *GQ* reports the amount as about $400,000, Felder, in an AI on May 9, 1989, set the amount at about $300,000.

p. 146. Highest palimony settlement for Mitchelson: "The Dukes of Divorce"; also "Palimony Pays for 'Third Marvin,' Their Attorney."

p. 146. Reaping the benefits for years to come: "The Split Decision: $104,000 to Michelle Marvin, but Spoils Go to Many 'Victors.'"

Chapter Twenty (Pages 147–158)

Except as noted in the citations below, descriptions in Chapters Twenty and Twenty-One of the Vicki Morgan case were derived from various documents, pleadings, and depositions in *Vicki Morgan vs. Alfred Bloomingdale, et al.* (Docket No. C 417192, Superior Court of California, Los Angeles County). Michael G. Dave, Vicki's lawyer after she fired Mitchelson, made available her deposition and the full appeal record in her case.

Two books about Vicki Morgan were also used as sources for Chapters Twenty and Twenty-One, and are cited hereafter only by their titles: *Beautiful Bad Girl* (Santa Barbara Press, 1985), by Gordon Basichis; and *Vicki* (St. Martin's Press, 1986), by Joyce Milton and Ann Louise Bardach. Basichis was Vicki's lover at her death, and his book concentrates on the personal side of her life. I found the Milton-and-Bardach book's description of the legal aspects of Vicki's case to be far more useful.

I was given access to tape recordings of Vicki Morgan's telephone calls, and to personal diaries which she kept. Where material in Chapters Twenty and Twenty-One comes from either of those sources, it is cited here as "phone calls" or "diaries."

I was also given access to the interviews and contemporaneous notes of Jonathan Beaty, of *Time*, from the period when he was investigating the Vicki Morgan murder and its aftermath. Where such material is used in Chapters Twenty or Twenty-One, it is cited here as "Beaty notes."

p. 147. **Mitchelson tells Smilgis:** AI with Martha Smilgis, September 6, 1989.

p. 147. **Illegitimate son; three troubled marriages; heroin and freebase:** *Vicki, Beautiful Bad Girl,* and Beaty notes, respectively.

p. 148. **Skipped out on her when she was nine months old:** *Vicki.*

p. 148. **Died in front of her:** Beaty notes.

p. 148. **Alfred tried to "buy" her from husbands:** Beaty notes.

p. 148. **Create the perfect hostess and companion; arranged acting lessons:** Beaty notes.

p. 148. **Betsy spied Alfred with his mistress:** *Vicki.*

p. 148. **Vicki's friends and lovers:** *Vicki.*

p. 149. **Ordered Paul Caruso to sue Alfred; Caruso later sued her, but couldn't find her:** *Vicki.*

p. 149. **Bloomingdales get Watergate apartment; Albert becomes ill:** Beaty notes.

p. 149. **Vicki's allowance; Alfred gives her interest in deals, Showbiz Pizza; is discharged from hospital; Betsy just traveling the world:** Beaty notes.

p. 150. **Vicki goes back to Paul Caruso; he refuses:** *Vicki.*

p. 150. **Eloped with Carson:** Beaty notes.

p. 150. **Approved of Mitchelson's aggressive style:** Phone calls.

p. 150. **Mitchelson saw Vicki as an enigma:** *Vicki.*

p. 150. **Mitchelson kept her away from interviews:** AI with Smilgis, September 6, 1989.

p. 150. **Fox-trimmed coat from Cornfeld:** *Vicki.*

p. 150. **Mitchelson's description of Vicki:** Beaty notes.

p. 150. **"Quiet settlements":** The term is Mitchelson's.

p. 151. **Mitchelson met with Chodos; Chodos told him to forget it:** Phone calls.

p. 151. **Rhoden doing legal drafting:** AI with Rhoden, May 18, 1989.

p. 151. **Mitchelson's contingency:** Phone calls. Mitchelson told the Author on December 7, 1991 that his contingency was one third. From her taped phone conversations with others, however, it appears that she believed Mitchelson's contingency was one half.

p. 152. **Betsy's motivations not to settle:** *Vicki.*

p. 152. **Within a week, Alfred was dead:** Beaty notes.

p. 153. **Mitchelson took Vicki to lunch:** Beaty notes.

p. 153. **Vicki's renewed self confidence:** Diaries.

p. 153. **Mitchelson's conversation with Vicki:** Phone calls.

p. 154. **Vicki didn't think Mitchelson cared:** Diaries.

p. 154. **Vicki had known Lorraine Dave; Michael Dave handled her divorce:** *Vicki.*

p. 155. **Vicki complained to Dave:** Dairies.

p. 155. **Mitchelson's premonition:** Diaries.

p. 155. **Foreign Intelligence Advisory Board**: Beaty notes.

p. 155. **Mason's meeting with Mitchelson**: "Reagans Reportedly Seeking Bloomingdale Suit Settlement," *Los Angeles Times*, September 11, 1982, by Myrna Oliver.

p. 155. **The gist of Cohn's end of the conversation**: Phone calls.

p. 156. **Schlesinger divorce**: *Citizen Cohn* (Bantam Books, 1988), by Nicholas von Hoffman.

p. 156. **"James Bond of international lawsuits"**: "The Prince of Palimony," *New York* magazine, January 10, 1983, by Patricia Morrisroe.

p. 156. **Invited Mitchelson to party at "21"**: AI with Sy Presten, April 28, 1989.

p. 156. **Went to son's bar mitzvah, too**: AI with Presten, September 13, 1989.

p. 156. **Fee of more than $1 million**: AI with MM, January 30, 1990.

p. 156. **Vicki had been dubious**: Phone calls.

p. 156. **Mitchelson later told Vicki. . .** : Phone calls.

p. 156. **Vicki renewed her resolve**: *Vicki*.

p. 156. **Barens met with Vicki on three occasions**: Beaty notes.

p. 156. **Vicki didn't trust Barens**: *Vicki*.

p. 156. **Vicki goes to see Michael Dave**: Diaries.

p. 156. **Dave a "nobody lawyer"**: Phone calls.

p. 156. **Dave's analysis was sobering**: *Vicki*.

p. 156. **Mitchelson desperate to stay on the case; Dave saw some advantage to this**: Phone calls.

p. 156. **Publicity tactics caused Vicki grief**: Beaty notes.

p. 157. **They intended to make him give up half of his contingent fee; Mitchelson bit into the proposal**: Phone calls.

p. 157. **Mitchelson bragged that he had clout with Judge Markey**: Phone calls. Pressed about this, Mitchelson further explained in an interview with the Author on October 28, 1991: "I remember Markey asking me whether I was [still] in the case. I sensed that he was disappointed that I had been let go and replaced. I think he would have preferred us [Mitchelson and Rhoden] to stay on. That's my memory."

p. 157. **Markey categorically denied . . . (footnote)**: AI with Markey, November 7, 1991. Markey also said: "It's not my m.o. or style to talk to a lawyer about a pending case he's involved in. . . . I wouldn't say: 'Tell your client she shouldn't fire you!' I'm quite confident we didn't speak at all."

p. 157. **Kept pleading with Vicki; described Morgan Mason phone calls, etc.**: Phone calls.

p. 158. **Mitchelson told the newspapers his firing was a surprise**: "Vicki Fires Mitchelson," *New York Daily News*, September 16, 1982; "Bloomingdale Mistress Fires Mitchelson," *Los Angeles Times*, September 16, 1982, by Myrna Oliver.

Chapter Twenty-One (Pages 158–164)

(Note: See also the introductory source notes for Chapter Twenty.)

p. 159. **Mitchelson found that something to be proud of:** AI with MM, February 23, 1990.

p. 159. **Betsy dissolved interest in Showbiz Pizza:** *Vicki.*

p. 159. **Civil jury award (footnote):** *Vicki.*

p. 159. **Vicki signed contract, tried speaking lessons; was depressed; had previously been depressed; rented condo; moved in with Pancoast:** Beaty notes.

p. 159. **Pancoast's hospitalization; attempted suicide:** Beaty notes; also, *Vicki.*

p. 160. **Murder descriptions:** *Vicki.*

p. 160. **Bobby Steinberg's revelations about alleged sex tapes:** *Vicki.*

p. 161. **Incident at Pamela Mason's:** Beaty notees.

p. 161. **Deaver totally denied . . . (footnote):** AI with Deaver, November 27, 1991. Mitchelson replied: "All I know is what Morgan [Mason] said. . . . I just repeated what Morgan said [Deaver] said." (AI with MM, November 27, 1991.) Morgan Mason refused to be interviewed.

p. 161. **Mitchelson believed there were tapes; Vicki alluded to blackmail material:** AI with MM, February 23, 1990.

p. 161. **Conversation at Pamela Mason's:** Beaty notes.

p. 162. **"We talked about it for a long time,"** etc: Beaty notes.

p. 162. **"I think I discussed this with Roy":** AI with MM, February 23, 1990.

p. 162. **"People in high places":** AI with MM, February 23, 1990.

p. 162. **"Power from the top . . .":** Beaty notes.

p. 162. **Steinberg was in hot water:** *Vicki.*

p. 163. **Prosecution of Steinberg:** *People of the State of California vs. Robert K. Steinberg* (No. M 75420, Municipal Court, Beverly Hills).

p. 163. **"One of those strange, bizarre things":** AI with Robert Steinberg, September 29, 1989.

p. 163. **Beaty discovered more odd pieces of the puzzle; Barens's knowledge about the Vicki Morgan sex tapes; Barens's dealings with** *Time* **magazine:** AIs with Jonathan Beaty, May 19 and October 2, 1989. Also, Beaty notes.

p. 163. **Barens categorically denied . . . (footnote):** AI with Barens, December 6, 1991.

Chapter Twenty-Two (Pages 164–174)

The description of the Khashoggi case was derived from various published materials, including *The Richest Man in the World* (Warner Books, 1986), by Ronald Kessler; "Marvin Mitchelson Has Progressed from Palimony to Petro-Mony: Soraya Khashoggi Is Suing for $2 Billion," *People*, August 27, 1979, by Martha Smilgis; "Billions at Stake in Coast Divorce Battle," *New York Times*, November 27, 1979; "*Khashoggi vs. Khashoggi*: A Billion-Dollar Arab Divorce Thriller," *Los Angeles* magazine, July 1980, by Sally Ogle Davis and Ivor Davis; and "Khashoggi's Fall: A Crash in the Limo Lane," *Vanity Fair*, September 1989, by Dominick Dunne.

The description of the al-Fassi divorce and its aftermath was derived in substantial part from documents on file in Los Angeles Superior Court. Those cases are *Sheikha Dena al-Fassi vs. Sheikh Mohammed al-Fassi* (Docket No. D 63702); *Sir Leonard Joseph Knowles vs. Sheikha Dena al-Fassi, Marvin Morris Mitchelson, et al.* (Docket no. C 434856); *Melvyn B. Frumkes, P.A., vs. Sheikha Dena al-Feassi, Marvin Mitchelson, et al.* (Docket No. C 628403); and *Diana* (sic) *al-Fassi, Harold Rhoden, and Marvin M. Mitchelson vs. Max Fink, Cesar Lopez, Jr., C.L.J., Inc., et al.* (Docket No. C 552590). These cases are collectively referred to here as the "Fassi cases."

Descriptions of other lawsuits or liens filed against Mitchelson were derived from documents on file in Los Angeles Superior Court and in the Los Angeles County Recorder's Office.

Sources other than the above follow.

p. 166. "She made a deal. . . . We got peanuts!"; no fee in Jagger case: AI with Harold Rhoden, May 18, 1989.

p. 166. Judgment in the Fassi case: "Sheik's Wife Wins $81 Million: Award Called Record for a Marital Dispute," *Los Angeles Times*, June 4, 1983, by Myrna Oliver.

p. 167. Ethics of contingent-fee agreements: "Mitchelson Unmasked," *American Lawyer*, September 1988, by Amy Dockser and Gay Jervey; for requirements of California law, see 7 Cal.Jur.3d(Rev) 498, and *Coons vs. Kary*, 69 Cal.Rptr. 712.

p. 167. Mitchelson comments on contingent fees: AI with MM, December 5, 1989.

p. 168. Mitchelson lashes out at critics: AI with MM, February 23, 1990.

p. 168. Sold necklace for at least $50,000: AI with MM, January 6, 1990.

p. 170. "'If you don't pay for this funeral . . .'": Confidential source. Mitchelson acknowledged Groman's involvement in arranging his mother's funeral. He said he experienced denial about Sonia's death and that as a consequence of this it is "possible" that Groman was paid late. The fact that Sonia Mitchelson's estate was never probated also may have delayed the payment, he said. AI with MM, March 16, 1991.

p. 171. **Incident at MGM Grand**: AI with Linda Acaldo, March 18, 1989.

p. 171. **"He likes to gamble"**: AI with Martha Smilgis, December 29, 1989.

p. 171. **"Never won anything"**: AI with Acaldo, April 1, 1989.

p. 171. **Smilgis remembered Mitchelson at the Sands Hotel**: AI with Smilgis, September 6, 1989. Smilgis recalled that the gambling took place at Khashoggi's hotel but did not remember its name. Kessler's book says Khashoggi was using the Sands.

p. 171. **Loans from Pamela Rushworth**: Confidential source.

p. 172. **Money disputes between Mitchelson and Abe Pelter**: Confidential source. The lawsuit, which Mitchelson filed against Pelter, is on file in Los Angeles Superior Court. Mitchelson insisted he had no recollection of ever filing it. AI with MM, March 16, 1991.

p. 172. **Acaldo loaned her boss. . .** : AI with Acaldo, April 1, 1989. Mitchelson acknowledged the debt, but claimed the amount she was owed might not have been a loan, but, rather, an obligation of his to reimburse Acaldo for her Las Vegas expenses during the Mormon Will trial. AI with MM, March 16, 1991.

p. 172. **"He needed $100,000 . . ."**: AI with Acaldo, April 1, 1989. Mitchelson at first acknowledged the loan (AI with MM, March 16, 1991), but in a subsequent interview he indicated that its amount might only have been $50,000 (AI with MM, October 28, 1991).

p. 172. **"Shvartze's stole my money!"**: AI with Felder, May 9, 1989. Mitchelson confirmed he asked Felder to cash the check but did not address some of the other aspects of Felder's account. AI with MM, March 16, 1991.

p. 173. **Mitchelson's share of the Fassi transaction**: Real estate settlement statement from V. E. Pollard & Associates, April 30, 1986.

p. 173. **Default judgment had grown to $130 million**: AIs with MM, July 12 and September 25, 1989.

p. 173. **Incident with Beverly Hills Police**: MJS interview with Beverly Hills Police Lt. Curtis, August 23, 1989; Curtis was on the scene that night and prepared an incident report.

p. 174. **Mitchelson's attempts to collect from Mohammed**: AIs with MM, June 20 and September 25, 1989.

Chapter Twenty-Three (Pages 174–179)

The Author interviewed Richard Hirschfeld on June 22, 1989, at the Quality Inn in downtown Washington, D.C. Muhammad Ali was also present but did not participate in the interview. During this interview, Hirschfeld confirmed his participation in the bogus plot to assassinate Mitchelson, which was first revealed in a *Washington Post* article cited below.

p. 174. **Fassi a "nut case":** AI with Richard Hirschfeld, June 22, 1989.

p. 174. **Hirschfeld's early business and legal record:** "SEC Deals Blow to Ali's Boxing Camp," and "Tidewater Attorney's Life Has 'Gatsby-esque' Overtones," *Washington Post*, October 29, 1984 (as to both), by Nina Martin; also, "Muhammad Ali's Unlikely Match," *Washington Post*, May 18, 1989, by John Mintz.

p. 176. **Weapons "deal" with Marcos:** "Please Speak into the Microphone," *Time*, July 20, 1987; "New Marcos Restrictions Discussed," *Washington Post*, July 10, 1987.

p. 176. **5 percent commission:** UPI, July 13, 1987.

p. 177. **Salahuddin:** "Iran Ex-Attaché, Khomeini Foe, Slain in the U.S.," *New York Times*, July 23, 1980 by Robert Pear; "Two Held in Slaying of Iranian in U.S. and Third Is Sought," *New York Times*, July 24, 1980 by A.O. Sulzberger, Jr.; "The Call of Islam Changed Life of Slaying Suspect," *New York Times*, August 8, 1980; "Four Indicted in '80 Murder of Iranian Press Aide," *New York Times*, July 17, 1981, by Robert Pear.

p. 177. **Knew where Terry Waite was:** AI with Hirschfeld, June 22, 1989.

p. 178. **Rutherford's letter to Hirschfeld:** First revealed in "Hirschfeld and the 'Assassination' Lure," *Washington Post*, May 18, 1989, by John Mintz. Mintz later provided a copy of the letter. The name of the sender and the date were blacked out. Ruth Marcus of the *Washington Post* supplied the date. Rutherford, in an interview with the Author on July 10, 1989, refused to discuss whether he sent the letter, but Hirschfeld (June 22, 1989) said it was from Rutherford.

p. 178. **Rutherford's discussions with Hirschfeld, Fassi:** AI with Rutherford, July 10, 1989.

p. 178. **Hirschfeld met with FBI agents:** AI with Hirschfeld, June 22, 1989.

p. 178. **How Hirschfeld directed the action; Salahuddin would have shot Mitchelson for $10,000:** AI with Hirschfeld, June 22, 1989.

p. 178. **Mitchelson didn't know he would be the bait:** AI with Hirschfeld, June 22, 1989.

p. 178. **Justice Department said it had no files, acted like the whole thing never happened:** AI with FOI Officer, United States Marshals Service, December 4, 1989. A formal Freedom of Information Act request was first made by the Author on August 14, 1989. Revised requests and appeals were subsequently made. In response, both the U.S. Department of Justice and the Marshals Service consistently and repeatedly denied possessing any records whatsoever relating to the plot Hirschfeld and Rutherford both described—in spite of the existence of at least one government letter to Hirschfeld. After conducting her own search for pertinent records, the FOI Officer at the

Marshals Service concluded that any pertinent documents had been destroyed.

p. 179. Claimed Salahuddin was where Terry Waite was: AI with Hirschfeld, June 22, 1989.

p. 179. Mitchelson's reaction: AI with MM, May 17, 1989.

Chapter Twenty-Four (Pages 179–193)

Except as otherwise noted in the citations below, the description of the Merrick divorce case was derived from documents, declarations, letters, and a police report relating to one or more of the following cases: *Karen Merrick, on Behalf of David Merrick, vs. Morton Mitosky* (New York Supreme Court, New York County, Index No. 09749/83); *Morton J. Mitosky, Petitioner for the Appointment of a Conservator of the Property of David Merrick, Proposed Conservatee* (New York Supreme Court, New York County, Index No. 90052/83); and *Karen Prunczik Merrick vs. Morton J. Mitosky and Etan Merrick, Co-Conservators, and David Merrick* (New York Supreme Court, New York County, Index No. 20229/84).

Except as otherwise noted in the citations below, the descriptions of the Perelman-Kasen relationship, its breakup, and its aftermath were derived from complaints, documents, deposition transcripts, and related materials from the following cases: *Susan Kasen vs. Ronald O. Perelman* (New York Supreme Court, New York County, Index No. 91339/83); *Ronald O. Perelman vs. Susan Kasen* (New York Supreme Court, New York County, Index No. 01414/84); and *Susan Kasen vs. Stuart M. Berger* (New York Supreme Court, New York County, Index No. 11988/84).

p. 179. Description of the Pulitzer case: "The Revelations of Roxanne Pulitzer: After the *Playboy* Photos, Telling Her Story About the Divorce," *Washington Post*, May 9, 1985, by Stephanie Mansfield.

p. 179. Mitchelson let it be known that he was available: *The Prize Pulitzer* (Villard Books, 1987), by Roxanne Pulitzer with Kathleen Maxa.

p. 180. Mitchelson billed her $7,000; she refused to pay: *The Prize Pulitzer*.

p. 180. Merrick prided himself. . . : "Scrooged," *Vanity Fair*, December 1989, by Leslie Bennetts.

p. 180. Prunzcik played Anytime Annie: "Scrooged."

p. 181. "He told me, 'You never got paid right'": AI with Raoul Felder, September 13, 1989.

p. 181. Felder received $91,000, considered it chump change; called Merrick a mean guy (footnote): Respectively, AI with Felder, September 13, 1989, and "The Sultan of Splitsville: Divorce Lawyer

Raoul Lionel Felder, Making Headlines Off Heartache," *Washington Post*, November 21, 1988, by Howard Kurtz.

p. 181. **"Get me out of here!"**: AI with Morton Mitosky, July 19, 1989.

p. 181. **Spirited Merrick to Etan's**: AI with Mitosky, July 19, 1989.

p. 181. **"The next thing we know"**: AI with Felder, May 9, 1989.

p. 181. **"She still loves Merrick"**: "Merrick Mess," UPI, May 5, 1983.

pp. 181–182. **Felder's description of the Merrick hearing**: AI with Felder, May 9, 1989.

p. 182. **Mitchelson insisted that Prunczik was satisfied**: AI with MM, January 30, 1990.

p. 183. **Mitchelson wanted to see Merrick, Merrick said no; tickets to 42nd Street**: AI with Felder, May 9, 1989.

p. 183. **Wanted to kill Etan**: "Scrooged."

p. 183. **Montie Montana case**: Various newspaper and broadcast accounts of the case, including "Horsing Around," Saugus *Enterprise* (Calif.), October 17, 1984, and "Couple Isn't Horsin' Around With Nagging Custody Issue," *New York Post*, December 11, 1984.

p. 184. **Paid in cash**: Confidential source.

p. 185. **Perelman and wife were social scene fixtures**: "The '80s Are Over, and Ron Perelman Now Is a 'Builder,'" *Wall Street Journal*, March 27, 1990, by Randall Smith and David Wessel.

p. 185. **Perelman was one of the richest men. . .** : "The Perils of Perelman," *Forbes* magazine, December 10, 1990.

p. 186. **Mitchelson's descriptions of the negotiations**: AI with MM, May 7, 1990.

p. 186. **Perelman's palimony agreement**: The agreement itself was an exhibit in the subsequent court case. It was also the subject of an article, "Exec Fights $1M Bill For Love," *New York Post*, June 29, 1984, by Hal Davis.

p. 187. **"Big case!"**: AI with MM, January 30, 1990.

p. 188. **Mitchelson astounded**: AI with MM, May 7, 1990.

p. 188. **Property worth $2 million**: AI with MM, April 29, 1990.

p. 188. **"I adore Marvin"**: AI with Susan Kasen, April 5, 1990. Kasen refused otherwise to discuss anything.

p. 188. **"God, has Roy got balls!"**: AI with MM, March 18, 1990.

p. 188. **Saw Perelman at "Phantom"**: May 7, 1990.

p. 188. **Age of Kathleen Markey Perdue**: This and various other facts relating to her divorce were derived from *Franklin P. Perdue vs. Kathleen Markey Perdue* (Docket No. 88CV0723, Circuit Court for Wicomico County, Maryland).

p. 188. **Received at least $2 million**: AI with MM, April 29, 1990; also, AI with Martha Smilgis, December 29, 1989.

p. 189. **Smilgis's comments about meeting Kathleen**: AI with Smilgis, December 29, 1989.

p. 189. **Frank Perdue chased Kathleen:** "Strange Bird," *Washingtonian*, December 1989, by Ramsey Flynn. This article also proved to be an excellent general source on Frank Perdue's background.

p. 189. **Mitchelson had to get around a prenuptial agreement:** AI with MM, January 30, 1990.

p. 189. **Earlier "quiet settlement" with Perdue:** AI with MM, February 10, 1990.

p. 189. **"Quiet settlement" with Clint Murchison:** AI with MM, July 25, 1990.

p. 189. **Saw Collins divorce as a script from "L.A. Law":** "Divorce, American Style," *Rolling Stone*, July 14, 1988, by Corbin Bernsen.

pp. 189–190. **Was only about validity of prenuptial agreement; Steinschriber didn't think it mattered either way:** "Joan Collins, Peter Holm End Long Legal Rift with 4-½ Hours of Bargaining," *Los Angeles Times*, February 9, 1988.

p. 190. **"It's a theatrical performance":** AI with Frank Steinschriber, May 19, 1989.

p. 190. **Holm picketed:** UPI, July 17, 1987.

p. 191. **Romina Danielson's testimony:** "Divorce, American Style." See also, "Return of the Passion Flower," *Philadelphia Inquirer*, August 2, 1988, by Ann Kolson.

p. 192. **Steinschriber's comments:** AI with Frank Steinschriber, May 19, 1989.

p. 192. **Cultivated friends in high places, etc.:** "Two Hundred Friends to Toast Reagans at a Secluded Estate," *Los Angeles Times*, February 1, 1989, by Marylouise Oates.

p. 192. **Al-Midani's extensive holdings:** AI with Hassan Saade (brother of Edith al-Midani), October 3, 1989.

p. 192. **Marriage deteriorated; Edith sued in California:** AI with Saade, October 3, 1989. The docket in *Edith Al-Midani vs. Mouaffack al-Midani* (Docket No. D 179635, Superior Court of California, Los Angeles County) was used to establish the rough timing of events, but the file itself has been sealed and no documents were available.

p. 192. **Al-Midani divorce case would be business prosposition for Hassan Saade:** *Walid Saadeh vs. Edith Saade al-Midani, et al.* (Docket No. C 737575, Superior Court of California, Los Angeles County).

p. 192. **Gruen invited Mitchelson into the case; they split a 10 percent contingency:** Declaration of Evelyn Gruen in *Evelyn J. Gruen vs. Marvin M. Mitchelson, et al.* (Docket No. C 651738, Superior Court of California, Los Angeles County).

p. 193. **Gruen claimed Mitchelson intended to take the whole fee for himself:** *Gruen vs. Mitchelson.*

p. 193. **Mitchelson, Gruen accuse each other of bad faith (footnote):** Declarations in *Gruen vs. Mitchelson.*

p. 193. Was a case of "go screw yourself": AI with Gruen, October 3, 1989.

p. 193. Sought injunction; recounted tax problems: Declaration of Gruen in *Gruen vs. Mitchelson.*

p. 193. Settlement in excess of $20 million: *Saadeh vs. al-Midani.*

PART FIVE: A GOOD LUCK CHARM

Much of Part Five came either from investigative reports prepared by various public and private sources, or from confidential sources. To preserve confidentiality, information thus obtained is not cited below.

Chapter Twenty-Five (Pages 197–203)

p. 197. Called Nina his good luck charm: AI with Evelyn Gruen, October 3, 1989.

p. 197. "An aging nymphette:" AI with Gruen, October 3, 1989.

p. 198. "She's a wrist slitter": AI with MM, March 18, 1990.

p. 198. Sotheby's auction: "The Story in Stones" (Editorial), *New York Times,* March 22, 1987; "Windsor Jewels Bring an Auction Record," *New York Times,* April 3, 1987, by Francis X. Clines; "The Windsor Epilogue," *Vanity Fair,* August 1987, by Dominick Dunne.

p. 198. Mitchelson professed not to be able to account for Nina's presence at the auction: AI with MM, February 23, 1990.

p. 198. Amounts spent on the jewels: From court documents in *Sotheby's S.A., Geneve, vs. Marvin M. Mitchelson* (Docket No. 88-0471, United States District Court, Central District of California).

p. 199. Nina's palimony suit against Mitchelson: *Nina Iliescu vs. Marvin M. Mitchelson* (Docket No. EC 002614, Superior Court of California, Los Angeles County).

p. 199. Sinister force, other Mitchelson comments about the auction: AI with MM, February 23, 1990.

p. 200. Necklace's checkered history: Nina admired the bib necklace in a photograph that appeared in *The Jewels of the Duchess of Windsor* (Vendome Press, 1987), by John Culme and Nicholas Rayner, a coffee-table book. Marcella Mitchelson's photograph, wearing the bib necklace and sitting on a sofa at the family home, appeared in *People* below Mitchelson's and Iliescu's; see "Queen of Diamonds," *People,* April 27, 1987, by Brad Darrach.

p. 200. Shoved the jewels: AI with Gruen, October 3, 1989.

p. 201. "My mother, God bless her," etc.: AI with MM, January 6, 1990.

p. 201. Fastest thinker on feet: AI with MM, February 23, 1990.

p. 201. Sotheby's litigation against Mitchelson, and his various responses: Documents from the extensive litigation file in *Sotheby's S.A., Geneve, vs. Marvin M. Mitchelson.*

Repayment of Sotheby's: On July 2, 1991, various Mitchelson family members, through a series of transactions, effectively terminated what the federal court had earlier characterized as the "purported Sonia Mitchelson Trust" that owned Mitchelson's castle on Sweetzer Avenue. Thereafter, the castle was transferred to Mitchelson and his wife and son, who refinanced the property for $1,995,000. (Documents on file at Recorder's Office for Los Angeles County.) Mitchelson valued his mansion, with its three acres of grounds, at between $5 million and $7 million. (AI with MM, March 16, 1991.) Some $900,000 from the proceeds of the refinancing went directly to pay off Sotheby's. (Escrow Consultants, Inc. settlement sheet dated June 13, 1991.) The remainder due Sotheby's was paid out of Mitchelson's fee from the final *Christian* settlement. (Confidential source.) In AI with MM, October 28, 1991, Mitchelson affirmed that the *Christian* settlement and the mortgage refinancing provided the sources for paying off Sotheby's.

p. 201. "Mitchelson hedged his answers": Questioned by a Customs agent as to why the jewels hadn't been declared, Mitchelson replied: 1.) he'd seen them on display in New York City and thought they didn't need to clear Customs again; 2.) they were antiquities and thus non-declarable; and 3.) he thought Sotheby's would bill him for the Customs duties, if any, at the same time they billed him for the jewels.

p. 201. Never knowingly smuggled: AI with MM, July 12, 1989.

p. 202. Joan Shepherd case: AI with Joan Shepherd, December 29, 1989; also, "Celebrity Divorce Settlements: Pairs Who Trump the Trumps," *San Jose Mercury*, February 16, 1990, by the *New York Daily News*. Shepherd was married for 14 years to a popular Japanese folk singer named Masao Sen. She once was a vocalist with the Glenn Miller Orchestra.

p. 202. He asked for Hawaii property; she paid him $1.1 million instead; would have paid $5 million: AI with Shepherd, December 29, 1989.

p. 202. Sotheby's mangaged to get *Christian* fee: AI with Harold Rhoden, May 18, 1989.

p. 202. The *Christian* judgment (footnote): AI with Rhoden, May 18, 1989. Subsequently, the California 2nd District Court of Appeal in Los Angeles upheld the $5.5 million judgement on June 17, 1991. ("$5 Million Award to Lover of Rock Hudson Upheld," *Los Angeles Times*, June 18, 1991). By then, however, a major deep pocket in the case, Aetna Casualty & Surety Co., had been ruled not liable for any part of the judgment. ("Atena Ruled Not Liable in Hudson

Suit," *Los Angeles Times*, November 7, 1990.) Not long after the appeals court ruling, the Hudson estate settled with Christian for an undisclosed amount. AI with MM, October 28, 1991.

p. 203. "Don't let the guards get anything:" AI with MM, October 28, 1991.

p. 203. Clerk came to office twice a day: "Mitchelson's Checks Are Not in the Mail," *American Lawyer*, December 1990.

p. 203. "Voracious, greedy people": AI with MM, March 18, 1990.

Chapter Twenty-Six (Pages 204–212)

p. 204. Raoul Felder remembered: AI with Felder, May 9, 1989.

p. 204. Mitchelson's representation of Veronica Buss; her assessment of Mitchelson; his freebasing: AIs with Buss, September 19, September 21, and October 1, 1989; documents in *Veronica Buss vs. Jerry Buss* (Docket No. C 449427, Superior Court of California, Los Angeles County); and various newspaper accounts about the Buss divorce litigation and Buss's career, including "Buss's Wife Sues to Annul Marriage; Bigamy Alleged," *Los Angeles Times*, April 15, 1983, by Myrna Oliver.

p. 207. Lydia Criss's background: "'Cat Man' Peter Criss Ends Lydia's Marital Bliss with a Million-Dollar Kiss-Off," *People*, October 1, 1979, by Martha Smilgis.

p. 207. Presten arranged celebration at Nirvana: AI with Criss, September 11, 1989.

p. 207. Criss got a $500,000 settlement: AI with Criss, September 11, 1989; AI with MM, February 21, 1990.

p. 207. Mitchelson refused to answer drug allegations: Mitchelson's deposition of June 4, 1982 in the case of *Lydia Criscoula vs. Marvin M. Mitchelson* (Docket No. 81 Civ. 3869, United States District Court, Southern District of New York).

p. 207. "If I knew you didn't have insurance": AI with MM, February 10, 1990.

p. 207. Told client to act like a lesbian: Los Angeles district attorney's office report.

p. 208. "You deal with a lot of crazies": February 21, 1990.

p. 208. Nancy Michelle Vincent told the LAPD about Mitchelson: LAPD report.

pp. 208–209. Dr. Milton Reder's medical practice, actions by N.Y. authorities: AI with Dr. Thomas Coffey, director, New York State Department of Health Bureau of Controlled Substances, September 7, 1989; AI with Dr. Milton Reder, September 12, 1989. Reder's clients are listed in *Miracles on Park Avenue* (Lyle Stuart, 1986), by Albert B. Gerber.

p. 209. Background on the IRS's Criminal Investigations Division: A

Law Unto Itself: Power, Politics, and the IRS (Random House, 1989), by David Burnham.

pp. 209–210. Surveillance of Mitchelson: Mitchelson said he could not recall knowing anyone by the names of those whose homes he was followed to. (AI with MM, March 16, 1991). In separate interviews, however, all the residents acknowledged knowing Mitchelson. (AIs of confidential sources.)

Chapter Twenty-Seven (Pages 212–219)

p. 212. Lived on Social Security and Medicare: Kristin Barrett-Whitney letter to LAPD, August 24, 1989.

p. 213. Barrett-Whitney aliases: From *Kristen Barrett-Whitney vs. Donald L. Chiapetti et al.* (Docket No. C 573124, Superior Court of Arizona, Maricopa County), and from Mitchelson's answer and cross-complaint in *Kristen Barrett-Whitney vs. Marvin M. Mitchelson* (Docket No. WEC 108676, Superior Court of California, Los Angeles County).

p. 213. Mitchelson called her extortionist: Mitchelson cross-complaint.

p. 213. Barrett-Whitney revealed Chase Revel's criminal past: Affidavit for Search Warrant, Search Warrant, and Return to Search Warrant (Search Warrant No. 26535), all prepared by District Attorney Senior Investigator Laurence A. Rooker. Rooker's investigation resulted in a felony complaint, *People of the State of California vs. John Leonard Burke, aka Chase Ricaro Revel, aka Jacques Victor Baron* (Docket No. A 788525, Superior Court of California, Los Angeles County).

p. 213. Revel's criminal record: "Entrepreneur Had Unusual Capital-Raising Technique," *Los Angeles Times*, August 1, 1986, by Ted Rohrlich; "Entrepreneur Magazine's Revel Arrested," *Los Angeles Times*, August 8, 1986, by Ted Rohrlich and Boris Yaro; "LV's Weird Bank Bandit Eludes Police Dragnet," *Las Vegas Review-Journal*, March 13, 1964; "Vegas 'Gossip Columnist' Admits Bank Extortion, Fills Up on Caviar," *Houston Chronicle*, April 25, 1964, by Arthur Byrd; "Crafty Crook Robs Bank by Messenger," *Houston Post*, April 25, 1964; *U.S. vs. John Leonard Burke* (United States District Court for Nevada, Docket No. 64-H-94), for bank robbery, filed May 21, 1964; and *U.S. vs. John Leonard Burke* (United States District Court for Southern Texas, Docket No. 64-H-81), for bank robbery, filed April 25, 1964.

p. 214. Taped confrontations between Mitchelson and Barrett-Whitney: LAPD transcripts.

p. 215. Couldn't erase smell of Mitchelson: Statement of Barrett-Whitney to Los Angeles County grand jury, October 14, 1986.

p. 216. "I'd love to see. . . . Sumbitch is guilty": AI with Robert Kestler, March 28, 1989.

p. 216. **She flew to New York. . . :** Confidential source.

p. 216. **Pierce O'Donnell's background:** O'Donnell dissolved his own small law firm in 1988 to help found the Los Angeles office of New York's Kaye, Scholer, Fierman, Hays & Handler. Soon, he was in the headlines again, filing suit on behalf of Art Buchwald against Paramount Pictures Corporation. Buchwald sought a share of the profits from the Eddie Murphy hit movie *Coming to America.* (See "Pierce O'Donnell Pans 'Fatal Subtraction'," *American Lawyer,* March 1991, by Shahram Victory.)

p. 216. **NOW tried to raise hell:** AI with Shireen Miles, April 14, 1989.

p. 216. **Publicity stung D.A.'s office:** "D.A. Won't Prosecute Mitchelson in Rape Case; State to Open Inquiry," *Los Angeles Times,* January 21, 1987, by Ted Rohrlich; "Grand Juror Rips Judge, Prosecutors in Rape Case," *Los Angeles Times,* May 15, 1987, by Ted Rohrlich.

p. 217. **Garcetti's comments:** AI with Gilbert Garcetti, March 31, 1989.

p. 217. **D.A.'s plea bargain with Revel (footnote):** Documents in *People vs. John Leonard Burke, aka Chase Revel.*

p. 218. **Acaldo warns of possible conflict of interest:** AI with Linda Acaldo, April 1, 1989.

p. 218. **Acaldo's interview by other deputy D.A.'s:** Audio tape recording of Acaldo being interviewed by Deputy L.A. District Attorneys Ron Ross and Stephen Sitkoff, August 5, 1986.

p. 218. **Barrett-Whitney's malpractice suit against O'Donnell:** *Kristen Whitney* (sic) *vs. Pierce O'Donnell et al.* (Docket No. SC 004889, Superior Court of California, Los Angeles County), filed November 21, 1990.

p. 219. **Barrett-Whitney makes threat against Mitchelson:** LAPD report.

p. 219. **New rape allegations:** LAPD report.

Chapter Twenty-Eight (Pages 220–227)

p. 220. **Arbitration in French case:** "Lawyer Cleared in Rape Suit," *New York Times,* August 2, 1988.

p. 220. **Daye Shinn discipline, indictment:** California Bar records; also "Bugliosi and Shinn Indicted on Perjury Charges in Farr Case," *Los Angeles Times,* June 29, 1974, and "Charges of Perjury by Shinn Dismissed," *Los Angeles Times,* December 5, 1974, by Myrna Oliver.

p. 220. **French vs. Mitchelson** trial: Documents, depositions, and evidentiary materials in *Patricia French vs. Marvin M. Mitchelson* (Docket No. C 452183, Superior Court of California, Los Angeles

County); also MJS trial notes and AI of Harold Rhoden, May 18, 1989.

p. 222. **$462,400-a-year lifestyle**: Report of Rootenberg, Rosenthal & Getz, CPAs, prepared April 13, 1984 in the case of *MacDonald vs. MacDonald*.

p. 222. **Paranoia about CIA**: Trial testimony in *Felicia MacDonald vs. Marvin M. Mitchelson* (Docket No. C 539106, Superior Court of California, Los Angeles), from MJS trial notes, July 25 through August 3, 1989; also, "Mitchelson Testifies That Former Client Is Paranoid," *Los Angeles Herald-Examiner*, July 25, 1989.

p. 223. **Felicia MacDonald talking to Max Hugel**: AI with MM, October 28, 1991.

p. 223. **Sex with Mitchelson**: LAPD report and trial testimony.

p. 223. **"She's a ball breaker," etc.**: AI with MM, August 22, 1989.

p. 223. **Kolodny later sued her**: *Stephen A. Kolodny vs. Felicia Gordon, formerly known as Felicia MacDonald* (Docket No. C 729904, Superior Court of California, Los Angeles County).

p. 223. **"It was like Peyton Place"**: AI with Michael Krycler, January 6, 1990.

p. 223. **Barrett-Whitney vowed to get Mitchelson**: AI with Barrett-Whitney, August 15, 1989.

p. 224. **Incident with flowers**: AIs with Barrett-Whitney, August 15, 1989, and Patricia French, August 20, 1989.

p. 224. **MacDonald trial testimony**: MJS notes.

p. 225. **Mitchelson comments**: AI with MM, February 21, 1990.

p. 225. **Commotion in hallway**: MJS trial notes; also, "Mitchelson Wins Latest Big Case: His Own," *Los Angeles Herald-Examiner*, August 4, 1989, by Faye Fiore.

p. 226. **Rhoden plane crash**: AI with Don Llorente, of the National Transportation Safety Board, July 7, 1989; NTSB Report of A. D. Llorente, July 28, 1989; "Rock Hudson Case Lawyer One of Three Air Crash Victims," *Los Angeles Times*, June 24, 1989, by Gabe Fuentes, and related articles; Federal Aviation Administration transcripts provided to MJS pursuant to a Freedom of Information Act request.

p. 227. **Mitchelson on Rhoden**: AIs with MM, July 12, 1989 and January 19, 1990.

p. 227. **Tashi Grady's premonition**: AI with Tashi Grady, May 10, 1990.

Chapter Twenty-Nine (Pages 227–236)

p. 227. **Telephone . . . rang less often**: AI with MM, October 28, 1991.

p. 227. **Supplying illegal drugs**: "Carrie Leigh Makes Drug Allegations," *Philadelphia Inquirer*, July 8, 1988.

p. 228. **Preparation of the the "60 Mintutes" broadcast:** Derived from AIs with Chuck Lewis in 1989 on March 7, 16, 24, 27, 28, and 29; April 18; May 1 and 12; June 5; July 17; August 20, 22, and 31; October 13; November 30; and December 1. During these interviews, Lewis had available to him extensive contemporaneous notes about his work on the Mitchelson story.

p. 234. **"Those three dogs. . . . I don't even know the woman!":** AI with MM, February 17, 1989.

p. 234. **Felder's conversation; Mitchelson fears a bug:** AI with Raoul Felder, May 9, 1989.

p. 235. **Mitchelson in a state of shock; derides Sitkoff; defends wardrobe:** AI with MM, December 5, 1989.

p. 236. **"I'd like to think. . . . So what could my mother have prevented?"** AI with MM, February 21, 1991.

Chapter Thirty (Pages 236–244)

p. 236. **State Bar expected resistance; "I don't give up":** AI with Victoria Molloy, March 30, 1989.

p. 236. **State Bar lassitude:** The most detailed examination of the Bar's problems can be found in "The Brotherhood: Justice for Lawyers," a six-part series published in the *San Francisco Examiner* from March 24 through 29, 1985, by K. Connie Kang and James A. Finefrock.

p. 237. **Only slightly more likely:** In 1984, there were 11 disbarments in California, according to the *Examiner* series. From 1968 to 1984, according to the Author's research, an average of seven murderers per year were sent to Death Row in California.

p. 237. **Fellmeth coments:** AI with Robert Fellmeth, October 2, 1989.

p. 238. **Molloy's comments:** AI with Molloy, March 30, 1989.

p. 238. **State Bar complaints against Mitchelson:** Public documents in four State Bar proceedings against Mitchelson (Case Nos. 84-O-13094; 85-O-12124; 88-O-12184; and 88-O-13160).

p. 239. **Rhoden's comments about disbarment:** AI with Harold Rhoden, May 18, 1989.

p. 239. **Symbolic importance of the proceeding:** AI with Fellmeth, October 2, 1989.

p. 239. **Background of Margolis:** AI with Arthur Margolis, May 14, 1989.

p. 240. **Molloy's tough talk:** AI with Molloy, March 30, 1989.

p. 240. **"If they've got some little guy":** AI with Ted Cohen, March 30, 1989.

p. 242. **"Mike Williams" meets with Mitchelson:** According to a D.A. investigator's report prepared later, the meeting may have occurred on January 5 rather than January 8.

p. 243. **Thomas Molloy's attempt to sell information to Mitchelson:**

Described in various public documents, including motions filed by Mitchelson with the State Bar Court on May 1, 1990 and December 11, 1991. Copies of the letters Molloy sent to Mitchelson were included in Mitchelson's May 1 motion. Victoria Molloy refused to discuss the incident and its aftermath. (AI with Victoria Molloy, November 27, 1991.)

p. 243. **The sting operation directed at "Mike Wiliams":** D.A.'s office report.

p. 243. **Thomas Molloy's access to State Bar documents:** AI with Ron Magnuson, an examiner in the State Bar's Office of Trial Counsel, November 21, 1991. Also, D.A.'s office report.

p. 243. **"The authorities simultaneously confronted . . .":** AI with Magnuson, November 21, 1991. Magnuson stated that Victoria and Thomas Molloy shared a house, and that Thomas Molloy had shown the two Bar documents to Olsen as evidence of what else he could provide. This is affirmed by a contemporaneous account of the meeting prepared by an investigator in the D.A.'s office.

p. 243. **Molloy tried to talk his way out of trouble:** D.A.'s office report.

p. 243. **". . . already on probation . . .":** Judgments Adjudicating Guilt in Case Nos. 0338203D and 0331841D, *State of Texas vs. Thomas Scott Molloy* (Criminal District Court of Texas, Tarrant County); also, AI with Ruth White, District Clerk's Office, Tarrant County Justice Center, Fort Worth, Texas, December 9, 1991.

p. 244. **Mitchelson expands discovery:** "State Bar Court Lets Mitchelson Expand Discovery," *Los Angeles Daily Journal*, June 28, 1990, by G.M. Bush.

Chapter Thirty-One (Pages 244–246)

p. 245. **Last visit to Roy Cohn:** AI with Martha Smilgis, September 13, 1989.

POSTSCRIPT (PAGE 247)

p. 247. **Hirschfeld's criminal convictions:** "Hirschfeld Convicted of Three Fraud Counts," UPI, March 6, 1991. "Matching a Name to the Ali Voice; Documents Point to Boxer's Aide," *Washington Post*, April 17, 1991, by John Mintz.

p. 247. **Still in jail:** AI with secretary to Albert Krieger of Miami (Hirschfeld's lawyer), November 25, 1991.

p. 247. **Thomas Molloy's crimes:** Judgment on Plea of Guilty or Nolo Contendere, *State of Texas vs. Thomas Scott Molloy* (Docket No. 0440674R, Criminal District Court of Texas, Tarrant County); Judgment on Jury Verdict of Guilty After Indictment, *State of Texas vs.*

Thomas Scott Molloy (Docket No. 0440643R, Criminal District Court of Texas, Tarrant County); AI with Ruth White, District Clerk's Office, Tarrant County Justice Center, Fort Worth, Texas, December 9, 1991; AI with David Richards, Molloy's attorney on appeal, December 9, 1991; AI with Timmie R. White, Molloy's attorney at trial, December 12, 1991.

p. 247. **Pancoast's death:** AI with Barens, December 6, 1991. See also, "Killer of Bloomingdale's Mistress Dies in Prison," *Los Angeles Times*, December 5, 1991.

p. 247. **Barrett-Whitney vs. Mitchelson rape trial:** MJS trial notes; "Mitchelson Accuser Tells About Abuse," *The Outlook* (Santa Monica, California), November 8, 1991; "Testimony: Mitchelson Raped Client," *The Outlook*, November 9, 1991; "Woman Says She's Still Haunted by Alleged Rape," *The Outlook*, November 13, 1991; "Witness Evaluates Mitchelson's Accuser," *The Outlook*, November 23, 1991; "Mitchelson Trial Over; Jury Rejects Rape Claim," *The Outlook*, November 28, 1991, by Pat Alston (as to all *Outlook* articles); "Mitchelson Cleared in Rape Suit," *Los Angeles Times*, November 28, 1991; "Mitchelson Cleared of Rape Charge," *San Francisco Chronicle*, November 28, 1991; "Marvin Mitchelson Found Innocent," *Washington Post*, November 29, 1991.

p. 247. **"I told ya I didn't do it":** MM message on Author's telephone answering machine, November 27, 1991.

Index

ABOUT THE AUTHOR

John A. Jenkins has been writing from Washington, D.C. about the law and lawyers since 1971, when, shortly before his graduation from the University of Maryland College of Journalism, he went to work as a reporter covering the Justice Department for a prominent legal publisher. Four years later, his magazine writing career began with a series of investigative articles about the legal profession for the *Washington Monthly*. Since then, he has written widely about legal matters, and has been a regular contributor to *The New York Times Magazine*. His articles have appeared in many other newspapers and national magazines in the United States and abroad, and his reporting has won six major journalism awards, including four Certificates of Merit from the American Bar Association Gavel Awards, one of the highest honors in legal journalism. His first book, *The Litigators*, was published in 1989. He lives in Washington, D.C. with his wife, Susan, and their children.